M000221626

This series of commentaries ... ......... ........... ... ....... .... .... biblical understanding and pastoral insights. This current volume on the Gospel of Luke is no different. Thabiti understands the text of the Gospel and makes application of the text with a soulful conscience held captive by the text. Students of the Gospel of Luke will find a faithful teacher in this refreshingly new volume on the old, old story.

**Anthony J. Carter**, lead pastor of East Point Church, Atlanta, Georgia

While reading Thabiti's commentary on Luke, I kept saying to myself, we really needed this commentary and we really needed it to be written by Thabiti. Thabiti's expositional prowess and pastoral focus, along with vivid and lively illustrations, make this commentary a must read for any study of the Gospel of Luke. Pastors, Sunday school teachers, Bible study leaders, and family worship leaders will all find Thabiti's work on Luke useful. This commentary on Luke has quickly become a favorite in my library; it will be in yours as well.

**Louis C. Love Jr.**, pastor of New Life Fellowship Church, Waukegan, Illinois

Thabiti shows through this book that he is a shepherd. I was being shepherded while reading through it. The way God has gifted him to capture the ancient truth of Scripture and engage very contemporary yet timeless issues is masterful. In a book like Luke where people can feel they have heard everything, seen everything, and know everything, Thabiti frames it in ways that draw us back into the narrative of our Lord's incarnation as the Son of Man. Every pastor and parishioner needs this in their library! Lastly, I have the added excitement that a black theologian is penning a commentary. I'm thankful for this work and this series that has taken up the challenge to get qualified writers period, but particularly black writers who are trusted to contribute beyond tokenism.

**Eric Mason**, founder and pastor of Epiphany Fellowship, Philadelphia, Pennsylvania

I am often asked by members of my church for advice on good commentaries for their personal study. And though I may give them the ones I think that are solid, yet I also want them to discern in their reading what makes this such a good commentary. The feedback I typically get is that the commentary clearly explained the text, gave good historical and cultural background information, and was very practical. This volume on the Gospel of Luke in the Christ-Centered Expositional Commentary series contains these elements. Pastor Thabiti's exposition of this Gospel account aims at the heart of Luke's purpose in getting the reader to know Jesus more intimately.

**Victor Sholar**, pastor of Main Street Baptist Church, Lexington, Kentucky

CHRIST-CENTERED

Exposition

NT / COMMENTARY FEATURING

AUTHOR **Thabiti Anyabwile**

SERIES EDITORS **David Platt, Daniel L. Akin, and Tony Merida**

# CHRIST-CENTERED

# Exposition

## EXALTING JESUS IN

## LUKE

HOLMAN®

REFERENCE

NASHVILLE, TENNESSEE

Christ-Centered Exposition Commentary: Exalting Jesus in Luke
© Copyright 2018 by Thabiti Anyabwile

B&H Publishing Group
Nashville, Tennessee
All rights reserved.

ISBN: 978-0-8054-9746-5

Dewey Decimal Classification: 220.7
Subject Heading: BIBLE. N.T. LUKE—
COMMENTARIES\JESUS CHRIST

Unless otherwise noted, all Scripture quotations are from the
Christian Standard Bible® Copyright 1999, 2000, 2002, 2003,
2009, 2017 by Holman Bible Publishers. Used by permission.

Scripture passages marked ESV are taken from The ESV® Bible (The
Holy Bible, English Standard Version®). ESV® Permanent Text Edition®
(2016). Copyright © 2001 by Crossway, a publishing ministry of Good
News Publishers. The ESV® text has been reproduced in cooperation
with and by permission of Good News Publishers. Unauthorized
reproduction of this publication is prohibited. All rights reserved.

Scripture passages marked KJV are taken from
the King James Version of the Bible.

Scripture passages marked NKJV are taken from the
New King James Version®. Copyright © 1982 by Thomas
Nelson. Used by permission. All rights reserved.

Scripture quotations marked NLT are taken from the Holy
Bible, New Living Translation, copyright © 1996, 2004, 2007 by
Tyndale House Foundation. Used by permission of Tyndale House
Publishers, Inc., Carol Stream, Illinois 60188. All rights reserved.

Printed in the United States of America

1 2 3 4 5 6 7 8 9 10 • 23 22 21 20 19 18

SB

# SERIES DEDICATION

Dedicated to Adrian Rogers and John Piper. They have taught us to love the gospel of Jesus Christ, to preach the Bible as the inerrant Word of God, to pastor the church for which our Savior died, and to have a passion to see all nations gladly worship the Lamb.

—David Platt, Tony Merida, and Danny Akin
March 2013

# AUTHOR'S DEDICATION

*Afterward he was traveling from one town and village to another, preaching and telling the good news of the kingdom of God. The Twelve were with him, and also some women who had been healed of evil spirits and sicknesses: Mary, called Magdalene (seven demons had come out of her); Joanna the wife of Chuza, Herod's steward; Susanna; and many others who were supporting them from their possessions.* (Luke 8:1-3)

To those faithful women who have served the Lord since the days of Jesus's earthly life and those faithful women who have provided for me out of their means: my mother, Frances; my sisters: Sissy, Dee Dee, and Blossom; my wife, Kristie; my daughters: Eden and Afiya; the sister saints who have held it down over the years: Phshikie, Nadia, Kimberly, Ruby; Maxine, Connie D., Adrienne, Kasey, Joylane; Maria, Bev, Dawn, Darlene, Meg, Denise, Linda; Eli, Tiffany, Bari, Ka, Connie B., Stephanie, Jhonna, Carol, Wanda, Deborah, Cathy, and so many others I should not have begun this list. I praise God for you women. Without you there would be no me.

# TABLE OF CONTENTS

# SERIES INTRODUCTION

Augustine said, "Where Scripture speaks, God speaks." The editors of the Christ-Centered Exposition Commentary series believe that where God speaks, the pastor must speak. God speaks through His written Word. We must speak from that Word. We believe the Bible is God breathed, authoritative, inerrant, sufficient, understandable, necessary, and timeless. We also affirm that the Bible is a Christ-centered book; that is, it contains a unified story of redemptive history of which Jesus is the hero. Because of this Christ-centered trajectory that runs from Genesis 1 through Revelation 22, we believe the Bible has a corresponding global-missions thrust. From beginning to end, we see God's mission as one of making worshipers of Christ from every tribe and tongue worked out through this redemptive drama in Scripture. To that end we must preach the Word.

In addition to these distinct convictions, the Christ-Centered Exposition Commentary series has some distinguishing characteristics. First, this series seeks to display exegetical accuracy. What the Bible says is what we want to say. While not every volume in the series will be a verse-by-verse commentary, we nevertheless desire to handle the text carefully and explain it rightly. Those who teach and preach bear the heavy responsibility of saying what God has said in His Word and declaring what God has done in Christ. We desire to handle God's Word faithfully, knowing that we must give an account for how we have fulfilled this holy calling (Jas 3:1).

Second, the Christ-Centered Exposition Commentary series has pastors in view. While we hope others will read this series, such as parents, teachers, small-group leaders, and student ministers, we desire to provide a commentary busy pastors will use for weekly preparation of biblically faithful and gospel-saturated sermons. This series is not academic in nature. Our aim is to present a readable and pastoral style of commentaries. We believe this aim will serve the church of the Lord Jesus Christ.

Third, we want the Christ-Centered Exposition Commentary series to be known for the inclusion of helpful illustrations and theologically driven applications. Many commentaries offer no help in illustrations, and few offer any kind of help in application. Often those that do offer illustrative material and application unfortunately give little serious attention to the text. While giving ourselves primarily to explanation, we also hope to serve readers by providing inspiring and illuminating illustrations coupled with timely and timeless application.

Finally, as the name suggests, the editors seek to exalt Jesus from every book of the Bible. In saying this, we are not commending wild allegory or fanciful typology. We certainly believe we must be constrained to the meaning intended by the divine Author Himself, the Holy Spirit of God. However, we also believe the Bible has a messianic focus, and our hope is that the individual authors will exalt Christ from particular texts. Luke 24:25-27,44-47 and John 5:39,46 inform both our hermeneutics and our homiletics. Not every author will do this the same way or have the same degree of Christ-centered emphasis. That is fine with us. We believe faithful exposition that is Christ centered is not monolithic. We do believe, however, that we must read the whole Bible as Christian Scripture. Therefore, our aim is both to honor the historical particularity of each biblical passage and to highlight its intrinsic connection to the Redeemer.

The editors are indebted to the contributors of each volume. The reader will detect a unique style from each writer, and we celebrate these unique gifts and traits. While distinctive in their approaches, the authors share a common characteristic in that they are pastoral theologians. They love the church, and they regularly preach and teach God's Word to God's people. Further, many of these contributors are younger voices. We think these new, fresh voices can serve the church well, especially among a rising generation that has the task of proclaiming the Word of Christ and the Christ of the Word to the lost world.

We hope and pray this series will serve the body of Christ well in these ways until our Savior returns in glory. If it does, we will have succeeded in our assignment.

David Platt
Daniel L. Akin
Tony Merida
*Series Editors*
February 2013

# Luke

# Introduction

# A Certain Faith

## LUKE 1:1-4

**Main Idea:** A belief isn't worth having if you can't be certain it is true. Christianity is the only certain and therefore trustworthy faith.

I. **Why Does Luke Write His Gospel?**
   A. A biblical faith
   B. A historical faith
   C. A verifiable faith
II. **How Does Luke Order His Gospel?**
   A. Chronological order
   B. Geographic order
   C. Dramatic order
   D. Theological order

The powerful and penetrating writing of Ta-Nehisi Coates challenges me. I think Coates captivates so many readers because of his plain and sometimes painful statement of things. As a writer, he strikes me as someone attempting to be honest—bald and bare honesty, no sheltering hats or pretty clothes, just the full truth as he sees it.

Coates writes with a rare certainty—even about religious things. In his book *Between the World and Me* Coates retells the story of a young man in Baltimore pulling a gun on him when he was a child. He then offers these words:

> I could not retreat, as did so many, into the church and its mysteries. My parents rejected all dogmas. We spurned the holidays marketed by the people who wanted to be white. We would not stand for their anthems. We would not kneel before their God. And so I had no sense that any just God was on my side. "The meek shall inherit the earth" meant nothing to me. The meek were battered in West Baltimore, stomped out at Walbrook Junction, bashed up on Park Heights, and raped in the showers of the city jail. My understanding of the universe was physical, and its moral arc bent toward chaos then concluded in a box. (Coates, *Between the World and Me*, 28)

Later in the book Coates writes, "You must resist the common urge toward the comforting narrative of divine law, toward fairy tales that imply some irrepressible justice" (*Between the World and Me*, 70). It's not merely that faith claims were no comfort to Coates; rather, those claims must be *resisted*. He continues:

> Raised conscious, in rejection of a Christian God, I could see no higher purpose in Prince's death. I believed, and still do, that our bodies are our selves, that my soul is the voltage conducted through neurons and nerves, and that my spirit is my flesh. (ibid., 79)

What strikes me about Coates's writing on religious matters isn't his atheism. I am not surprised by unbelief. I have lived in unbelief enough years to understand something of its grip. What surprises me is how *certain* he is *in his unbelief*. Ironically, while rejecting Christian faith, he cannot help but make faith claims of his own—even if they are non-religious claims. He writes, "I *believed*, and still do."

Here's the truth: We cannot live without belief of some sort. We may believe in God, or we may believe, as Coates, in our bodies and a material universe that has no meaning. In either case we are believers. There are no unbelievers in the world, just people who believe in different things.

In such a world certainty becomes a rare and precious gift. The quest for certainty poses real dangers. We can give up on the quest prematurely, concluding that certainty itself is a hoax. Or we can be certain about things that are wrong or false. We all face that danger. So we're left with a question: Can we be sure that what we believe is true?

## Why Does Luke Write His Gospel?

The Gospel of Luke belongs to what we call "the Synoptic Gospels"—Matthew, Mark, and Luke. They "see" (optic) "together" (syn-). They tell the same basic story about the Lord Jesus Christ. There are places where one of the Gospel writers includes stories or teachings that the others do not, but by and large they relay the truth about Jesus's life and ministry from the same vantage point.

A man named Luke wrote what we call the Gospel of Luke and its sequel, the book of Acts. In Colossians 4:10-14 the apostle Paul lists people who were partners with him in the ministry. He first lists Aristarchus, Mark, and Justus, and says of them, "These alone of the circumcised are my coworkers for the kingdom of God, and they have been a comfort to me" (v. 11). These were Paul's Jewish partners. Then Paul lists Epaphras and describes him as "one of you" (v. 12)—a Colossian. And finally Paul refers to "Luke, the dearly loved physician" (v. 14), letting us know that Luke was (a) a companion of Paul's, (b) a physician, and (c) a Gentile.

Luke opens his Gospel by telling us his purpose in verses 3-4. "Theophilus" (v. 3), the name of the addressee, literally means "lover of God." It could be a name for an actual person; Luke addresses him in Acts 1:1 as well. Or it could be a code name for the entire church. In either case Luke intends his Gospel to provide believers "certainty" (v. 1) in the things they have been taught about Jesus Christ and the Christian faith.

Can we be certain of the teachings of a faith? Is not faith something you just believe without certainty? Is not faith a leap into nothingness? And is it not proud and arrogant to think your faith is certain and others are wrong?

The Christian claim is that the things the Bible teaches about Jesus are true and certain. We take this position for three reasons.

### A Biblical Faith

First, we may be certain because Christianity is a biblical faith. That's what Luke means when he says in verse 1 that certain events "have been fulfilled among us." The word "fulfilled" has the sense of something being "accomplished" (ESV). Why that word choice? Why "fulfilled" or "accomplished" rather than merely "happened"?

Luke is referring to the promises of the Old Testament, the Jewish Scriptures. One simple way of understanding the Bible's organization is to think of the Old Testament as "promises made" and the New Testament as "promises kept." The Old Testament looks forward to God's keeping promises he made to men like Abraham, Isaac, Jacob, and King David. The New Testament books, like Luke's Gospel, record for us how God kept or fulfilled those promises.

Now, if Christianity is "certain," then we should expect it to finish or fulfill all the promises made in the Old Testament. We should expect the Christian claims to be thoroughly rooted in previous biblical promises. We should expect the New Testament to be more than current events. These are not things that "just happened." These are foreseen and fore-promised events that have now come to pass. One of the major themes of Luke's Gospel is his emphasis on the plan of God and its fulfillment in Jesus Christ.

In fact, when Luke sets out to give us certainty by showing us how Jesus fulfills the promises of God, he reads and studies the Old Testament exactly the way Jesus himself did while on earth with his disciples. Luke 24:44-48 forms a bookend with 1:1-4, emphasizing the same idea that biblical promises are being fulfilled.

> *He told them, "These are my words that I spoke to you while I was still with you—that everything written about me in the Law of Moses, the Prophets, and the Psalms* [the entire Old Testament] *must be fulfilled." Then he opened their minds to understand the Scriptures. He also said to them, "This is what is written: The Messiah would suffer and rise from the dead the third day, and repentance for forgiveness of sins would be proclaimed in his name to all the nations, beginning at Jerusalem. You are witnesses of these things."*

Two of the key words in Luke 24 are also in Luke 1: "fulfilled" (v. 44) and "witnesses" (v. 48). The entire Gospel is about God's accomplishing his plan and humans seeing him do it.

What is God's plan? The heart of biblical faith is the person and work of Jesus Christ—it is the gospel message.

We may be certain of the Christian faith because Christianity is a biblical faith.

You may object, "Wait a minute! That's circular reasoning. You can't say Christianity is certain by saying, 'The Bible says so.'" You are correct. I mean, people could make up religious ideas and stories, right? Or they could just be mistaken about what they saw since that was a prescientific era, right?

If all we had were circular references to the Bible, we would not have much. But the fulfillment of the Bible's promises and prophecies is not the only reason we believe in the certainty of the faith.

### A Historical Faith

Second, we may be certain because the Christian faith is a historical faith. Luke points to evidence *outside* the Bible for believing what is *inside* the Bible. Verse 2 specifically refers to those who were "eyewitnesses . . . of the word." That refers to all the people at the time who saw these things. He refers also to the apostles who were "servants of the word" and companions with Jesus. This is not third-person hearsay.

In the Gospels we have eyewitness evidence admissible in a court of law. In fact, some scholars believe Luke and Acts are companion volumes written as a legal brief in defense of the apostle Paul. If this forms part of a legal brief, then Luke roots his account in *evidence*, not imagination.

This is a major difference between Christianity and every other major world religion. I wavered between agnosticism and atheism as a young man in my mid-twenties. That time of uncertainty followed a period when I lived as a practicing Muslim. I feel as if I have been around the religious block! In Islam there is so much certitude. Muslims are convinced that Islam is the final religion and culmination of all religions and that Muhammad is the final prophet and greatest of all prophets. Do you know what there is little of in Islam? There's little external historical evidence for its religious claims. For example, every Muslim believes in Muhammad being miraculously transported to Jerusalem and from there into heaven. That's why Muslims claim the Dome of the Rock and the temple grounds in Jerusalem as a holy site. Yet there is no historical evidence that Muhammad ever went to Jerusalem. None. It's the stuff of dreams; it's not the stuff of history. In Christianity we're receiving history fulfilled in view of all.

The things we claim as Christians were not done in secret. They were done in space and time and leave a historical footprint. Consider how Luke gives us specific historical dates and figures as he recounts the life of Jesus:

> *In the days of King Herod of Judea, there was a priest of Abijah's division named Zechariah.* (1:5)

> *In those days a decree went out from Caesar Augustus that the whole empire should be registered. This first registration took place while Quirinius was governing Syria.* (2:1-2)

> *In the fifteenth year of the reign of Tiberius Caesar, while Pontius Pilate was governor of Judea, Herod was tetrarch of Galilee, his brother Philip tetrarch of the region of Iturea and Trachonitis, and Lysanias tetrarch of Abilene, during the high priesthood of Annas and Caiaphas, . . .* (3:1-2)

What do these passages have in common? They give us the specific names of actual people and places. They also give us specific time references. This means we are not left dependent on the Bible's claims to have certainty. We can look outside the Bible to test what is inside the Bible.

Archaeology and history both confirm the accuracy of Luke's account. In fact, whenever archaeology makes a discovery, it tends to confirm the accuracy of the biblical text. And time and again those who have examined Luke for historical accuracy have found the text completely reliable. It is as if God not only put his word on paper; he also carved it into stones. For our certainty God left us a record inside and outside the Bible.

## A Verifiable Faith

Which brings us to a third reason for our certainty. Christianity presents a verifiable faith. Luke's Gospel is a "carefully investigated . . . orderly sequence" (v. 1).

Many others had written accounts (v. 1). We have three other divinely inspired accounts in the Bible: Matthew, Mark, and John. But Luke may not be limiting his reference to just those accounts. "Many" is a wide word. Though "many" have tried to write a narrative, only four have been recognized as Scripture. From the start of Christianity, Christ's followers have set his teaching and life to writing. The early church attempted to be a biblically literate church.

And they were careful about what they accepted. They rejected the false Gospels that were not associated with an apostle and often written very late. You may hear of the so-called lost books of the Bible. Those "lost books" include things like the Gospel of Thomas. Do not let such writings trouble you. The early church worked prayerfully and faithfully to preserve God's Word. They had five tests for whether a writing should be part of the canon of Scripture:

1. Was the book written by a prophet of God?
2. Was the writer authenticated by miracles to confirm his message?
3. Does the book tell the truth about God, with no falsehood or contradiction?
4. Does the book evince a divine capacity to transform lives?
5. Was the book accepted as God's Word by the people to whom it was first delivered?

These tests help us establish what should be regarded as Scripture. These tests give us a foundation for rejecting the Apocrypha, those books dated between the close of the Old Testament and the opening of the New Testament. Roman Catholics include these books in their Bibles, but these books were never accepted by first-century Jews or the early church. They fail the test of canonicity, and so we reject them as Scripture, however useful or edifying they may be in other ways. These tests help us assess and reject later books falsely attributed to apostles, like the so-called Gospel of Thomas and others.

Because the church wrestled through these questions of canonicity, we can be confident that the sixty-six books of the Protestant Bible are the same books used by the early church. We see this same carefulness in the Gospel of Luke, which, by the way, was always received by the early church as Scripture—even by heretics like Marcion. Marcion was the "Edward Scissorhands" of the early church, famous for cutting out parts of the Bible he did not like. As it turns out, he did not like most of the Bible. But even Marcion accepted Luke's Gospel as Scripture.

What am I saying with all of this? Christianity can be tested. Because it can be tested, it can be trusted.

What sets the Gospel of Luke apart is Luke's critical and logical analysis. The Gospel of Luke is a kind of investigative journalism. He "carefully investigated everything from the very first." He was not an eyewitness, but he apparently interviewed the eyewitnesses. That is why Luke's Gospel includes unique incidents like the conversation between Mary and Elizabeth when the two women were pregnant, the Magnificat (the song Mary sings when she visits Elizabeth), and the details about Jesus as a twelve-year-old boy. How would Luke know these things? He likely had access to Mary and others who knew these details. Luke has been *investigating, verifying, testing* the truth as he compiles the narrative.

If you have ever been told that to be a Christian "you must check your mind at the door," I am here to tell you somebody lied to you. Bring your mind to this book, and both your mind and your heart will be satisfied. To be a Christian is to be a thinking being and to think most deeply about the most profound things—the nature of God and the ways of God in the universe. Do not check your mind at the door. If you ever meet a pastor who gives you that impression, find yourself another pastor and another church. Was it not the Lord himself who told us that we are to love the Lord our God with all our heart, soul, *mind*, and strength? Bring your brain to church. You'll be lost without it! Bring your mind and open it to the truth of God's Word.

Our faith can be tested because it is a historical faith with external evidence. Consequently, when we talk about Christianity, we are not talking about mythology, superstitions, or man-made traditions. We are talking about truth. I stress that because some people think any religious claim must be a myth or legend. But when they say that about Christianity, they prove they don't know much about mythology!

C. S. Lewis was a student of literature, including mythology. Lewis came to faith in Christ late in life. He knew what it was to study literature as a non-Christian and what it was to appreciate literature as a Christian. He addressed the notion that Christianity is mythology head-on.

> All I am in private life is a literary critic and historian, that's my job. And I am prepared to say on that basis if anyone thinks the Gospels are either legend or novels, then that person is simply showing his incompetence as a literary critic. I've read a great many novels and I know a fair amount about the legends that grew up among early people, and I know perfectly well the Gospels are not that kind of stuff. (*Christian Reflections*, 209)

In another place Lewis writes,

> Now, as a literary historian, I am perfectly convinced that whatever else the Gospels are they are not legends. I have read a great deal of legend and I am quite clear that they are not the same sort of thing. They are not artistic enough to be legends. From an imaginative point of view they are clumsy; they don't work up to things properly. (*God in the Dock*, 169)

What is Lewis saying? He's saying that you can tell a work of fiction or legend when you read it. Legends have the feel and scent of *unreal*-ity. Legends have a fantastical quality about them. Lewis, who taught at Oxford for many years, knew his legends and myths. He assures us that the Gospels feel and smell like reality because they present the gritty truth about life.

If you are considering the claims of Christianity, let me give you a tip. The only religion you have to test, the only religion you *can* test, is Christianity. Test it with your whole mind. Test it with your whole heart. Ask all of your questions. Go honestly to the answers. If you find Christianity lacking, then walk away from it. And you can walk away from all religions in the world. But if you find it compelling, then submit yourself to it. Trust it. It will be the only religion you need.

The reason you may walk away from all other religions if you reject Christianity is Christianity makes a unique claim among all the world's faiths. All other religions teach humanity how we may climb up to God; Christianity teaches, This is how God came down to you. It's the only faith where God in his great love and mercy wraps himself in our humanity, lives in our places, suffers and dies for us, then rises for our forgiveness and right standing with God. As a consequence, all who believe in the Son of God are reconciled to God, forgiven their sins, and joined together with God by faith. Those who believe in Christ will most certainly see God face-to-face on the day when time is ended and eternity begins. No one else promises that—not Buddha or Muhammad, not Zoroastrianism or any other religion. Only Jesus promises this.

Test it. Seek him. Look for the truth while it may be found. The Truth will find you and keep you.

If you are not yet a Christian, I ask, Do your beliefs offer you this kind of certainty? What do you believe about God? About Jesus? About the purpose of life and what happens after death? Is what you believe *certain* to be true? I am not asking if you *feel* certain about what you believe. I am asking you something about the *beliefs themselves*. Are the *beliefs* certain to be true? Can you verify them with history, eyewitness accounts, or fulfilled prophecy? Or is the only authority for your belief the fact that you believe it and imagine or want it to be so?

Here's the key question: Do you really want to base your life and risk all of heaven and hell on your own thoughts?

Before you risk your soul on your own thoughts, you should consider at least two things. Consider how little we know as limited, imperfect human beings. Then consider the biblical and historical evidence for Christianity.

Friend, the only things worth believing are true things. Religions can be beautiful and contain a lot of good. But if they are false, then they are futile. A person's faith is only as good as the object he rests his faith on. We can be confident in what we believe only if what we believe is true. What Christianity offers is a faith that is biblically, historically, and verifiably true and therefore trustworthy.

Believe the gospel of Jesus Christ because it is true. That is the only reason to do so.

## How Does Luke Order His Gospel?

Luke tells us he has set out to write an "orderly sequence." He means to give his story structure. As we work our way through the Gospel we can see something of the order Luke has given it.

### Chronological Order

While the narrative is not strictly chronological, it has a chronological flow. We might divide the Gospel into four sections:

- Before Jesus's birth to age twelve (chs. 1–2)
- Beginning public ministry (chs. 3–9)
- Training his disciples and teaching about the kingdom (chs. 10–19)
- Betrayal, crucifixion, and resurrection (chs. 20–24)

### Geographic Order

Second, the Gospel of Luke follows a geographic order. In chapters 1–9 the bulk of the action takes place in and **around Galilee**. Galilee included Jesus's hometown area and his ministry headquarters in Capernaum.

Chapters 9–19 find Jesus on the move, **traveling to Jerusalem** (9:51). Though the Lord enters many towns and villages, Jerusalem looms in the distance as his ultimate destination. Every step Jesus takes brings him closer to his cross.

- *As they were traveling on the road . . .* (9:57).
- *While they were traveling . . .* (10:38).
- *He went through one town and village after another, teaching and making his way to Jerusalem* (13:22).
- *Then he took the Twelve aside and told them, "See, we are going up to Jerusalem. Everything that is written through the prophets about the Son of Man will be accomplished"* (18:31).
- *As he approached Jericho . . .* (18:35).
- *He entered Jericho and was passing through* (19:1).
- *When he had said these things, he went on ahead, going up to Jerusalem* (19:28).

The remainder of the Gospel (chs. 19–24) takes place **in Jerusalem**.

*Dramatic Order*

This geographical movement helps reveal the drama of the text. While Jesus moves, he moves into greater conflict and toward his earthly purpose.

In Galilee (chs. 1–9) Jesus lives at **the height of popularity**. The people seem to love him. He has a spreading fame. As a boy in the temple ,he amazes the religious leaders with his knowledge (ch. 2). John the Baptist announces him as the promised Messiah (ch. 3). Then Jesus begins his public ministry by defeating the temptations of Satan in the wilderness and reading the scroll of Isaiah as autobiography (ch. 4). He goes on to heal various people and call his first disciples (chs. 5–9). He begins to teach about the kingdom of God. The people received all of this with gladness.

The mood changes when he begins to journey toward Jerusalem in chapter 9. The Lord begins to face **opposition and rejection**. In chapter 11 people accuse him of casting out demons by the power of Satan and ask for a sign to prove he is the Messiah. So Jesus calls them a wicked and perverse generation. The Lord begins to warn openly against the scribes and Pharisees (ch. 12). He once privately warned his disciples about them; now he calls them hypocrites openly. He also begins to stress that repentance from sin is imperative for escaping hell (13:1-5). People must follow him, or they are not worthy of the kingdom of God (14:25-27,33). These confrontations go on until 19:45-48, when Jesus forcefully cleanses the temple.

In Jerusalem things turn murderous. Jesus openly teaches in the temple every day. But behind closed doors the religious leaders plot to kill him (ch. 22). The ones who should have recognized him and told the people "This is the one" put thirty pieces of silver as a bounty on his head. One of his twelve disciples, Judas Iscariot, sold the Lord out, and his other followers denied him after he was arrested (ch. 22). The religious leaders put the Lord through a sham trial before crucifying him just as he had predicted they would (ch. 23). But that is not the end of the story! After being put to death for claiming to be the promised Messiah, three days later God raised Jesus from the dead—defeating death and hell, the grave and condemnation (ch. 24).

## Theological Order

Finally, Luke's Gospel contains a theological order. Luke 1–6 and 10–18 present to us **Jesus Christ the Great Prophet**. In these sections we meet Jesus as the one who teaches the very word of God, who John 1 tells us is the Word of God in the flesh. The Lord Jesus is the one who teaches the word of God perfectly and fearlessly even in the face of opposition (13:31-34). Picture the Lord Jesus, arms stretched out over the entire globe, crying out not only to ancient Jerusalem but to all the neighborhoods of your city, to all people everywhere. The Prophet calls the nations to come to him. He cries out, "How I stretch my arms to you. I would receive you, but you're not willing." He says, "I have been crucified, resurrected, ascended into heaven where I now reign. What more proof do you need that I am the Son of God and that I save sinners from condemnation? Oh, come to me!" Here stands the Great Prophet of God giving the word of God that the life of God might inhabit the souls of men!

In chapters 7–9 Luke also presents the Lord Jesus to us as **the Great Priest of God**. In those chapters we see Jesus healing the broken, cleansing lepers, and forgiving sinners. Luke 6:17-19 provides a good summary of our Lord's priestly ministry. In the Old Testament worship in Israel, the law required unclean people to present themselves to the priests for inspection before they could worship with Israel or live in the city gates. If they were found unclean, they were forced to live outside the city and away from contact with others for the duration of their uncleanness. Think of it as an ancient quarantine against disease. Once the uncleanness passed, they had to present themselves to the priests for inspection before resuming life with the covenant people of God. The Levitical priests had no power to make a man clean, only to pronounce whether they were or not. But when people came to Jesus, they were not quarantined but cleansed, healed, and forgiven! The Lord Jesus is the real Great High Priest who makes us clean and whole.

One of the things I love about Luke's Gospel is Jesus most often serves as High Priest to lowly people. He comes in tenderness and compassion to those society has forgotten, those who are left out. He has sharp words for the religious elites, the rich and powerful. He does not have to cozy up with elites of this world. He preaches to them that they should repent or perish; then he leaves them. He goes in great tenderness to the thieves and lepers. He eats in the homes of tax collectors and accepts worship from prostitutes. I love that Luke shows us a Savior who goes to the broken and makes them beautiful.

Luke shows us that Jesus loves women. Luke often takes a woman of questionable background and places her in the context of men professing to be holy. Think, for example, of the woman who anoints the Lord with oil and washes his feet with her tears. Sitting across from her and the Lord is the owner of the house, Simon, a strict Pharisee indignant at the scene. He said to himself, "This man, if he were a prophet, would know who and what kind of woman this is who is touching him—she's a sinner!" (7:39). Jesus, knowing Simon's heart, uses the woman's devotion to him to expose the self-righteousness of the Pharisee. The woman is honored and cared for.

Luke 8:1-3 shows us women playing a vital trustee role in our Lord's earthly ministry. The Savior does not skip over people society likes to overlook. He stops. He loves them. He heals them. And he uses them in his kingdom.

Luke also shows us that **Jesus is King** (chs. 19–24). Luke 20:41-44 includes an argument wherein religious leaders attempt to snare Jesus with a trick question. The Lord's answer is a "mic drop" that ends all debate before he enters Jerusalem. The Lord uses the Psalms to show the beauty and intricacy of Scripture. Jesus uses David's words to prove that the Messiah would not only be a descendant of David but also be David's Lord who sits at God's right hand. The son of man would also be the Son of God. The Son of David would be none other than the King of kings himself, the second person of the Trinity. This King comes into the world not only as King but also as sacrifice and servant. Luke holds out to us the certainty that Jesus Christ is the Great Prophet, Priest, and King who redeems from their sin those who believe in him.

## Conclusion

As we travel with Luke through his Gospel, I pray that we travel to Jesus, the main point of the Gospel. I pray we get to know him better and love him more than we ever have.

If you are not yet a Christian, you may begin to know him now by repenting of your sins and placing your faith in Jesus as your Lord and God. He will not forsake you. He will save you.

## Reflect and Discuss

1. What is certainty?
2. In what ways is certainty important or unimportant to daily life?
3. Can we have certainty in matters of faith and religion?
4. How is religious certainty like or different from scientific claims to certainty?
5. What effect does uncertainty tend to have on us?
6. What is the difference between certainty and arrogance? Can one be certain without being intolerant or proud?
7. Can you recall a time when uncertainty gave way to certainty? What was that like? What difference did it make to you?
8. Luke aims to give his readers certainty about the things taught about Christ. Which test of certainty—biblical fulfillment or historical reliability—helps you most and why?
9. How might Luke's prologue be useful in defending the Christian faith against the idea that it is mythology?
10. Can you think of anyone who struggles with certainty about the claims of Christ? Prayerfully consider reading the Gospel of Luke with that person in order to help that person gain certainty.

# Jesus Was a Fetus

## LUKE 1:5-56

**Main Idea:** God always accomplishes his plan for his people. These scenes reveal for us two basic ways to respond to this truth.

I. **We May Respond to God's Plan in Unbelief (1:5-25).**
   A. Introduction of Zechariah and Elizabeth (1:5-7)
   B. Serving God through disappointment
   C. Gabriel's visit and prophecy (1:8-17)
   D. Zechariah's response (1:18)
   E. Gabriel's rebuke (1:19-25)
II. **We May Believe God's Plan Even When We Don't Understand (1:26-38).**
   A. Introduction to Mary and Joseph (1:26-27)
   B. Gabriel's greeting (1:28-33)
   C. Mary's response (1:34)
   D. Gabriel's explanation (1:35-37)
   E. Mary's faith (1:38)
III. **We Should Praise God for His Work Even Before It's Completed (1:39-56).**
   A. Elizabeth's confession (1:41-45)
   B. Mary's song (1:46-56)

Fifty-seven million. Do you know what that number represents? Before I tell you, I want you to know I am not trying to be political or unkind. The American public has politicized this issue to death with little fruit to show for it. So I'm not trying to be harsh or partisan. This issue should elicit the deepest wells of compassion because the number represents much pain and strife.

I give you the number in case you do not know. I give you the number so the scope of the issue is clear. I give you the number because I hope you will see its connection with God's work in the world.

In 1973, *Roe v. Wade* made unrestricted abortion a right in the United States. As of January 2015, some forty-three years later, the total number of reported abortions performed in the United States had reached 57,762,169.

Researchers classify approximately five of ten pregnancies in the United States as "unwanted pregnancies"—a hideous term. Of those, 40 percent end in abortion. Those percentages yield the fifty-seven million total.

If that number had been true in the first century, how might it have affected God's plan? If Mary, Joseph, and the first-century world lived in a context like today's United States, how do you imagine abortion laws might have impacted God's plan to redeem sinners?

Our text covers two miraculous pregnancies. In verses 5-25 God miraculously opens the womb of an old woman named Elizabeth. In verses 26-38 God miraculously opens the womb of a virgin girl named Mary. Both scenes follow the same pattern: the angel Gabriel appears, he announces the miracle, the people have questions, then Gabriel further explains God's plan. Our text concludes with Mary and Elizabeth together, praising God (vv. 39-56).

Luke does not begin his Gospel with a full-grown Jesus or even with an infant Jesus. Luke begins his Gospel in the wombs of two women. In doing so Luke tells us about the dignity and importance of pregnancy and children. He illustrates how God in infinite wisdom placed the weight of his entire plan of redemption on the back of an unborn baby.

## We May Respond to God's Plan in Unbelief
### LUKE 1:5-25

*Introduction of Zechariah and Elizabeth (1:5-7)*

*Context.* Verses 5-7 introduce us to Zechariah and Elizabeth. Verse 5 says they lived during "the days of King Herod of Judea." This is Herod the Great, who ruled from 37 to 34 BC. Herod was a puppet king put in place by Rome. This was not a peaceful time in Israel. They were a defeated people watching a foreign power occupy their land. It was a time of longing for deliverance.

*Character.* Zechariah and Elizabeth descended from Aaron, Moses's brother, the father of the priesthood in Israel. Elizabeth was "from the daughters of Aaron" (v. 5), and Zechariah was "a priest of Abijah's division" (v. 5), which means his people served the temple from the time of King David (1 Chr 24:10). As for character (v. 6), "Both were righteous in God's sight, living without blame according to all the commands and requirements of the Lord." They were faithful even into old age. Oh, to have God remember us all this way!

*Challenge.* We are meant to understand the sadness of this situation. They were righteous, but they were childless (v. 7). And they probably wondered why they were childless if they were righteous, or if they were truly righteous since they were childless. You know the human tendency to conflate God's approval with our blessing. That tendency remains common, but it is wrong. Elizabeth must have felt broken and to blame. She was the one who was barren. What a desert-like word. Dry. Cracked. Lifeless.

When she was a younger woman, newly married to Zechariah, no doubt well-meaning people probably asked, "When are you going to have children?" As she began to age, they then began to say with concern in their voice, "We are praying for you." Now in old age, they whisper around her, "She can't have children." You could probably see the concern on their faces. Imagine how difficult it might have been for her to rejoice in the pregnancy of other women without feeling sorrow for her own barrenness. Elizabeth was well aware of what she called her "disgrace among the people" (v. 25). She felt stigma and shame.

They were now "well along in years" (v. 7). So, at some point in life, Elizabeth and Zechariah had to adjust to the reality that their *could not* have children was, in fact, a *would not* have children.

## Serving God through Disappointment

While I was serving in the Cayman Islands, a middle-aged woman once asked if she could meet with me. She'd been attending church services for a few weeks, and a cloud of sadness hung over her. When she came to my office, she told me she had one son but had suffered six or seven miscarriages. She had one question: "Why is God punishing me?"

Our disappointments will either make us bitter or make us better. Our disappointments have a way of producing terrible theology and denials of God's goodness. That morning I told this depressed woman, "Though I cannot explain why God has entrusted you with so much suffering, I know God is good." My words seemed to her an empty platitude. In Elizabeth and Zechariah's case, the striking thing is that they handled a lifelong disappointment and social shame with righteousness and blamelessness before God. They served God even though they did not have what they wanted.

Being righteous and blameless does not mean a challenge-free life, exemption from heartaches, or that every desire will be granted. If you serve God for what you can get, then you actually serve yourself. That, beloved, is the prosperity gospel, not the biblical gospel. The righteous person is not free from suffering because he serves the Lord. We do not get everything we want just because we live well. We may live well past the years of possibility without receiving our hope; but if we are God's people, we will live righteously anyway because God is our hope.

Elizabeth and Zechariah endured this test. Their examples provoke us to ask, Will we serve God faithfully through our disappointments? No child. No husband. No dream job. No dream house or car. Will God mean more to us than all those things though we receive none of them?

## Gabriel's Visit and Prophecy (1:8-17)

Verses 8-10 zero in on Zechariah the priest. His division has been called up to the temple in Jerusalem to serve their rotation as priests (see 1 Chr 24). This happened twice a year. But something special happened during this rotation. Zechariah "was chosen . . . to enter the sanctuary of the Lord" (v. 9). Because there were so many priests serving the temple, such service was a once-in-a-lifetime thing. God worked providentially to extend this special privilege to this aged priest. Zechariah would have the honor of going into the holy place before the presence of God and burning the incense during the sacrifice.

During this period of focused worship, an angel appeared to him. Angels are glorious creatures, majestic and awesome! They strike fear into the hearts of even the righteous! They are so awesome and powerful that two things often happen when they show up. Some people mistake angels for God himself. Some people are overcome with fear before these great beings. Zechariah experienced the latter.

Incidentally, one reason I don't believe stories about people seeing angels and feeling all warm and fuzzy inside is because of scenes like this. Persons in the Bible who see an angel cover their eyes, hide their faces, and fear for their lives!

But angels are also messengers. According to Acts 7:53 angels deliver God's word—which is what the angel of the Lord does in verses 13-17. What a wonderful message this is! God says through Gabriel seven things:

1. "Do not be afraid" (v. 13). That alone comforts the Lord's people—the assurance that the Lord is on their side.

2. "Your prayer has been heard" (v. 13). Which prayer? His prayer for a son: "Your wife Elizabeth will bear you a son, and you will name him John" (v. 13). Given Zechariah's response in verse 18, I do not think Zechariah was praying for a son at that moment. I think the angel delivered an answer to prayers prayed long ago and now almost forgotten, maybe abandoned. Maybe Zechariah thought God had not heard or had forgotten. He did not realize God records our prayers in a book. In the fullness of time, God sent the angel to say, "I heard you. I have you in mind." God had stored his prayers until this dramatic moment in his plan of salvation. God was so interested and delighted in Zechariah's prayers he gave the baby a name for him!

3. "There will be joy and delight for you, and many will rejoice at his birth" (v. 14). If we stopped right there, these three statements would include almost everything human beings want: not to be afraid, to have a family, and to be happy. Oh how often we settle for so small a prize from God. But the angel went on.

4. "For he will be great in the sight of the Lord" (v. 15). God will have a special regard for this child. He will be a mighty man of God.

5. "He will be filled with the Holy Spirit while still in his mother's womb" (v. 15). This means the child John, from conception, will be controlled by God the Holy Spirit. So he must not drink alcohol; nothing else should control him. Verse 15 teaches the same idea we find in Ephesians 5:18: "Don't get drunk with wine, . . . but be filled by the Spirit." Why was John anointed with the Spirit of God?

6. "He will turn many of the children of Israel to the Lord their God" (v. 16). God will use Zechariah's son to ignite a revival in Israel.

7. "He [John] will go before him [the Lord] in the spirit and power of Elijah, to turn the hearts of fathers to their children, and the disobedient to the understanding of the righteous, to make ready for the Lord a prepared people" (v. 17).

The angel's speaking to Zechariah in the temple was a historic and unique moment in the history of salvation. Not since the last words of the last book of the Old Testament (Malachi) had God spoken. That was over four hundred years ago. God can give you the silent treatment when he wants to. And now through the angel Gabriel, God breaks his silence and speaks to an old man.

What does God say when he begins speaking again? He picks up where he left off, with the last words spoken four hundred years ago in Malachi 4:5-6. God made promises in the Old Testament that he now begins to fulfill in the New Testament. He sends John as another Elijah who will prepare the way for the coming of the Messiah. God now sends his long-awaited Savior to his people!

### Zechariah's Response (1:18)

The angel brings really good news to Zechariah, but Zechariah's response is, "How can I know this?" Seeing and hearing an angel is not enough? You want more proof!?

When our eyes are on our problems—in Zechariah's case, his old age—we will not receive God's word or trust God's power. We can't think our problems are great and God's power is great at the same time. We will exalt one a little bit more than the other. Trying to exalt our problems and God's power is like attempting to serve money and God at the same time. We cannot do it. We can be so focused on our problems we can't hear God's promises and we fail to believe God's power.

Did you know you can block out the noonday sun with a quarter? All you have to do is bring the quarter right up to your eye. We sometimes hold our problems and limitations to our eyes in that way, bringing them so close to our eyes we cannot see the great, glowing sun of God's promises and God's power.

When our eyes are on our problems, we will not remember God's Word and how it applies to us. Why did Zechariah not remember Abraham in Genesis 17:17? Abraham was in the same situation—wanting a child but he and his wife were far too old. God gave Abraham and Sarah a son when they were nearly a hundred years old! Zechariah should have remembered God's word, but he was focused on his limitation instead.

So Zechariah wants more proof than the Scriptures and more proof than an angel visiting him. He wants proof rather than the promise. In that way this righteous man walks by sight, not by faith.

We can be righteous persons in the holiest places, carrying out the holiest acts of worship, and not believe God! Unbelief is that sneaky! It can slither right into the middle of spiritual worship. You can be a preacher preaching the gospel and not believe anyone will be saved. You can be an evangelist on the street corner and not believe anyone will listen. You can be married and not believe your spouse is a gift from the Lord. We can pray for our heart's deepest desire, and laced in the marrow of our prayer is a sneaky unbelief. That was Zechariah, and that is many of us.

This lesson applies to older Christians in particular. Don't let age hinder you from God's work in and through you. You are not forgotten in God's plans any more than Elizabeth and Zechariah were forgotten. You are a vital part of God's plan in the church. In fact, without you we cannot do the one thing Christ commands in Matthew 28:18-20—make disciples. Christ has ordered things in his church in such a way that the older persons among us are meant to teach the younger (Titus 2:1-10). You are not simply "along for the ride." We do not want to put you in a corner and forget about you. It is to our shame that older persons are forgotten in society. We want to treasure you. We want to remind you of God's plan for your life. We want to see you active and involved in all God has for us as his church.

You will feel as if young people have passed you by. You may feel that you have little to contribute. You may think you're too old now. Let me encourage you: Don't make your age a quarter you hold to your eye and forget the power of God. Keep living for God and serving him with the strength and the wisdom he supplies!

## Gabriel's Rebuke (1:19-25)

In verses 19-20 the angel is like, "Man, don't you know who I am? Don't you know who I work for? You want a sign? I tell you what, since you like to question God's word, I will close your mouth until the whole promise is fulfilled."

Do not make God close your mouth because of unbelief. If the choice is between human creatures questioning God's word or God's word closing our mouths, guess which one will come to pass? God's word will stand. In fact, on the final day, the day of judgment, every mouth will be closed. There will be no rebuttal, no rejoinder or appeal. The God of the universe will do all things well, including administering justice on that final day. So it's better to receive and share his word rather than doubt it. Zechariah found that out the hard way.

Zechariah had to learn sign language while he was in the temple! All he could do was gesture and go home (vv. 21-23). The people knew he had seen a vision. Elizabeth conceived just as God had said through the angel Gabriel (vv. 24-25).

# We May Believe God's Plan Even When We Don't Understand

## LUKE 1:26-38

This is what we learn from Gabriel's second visit and second prophecy.

### Introduction of Mary and Joseph (1:26-27)

It's six months after Elizabeth had conceived. Now we've moved from Jerusalem north to the region of Galilee to a city called Nazareth. We've switched from the religious capital of the country to a small, backwater town with a bad reputation. "Can anything good come out of Nazareth?" (John 1:46). We're told in verse 27 that this young woman, Mary, was a virgin engaged to Joseph, a descendant of King David. To be engaged in those days was stronger than in our day. You couldn't break an engagement without getting a divorce for sexual immorality.

Zechariah and Elizabeth are at the end of their long lives, while Mary and Joseph are beginning theirs. What God does in the world has nothing to do with our ages or our hometowns. God uses whomever he wills.

### Gabriel's Greeting (1:28-33)

Gabriel greets Mary with words of grace, really (v. 28). God is smiling on this young, unknown girl. We might be tempted to think Zechariah was chosen because he was righteous and a priest. The angel's greeting to Mary reveals she is chosen solely as a matter of God's grace.

Mary doesn't understand the angel's greeting. She "was deeply troubled" by it and tried to figure out what kind of greeting it was (v. 29). How could she, an unknown young woman, be so described by God? Did you ever feel like your life is too small for God to notice, too insignificant for God to be aware of you? Perhaps that's how Mary felt.

Just as with Zechariah, the angel explains his message (vv. 30-33). Not only would Zechariah and Elizabeth give birth to the promised forerunner, but Mary would give birth to the promised Savior.

- Gabriel promises she too will conceive.
- She should name him Jesus, which according to Matthew 1:21 implies, "He will save his people from their sins."
- Mary's son will actually be "the Son of the Most High" (v. 32). He will be God's own Son. This is more than any human could ever have imagined or dreamed.

- This Son will fulfill the promise made to King David hundreds of years earlier (2 Sam 7). This will be David's son who rules over Israel forever in an everlasting kingdom.

## Mary's Response (1:34)

Now Mary *sounds* a lot like Zechariah when she replies in verse 34, but apparently there's no unbelief in her question. She's not asking, "*Can* you do it?" She's asking, "*How* will you do it?" Her question builds on faith, not unbelief. This is why Gabriel does not rebuke.

## Gabriel's Explanation (1:35-37)

To this young girl in a rural countryside, God through Gabriel reveals two of the greatest mysteries in the universe: the incarnation and the Trinity (v. 35):

> The Holy Spirit will come upon you, and the power of the Most High will overshadow you. Therefore, the holy one to be born will be called the Son of God." He refers to God the Father, God the Son, and God the Holy Spirit each having a part. But it's God the Son who will take on himself human flesh in the humility of a babe.

When God says the Holy Spirit "will come upon" Mary, he does not mean God impregnated Mary, as some Muslims slanderously believe of Christians. What a blasphemous thought! "Come upon" brings to mind Genesis 1:2, where the Holy Spirit was "hovering over" the face of the deep in creation. It's what Jesus is quoted as saying in Hebrews 10:5: "As he was coming into the world, he said: 'You did not desire sacrifice and offering, but you prepared a body for me.'" By the power of the Holy Spirit and the power of God the Father, a body was prepared for God the Son who would be brought forth by Mary.

Because Christ is fully God and fully man, he is the perfect Savior. He needed to be God to supply the righteousness humans could not achieve. He needed to be man to supply to God the sacrifice we owe. So he became the only mediator between God and man—the God-man, Christ Jesus. He is the only way for men to come to God.

We don't have to stumble at Jesus's deity and humanity. The angel assures Mary and assures us, "Nothing will be impossible with God" (v. 37). The moment you admit the existence of God, you must deny the impossible. With God it's nothing that a barren woman and a virgin woman would both conceive. In fact, that's just like God!

*Mary's Faith (1:38)*

Now contrast Mary's response to Zechariah's. Zechariah stumbled in unbelief. Mary yields in faith. Doesn't she sound a lot like Isaiah saying, "Here I am. Send me" (Isa 6:8)? Doesn't she sound a lot like Esther saying, "If I perish, I perish" (Esth 4:16)? Doesn't she sound a lot like Ruth saying to Naomi, "Your people will be my people, and your God will be my God" (Ruth 1:16)? It brings to mind Job's, "Even if he kills me, I will hope in him" (Job 13:15). It reminds us of Jesus in the garden of Gethsemane praying, "Father, . . . not my will, but yours, be done" (Luke 22:42). This is how faithful people respond to God's plan, even when they do not understand it.

What must Mary have thought about the Lord's plan? The only way a person can genuinely say what Mary says is to believe that God's plan is better than our plans for ourselves. When Mary responds in faith, she faces the potential of public shame. She faces the prospect of a divorce or a broken betrothal and never marrying. She would likely wear the scarlet letter of her day and be forced from home and family. She would be destitute.

Mary would face the same prospect that women face today when unfaithful men abandon them. Statistically, a woman ends up in poverty. Their lives are doubly hard. This is why we brothers must care for our women and children. Even if it breaks us, never let us forsake them.

Though she faced all of this, Mary spoke in faith. She concluded, "Whatever your will is for me, let it be." Like Mary, we can't truly be servants of Christ unless we accept his plan for our lives. He cannot be our Lord if we insist on ruling ourselves. If he is Lord, then we are servants—glad servants of God. This is how faith replies to grace. When God promises you a Savior, say, "Let me have him!" When God announces his plan for your life, say, "Amen! Let it be so! Not my will, but your will be done, God!"

Do we have this kind of faith? I pray we do. To express this kind of faith, must we renew our commitment to the Lord in some way? I pray we will.

## We Should Praise God for His Work Even Before It's Completed

### LUKE 1:39-56

Mary learned from Gabriel that her cousin Elizabeth was six months pregnant. Elizabeth had kept her pregnancy hidden for five months

(v. 24). Now Mary knows, and she travels to the hill country in Judah to visit her cousin.

These two women meet together and erupt with joy. They're not just joyful because they're both having babies. No. They know the Lord has shown them favor. They know the inside scoop on God's plans for their children. Their joy is supernatural.

### Elizabeth's Confession (1:41-45)

By the filling of the Holy Spirit, Elizabeth gets loud and blesses Mary as well as her baby Jesus in the womb. Apparently Elizabeth receives a revelation from God. Once Mary walks into the room, Elizabeth announces without prior communication that Mary carries her Lord. Elizabeth knows that Mary has believed the word she received from the Lord. Even the fetus John leaps for joy in his mother's womb when Mary, carrying Jesus, enters.

It's customary for us to think the first to confess that Jesus is the Christ was Peter. Actually, the first to make this confession is the older woman, Elizabeth, who confesses Jesus is Lord even before Jesus is born.

How did she know this? "Jesus is Lord" is the earliest of the Christian confessions. Paul tells us that no one can truly call Jesus "Lord" unless the Spirit gives him the ability (1 Cor 12:3). The Spirit gives Elizabeth that ability, and he gives that ability to everyone who believes in Christ. In the power of the Spirit, we should proclaim it loudly to all who will listen. From the four corners of the block to the four corners of the globe, let us follow Elizabeth's example and proclaim him as Lord to everyone!

Elizabeth knows that God's fulfillment is at hand, and Mary has believed it too (v. 45). God has a plan. Our most basic part in the plan is to believe it. These women are models of faith. They believe before the plan is fulfilled. How can we not believe him after it is fulfilled?

### Mary's Song (1:46-56)

After Elizabeth makes her confession, Mary sings her song. It's a beautiful song filled with hope and rich truth about God.

Mary rejoices in the Lord (vv. 46-48). Why? Because God her Savior "looked with favor on the humble condition of his servant" (v. 48). That is what God is like. He is close to the broken and the lowly.

Mary sees herself as blessed (vv. 48-49). Generations will call her blessed. Hasn't that happened for centuries now? She's no longer confused about what it means to find favor with God. However, the nations don't call Mary blessed because of anything she has done. They call her blessed "because the Mighty One has done great things for [her], and his name is holy" (v. 49). The point is God, not Mary. There's not the slightest hint of Mary worship, or Mariolatry, in this passage. Our Catholic friends err significantly when they exalt Mary to comediator with Christ. Mary herself exalted *God* for his greatness.

Anyone who would love and respect God will find mercy with God. "From generation to generation" (v. 50) means God's mercy reaches down to our time and place, too.

Verses 51-53 give us the signs that God's mercy is for all. There are no more virgin births, and we're unlikely to be in a Jewish temple when an angel visits; but we can see the work of God every day. That's what Mary celebrates. Don't ask God for a sign his promise will be fulfilled. We are simply to look around to see fulfillment. Signs are posted everywhere for all us "nobodies." God scatters the proud (v. 51). God topples the mighty (v. 52). God sends the rich away empty (v. 53). But the Lord exalts the lowly—that's the projects and the hoods (v. 52). He fills the hungry (v. 53). If we would know the riches of God's mercy, we simply need to admit the poverty of our lives.

Mary has confidence that God fulfills his plans and keeps his promises (vv. 54-55). He has helped Israel. He has remembered his mercy. All that he said to Abraham and Abraham's descendants is about to come to pass. And indeed it did. Christ was born as promised. He lived a sinless life. He offered righteousness to God in our place. He died a sinner's death, suffering the wrath of God in our place on Calvary's cross. He satisfied God's anger, and three days later God raised him from the dead—proving that the Father accepted the Son's sacrifice on our behalf. Now God calls all men everywhere to repent of their sins and to trust in Jesus as their Lord and Savior. The Father's mercy comes to us through his Son.

We should praise God for keeping his promises even before we see the promises fulfilled. That's what these women of faith do. His mercy endures forever.

## Conclusion

What do you think is Mary and Elizabeth's view of children in the womb? The least we can say is that they think life is a special gift from God and that the fetus is a baby.

From the beginning God planned to carry out his plan to save the world by the birth of a child. Genesis 3:15 says the offspring of the woman would crush the serpent's head. The Son of God entered the world through pregnancy and childbirth. That fact fills pregnancy, gestation, and childbirth with incalculable dignity and meaning! The infinite God came into the world through the close spaces of a human womb, making the womb and all that's in it sacred!

Had Mary and Elizabeth lived under *Roe v. Wade*, the plan of God to save the world would have been in jeopardy from the angel's announcement to her. She would have had a line of people ready to tell her to abort the baby. We think our age is more advanced and scientific. Well, these "primitive people" recognized from the start something our culture works hard to deny: the fetus is a baby. If it's a baby when you miscarry, it's a baby when you abort.

Praise God Christ was not born in modern-day America. Praise God for pregnancy! Praise God our Savior was born!

## Reflect and Discuss

1. What do the miraculous pregnancies of Mary and Elizabeth teach us about the power of God? What do they teach us about how God works in the world?

2. Does the fact that Christ came into the world through the normal process of childbirth affect how you view pregnancy and children? If so, how?

3. Zechariah and Mary have similar experiences with the angel Gabriel. How do their responses differ, and what is the consequence?

4. Zechariah was a righteous man, but he stumbled in unbelief. How common a problem do you think unbelief is among Christians?

5. Can you describe a time when you struggled to believe a promise of God or a part of God's Word?

6. What kinds of things have helped you in your battle against unbelief?

7. The angel announced to Mary a difficult thing to comprehend. Can you remember a time when you found God's Word or promise difficult to believe? How were you able to express faith despite the difficulty?

8. Israel waited a long time before God fulfilled his promise of a Messiah. Have you ever had to wait a long time for God to fulfill a promise in his Word? Did you find it difficult to wait? What was difficult and what was helpful to you?

9. In this section of Luke's Gospel, older persons figure prominently in the life of Christ. What do they teach us about faith and the role of older persons in the church today?

10. How can you praise God right now for some unfulfilled promise or some aspect of his work in the world that you don't yet understand?

# Getting to Know Jesus

# The Savior, Christ, and Lord

## LUKE 1:57–2:20

**Main Idea:** Our response to the birth of Christ should be to teach, treasure, and tell.

---

I. **God's Mercy Means Joy and Praise for Elizabeth and Zechariah (1:57-66,80).**
   A. Mercy brings joy to Elizabeth (1:57-58).
   B. Mercy brings praise for Zechariah (1:59-66).
   C. Suffering and enduring God's chastisement
   D. Lessons to parents and children (1:66,80)

II. **God's Mercy Means Salvation and Worship for Israel (1:67-79).**
   A. The plan of salvation (1:68-73)
   B. The purpose of salvation (1:72-75)
   C. The prophet of salvation (1:76-77)
   D. The peace of salvation (1:77-79)

III. **God's Mercy Means the Highest Glory through Jesus Christ (2:1-20).**
   A. A lowly birth (2:1-7)
   B. Humility before glory
   C. Glory in the highest (2:8-20)

---

Soul music began largely as a genre focusing on ballads. The pioneers of soul were "crooners," bellowing out sultry lyrics for lovers. Marvin Gaye was perhaps one of the most famous soul singers of his era. Gaye—who grew up in a pastor's home in the Deanwood neighborhood of Washington, D.C.—became the poster boy of smooth, sultry, romantic sound with hits like "How Sweet It Is to Be Loved by You," "I Heard It through the Grapevine," and with Tammi Terrell "Ain't No Mountain High Enough" and "You're All I Need to Get By."

However, by the 1960s many artists and genres of music became more concerned with the political issues and causes of the day, including Marvin Gaye. Gaye released a string of chart-topping hits like his 1971 tune "What's Going On?," "Inner City Blues: Makes Me Wanna Holla," and "Mercy, Mercy Me."

"What's Going On?" and "Mercy, Mercy Me" captured the anguished cry of a disenchanted and disenfranchised generation. The songs were urban laments, longing for an almost mythic day when things like hunger and war would cease to exist.

In other ways the songs gave voice to a question—a prayer, really—that almost irrepressibly escapes one's lips amid life's turmoil. Gaye seemed to be crying out with his generation for mercy. The cry for mercy is as old as humanity's fall in the garden. It's been uttered, whispered, and yelled in every generation among every people since sin entered the world. When we reach those limits, something in us looks for mercy.

Luke 1:57–2:20 contains two natural births, two supernatural messages from God, and one main point. This passage of Scripture reveals that Jesus is the Savior. That's good news for humanity, for great mercy comes from a great God and his Savior.

## God's Mercy Means Joy and Praise for Elizabeth and Zechariah
### LUKE 1:57-66

*Mercy Brings Joy to Elizabeth (1:57-58)*

Nine months have passed since the angel Gabriel visited Zechariah in the temple and promised that he and Elizabeth would have a son. Things happened just as the angel said they would. The simple words of verse 57 remind us that we can trust God's word because God's word is true.

Part of what the angel promised in 1:14 is that "many will rejoice at his birth." Verse 58 partially fulfills that promise. Picture the scene. You have this old woman, well past the years of childbearing, who had suffered the reproach of being childless, now finally giving birth. What no one thought would happen has finally happened. Neighbors and relatives had given up, too. Their hopes for Elizabeth had long faded. And now, here she is with a baby boy! Everyone is rejoicing with her.

Here's the important thing the people recognized: "The Lord had shown [Elizabeth] his great mercy" (v. 58). This was no regular circumstance. God was involved. God was showing part of his character—specifically his mercy. God shows mercy when he punishes us less than our sins deserve. God shows mercy when he relieves us of our suffering. That's what he does for Elizabeth in the birth of John. J. C. Ryle wrote,

There was mercy in bringing her safely through her time of
trial. There was mercy in making her the mother of a living
child. Happy are those family circles, whose births are viewed
in this light—as special instances of the mercy of the Lord.
(*Luke*, 1:30–31)

All children are gifts of God's mercy—no matter the circumstance.
Psalm 127:3 declares, "Sons are indeed a heritage from the Lord,
offspring, a reward." We all should receive children with the joy that
Elizabeth received John. We all should recognize children as God's
mercy to us.

### Mercy Brings Praise for Zechariah (1:59-66)

Zechariah and Elizabeth were faithful in their obedience to God so
"they came to circumcise the child on the eighth day" (v. 59). God commanded that all the male children of Israel be circumcised when they
were eight days old. Circumcision was the sign of God's covenant relationship with Israel. Apparently, Jewish families at the time of Christ
held the ceremony of circumcision in the home with family and friends.

And, apparently, they named the child on the eighth day at his circumcision. All the family and friends just know the boy is going to be
a "junior" (v. 59). Funny how the extended family assumed they could
name the child as if it's theirs! But maybe they were thinking the best.
Maybe they were thinking, *They've tried for so long. They're so advanced in*
*years now. Surely they'll name the child Zechariah and keep the father's name*
*alive.*

But the people are unaware of what God has said through Gabriel.
They do not know that God has already named the child. Naming was
sometimes associated with dominion or rule; this child will be under
God's rule, not man's.

Elizabeth speaks up (v. 60). That should have ended it, but the family pushes back. They're like, "What kind of name is 'John'? No, we
don't like that." Then they try to pull rank by motioning to Zechariah.
The fact that they make signs indicates that not only did the angel
close Zechariah's mouth; he also closed John's ears. For nine months
now, Zechariah could not hear or speak. He has had to make some
adjustments. That is why a writing tablet was handy (v. 63). In Greek
the emphasis on what he writes is on "John." More literally Zechariah
writes, "*John* is his name."

At that precise moment of faith and obedience, in mercy God lifted his punishment and freed Zechariah's mouth. And praise came flying out! As Ryle put it,

> He shews that his nine months' dumbness had not been inflicted on him in vain. He is no longer faithless, but believing. He now believes every word that Gabriel had spoken to him, and every word of his message shall be obeyed.
>
> Let us take heed that affliction does us good, as it did to Zecharias. . . . "Sanctified afflictions" . . . are "spiritual promotions." The sorrow that humbles us, and drives us nearer to God, is a blessing, and a downright gain. No case is more hopeless than that of a man who, in time of affliction, turns his back upon God. (*Luke*, 1:32)

Zechariah's praise is contagious. All the neighbors are in awe of God (v. 65). Those who were there talked about it everywhere, and everyone who heard the report knew something miraculous and supernatural was happening (v. 66).

## Suffering and Enduring God's Chastisement

Our suffering will make us either bitter or better. It made Zechariah better. "Zacharias had learned, probably, more about his own heart, and about God, than he ever knew before" (Ryle, *Luke*, 1:32). The proof of that is the praise for God that leaped from his mouth that day.

How are we handling our suffering? Is it working in us deeper thoughts of God's goodness or harder thoughts about our circumstance? Are we growing warmer or colder toward God?

## Lessons to Parents and Children (1:66,80)

The people at John's circumcision and naming ceremony knew God was at work among them. Verse 66 says, "For, indeed, the Lord's hand was with him." They had a sense that God was at work through John. What a beautiful sentence that is, isn't it?

What does that look like? How can we recognize it? Look at the first part of verse 80: "The child grew up and became spiritually strong." When God's hand is on our children, they grow and become strong—not just in body but, more importantly, in spirit. Their whole being matures into spiritual strength before the Lord as he guides and protects them.

God's hand was with John. That is part of what it means that John "was in the wilderness until the day of his public appearance to Israel" (v. 80). The wilderness is where prophets are prepared for the hardship of public ministry. That part of verse 80 is unique to John, but doesn't the first part of verse 80 call us to want the last part of verse 66 for our children? Don't we want God's loving, powerful hand to make our children spiritually strong? And the children of the church? And the children of the community?

Once again J. C. Ryle offers penetrating insight:

> This is the portion that we ought to seek for our children. It is the best portion, the happiest portion, the only portion that can never be lost, and will endure beyond the grave. It is good to have over them "the hand" of teachers and instructors; but it is better still to have "the hand of the Lord." We may be thankful if they obtain the patronage of the great and the rich. But we ought to care far more for their obtaining the favour of God. The hand of the Lord is a thousand times better than the hand of Herod. The one is weak, foolish, and uncertain; caressing today, and beheading to-morrow. The other is almighty, all-wise, and unchangeable. Where it holds it holds for evermore. Let us bless God that the Lord never changes. What he was in John the Baptist's days, he is now. What he did for the son of Zacharias, he can do for our boys and girls. But he waits to be entreated. If we would have the hand of the Lord with our children, we must diligently seek it. (*Luke*, 1:33)

God waits to be asked. We must diligently seek his hand on our children's lives. So let us pray like we never have for the hand of the Lord to be on our children.

God's mercy means joy and praise for Elizabeth and Zechariah. It means the same for us if we receive it.

## God's Mercy Means Salvation and Worship for Israel
### LUKE 1:67-79

This is what we learn in Zechariah's prophecy. *God in his mercy has sent salvation to his people.* That dominant idea finds expression in four parts.

## The Plan of Salvation (1:68-73)

Zechariah blesses or praises God because God has visited and redeemed his people with a strong salvation. A "horn" is used in the Bible to symbolize strength or power. This is the powerful salvation for Israel that was promised to come through David, that was prophesied through the prophets of old, and that in verses 72-73 goes all the way back to the "fathers," or patriarchs, and to Abraham. This salvation is an act of mercy (v. 72). God saves us to prove his mercy. The entire Bible—from Abraham to the prophets down to King David—is about this one thing: salvation. The Bible has one story: God visiting or coming to get his people. That was and is the plan.

This salvation has multiple parts to it. One part, as verse 71 puts it, is to save Israel from their enemies and from the hand of all their haters. This is an actual, political, physical rescue. But that's not all.

## The Purpose of Salvation (1:72-75)

The goal of their physical deliverance was not simply their physical freedom. The goal was worship. This is the New Testament version of what God told Moses to tell Pharaoh: "Let my people go, *so that they may worship me*" (Exod 7:16; emphasis added).

God saves so that we might worship. Freedom is a good goal, but it's not the ultimate goal. The freedom God seems most interested in is the freedom to worship him. Just as Zechariah worshiped God when God mercifully opened Zechariah's mouth and ears, so all Israel is to praise and glorify God for the salvation he brings.

## The Prophet of Salvation (1:76-77)

Zechariah now prophesies about John. John will be great. He will be called a prophet of God. He will be unique among the prophets because he will be the forerunner. He will soften the ground. He will till the soil of Israel's heart. He will not be the Savior, but John will make things ready for the Savior by teaching people how they are to be saved. John will be a giant index finger pointing the way to God's salvation from sin.

Zechariah's prophecy defines John's life in relationship to Jesus's life and mission. Beloved, all lasting meaning is found when we define our lives this way. Greatness comes from serving the Lord, not from serving ourselves. Greatness comes when we, like John, say, "We must decrease; Jesus must increase" (see John 3:30). The prophet of salvation never replaces the bringer of salvation.

### The Peace of Salvation (1:77-79)

Zechariah begins to describe the effect of this salvation on the people.

*First, this salvation is ultimately spiritual and personal.* It involves "the forgiveness of their sins" (v. 77). Why must sin be forgiven? Why is sin a problem? Because it is an offense against God, who is holy. God in his holiness and anger will punish the sinner forever unless they are forgiven. When we talk about being "saved," we should ask, "Saved from what?" The Bible's answer is, "Saved from God." We need to be rescued from God's coming judgment against the world. Unless we are rescued, we will suffer punishment in hell forever. Have you escaped God's condemnation? Do you know how?

*Second, this salvation is by God's mercy.* Verse 78 says it is "because of our God's merciful compassion." That's the only reason anyone is ever forgiven of sin: mercy. You cannot earn forgiveness. You cannot demand forgiveness. You cannot swap forgiveness with a trade. There would be no peace in salvation if we had to earn, demand, or buy forgiveness. We would only worry if we had done enough, if we were strong enough, or if we had paid enough. Forgiveness comes only by mercy. Which means forgiveness is free and undeserved. The only step we can take to find forgiveness with God is to ask for it. Beg for mercy, and God will show it. Confess your sin, and he is faithful to forgive it (1 John 1:9).

*Third, this salvation brings light.* Verses 78-79 declare, "The dawn from on high will visit us to shine on those who live in darkness and the shadow of death." Through the mercy of our God, we receive light. This light is Christ himself. He is the sunrise, or you may have a translation that says the "dayspring" (KJV). In our sin we sit in darkness like prisoners locked in an underground dungeon. But when Christ comes into our hearts, he brings light. All of a sudden everything shines. Darkness flees. Death is defeated. "The way of peace" (v. 79) refers to an entire life of peace. Salvation brings peace. Peace with God. Peace with man. Peace within ourselves.

Do you have this peace? Has the sunrise dawned in your soul yet?

# God's Mercy Means the Highest Glory through Jesus Christ
## LUKE 2:1-20

Glory is not the first word you think of when you think of Jesus's birth.

## A Lowly Birth (2:1-7)

*First, Jesus is born when Israel is under Roman rule.* Caesar Augustus and Quirinius are in positions of power. God's people are an oppressed people. Oppressed people don't have glory or power or honor to speak of.

Though that is true, it is not the highest truth. There is an invisible power behind and over these human rulers. They do not know it, but God uses Caesar and Quirinius to fulfill what he promised long ago. In Malachi 5:2, four hundred years before the birth of Christ, God told his people the Messiah would be born in Bethlehem of Judea. Joseph and Mary start out in Nazareth of Galilee (v. 4). God uses the emperor's census to move them back to Joseph's hometown—Bethlehem.

God's people need never fear the laws of men. Over those laws are the laws of God. Even when men rule for their own ends, God is at work to fulfill his plan.

*Second, Jesus is born where no child should be born* (vv. 6-7). The God of the universe is laid in an animal's feeding trough. There is no glory in that. We think of something the Lord would later say: "Foxes have dens, and birds of the sky have nests, but the Son of Man has no place to lay his head" (9:58; Matt 8:20). That was the Savior's lifelong testimony.

Nothing about this scene says "glory." But there is much in this scene to instruct us.

## Humility before Glory

Before there is glory, there must first be humility. That is the way the kingdom of God operates. The first will be last, and the last will be first (Mark 10:31). God opposes the proud but gives grace to the humble (Jas 4:6; 1 Pet 5:5). Humble yourself before the Lord, and in due time he will exalt you (Jas 4:10). In the kingdom of God, first comes humility then comes glory. We see this modeled for us right from the Savior's birth. True greatness is not always visible greatness.

The incarnation of the Son of God in an animal's feeding trough puts our glory-craving hearts in check. Matthew Henry rightly observed,

He well knew how unwilling we are to be meanly lodged,
clothed, or fed; how we desire to have our children decorated
and indulged; how apt the poor are to envy the rich, and how
prone the rich to disdain the poor. But when we by faith view
the Son of God being made man and lying in a manger, our
vanity, ambition, and envy are checked. We cannot, with this
object rightly before us, seek great things for ourselves or our
children. (*Commentary*, 5:257)

## Glory in the Highest (2:8-20)

We do not see the glory of this passage until we learn what the shepherds
learn. They are out at night keeping watch over their flock (v. 8). This is
not glorious work. This is not the best shift. Shepherds had bad reputations. The nature of their work meant they could not observe Israel's
ceremonial laws. They were considered unreliable and could not give
testimony in the law courts. They were a despised class of people.

On that night "an angel of the Lord stood before them" (v. 9). The
dark night runs away from the shining light of God's glory. And they
were filled with fear; awe and reverence grip their hearts.

To these lowly men, the angel gives the highest theology (vv. 10-12).
These despised shepherds are the first to receive the announcement
of the gospel. These men are the first to learn of "great joy for all the
people." They understand that the gospel is not just for Israel but for all
the nations, that all may have this joy.

These despised men hear the most wonderful thing about how this
joy comes. It comes through the birth of "a Savior . . . who is the Messiah,
the Lord" (v. 11). This is the only time in the Gospels this phrase is used.
It's the only time we see all the titles of Jesus brought together—Savior,
Messiah, Lord. He will save his people from their sins. Jesus is the Christ,
the Messiah promised to Israel. And most staggeringly of all, he is Lord.
He is God. He is Maker of all. He is Ruler of all. The angels not only give
the gospel to the shepherds; they give the true identity of Christ.

It seems God believes high theology should be given to low people.
That's why we want to teach as robustly as we can the deep truths of
God. We do not want to be unnecessarily complex. The angels speak
plainly here, but they use plain speech to convey deep truth. That is
what preaching should do. It's what it should do for poor and despised
people. Nothing about poverty prevents people from knowing God well.
Nothing about class determines what people can afford to know about

God. The fullness of the gospel goes to the poor just as it would to anyone. The truth is that Luke shows us that the poor receive it, not the educated, powerful, and rich. As J. C. Ryle put it,

> Let us beware of despising the poor, because of their poverty. Their condition is one which the Son of God has sanctified and honored, by taking it voluntarily on Himself. God is no respecter of people. He looks at the hearts of men, and not at their incomes. Let us never be ashamed of the *affliction of poverty*, if God thinks fit to lay it upon us. To be godless and covetous is disgraceful, but it is no disgrace to be poor. A lowly dwelling place, and coarse food, and a hard bed, are not pleasing to flesh and blood. But they are the portion which the Lord Jesus Himself willingly accepted from the day of His entrance into the world. Wealth ruins far more souls than poverty. When the love of money begins to creep over us, let us think of the manger at Bethlehem, and of Him who was laid in it. Such thoughts may deliver us from much harm. (*Luke*, 1:141)

When the angel had finished preaching the gospel to the shepherds, the angelic choir came on for a closing hymn. Then God revealed his glory (v. 14). God's mercy to men brings God's highest glory in heaven.

Luke 2:15-18 remind us of 1:65-66. The shepherds visit baby Jesus and his earthly parents in the stable. They tell everyone what they've seen and heard. People are amazed.

## Conclusion

Verses 17-20 lay for us a pattern to be repeated by disciples of the Lord throughout all generations. The shepherds teach others what they heard and saw. Mary treasures it in her heart. Then the shepherds return home to tell others of the glory of God. From the time of the Savior's birth, those receiving the Savior have followed this pattern of teach, treasure, and tell. Can there be any other response to God's mercy in Jesus Christ? Can there be any other response to seeing the glory of God? Let us teach it, treasure it, and tell it abroad forever.

## Reflect and Discuss

1. Have you ever been in a situation where you needed mercy? What was it like?
2. What difference did receiving mercy make for you? Did it bring you joy or relief?
3. How would you say you handle suffering? Does suffering tend to produce in you deeper thoughts of God's goodness or hard thoughts toward God?
4. In Luke 1:68-79, how does God show mercy to Israel and the world? What goal or purpose does God have in mind for man's salvation?
5. How does God's mercy reveal his glory?
6. In what ways should our Lord's incarnation humble us?
7. Can you think of three persons to teach about the Lord and his salvation? How will you share with them? Write down your plan, including when you hope to share and what you hope to say. Do you treasure these things in your own heart?

# A Growing Boy

## LUKE 2:21-52

**Main Idea:** We grow in wisdom and favor as we are surrounded by godliness.

---

I.   **Righteous Parents (2:21-24)**
II.  **Revealed Purpose (2:25-40)**
    A.  Simeon
    B.  Anna
    C.  Simeon's prophecy
    D.  The gospel
    E.  Anna's preaching
    F.  Passing on a revealed purpose
    G.  Women like Anna among us
III. **Responsible Parents (2:41-52)**

---

Luke belongs to the Synoptic Gospels along with Matthew and Mark. As mentioned earlier (p. 4), the term *synoptic* means to "see together." These three Gospels tell the story of our Lord's earthly life from largely the same perspective.

But the Synoptic Gospels do not teach us a great deal about our Lord's childhood. Almost everything we know about the childhood of Christ comes from Luke 1–2. In Luke 1:5-56 we considered the pregnancy narrative, where Mary and Elizabeth were miraculously enabled to conceive children. There we saw that Jesus was a fetus. In our last chapter we considered the birth of the Lord Jesus Christ. As we get to know Jesus in these opening chapters, we witness the amazing humility of our Savior. The Lord of glory himself, infinite in majesty, lay in the womb of a young virgin. The one who is "sustaining all things by his powerful word" (Heb 1:3) did so while lying in a manger.

From this text we wish to get to know Jesus as a growing boy. Luke 2:21-52 covers three scenes. The first scene begins in verse 21 when Jesus is eight days old and is about to be circumcised. The second scene begins in verse 22. The reference to "the days of their purification," according to Old Testament law, puts us at thirty-three days after

Jesus's birth. So verses 22-40 give us a glimpse of Jesus as a one-month-
old. Verses 41-52 give us the third scene when Jesus is around twelve
years old.

The opening chapters of Luke's Gospel reveal nearly everything we
know about our Lord's first twelve years on earth. Luke tells us "the boy
grew up and became strong, filled with wisdom, and God's grace was on
him" (v. 40), and "Jesus increased in wisdom and stature, and in favor
with God and with people" (v. 52).

Three factors contributed to Jesus's wisdom and stature before God
and man. I trust our children need these three factors as well.

## Righteous Parents
### LUKE 2:21-24

Naturally speaking, how did Jesus grow in wisdom and stature before
God and man? First, Jesus had righteous parents. Mary and Joseph's
obedience reflects righteousness in two ways.

*First, Mary and Joseph show their righteousness by obeying the angel's
instruction* to name the baby "Jesus." That was an act of "the obedience
of faith" (Rom 1:5).

Luke 1:26-38 records the angel Gabriel appearing to Mary and
announcing that the virgin would conceive a child. The saying at first
troubled her (1:29), but she believed God. According to Matthew 1:18-
25, Joseph initially thought Mary had been unfaithful. The Bible calls
him a "righteous man" (v. 19) who planned to quietly divorce Mary to
save her from public embarrassment. But then an angel appeared to
Joseph in a dream. The angel told Joseph to take Mary as his wife and
that the child was conceived in her from the Holy Spirit (Matt 1:20).

The angel told both Mary and Joseph independently what was to be
the baby's name: "Jesus." Matthew 1:21 gives us the reason for the name:
"He will save his people from their sins." In Luke 2:21 we see the young
couple completing their obedience to God's will by naming the baby
"Jesus."

Could you imagine Mary and Joseph naming the baby with some
other name? How would they teach Jesus to honor the Lord if they
refused to honor God themselves? But because they obeyed God in
naming Jesus, every time they called their son's name, the name itself
was a reminder of their following the Lord and a reminder of Jesus's
calling to save. Each time they called Jesus's name, Mary and Joseph

remembered the angel's visit and God's plan. Calling their son "Jesus" reminds them God had visited his people.

*Second, they show their righteousness by obeying the law of God.* They respond not only to supernatural revelation of the angel but also to the written Word of God. Sometimes Christians feel certain God has "told them" something, but then they cannot square that personal "word" with the Bible. In such cases we can be sure God has not told them such a thing. Mary and Joseph have the unusual revelation from the angel but also the "regular" revelation of the Scriptures. They believe and obey God's Word.

Verses 21-24 are rooted in the Mosaic law. Leviticus 12 gave instruction for regaining purity after the birth of a child.

> The LORD spoke to Moses: *"Tell the Israelites: When a woman becomes pregnant and gives birth to a male child, she will be unclean seven days, as she is during the days of her menstrual impurity. The flesh of his foreskin must be circumcised on the eighth day. She will continue in purification from her bleeding for thirty-three days. She must not touch any holy thing or go into the sanctuary until completing her days of purification.* . . .
>
> *"When her days of purification are complete, whether for a son or daughter, she is to bring to the priest at the entrance to the tent of meeting a year-old male lamb for a burnt offering, and a young pigeon or a turtledove for a sin offering. He will present them before the LORD and make atonement on her behalf; she will be clean from her discharge of blood. This is the law for a woman giving birth, whether to a male or female. But if she doesn't have sufficient means for a sheep, she may take two turtledoves or two young pigeons, one for a burnt offering and the other for a sin offering. Then the priest will make atonement on her behalf, and she will be clean."* (12:1-4,6-8)

Mary and Joseph carefully follow the law and time line of Leviticus 12. They circumcise Jesus on the eighth day (Luke 2:21) and take him to Jerusalem to present him to God (v. 22). Verse 23 reminds us that the baby already belonged to God. In the exodus out of Egypt, when God spared the lives of all Israel's firstborn children, God also laid claim to the firstborn as his own. They were "dedicated to the Lord." Mary and Joseph make their obedience complete by offering in worship what the Lord required (v. 24).

Naturally speaking, the first reason Jesus grew in wisdom and favor with God was that he had righteous earthly parents. They obeyed God. We parents have tremendous influence on our children. What they regard as plausible in the faith is often shaped by our faith. Their inconsistencies and hypocrisies are often seen in us first, are they not? This is why believing, righteous, obedient parents are a tremendous blessing to any child. Our obedience creates a context for a growing child to see the need for his own obedience to the Father.

Parents, is our obedience to the Word of the Lord as consistent and thorough as Mary and Joseph's? What do our children learn about serving God as they watch us?

*A theology of poverty.* The two turtledoves or the two young pigeons were to be offered if a family could not afford to offer a lamb and a turtledove (v. 24; Lev 12:6-8). In other words, Jesus was born into poverty. What does it mean that the Savior of the world, the Son of God, was born to a poor mother and family? I think it implies at least seven things:

1. Poverty is not a sin.
2. Poverty is not God's disapproval.
3. Poverty does not prevent a person from worshiping God.
4. Poverty does not necessarily doom a person to poverty forever.
5. Poverty does not excuse unrighteousness.
6. Poverty is not shameful in and of itself.
7. Poverty is a cross that God entrusts to some people for a time.

If some teacher or preacher tries to convince you that poverty is a sin, that poverty is God's condemnation of you, that you have to give a certain amount of money to worship God, or that poverty excuses your sin, then do not listen to that teacher. Remember Jesus. Jesus and his family were poor, and none of those things were true of him. Jesus was not in sin. God the Father was well pleased with him.

Now poverty is hard. There are a lot of temptations and a lot of suffering in poverty. Poverty is a cross. But for many of us, that God should place us in poverty is a grace that saves us when riches would destroy us. We tend to think poverty is only a curse, but it may be God spares us things worse than poverty. Proverbs 28:6 reads, "Better the poor person who lives with integrity than the rich one who distorts right and wrong." Or, as Ecclesiastes 4:13 puts it, "Better is a poor but wise youth than an old but foolish king who no longer pays attention to warnings."

Christian, let us be sure we never despise poor people. How easily do pride and condescension infiltrate our attitudes toward the poor? J. C. Ryle's comments on poverty as quoted in the previous section are also appropriate here (see p. 40). If we despise the poor, we show we would have likely despised the boy Jesus himself. Our Lord was poor and has infused righteous poverty with dignity and holiness.

And let us not be deceived by riches. Wealth may be our greatest trial. So let us pray the prayer of Agur: "Give me neither poverty nor wealth" (Prov 30:8). Both poverty and wealth have their own temptations. Let us beware of them both.

Parents, righteousness—even in poverty—makes a huge difference in the lives of children. It's not about what we can give our children in material things but how we model for them faithful obedience in service to the Lord. If we give our children that example, then we will give them everything they need for life and godliness. If we teach our children the Scriptures, then it will be said that our children have "wisdom for salvation" because of the nature of the Scriptures (2 Tim 3:15). If we give our children the treasure of the Scriptures, then we give them spiritual wealth for a lifetime and eternity.

You may be thinking, *I'm a parent and I'm not righteous like Mary and Joseph.* I have more good news for you. While you yet breathe, you have opportunity to confess and repent of unrighteousness. You have opportunity to recognize your failings and sins. There's nothing like parenthood to make us insecure about our inability. We all stumble in many ways in our parenting. Yet it is the nature of God to deal graciously with us—even parents who sin. There is no failing in our parenting life that Christ has not overcome if we will confess and repent of those sins and seek righteousness in Christ alone.

As a local church, can we follow the Lord's pattern of incarnation? Christ lived as a poor boy among poor people. Can we plant our lives in the community among the poor as the Savior did? I realize that Jesus was the Messiah and we are not—we must not get a Messiah complex—but can we embrace this posture of service, humility, and love? Can we take a similar place among the poor, living in the neighborhood?

Jesus grew in wisdom and favor with God and man because he had righteous parents.

## Revealed Purpose
### LUKE 2:25-40

### Simeon

Verses 25-40 introduce us to Simeon and Anna. Like Mary and Joseph, Simeon was dedicated to obeying God's word. And he was full of faith—he was waiting for God to fulfill his promise to comfort or console Israel with a Savior (Isa 40:1; 57:18). He believed God's word of promise. And he had that rare gift for this period in history—he was filled with the Holy Spirit. This old man was controlled by God and empowered to serve. By the Holy Spirit, God promised Simeon that he would not die before seeing the Messiah (v. 26).

### Anna

If you ever want a picture of true devotion and godliness, look at Anna. She's a prophetess, which was not unusual in the Old Testament. From time to time God raised up women who spoke his word on his behalf. Anna was such a woman. Now this is a not a passage that justifies women pastors. People sometimes do that with the Old Testament prophetess Deborah, and it could be tempting to do that with Anna. But Anna, as a prophetess, was not called to lead Israel in worship—that was the job of qualified male priests even in the Old Testament. Plus, there are clear passages in the New Testament epistles that prohibit women from serving as pastors or elders. We should interpret the historical narratives in light of the teaching letters. Anna is a prophetess.

Anna is also "well along in years." Not only that, for eighty-four years she lived as a single woman following the death of her husband. Apparently she married young and was widowed young. You'd have to think she's over a hundred years old if she married around age sixteen.

### Simeon's Prophecy

Verses 27-35 record Simeon's prophecy regarding Jesus. Imagine this old man's elation. He was at home carrying on his day—perhaps in prayer or some other activity. Then, unexpectedly, he has a strong urge and leading to go to the temple. With each step the leading gets stronger until, even as an old man, he was nearly running to get there. He saw Jesus in his parents' arms and he knew. He knew! This was the long-awaited comfort of Israel, the promised Savior. He took the one-month-old baby out of their arms and brought him close to his chest. Looking into the face of Christ, by the inspiration of the Holy Spirit, Simeon blessed Jesus with a prophecy.

Simeon blessed God for keeping the promise to let him see the Messiah (vv. 29-30). Imagine the peace and the deep satisfaction at seeing the promise fulfilled. Simeon's soul found rest as the infant Christ rested in his old arms. Simeon was basically saying, "Lord, you can take me now. My work is done. You kept your word."

In verses 31-32 Simeon reveals the purpose for which Christ was born. The consolation of Israel is also the light of the world. This babe will bring the light and glory of salvation not only to the Jews but also to the Gentiles. He is to be the Savior of the world! All the nations will come to him for light and life. Simeon has a 1-16 moment, the Gospel equivalent of Paul's declaration in Romans 1:16 that he is "not ashamed of the gospel, because it is the power of God for salvation to everyone who believes, first to the Jew, and also to the Greek."

Simeon is not finished. The gladness of verses 31 and 32 come also with hints of sorrow in verses 34-35. The old man turned his cloudy eyes to the parents. Simeon blessed them with strange words. This child will be a light, but he will be the kind of light that exposes. Because he exposes, he will face opposition. That opposition will be a violent piercing—a piercing that will penetrate his mother's heart also.

## The Gospel

Simeon sees the salvation from the Lord in his arms, and he glimpses Calvary as well. In time, the poor will be lifted up and the wealthy, powerful religious leaders will fall. In time, this child will grow and an entire nation—an entire world!—will have to decide to either follow him or oppose him. Hearts will be revealed. God will see. Condemnation and salvation will come in one Savior sacrificed on a cross.

Jesus still exposes hearts and provokes opposition. Perhaps you don't know what you think about Jesus. Maybe you're aware of your slight opposition to him, but you don't really know where it comes from or how it got there. It could have gotten there by any number of things you've been taught over the years. But the ultimate source of that opposition is your sin nature. You were born that way. All of us were. In our sin we have this opposition to Christ, to his claim on our lives, to his lordship and deity. And so we rebel against him.

But that rebellion will be put down. God will not always strive with us in our sin. If we continue in it, we will fall—or, rather, be pulled down by God. Christ was sent to save us and bring us into his light, but men love darkness rather than the light (John 3:19). Our deeds are evil, and we don't want to be found out.

But God knows. He sees us in our sin. He sends us a Savior in Jesus Christ. Jesus is a Savior you either love or hate. The cross says he loves you. Unbelief and sin say we hate him. But repentance and faith say we love him. For our hate, we deserve and we receive death. For our love we don't deserve but we do receive life. Choose life. Choose Christ. Believe in him so that you might be saved.

## Anna's Preaching

If you believe the gospel, then tell others. What does Anna do in her old age? First, she thanks God. When you realize God has sent a Savior you ought to thank him. Don't be like the nine lepers Jesus healed who went off with no word of thanks. Be like the one leper who returned out of gratitude (17:11-19).

The Christian heart should be a grateful heart. And as much as I want to encourage older saints, I also want to provide a respectful word of admonishment. Sometimes age has a way of making people bitter rather than thankful. There are churches filled with older saints, but they're not like Anna. They're hard. Their faces are shriveled in peevishness and unkindness. So my encouragement is this: Don't let that be you and me. As we age, let us become more expert in giving God thanks for thousands of days of fresh mercy he has shown us. Anna gives thanks for her Savior.

Second, Anna starts gossiping the gospel. There were others longing for a salvation who did not know it had already come. I love Anna. She decided, *I am going to go tell it on the mountain. I am going to tell it everywhere: that Jesus Christ is born.* Anna becomes an evangelist. She uses her gift and call as a prophetess to declare the good news of Jesus's birth.

She believes, and so she speaks. In speaking of Jesus, she becomes a real promoter of Jesus. She encourages others to trust in him.

## Passing on a Revealed Purpose

This is Jesus's revealed purpose: to save his people from their sin—both Jew and Gentile. He grew in wisdom and favor with God because from infancy he had people speaking this over his life. In supernatural ways and in ways as natural as his name, the Lord Jesus was constantly reminded of his purpose.

Jesus is the only Savior, so no one else has that purpose. I know you love your kids, but they're not perfect. They can't *be* the Savior; they *need* a Savior. That's the revealed purpose for them.

Our kids do better when they have even a general sense of God's purpose for their lives. Notice verse 33: "His father and mother were amazed at what was being said about him." They are blown away. They don't yet understand all that's being said—which is an encouragement for parents everywhere. We don't have to have all the details about our children's future. We don't have to have any of the details, and many things may leave us wondering. But we do know this: Our children were made to know and love God through faith in Christ. We know they were given to us so we might shepherd them to Christ.

How wonderful it is to tell our children they are loved by God— that God proved his love for them in that while they were sinners (even before they were born!), Christ came into the world and died for them. What a difference it makes to the sense of purpose, worth, and dignity of a child to know they're loved—and loved most by God. Every parent can give a child that gift. We have reason to believe that every child who receives that sense of purpose will grow in wisdom before God.

## Women like Anna among Us

Oh, what a blessing this woman must have been! Can you imagine what a resource she would be to younger women struggling with the desire to marry? Or how she could identify with the grieving widows in the community? And what a model of fruitful old age she is! Every day she's in the temple worshiping, fasting, praying—"night and day"! And we think we've served the Lord because we attended a long service on Sunday morning or got to the football game after kickoff. Doesn't she put us to shame? Doesn't she prove that you never age out of worshiping God?

I know we have some women like Anna among us. There are older sisters going hard after God. When we talk about planting a new church, really being rooted in the neighborhood, seeking the welfare of our neighbors, some of the first people to step up were women like Anna!

Christianity is *not* "a young man's religion." Church planting is *not* a young, cool, hipster activity. Christianity and church planting belong as much to old men and women like Simeon and Anna. Shame on the church for any ways we have shut out our older members. They are gifts from God meant to give the church family gravity, stability, wisdom, and faith. One wonders if the church isn't as weak as she sometimes is because she so often has no place for older people.

What did the growing boy Jesus have that our kids need? Righteous parents. Revealed purpose.

## Responsible Parents
### LUKE 2:41-52

We said earlier that Mary and Joseph were righteous parents. Our last scene shows that they were also responsible parents.

*They were responsible in religious devotion* (vv. 41-42). The boy Jesus is now twelve years old. For the past twelve years, his parents have taken him on this annual pilgrimage to worship during the Passover.

*They were responsible when it came to watching over Jesus.* Now, we might not think so since verses 43-44 tell us they left Jerusalem and forgot Jesus. If you're a parent and you've never left your child anywhere by mistake, the rest of us say, "Congratulations!" Kristie and I have left all three of our kids at church at one time or another. Driving separately, we each thought the child was with the other. But the kids are turning out OK—except for the fear of janitors turning off lights.

Mary and Joseph are so human! They spend five days looking for Jesus (vv. 44-46): They went a day's journey thinking he was with the group. They returned to Jerusalem—another day's journey. They searched for him in that big, crowded city for three days! You know they were distraught! They were probably quietly blaming each other. Joseph thinks, *What kind of mother loses the Son of God? Who does that? If there's one rule, make sure the Savior is in the caravan!* Mary thinks to herself, *Look at him looking at me. I know he blames me. But he is the man. He's supposed to take care of the family. It's his son. How could he leave his son in the city? I can't do everything. I packed up the tent, made breakfast, fixed us some lunch. The least he could have done was keep an eye on the boy.*

They lost Jesus, but they did not stop until they found him again. That's responsible parenting. Sometimes responsible parenting is better seen in how you respond to your failings than in your successes. They respond to this danger with parental care, urgency, and love.

When they find the boy Jesus, he is sitting where they always took him—in the temple for worship and teaching. That speaks to their responsibility as parents too. Young Jesus has done this so much that it's natural instinct for him. Verse 46 says Jesus sat among the teachers, listening and asking questions. He's holding court with his elders. Everyone was amazed when they heard his understanding and answers (v. 47). Even his parents were astonished when they saw him (v. 48). By age twelve, Jesus is the wisest person in the land.

But you know, no matter how special our children are, we still act like parents, don't we? Mary probably has that mixture of relief and fear. Because you're afraid, you can't help but scold the child even while you're trying to say "I love you." That's Mary in verse 48.

Verse 49 proves that responsible parenting can give our children a higher level of responsibility than we imagined. Jesus replied to Mary, "Why were you searching for me? Didn't you know that it was necessary for me to be in my Father's house?" In that sentence the twelve-year-old boy demonstrates profound understanding of his identity and purpose. He knows he is the Son of God. No one else would have spoken this way at that time. That's why no one understands him in verse 50.

Jesus makes clear that God is his Father. He makes clear that the Father's business is his business. He is not being rude. We know that because in verse 51 he humbly goes home with his parents and submits to them. He is simply making clear that he seeks God independently of his earthly parents. Worship is not for adults only. It's for twelve-year-olds and younger and everyone at every age.

## Teenagers and Preteens

*Many of you were converted at a young age.* We praise God for you. That's a wonderful testimony, and you should cherish it. God has granted you to seek him in your youth, just as the Lord Jesus sought the Father in his youth.

*Many of you converted before your parents* and had to learn the faith without them. That, too, is a tremendous grace from God. If your parents are not yet Christians, do not let that stop you from being about the Father's business. Do not let that stop you from believing. Seek the Lord right now. Repent and believe.

*Some of you have earthly parents who do not understand your faith.* That's a hard thing. But Jesus's parents didn't understand him. The Lord Jesus did not let that keep him from honoring his earthly parents as well as his heavenly Father. Do your best, with prayer and faith, to honor God and honor your parents. Submit to them as an act of submission to God.

*If you're one of those teenagers who think they know everything,* then know these two things also: (1) you're not the first to think you know everything, and (2) you don't know everything. Many of us adults thought we knew everything when we were teens and acted the same way. Many of us found out the hard way that we didn't know all that much. We didn't even know something as basic as this: The main way God gets his voice into your life is through the counsel and leadership of your parents. Your parents are the authority God has placed in your life for your blessing and your protection. When you honor your parents, you honor your God. They may not be good parents, so you may not be able to obey everything they say and do because you would then be disobeying God. When that happens, choose God. But resist the temptation to think you don't need to submit to your parents. Even Jesus, the Son of God, "the wisdom from God" (1 Cor 1:24), went home and submitted to his parents.

## Conclusion

What do growing kids need?

- Righteous parents
- Revealed purpose
- Responsible parents

These things were used in our Lord's young life to help him "increase in wisdom and in stature, and in favor with God and with people" (v. 52). Can we ask for anything more for our children?

## Reflect and Discuss

1. How does the meaning of your child's name remind you of your responsibility to be a righteous and responsible parent?
2. Has your child shown that he or she is watching your obedience and compromises? Have you ever apologized for your failures? How did that affect your child?
3. How can poverty be a blessing? How can wealth be a curse?
4. What lessons can a parent in poverty teach a child that will be valuable when that child grows up?
5. Have you seen opposition to Jesus and his church cause trouble in your life? How has he proven that faithfulness is worth all the trouble?

6. Think about older people you know who are gracious and happy like Anna and those who are angry and grumpy. How can we avoid becoming cranky and bitter as we age?
7. How did Mary and Joseph act responsibly as parents even when they left Jesus behind?

# The Only Savior, God's Son

## LUKE 3

**Main Idea:** We have the testimony of the people, the Father, and the test proving that Jesus is the Son of God and our Savior.

---

I.  **What Do the People Say (3:1-20)?**
    A.  John's public context (3:1-2)
    B.  John's public ministry (3:3-9)
    C.  John's practice in ministry (3:10-14)
    D.  John's personal identity (3:15-17)
    E.  John's persevering faithfulness (3:18-20)
II. **What Does the Father Say (3:21-22)?**
III. **What Does the Test Say (3:23-38)?**

---

Getting to know someone is not always easy. One of the most profound questions we will ever be asked is, "Who are you?" It is a simple question, yet it calls forth a lot more than a three-word answer. It is one of those questions in every culture and every place that people ask. In the Cayman Islands people ask you, "Who ya fa?" or "Who are you for?" which means, "Who are your people?" or "Where are you from?"

We have lots of ways of saying who we are or where we're from. My mother blazed the importance of this question on my preteen mind. Whenever I was around my father's side of the family, I would often shy away from people. But my mother would always say, "Boy, those are your daddy's people. You need to know your people."

Who your people are has a lot to do with how you answer "Who are you?" That's no less true of the Lord Jesus Christ. The question that runs through this Gospel is "Who is Jesus?" Who are his people? Where is he from? And that question has a lot to do with authenticating that Jesus is the Christ.

We live in the real world. We know that a question like "Who are your people?" can be difficult to answer. There is another saying I sometimes heard from my mother: "Mama's baby; Papa's maybe." Sometimes there may be some controversy around the parentage of the child, as was the case with Jesus. Mary was pregnant while only betrothed to Joseph, who had not known her. Because of this scandal, Joseph even considered putting her away quietly (see Matt 1:19) or calling off the engagement. Oftentimes in these kinds of circumstances, gossip swirls and questions are raised about the baby. Luke 3 answers three questions: What do the people say? What does the Father say? What does the test say?

When it comes to Jesus, we don't need Jerry Springer to prove paternity. We only need Luke 3. In this chapter we have the testimony of the people, the testimony of the Father, and the test itself: the genealogy of our Lord.

## What Do the People Say?
### LUKE 3:1-20

In verses 1-20 Luke introduces us to the public ministry of John the Baptist.

### John's Public Context (3:1-2)

Verses 1-2 provide the public context. John begins his public ministry in the fifteenth year of Tiberius Caesar. The Caesars were the rulers of the Roman world. Beneath Caesar was a governor named Pilate. And beneath Pilate were three tetrarchs who ruled various regions. Phillip ruled Iturea and Trochonitis, Lysanias ruled Abilene, and Herod ruled Galilee, Jesus's hometown area.

Not only does Luke introduce us to the political hierarchy of the Lord's Day; he also tells us about the religious hierarchy in verse 2. This all happened "during the high priesthood of Annas and Caiaphas."

Luke gives us the entire civil and religious order of Jewish society under Roman occupation. We are left to think these are the movers and shakers of Jesus's day, the power brokers. So the most striking point of verse 2 is that "God's word came to *John* the son of Zechariah in the wilderness" (emphasis added). It is interesting to follow where God's word goes. The word or revelation of God keeps going to the little people. It doesn't to the Caesars or even to the priests in their robes. It goes to shepherds in the fields keeping watch over their flock by night. It goes to a little virgin girl. It goes to old men and old women well past the age of bearing children. It goes to Zechariah's son, John, who doesn't love the world or follow the ways of the world; he lives in the wilderness.

Two things clue us in to John's prophetic status. First is the phrase "God's word came to John." That phrase is a formula from the Old

Testament frequently used of prophets. Second is the reference to John's being "in the wilderness." God often sends his servants into the wilderness to prepare them for the work of the ministry.

In Luke's Gospel little people are the heroes. That's a wonderful thing in a world and a Christian church where people are intoxicated with the powerful. We love the elites, the rich and the famous. This is why Christians sometimes get so excited when some rapper or entertainer becomes a Christian. We should rejoice with heaven at the repentance of every single sinner. But I suspect some Christians are happy because the person is rich and famous. We think somehow the credibility of the gospel is enhanced because the wealthy and the powerful believe.

God's ways are not our ways. His thoughts are not like our thoughts. Sitting higher and thinking higher, God looks lower to the little people. I believe verses 1-2 are a Gospel version of what we read in 1 Corinthians 1:26-29. Paul says God didn't choose the powerful, wise, and strong but the weak, foolish, and despised things to confound the world. That's what God is like.

### John's Public Ministry (3:3-9)

In verses 3-14 Luke turns to John's public ministry. Verse 3 summarizes his ministry. John "went into all the vicinity of the Jordan, proclaiming . . ." When the word comes, the preacher preaches. It is like fire shut up in his bones (see Jer 20:9).

I love John. He only has one good sermon. And the truth is every pastor only has one good sermon—the gospel of Jesus Christ. That is what John is preaching in "proclaiming a baptism of repentance for the forgiveness of sins" (v. 3).

Repentance simply means a change of mind, a change of heart, and a change of direction. All of us in our sins apart from Christ were driving toward the city of sin. But something happened, causing us to switch lanes and drive in the opposite direction. Now we drive with the city of sin in our rearview mirror as we head to the city of God. That is what repentance is—that turning in the heart and mind that results in a changing of direction of the entire life. John preaches his heart out: we must repent for the forgiveness of sins.

Repentance and forgiveness go together like hard work and a corner office. There is no forgiveness unless there is also repentance. To forgive is to cause two things to stand apart from each other, to separate them. In forgiveness we place the guilt and offense on one side, and we put the offending, guilty person on the other side. We relieve them of their guilt against us. The Bible says, "As far as the east is from the west, so far has [God] removed our transgressions from us" (Ps 103:12). This is what John preaches in the wilderness as people come to him.

John is a prophet who himself was prophesied. Seven hundred years before John, the prophet Isaiah told us there would be a forerunner who cleared the path and made ready for the coming of the Lord himself. Luke quotes Isaiah's comments (see Isa 40:4) about valleys being filled, mountains leveled, and crooked places made straight not because God is interested in transforming physical land. These are metaphors for a construction project in the human heart. These are vivid ways of describing repentance.

John has come to make the people ready for the coming of the Messiah. That readiness boils down to repentance from sin. Repentance looks like a deep alteration of the heart.

Verses 7-9 give us a glimpse into John's preaching. John's theology of repentance affected his proclamation. John's preaching was confrontational. People come to John to be baptized. These people are already sympathetic to the message. These are not the sinners going to party in clubs. These people are coming to do something religious. But John is well aware that you can be religious and be lost. You can engage in all kinds of external religious exercises and not be repentant. So John confronts them in verse 7, saying, "Brood of vipers!"

In our day we are told we must always be nice and never offend people. But right from the start John proclaims his warning. John knows there is a God who has appointed a day when he will pour out his anger and indignation against sin. The thing to really be worried about is the judgment of God, not the politeness of the preacher!

Sometimes the preacher does you the best favor when he gets in your face. He loves you best when he tells you the things that you don't want to hear but that are true and necessary for your soul. We need preachers who will tell us about our state before a holy God, even with words like "Brood of vipers!" Verse 18 tells us John's teaching was "good news." Luke describes this preaching as "exhortations," and it is for the wise who have ears to hear. John confronts them about their spiritual standing before God.

Moreover, John confronts them about the quality of their lives (v. 8). Repentance isn't simply mental. True repentance is accompanied by fruit, by good deeds.

This is how the gospel was preached from the earliest days. For example, the apostle Paul, testifying before King Agrippa, says that he preached "that they should repent and turn to God, and do works worthy of repentance" (Acts 26:20). There is no gospel preaching without the preaching of repentance—of turning from sin to God and demonstrating that turn in a new life. John confronts his audience about the quality of their lives.

John confronts his hearers about their possible futures. He warns in verse 9, "The ax is already at the root"—not at the branches or at the trunk of the trees. The ax is at the root, the sustaining source of the trees. The ax of God's judgment is already in motion, and it is aimed at the life-giving base of the nation of Israel.

This forerunner introduces us to a coming King who is also Judge. The fact that he is a Judge makes repentance so deeply necessary. Repentance brings salvation. The failure to repent brings damnation. There are only two ways to live. There are only two ways to face: either we face the condemnation that is to come, or we face the salvation in his Son. And here's the thing: this salvation is behind our backs. We must turn around from sin in order to see it.

Perhaps you have never repented of your sin. If you have never turned in mind and heart to agree with God about your sin and turned in mind, heart, and life to follow Jesus, then you may be religious or even raised in the church, but you are not yet a Christian. You may be offended that the preacher is calling you a sinner. If so, that's probably an indication that you don't understand your sin very deeply. You don't understand the necessity of your repentance. The true offense is not that your sin is being pointed out. The offense before God is that you don't acknowledge your sin.

And what has God done about sin? He has charged us nothing for his salvation. God sent his Son into the world to live a righteous life that we could not live. Christ came into the world voluntarily and died the death we deserve in order to pay the penalty for our sins. The wrath of God is absorbed by the Son of God on the cross so that sinners would not have to suffer that punishment if they trust in Christ. Three days later God raised Jesus from the grave to demonstrate that he had accepted the sacrifice of his Son on behalf of sinners.

All that is left to do—if we can call it "doing"—is to turn *from* our sin and turn *to* our Savior. Trust and follow him in order to receive the salvation of God. Do not get offended when God tells you he loves you and when he loves you enough to point out your sin then loves you enough to point you to his salvation. Do not be offended. Receive it—all of it.

### John's Practice in Ministry (3:10-14)

John maintains an interesting pattern of ministry. He not only confronts the people (vv. 7-9); he also counsels the people (vv. 10-14). After John preaches a blistering sermon, the people wish to know what they must do to be saved. As John MacArthur once put it, "Hard truth makes soft people" ("Question and Answer"). The hearts of the people have been softened.

John gives a general principle and a specific practice. The general principle: In response to the message of repentance, they should demonstrate their repentance by sharing (v. 11). Repentance includes ordinary, along-the-way kindness and generosity to others in need. In true repentance our eyes are opened. We see how generous God has been to us in Christ; then we look with similar kindness on our neighbors. We recognize those who have no coats and no food while we have multiple coats and full cupboards. Many of us spend minutes in our closets deciding which coat best matches our shoes. How many schoolchildren did we pass on our way who need a winter coat? How many homes did we pass in need of groceries? The repentant Christian life opens our eyes to these things. God has been generous to us, and we are compelled to care for others. In repentance we recognize that our abundance is to be shared in blessing our neighbors.

The church I shepherd has five objectives we call our "Five M's," and one of them is mercy. We want to be a congregation of people who show mercy to our neighbors. We think it an odd thing to be a Christian and to be indifferent to the suffering and needs of others. It's an odd thing to be Christian and to remain indifferent to poverty. So we wish to prove our repentance in a good Samaritan way (10:25-37). We want to be like the lepers who returned to the city to tell others the Lord had plundered the Syrians and left us the spoils (2 Kings 7).

We wish to reflect this generosity in our private and corporate lives. As the Lord gives us life and opportunity, we want to intentionally manifest this sharing attitude beyond the benevolence line of our budget or a temporary handout. We want this baked into our lives because we are repentant people who share.

Beyond this general principle there is also a specific practice. In verses 12-14 particular groups of persons speak up. We move from the nameless "crowds" in verse 10 to the "tax collectors" (v. 12) and "soldiers" (v. 14). They want to know "what should we do" in their specific cases.

John answers in a way that considers their vocations and the specific temptations unique to their vocations. He counsels the tax collectors and the soldiers not to use their positions for selfish advantage (vv. 13-14). Do not extort. Do not bully. Do not cheat others using the authority of the state. Do not use weapons to take from people; rather, be content with your wages.

Our Presbyterian friends have a wonderful way of expressing this aspect of repentance. The Westminster Confession of Faith (15.5) says, "Men ought not to content themselves with a general repentance, but it is every man's duty to endeavor to repent of his particular sins, particularly." Repentance causes us to examine our own lives with specificity. We must think about how we use our callings, our positions, and our privileges to either help or hurt, to sin or pursue righteousness.

We must get before the Lord and ask, "Who am I? What are my callings?" Then we must ask ourselves, "What are the particular temptations of my calling? What sins am I drawn toward given who I am and my station in life?" Then we must go on to ask ourselves, "Given those things, what does temptation look like for me?" We must repent of our particular sins, particularly.

Luke 3:7-14 insists that we understand repentance, for if we do not understand repentance, then we do not accurately understand the Christian life. As Martin Luther put it in his ninety-five theses, "When our Lord and Master Jesus Christ said, 'Repent' (Matt 4:17), he willed the entire life of believers to be one of repentance." In the Christian life we enter into a life of repentance, a life of ever turning toward that celestial city. Repentance is a wonderful Christian discipline.

### John's Personal Identity (3:15-17)

John's public ministry raises the question of John's personal identity. The people wonder just who John is. He is growing in their estimation. It is natural to exalt or esteem people when we recognize the good they have done for us. The crowds begin to wonder "whether John might be the Messiah" (v. 15).

John wishes to set the record straight immediately (v. 16). He tells them that his baptism was symbolic. The true baptism includes the gift of God himself—the Holy Spirit. John makes clear that the Messiah will bring God's fire of judgment.

Every preacher and pastor should follow John's example. Let us use all our fingers to point away from ourselves and to the Lord Jesus Christ. People will love and esteem faithful pastors. Sometimes they will appreciate their pastors too much or in improper ways. Let every faithful pastor work against that tendency in their people. The best way to help the people express proper affection is to emulate John by constantly pointing them to Jesus Christ the Lord. Make clear that we must decrease and Christ must increase. We cannot be great and Christ great too. We cannot worry about people loving our sermons when we should want them to love the Savior.

Our task is to point to Jesus that he might be great in the people's sight. We cannot point to him and to ourselves at the same time. Sometimes we must reorient the people so they see Jesus for who he really is. John the Baptist does that as he reminds the people of the winnowing shovel and the threshing floor. A winnowing shovel was used to separate wheat from the chaff. A farmer would toss the harvest into the air. The wheat would fall and the chaff would float on the breeze, thus separating the two. He would gather the wheat to be used, and he would gather the chaff to be burned as waste.

Christ's coming includes this kind of sifting. The Lord Jesus said it himself:

> *"From now on, five in one household will be divided: three against two, and two against three. They will be divided, father against son, son against father, mother against daughter, daughter against mother, mother-in-law against her daughter-in-law, and daughter-in-law against mother-in-law."* (12:52-53)

Christ plunges the winnowing shovel of the gospel into the world, and the wheat of faith is collected while the chaff of unbelief gets burned away in condemnation. Christians must bear faithful witness to Christ the Judge in a world that would rather Jesus were only a babe in a manger; they would only have Jesus be some wise teacher and consistently deny that he is Judge. Jesus is both the saving Lord who gives his life for sinners and the judging King who weighs us all.

## John's Persevering Faithfulness (3:18-20)

People are often wrong in their assessment of who Jesus is. The Christian's job is to make it plain. John gives us a model of persevering faithful witness. We see John's faithfulness in three things. First,

John remains faithful with the gospel itself (v. 18). He keeps preaching the good news. Second, we see his faithfulness no matter the audience (v. 19). He preached the same gospel to Herod the tetrarch. He does not bend the message to suit the itching ears of his hearers. Third, we see John's faithfulness no matter the cost (v. 20). For preaching the gospel without compromise to Herod, John finds himself locked up in prison. Before long, Herod will have John beheaded (Matt 14:1-2; Mark 6:14-29).

To bear faithful witness about Jesus requires us to be careful with the message of the gospel, to be lovingly confrontational with the people who hear it, and to pay the cost that Christ may call us to pay. That is the only way we make clear that Jesus is Lord in both our preaching and our pain, that we fear God and not man. This is God's calling on the Christian life and how the world will know who Jesus is.

Who do the people say or think Jesus is? They get it wrong. Who gets it right? Those who bear the message of Jesus Christ in the gospel. We must be faithful so the crowds will truly know him.

## What Does the Father Say?
### LUKE 3:21-22

What does the Father say about who Jesus is? That question gets answered in verses 21-22. We've heard John's testimony that Jesus is greater than him and that Jesus brings both salvation and condemnation. But what people say about Jesus does not settle the matter. We need other testimony. Here God the Father gives testimony.

Jesus submits himself to baptism. People sometimes wonder why Jesus was baptized if he did not sin and had no reason to repent. The other Gospel writers give us insight. In Matthew 3:15 Jesus explains to John that he must be baptized because "this is the way for us to fulfill all righteousness." The Lord Jesus Christ came into the world to fulfill all the righteous requirements of the law. We have broken all those righteous requirements. Here Jesus stands in our place not just as our sin bearer but also as our righteousness. All the active and positive obedience we owe God as his creatures, the Lord Jesus provides perfectly, even down to his willingness to be baptized by John for the remission of sins he had not committed.

John 1:29-34 also records the baptism of our Lord. Jesus participates in this baptism so that "he might be revealed to Israel" (John 1:31). Jesus submitted in order to demonstrate to Israel that he is the Savior they awaited. At his baptism a confirmation is given of this in heaven. Luke 3:21-22 records that the Holy Spirit, who is noncorporeal, who blows where he wills like the felt but unseen wind, takes the visible form of a dove as he descends on the Lord Jesus Christ.

Then the voice comes from heaven saying, "You are my beloved Son." The Father steps vocally out of glory to testify that the child about whom there had been some question is indeed his Son. The fullness of God in all three persons of the Trinity unites in revealing Jesus Christ as God's Son and Israel's Savior.

Christ Jesus, who had been the Father's Son from all eternity past, will be the Father's Son for all eternity future. And Christ is no displeasing, hardheaded boy. This young man of thirty years, who is God the Son incarnate, is the Son who pleases his Father. Do you wish to know what delights God? It is his Son. The Father looks at the Lord Jesus Christ, who has come into the world to take the place of sinners, and he concludes, "This Son of mine pleases me."

This is why all those who are "in Christ" by faith also have God as a Father who is pleased with them. The Father looks at the faithful, and he sees his Son. All the Son has done to please the Father has become ours through our union with Christ through faith in him. This is why Christians have every right to fight those nagging doubts and whispers that come along sometimes to suggest God is not happy with us. If we have made the hard choice of repenting of our sins and coming to God, we can expect to hear blessing from God, not condemnation. We do not have to shudder and cower for fear of a harsh word of rebuke from God. He gave us that rebuke to turn us away from sin. What we can joyfully and confidently expect to hear now that we are in Christ are words similar to those spoken at our Lord's baptism: "I am pleased with you because of Christ." All of our comfort, security before God, joy in his presence, sense of safety, and delight come from this marvelous statement from heaven. Jesus is God's Son, and God is pleased with him. Because we are in him through faith, God is pleased with us.

This text is obviously Trinitarian, isn't it? At Jesus's baptism all the persons of the Godhead are present. God the Son is baptized. God the Father speaks from heaven. God the Holy Spirit descends on the Son in the form of a dove. This one text stands in clear contrast against errors in understanding the nature of God. Some have taught that there is one God who takes different forms at different times. They say he is the Father in the Old Testament, then he takes the form of the Son in the New Testament, and at other times he takes the form of the Spirit. They argue God exists in these modes—which is false. That all three persons exist in the same scene at the same time means modalism cannot be true.

At other times people wrestling with the mystery of the Trinity have tried to subordinate one or the other in some way. So, for example, they argue that Jesus is less than God but more than man. Or they tell us that the Spirit is a force rather than a person. But that's false too. In this text we see the three persons, and yet there remains only one God. Each person is fully and eternally God.

Belief in the Trinity is one thing that makes us Christian. The historical Christian church has always understood the Trinity to be foundational to who God is and foundational to the faith. So those who deny the Trinity actually deny the Christian faith. They deny who God really is and by that denial prove they do not know God.

Indeed, those who actively and self-consciously deny the Trinity deny the gospel itself. Ephesians 1:3-14 gives us a Trinitarian understanding of God's work of redemption. It teaches us that the Father appoints our salvation, the Son accomplishes our salvation, and the Holy Spirit applies our salvation. Lose any one person in the Godhead, and the entire gospel house falls down.

Trinitarian teaching about the nature of God is for our delight. The reality of the Trinity mystifies us and exceeds our intelligence. But praise God! For if we could completely comprehend God, then he would not be God; we would be. Yet the Trinity is not meant to confound us as much as it is meant to delight us. This one true God exists in three persons—all of whom love us and all of whom participate in our salvation.

If we would know Jesus, we must know this God. This God tells us that Jesus—not John—is his Son with whom he is pleased.

## What Does the Test Say?
### LUKE 3:23-38

We have heard the testimony of John and the testimony of God the Father. Now in verses 23-38 we come to the testimony of the genealogy. If John's prophetic ministry answers the gossip about the identity of the Christ, and the Father divinely vouches for Jesus as his Son, then the genealogy is the DNA evidence proving that only Jesus is the Christ.

The Lord was about thirty years of age when he was baptized and began his public ministry. In the Old Testament, priests would begin their public ministry at age thirty. The Lord's example suggests we should be patient with baptizing persons. If the Lord could wait until he demonstrated some maturity, it is a good practice for us to do that with our children by not rushing them to the baptismal waters. The same could be said to men aspiring to pastoral ministry. If the Lord could wait until he was thirty, then young man at twenty-five, twenty-seven, thirty, and even thirty-five, you can wait too. You can be tested, endure, and learn something about patience.

Truthfully, everything I have ever rushed in my life I have messed up. If you are thinking, *Pastor, help me go to seminary or pursue pastoral ministry,* and you are in a hurry, then my question for you is, "Do you really want to be the next thing I rush?" You will need to learn patience in order to be an effective minister of the gospel; you may as well learn it as you wait for the Lord to prepare you and send you.

What is the purpose of the genealogy in Israel? Scattered throughout the Old Testament are these tracings of family trees and relationships. Genealogies have a threefold purpose. First, they prove who was Jewish and who was not. Such proof of Jewish ancestry was important because God's covenants were made with Israel. The promise of a deliverer was a promise made to Israel, and he would come from Israel (Deut 18:15,18).

Second, the genealogies prove who could or could not serve as priests. Only Levites could serve before the Lord in the tabernacle and the temple. When Israel left captivity and exile during the days of Nehemiah, they turned almost immediately to the genealogies to register the people returning from exile. Nehemiah 7:64 tells us some who sought to be registered were not found in the genealogies, "so they were disqualified from the priesthood." The entire priesthood prefigured the coming Savior who would be the Great High Priest.

Third, the genealogies prove who was or was not a "son of David." Do you remember the promise of 2 Samuel 7, when God promised to establish David's throne forever? David's son would be ruler over Israel and the hoped-for Messiah. But not just any son or descendant of David could fill that role. The genealogy also had to prove that anyone claiming to be Messiah was not descended from David through Jeconiah (Jer 22:24-30; 36:30-31). God declared that no one from Jeconiah's house would sit on David's throne.

This helps us understand some major differences between Matthew's genealogy and Luke's. Matthew's genealogy is abbreviated and stylistic. He divides his record into three generations of fourteen as he traces Joseph's lineage. He also breaks with Jewish convention by mentioning four women by name—and those were Gentile women.

Luke records a more exhaustive genealogy in a traditionally Jewish style. Luke's genealogy does not mention any women by name. Nevertheless, Luke's genealogy actually traces *Mary's* lineage. We infer that from Luke 3:23 where we read that Jesus "was *thought to be* the son of Joseph, son of Heli" (emphasis added).

If the Messiah must be Jewish, a male descendant of David, and not a son of Jeconiah, why does Matthew twice mention Jeconiah and include Gentile women in the genealogy? It's all very un-Jewish and dis-qualifying. Matthew writes his genealogy to prove Jesus's claim to be Messiah is *not* through Joseph. Perhaps that's why Matthew immediately follows his genealogy with the virgin birth (Matt 1:18-23).

Luke writes to show that Jesus *is* the Messiah promised by God and that his claim is fulfilled through his mother, Mary. This helps make sense of Genesis 3:15 and Isaiah 7:14, where we read that the *offspring of the woman* will strike the serpent's head, and "the *virgin will conceive* [and] have a son" (emphasis added). Luke's genealogy shows that Jesus fulfills all the criteria necessary for being Messiah. His claim is legiti-mate. The genealogy makes his claim a matter of public record.

No one else can establish their descent from David. In AD 70 the Roman army destroyed the temple in Jerusalem. They conquered and scattered Israel into captivity. The records of the genealogies and lines of descent were destroyed. Only here in the Gospel of Luke in the gene-alogy of chapter 3 do we receive the definitive evidence that the Messiah, the anointed one of God, is none other than Jesus Christ.

## Conclusion

The genealogy helps Luke fulfill his purpose in writing this Gospel. His desire is "to write to you in an orderly sequence . . . so that you may know the certainty of the things about which you have been instructed" (1:3-4). Fulfilling the requirements for Messiah cannot happen by chance or by choice. No way. We don't humanly control our births. We don't choose our parents. We can't set the time of our birth. Fulfillment of the criteria for Messiah cannot be manipulated or fabricated. That

Jesus meets all the criteria is a remarkable evidence of his rightful claim to be Lord and Savior

The genealogical record gives us a tremendous amount of certainty. Our certainty does not only rest on the prophetic report about John, nor does it only rest on the extraordinary and miraculous events at the Lord's baptism when heaven was opened and God spoke in a voice we have not heard. Here, traced and recorded over centuries, we have the answer to our introductory questions: Who ya fa? Where are you from? Jesus Christ is the King of kings, Lord of lords, and the only Savior, God's Son.

## Reflect and Discuss

1. Luke introduces us to John the Baptist. What was John's unique mission?
2. What do we learn about John's life and ministry that can inform our own?
3. How does the genealogy of our Lord help us have confidence that he really is the Messiah? Can anyone else provide this kind of genealogical evidence for being the Messiah?
4. Consider some of the persons in our Lord's family tree. Do you draw any encouragement about your own family when you consider some of the people in Jesus's family? Why or why not?

# Our Prophet, Priest, and King

## LUKE 4

**Main Idea:** Jesus meets our greatest needs when we recognize him as the Son of God and our Savior.

---

I.   **Our High Priest Overcomes Satan's Temptations for Us (4:1-13).**
II.  **Our Great Prophet Brings Good News of God's Salvation to Us (4:14-27).**
   A.   One dramatic reading of Scripture (4:16-20)
   B.   Two dramatic revelations from Scripture (4:21-27)
III. **Our King Uses His Authority to Bless Us (4:28-44).**
   A.   Authority in his teaching (4:31-32)
   B.   Authority over demons (4:33-37)
   C.   Authority over physical existence (4:38-40)

---

We get to know Jesus best by examining the Bible. And if we wish to know what God is like, we must look at his Son.

The greatest question about Jesus asked in the Bible is "Who is Jesus?" It's a good, basic question to ask. In the last chapter we saw that Jesus our Savior is the Son of God. That identity—Son of God—carries with it three offices. The Lord Jesus is priest, prophet, and king for the benefit of his people.

## Our High Priest Overcomes Satan's Temptations
### LUKE 4:1-13

Luke 4 includes two well-known passages of Scripture often appealed to by various sections of the Christian church. The first is the wilderness temptation of the Lord in verses 1-13. The Lord was baptized in chapter 3. That chapter concludes with our Lord's genealogy, in which the last words are "son of God" (v. 38).

Now we see the Holy Spirit lead Christ into the wilderness for forty days where he will be tempted by Satan himself. The main issue at stake in this temptation is the identity of Jesus, whether he truly is the Son of God. In verse 3 Satan comes to Jesus and says, "If you are the Son of God . . ." Again in verse 9 the serpent says, "If you are the Son of God . . ." The pressing issue in the passage is the question "Who is Jesus? Is he really the Son of God?"

The immediate context of this temptation harks back to others who were previously called "son of God." Adam receives mention in Luke 3:38. You will recall Satan's temptation of Adam in the garden, where Adam failed the test. Now Jesus is presented to us as the second Adam.

The passage also harks back to Hosea 11:1 where God calls Israel his "child" and declares, "Out of Egypt I called my son," referring to Israel. In Hosea 11:2, once God had delivered his people from bondage, they entered the wilderness where they worshiped the Baals and idols rather than God. Israel, too, failed to be God's perfect son, and their wilderness temptation lurks in the background of Luke 4 as well. But here we are finally presented with God's true Son and the true Israel, which is Christ.

Just as Adam had his garden of temptation, Jesus has his wilderness of temptation. Everything God has affirmed, Satan tries to negate. God calls Jesus his Son and produces the paternity test to prove it (ch. 3). Satan shows up to doubt and dispute it.

Satan seizes upon our Lord's human weakness. Verse 2 says Jesus "ate nothing during those days, and when they were over, he was hungry." Satan hates humanity. He loves (if Satan can love anything) to attack at our points of weakness. Three times over these forty days he attacks the Lord.

*First, the devil tempts Jesus with provision.* Verse 3: "If you are the Son of God, tell this stone to become bread." But Jesus quotes from Israel's wilderness wanderings in Deuteronomy 8:3: "It is written: 'Man must not live on bread alone'" (v. 4). Matthew adds, "but on every word that comes from the mouth of God" (4:4).

*Then Satan tempts Jesus with power.* Verses 5-7: "I will give you their splendor and all this authority, because it has been given over to me, and I can give it to anyone I want. If you, then, will worship me, all will be yours." Sometimes Christians debate whether Satan could really do this. I think that debate indicates we are not Jesus. The moment we begin to entertain whether Satan can deliver on a promise, we're already losing the spiritual battle. The Savior answers by quoting Deuteronomy 6:13: "It is written: 'Worship the Lord your God, and serve him only'" (v. 8).

Satan thrusts himself into the place of God, willing to bargain worship for power. But Christ reserves worship for God alone.

*Finally, Satan tempts Jesus with protection* in verses 9-11. Satan himself now begins to use Scripture. He twists Psalm 91:11-12. He turns God's word into an occasion not to trust God but to test God. Isn't it striking that after Jesus twice quotes the Scriptures, Satan thinks himself subtle enough to quote the Bible to the Lord and deceive even the Son of God. But our Lord again answers with Scripture in verse 12: "It is said: Do not test the Lord your God" (Deut 6:16). God is to be trusted, served, and worshiped. But he is not to be tested. Then Satan left Jesus until a later time.

In his own time and in a way that glorified the Father, Jesus received everything Satan tempted him with. Jesus would miraculously produce bread for the hungry masses, obtain all authority and splendor in heaven and earth through the cross and resurrection (Matt 28:18-20), and receive the service and worship of heaven's angels as he rules at the Father's right hand. Beloved, the best way to fight temptation is to realize we may receive what tempts us in a holy way if we wait on God's timing, trusting him.

In all of these temptations Jesus relies on God's Word. Our Lord quotes and trusts the Scriptures. From that fact we can deduce Jesus's view of the Bible. First, Jesus believes the Bible applies to our temptations. Second, Jesus believes the Bible to truly be the word of God. Third, our Lord believes in the inspiration and authority of the Scriptures. He does not equivocate or quibble but stands on God's Word.

Now typically at this point in the exposition, teachers encourage Christians to face their temptations by standing on God's Word. Preachers tell us if we hide God's Word in our hearts we will not sin against God (Deut 11:18; Ps 119:11). They tell us we are to live by every word that comes from the mouth of God (Deut 8:3; Matt 4:4). But no human boxing with Satan is likely to be as effective as Jesus in that fight. If Satan would try to twist Scripture and to twist the Lord's heart and mind, then you know he will try it with us. So resisting temptation cannot be *merely* a matter of "take two Bible verses and call me in the morning." We would need to know the Word as well as Jesus knows it in order to do what Jesus does here. It is probably not best to think of this as *primarily* a pattern for resisting temptation.

The question is: Why is this text given to us? Is it so that we may trust God's Word or trust God's Son? "Trust God's Word" is a secondary application. Jesus's perfect interpretation and obedience to God's Word reveals he is God's true Son. Satan is not so subtle that he can do with Jesus what he did with Adam and Eve in the garden. Satan is not so effective that he can cause the Christ, the Son of God, to grumble against God because of hunger the way he caused Israel to do so.

Our primary application is "Jesus is God's Son; trust him." The Lord endured temptation *in our place.* So in our temptation, we must flee to Christ! He conquered our adversary. The Son stands in our place to defeat the temptation that often defeats us. He does *not* do this to say, "OK, now, that's how you do it." As Jesus endures this temptation, he becomes our Great High Priest. That's what Hebrews 4:15 teaches us. He "has been tempted in every way as we are, yet without sin." Right now Jesus reigns in the heavens as a priest who can "sympathize with our weaknesses" (v. 15) and who now makes it possible for us to "approach the throne of grace with boldness, so that we may receive mercy and find grace to help us in our time of need" (v. 16). Our Lord didn't endure this so we would have a *model to follow.* He did this so we would have *mercy when falling.* Christ delivers us. He stands in as priest for us, offering both a sacrifice and righteousness for us.

The ultimate issue here is whether Jesus is the Son of God. That's why Satan keeps coming at him this way. Satan's real aim is to destroy Jesus's sonship so that he might destroy our salvation, for if Jesus were to fall in any of these temptations, he could not be the sinless sacrifice that takes away the sins of the world. So Satan unleashes the most relentless demonic assault in the history of creation, and Jesus remains faithful to his Father through it all. This is the second proof of Jesus's divine nature. No natural man could withstand such a demonic assault. Only God could.

Here the God-man passes the test that Adam and Eve failed. He survives temptation in the wilderness when Israel failed in the exodus. He passes the test that we have all failed. In doing so he becomes our ever-present help in times of need and temptation.

This means that in our temptations our best strategy is to run to Jesus. He is our strength. He is our shield. He is our High Priest who prays and intercedes for us. He is our victory and our confidence. However well we know the Word of God, let us not begin to think we know it so well that we don't need to first flee to Jesus, our High Priest who has overcome the tempter on our behalf.

# Our Great Prophet Brings Good News of Salvation to Us
## LUKE 4:14-27

Verses 14-15 tell us that Jesus was really popular. However, this isn't the praise that goes along with true worship. This is worldly popularity. Jesus is a celebrity. On a popular level, Jesus is the man. But they don't yet know him.

Jesus comes to Nazareth in verse 16. Nazareth is his hometown—"where he had been brought up." When he gets home, he immediately gets into his regular routine: "He entered the synagogue on the Sabbath day."

As an aside: Jesus went to synagogue regularly. It was his *usual custom*. We live in a day when a lot of Christian leaders and many ordinary Christians are telling us we don't need to be a part of the church or attend regularly. They tell us that the church has too many problems and that their faith is more genuine because they're *not* part of the institutional church. Now if Jesus went to synagogue every Sabbath, shouldn't the Christian go to church every Sunday? How are we going to be like Jesus if we're *customarily avoiding* the things Jesus *customarily attended*? The synagogue of Jesus's day was in worse shape than the churches of our day, and our Lord still attended.

Jesus is in the community where he grew up. He is in the synagogue among the religious. He is where he should have been known best.

### One Dramatic Reading of Scripture (4:16-20)

This is where Jesus preaches his first recorded public sermon in Luke's Gospel. It's a dramatic scene. He stands to read. They hand him the scroll of the prophet Isaiah. Jesus keeps unrolling it slowly, respectfully, until he gets down near the end of the scroll, what we would call Isaiah 61:1-2. Once Jesus reads this passage, he sits down, and everyone watches him. Can you feel the drama here? People lean in wondering, *What will he say?*

Isaiah 61 prophesies the coming Messiah who brings the salvation of God. Isaiah says that the Messiah is anointed to do one thing primarily: to preach. That's what a prophet does: he preaches the words and the promises of God. See the three mentions of preaching:

- "to *preach* good news to the poor" (v. 18; emphasis added),
- "to *proclaim* release to the captives and recovery of sight to the blind, to set free the oppressed" (v. 18; emphasis added), and
- "to *proclaim* the year of the Lord's favor" (v. 19; emphasis added).

Our Lord's use of the Isaiah passages provokes wide differences of opinion on how to interpret who he is and his mission. Sometimes people interpret this quotation as a political statement. They view Jesus as a social and political revolutionary because of the reference to liberating the poor and oppressed. They understand this passage to have implications for the mission of the church in alleviating the suffering of people who are actually poor and imprisoned.

Some other Christians view the quotation in spiritual terms. They view the passage as a picture of the coming spiritual salvation from the Lord. In this view the "poor," "blind," and "oppressed" are so because of sin. Isaiah 61 certainly has in mind this salvific meaning (see Isa 61:2,4,7-8). This salvation anticipates a time when all the people's spiritual brokenness, spiritual poverty, spiritual imprisonment, spiritual blindness, and spiritual oppression because of sin will be restored and reversed by God's "favor" or grace *through preaching.*

While Isaiah 61 foresees a salvific fulfillment, it is also certain that this text cannot mean *less than* the gospel going to poor people, the imprisoned, and the oppressed. I think we're best helped to understand this text if we *first* remember it's about Jesus and not about us. This is Jesus saying to us that the prophecy in Isaiah refers to his own life and ministry. Whatever the text means, the prophecy was fulfilled *on that day* when Jesus preached this sermon. He says, "*Today as you listen,* this Scripture has been fulfilled" (Luke 4:21; emphasis added). Christ is the Messiah, the prophet who brings the announcement of God's kingdom breaking into the world.

The "poor" here are certainly the poor who are impoverished by their sin. But it's not less than the poor who are impoverished in the world. Throughout Luke's Gospel the people who respond most fervently and quickly to the message of Jesus are the materially poor, the destitute, and the beggars. The "blind" are certainly those who are spiritually blinded by the god of this age (2 Cor 4:4), but the reference includes blind Bartimaeus, who though he couldn't see physically, could see spiritually. Bartimaeus knew that Jesus is the Christ, the Son of David. Despite his physical limitations Bartimaeus recognized the spiritual reality that Christ is the great prophet who brings the messianic kingdom of God.

The second thing to recognize is that Jesus did, in fact, go to these kinds of people and proclaim, preach, and teach the kingdom of God. The primary means of setting people free in whatever their social or political circumstance is the proclamation of the gospel. But that means the gospel has to be so real a gospel that it addresses people in their social and political position. The gospel cannot be abstracted from the real conditions of the people it addresses. Israel was under Roman occupation. Israel was oppressed. Israel was crushed beneath the heel of the Caesars. And Christ came to them preaching the gospel of the kingdom—not the kingdom of Caesar but of another world. He gave hope to a people broken by the rule of men.

The gospel we preach cannot be an escapist, pie-in-the-sky gospel; it must be a gospel acquainted with pain, roughened by grit, and smelling like marginalized people. The gospel must enter the world as it is and proclaim to broken people a healing Savior.

So our challenge is not to be Jesus—either in our temptation, as though we are as clever and capable with the word as Christ, or in our evangelism, as if we are messiahs entering a neighborhood to set people free. Our challenge is to point to the one who does set free, the one who enters temptation to purchase our victory, the one who has come into our broken world with the promise of rescue and deliverance. His promise comes to people while they are in their misery. That's why it's good news. That's why the angels shout, "Joy to the world!" That's why the gospel gives life: it reaches people in their barrenness.

Our task is not to form a holy huddle or celebrate sublime things about Christ. Our task is not to swell our heads with theology and Bible knowledge. Our task is to, yes, feed on Christ, but also to find beggars and tell them where there is bread. We must find fellow lepers and tell them where there is cleansing. We must remember we were the lepers who woke up to find the enemy camp already abandoned. We needed the victory, but we didn't earn it. Like people glad to have found what they most desperately needed, our task is to go to our neighbors and tell them there is a Savior who supplies all their needs, too.

Will we embrace this calling really, practically, daily? We could put a church anywhere, on any block or in any neighborhood. New churches are springing up all over our city, most of them in already redeveloped sections where "urban" has come to mean "chic." *Urban* now means "gentrified, redeveloped, and renewed." May the Lord prosper those churches. But we must be convinced that God very much means to insert a colony of heaven in the neighborhoods that are not redeveloped, in sections of the city where windows are broken, bottles are strewn across streets, and neighbors are using PCP, selling their bodies, and exhibiting their brokenness in all manner of sin. The Lord means that colony to announce to those neighborhoods and neighbors there is a Savior tempted like you who gave his life for your salvation. His name is Jesus, the Son of God, crucified for our sins, buried, and raised three days later for our justification.

We are meant to announce to the blind that, if they believe in this Jesus, they may never see with their physical eyes in this life, but they will see glories they cannot imagine. We are meant to announce to prisoners that they may still be required to serve lifelong sentences, but they will be free inside that jail if they believe. We must tell the poor they may not receive riches and may have to serve the Lord the rest of their lives in poverty, but in glory they will receive riches they cannot imagine. Christ Jesus intends for us to go to our neighborhood and neighbors to make this known. This is why God put your church where it is and why you should also plant more churches in other neighborhoods across your city.

## Two Dramatic Revelations from Scripture (4:21-27)

First, Jesus explains the text. It's a one-sentence sermon that explodes in your ear every couple of words. I imagine he said verse 21 slowly, clearly, and loudly.

- *"Today"*—not in Isaiah's day but in their day, on that very day
- *"as you listen"*—right in front of you, with my words, in person, not by secondhand hearsay
- *"this Scripture"*—the announcement of God's salvation promised long ago
- *"has been fulfilled"*—completed, brought to pass, come true

In this one sentence Jesus proclaims that he is *the Messiah who brings this great salvation that was promised to Israel.*

The people enjoy the sermon, but they don't see the Savior! They think Jesus is a nice preacher, but they are too familiar with him. All they see is "Joseph's son" (v. 22). They miss the fulfillment of the Scripture and only see a hometown boy who has made good.

Sometimes the truth is hidden in plain sight. Sometimes the familiar hides the fantastic. That's why most automobile accidents happen within a few blocks of the driver's home. They get close to home, and they assume everything is as it's always been so they don't see the unusual thing going on with the other driver. Familiarity is why most household accidents happen in the bathroom. We're so comfortable and familiar that we don't see the wet floor.

Familiarity is why a lot of people don't recognize Jesus as their Messiah. They've had just enough Bible to make them think they know, so they're not looking any deeper. They're familiar with Sunday School Bible stories. They've come to church at Easter and Christmas. They've heard a little bit on TV or in the barbershop. So they've become familiar, and they don't see. Don't be too familiar with Jesus. Look hard. Listen long. Be certain you recognize him for who he is. He is someone who gets deeper the deeper you look.

Jesus goes on to anticipate what the people are thinking (v. 23). Jesus sees them even though they don't see him. Jesus says a day is coming when they will say to him, "Doctor, heal yourself!" We can't help but think of the religious leaders at Jesus's crucifixion when they mockingly say, "He saved others; let him save himself if this is God's Messiah" (23:35). That day is coming, but right now they want him to do in Nazareth, his hometown, what he did in Capernaum. They want him to put Nazareth first and minister there. They want him to prove himself by working miracles and putting Israel first. It's the response of pride and unbelief. It's self-importance and entitlement.

Jesus finds no honor in their response (v. 24). They're not going to honor him here. Familiarity breeds contempt. To them he is always going to be "Joseph's son."

You see, beloved, it's dishonoring Jesus to call him something less than he really is. Muslims say they honor Jesus as a great prophet, but they dishonor him by denying he is the Son of God. Hindus say they honor Jesus by worshiping him as one of thousands of gods, but they dishonor him by not seeing that he is the only true God and all others are idols. Some people think they honor Jesus by saying, "He is a good moral teacher," but they dishonor him by refusing to see he is the Savior of the world.

To honor Jesus, you have to receive him as he really is: the Messiah and Son of God who alone rescues sinners from God's wrath and makes those same sinners righteous in God's sight.

Then comes the second dramatic revelation. Not only does the audience in the synagogue not accept him as Messiah, but *the Gentiles will be brought in while Israel is cut off.* He gives them two analogies from their history.

- He reminds them of the widows in Elijah's day (vv. 25-26). Though there were many widows in Israel, God sent Elijah to the widow of Zarapheth in Sidon.
- Jesus reminds them of Elisha, Elijah's successor (v. 27). There were many lepers in Israel in Elisha's day, but God sent Elisha to heal Naaman, a Syrian.

Sidon and Syria were *Gentile* lands and people. Jesus is saying God's salvation passed over Israel and went to the "unclean" Gentiles. Israel rejected their prophets, but the Gentiles received them and were saved. Now we remember the last words of Isaiah 61: "For as the earth produces its growth, and as a garden enables what is sown to spring up, so the Lord God will cause righteousness and praise to spring up before all the nations" (v. 11). God always intended to save people from every nation and ethnic group and language group, not just from Israel. As Paul explains in Romans, the Gentiles have been grafted into God's salvation because the Israelites have been broken off (Rom 11:17). That is what Jesus preaches here: Israel will be cut off and the Gentiles brought in.

God's salvation is for all nations. It's for everyone who will receive Jesus Christ as their Lord and God.

I think Luke 4 compels us to consider if we're like the people in the synagogue who miss Jesus. Perhaps we've been brought up in church the way they were raised in synagogue. We know the language of the church. We know the culture and the rituals. We know the routine, but we don't know Jesus. I think Jesus's sermon is aimed at nominal believers, at people who assume they are God's people but have no living, saving knowledge of Jesus Christ. And the Lord's application to them and to us is you can miss God's salvation if you fail to recognize Jesus. Perhaps you have not thought of Jesus as necessary to your salvation and forgiveness with God. You have not thought of him as the one who provides you righteousness and pays the penalty for your sin. Today is the day of salvation. Today this salvation is preached in your hearing, just as it was then. Believe on Jesus. Trust him. Repent of sin, come to him in faith, and you will be saved. Do not miss the salvation he brings.

## Our King Exercises His Authority for Our Blessing
### LUKE 4:28-44

The Israelites reject him (vv. 28-29). Ironically, the people try to put Jesus in the same position that Satan tried to tempt him with—to throw the Lord down from a height. Then the people get a miracle but not like the ones in Capernaum—like they want him to do (v. 23). Jesus passes right through them unharmed. I wonder what they thought when that happened? *Come here! Grab him! Hold him!* Jesus never said a word.

As far as we know, the Lord never returned to Nazareth. The Gospels do not record him entering his hometown again. Some rejections are final.

My non-Christian friend, don't look to Jesus to do parlor tricks to satisfy your unbelief. You're called to take him at his word, to believe his teaching. In his word the Lord reveals himself. When he tells you that he brings God's salvation to the nations, believe him. Trust him. Don't reject him, or he may reject you in the end. That's why we plead with you: believe on the Lord Jesus Christ so you may be saved!

Following the people's rejection in Nazareth, Jesus moves down to Capernaum. Capernaum was Jesus's ministry headquarters. It's where Peter lived with his family. At Capernaum Jesus reveals something more about what it means for him to be the Son of God. Jesus repeatedly demonstrates that as the unique Son of God he has authority over all things.

In our text the Son of God is a King with authority in three domains.

### Authority in His Teaching (4:31-32)

Matthew 7:29 says Jesus's teaching was not like the scribes and Pharisees, who taught a lot of speculation and doubt. Jesus's teaching came with exclamation marks and with power. He taught as if he had the ability and the right to define and proclaim the words of God. And he did!

There is certainty and confidence in his message. Our Lord taught the Old Testament like it was his autobiography. There is power in his words—so much so that outwardly religious people are amazed! Do you know how difficult it is to amaze outwardly religious people? They have heard and seen it all. But as Jesus thunders in preaching, their hearts respond. They had never seen or heard a teacher like Jesus with such authority in his teaching.

### Authority over Demons (4:33-37)

Do not pass verse 33 too fast. There is a sad irony here. You run into the devil in the most surprising places, don't you? You do not expect to find demon-possessed people in a synagogue or church. Hollywood has us thinking we find demons in graveyards or dark forests. Satan makes us look at the dead while he takes over the living. Satan took over a man and took him to church! We do not have to go farther than the assembly of God's people to find evidence of the enemy's work. Satan loves to oppose Christ's work right where the Lord is meant to be worshiped.

Here this man is in the synagogue screaming. The religious people had no answer. But with a command the Lord Jesus Christ ruled over this evil spirit (v. 35). He has the power and the right to control even the forces of darkness, to command Satan and his minions.

That is why, in verse 36, "Amazement came over them all." When you think about what a demon is, this really is amazing. A demon is a fallen angel who rebelled with Satan against God and was cast from heaven. Demons are committed to opposing God's rule and everything God does. They hate God and hate God's people. Their entire mission is to resist God. But when Jesus speaks, demons tremble!

Dualism is the idea that good and evil are locked in a struggle and the battle is almost equal. But the Christian worldview does not allow any such thinking. There is Jesus—King of kings and Lord of lords with all authority in heaven and on earth. He always wins! He rules over even the demonic powers!

### Authority over Physical Existence (4:38-40)

Jesus shows this authority primarily through his healing ministry. The Lord heals Simon Peter's mother-in-law (vv. 38-39). When Luke refers to a "high fever" (v. 38), he speaks with a physician's concern and insight. This is no common cold or flu bug. This woman is down and out. The fever must have been desperate because "they asked him about her" (v. 38). They're asking for a miracle. "So he stood over her and rebuked the fever, and it left her" (v. 39). Fevers do not have ears or minds. Fevers are not sentient beings. But the Son of God speaks to this virus or whatever causes the fever, and this unhearing, unthinking thing obeys him! What power!

This was no fluke or fraud. The Lord healed "various diseases" (v. 40). He is not healing those vague, unverifiable kinds of sicknesses. This is not a tent revival featuring a fake healer planting people in the audience. The Lord healed "each one" (v. 40). He did not turn anybody away. He did not sell tickets or ask for an offering. He sat there well into sunset, and he personally laid hands on every person who came to him, and they were healed.

Every disease, every person . . . healed. I often wonder why people who claim to have healing powers and gifts do not simply go to hospitals and heal the sick. Why must they rent stadiums, sell tickets, and have cameras filming them? There is something demonic about that. If you have the ability to heal but you use it as a means of building a name for yourself or lining your pockets with money, then you are not doing the Lord's work.

When Jesus heals, there is no fakery. Satan always has counterfeits, but Jesus is the real deal. He is the Son of God, the King of kings, and he has authority in his teaching, authority over demons, and authority over physical existence.

In this text of Scripture, between the people and the demons, who understands the truth about Jesus? It was the demons! The demon cried out, "I know who you are—the Holy One of God!" (v. 34). Luke tells us, "Demons were coming out of many, shouting and saying, 'You are the Son of God!' But he rebuked them and would not allow them to speak, because they knew he was the Christ" (v. 41). The evil spirits get it right. They know Jesus is "the Holy One of God"—another way of referring to Jesus as the Messiah, the chosen Savior of the world. *Demons* know this.

Beloved, do not let demons that cannot be saved acknowledge more about Jesus than you whom he came to save. Demons have sense enough to ask, "Have you come to destroy us?" (v. 34). The demons knew he would; their only concern was when. They did not assume they had unlimited time to carry on their wickedness. They knew their days were numbered.

The days of sinful man's rebellion are numbered too. You will either end your rebellion by repenting now of your sin, confessing it to God, and asking for his forgiveness through Jesus Christ, or Jesus will end your rebellion by demonstrating his holiness in condemnation. My friend, don't sit here in your sins and fail to ask the Lord, "Will you destroy me because of my sin?" The wise man repents. The wise man turns to Jesus. The wise man recognizes that Jesus is the Son of God, the chosen one of God. Be wise. Recognize Jesus. Come to him while you may be saved. I plead with you, before it's too late, before you die in your sin and face the Lord's judgment, repent and believe. Do not allow an evil spirit to respond more honestly to Jesus than you.

Christian, the response of these demons has much to teach us, too. Look how loudly they proclaim that Jesus is the Holy One of God and the Son of God: "with a loud voice" (v. 33); "shouting" (v. 41). That's how demons acknowledge Jesus. Do we acknowledge Jesus as loudly? Or are we in some measure ashamed to proclaim his name? We must not allow demons to proclaim Christ more boldly than we do. If we are ashamed of Jesus before men, he will be ashamed of us before his Father in heaven (Mark 8:38; Luke 9:26).

And, Christian, consider how the demons obey Jesus. Are we quicker and more joyful in our obedience to Jesus than demons are? They obey him because he exercises raw authority toward them. Toward us he shows love. How much more should we who have been loved by God through Jesus his Son show our love toward him in a quick, glad, full obedience?

Beloved, let us resolve not to allow demons to acknowledge and obey Jesus more loudly and more quickly than we acknowledge and obey the Lord who loves us and gave his life for us.

## Conclusion

In Luke 4 Jesus came preaching the good news of the kingdom throughout the region of Galilee. That same gospel is preached in our day. We still live in "the year of God's favor" (v. 19). This is a day not to be wasted but treasured. Drink in the realization that Christ is for us Prophet, Priest, and King. He has endured every temptation that all humanity would have failed. He has brought the good news of salvation that all humanity needed. He has exercised his kingship for the blessing of all who have been broken by the fall. Christ is for us the sufficient and only Savior. And this Jesus, who is your Messiah and who has authority over all things, loves you. Hope in him and trust his love.

## Reflect and Discuss

1. Do you believe Jesus is the Son of God? Why or why not?
2. What temptations commonly attack you? How are you fighting those temptations?
3. How might fleeing to Christ help you in times of temptation? How would fleeing to Christ differ from fighting those battles in your own strength?
4. Jesus came preaching the good news of the kingdom of heaven. What does our Lord's emphasis teach us about the importance of preaching and evangelism?
5. Do you think all Christians have a responsibility to preach the gospel to persons who are poor, blind, imprisoned, etc.? Why or why not?

6. How might you take part in seeing the gospel reach persons who are poor, are captive, or have disabilities?
7. Why do you think demons recognized Jesus's true identity before the people did?
8. In this chapter we see Jesus as Prophet, Priest, and King. Which of those mediatorial offices seems most dear to you right now? Why?

# The Holy One of God

## LUKE 5:1-32

**Main Idea:** Holiness in Christ is surprisingly more powerful than we think.

---

I.   Jesus Has a Holiness That Exposes Us to Ourselves (5:1-11).
II.  Jesus Has a Holiness That Cleanses Us before God (5:12-16).
III. Jesus Has a Holiness That Legitimately Forgives Sin (5:17-26).
IV.  Jesus Has a Holiness That Calls Sinners to Repentance (5:27-32).

---

When you think of "holiness," what comes to mind? For many people images of a Buddhist monk come to mind—perhaps a clean-shaven man, dressed in robes, a kind smile, devout in religious activity. Maybe you think of Mahatma Gandhi—clothed in a robe, slightly bent, a little wasted away from fasting or protesting. Or perhaps you don't think of a person but a particular posture. The holy person is a person separated from everything that is unclean, morally wrong, and displeasing to God. The holy person may be known by the things from which they abstain or reject. In their abstinence from what is unclean and polluted, we come to regard them as holy.

What if another kind of holiness exists? What if we defined holiness not so much by what it avoids or by its religious activity and habits? What if there exists a holiness that is both transcendent and transformative? Suppose there is a holiness that makes contact with the world and *by that contact* transforms the world.

Recall the profession of one of the demons in Luke 4. On seeing Jesus it cried out, "I know who you are—*the Holy One of God!* (v. 4; emphasis added). We want to know the Lord Jesus as "the Holy One of God" in his surprising, transformative holiness.

## Jesus Has a Holiness That Exposes Us to Ourselves
### LUKE 5:1-11

Our text begins with a fishing story. It's not the kind of tall-tale fishing story men usually tell. You know, "It was *this* big!" Have you ever noticed that in those kinds of fishing stories the fisherman is always alone, nobody is there to see it, the fish gets bigger with each telling, and the fish always gets away?

This story in Luke's Gospel is not like those tall tales. Here's how it happened: "The crowd was pressing in on Jesus to hear God's word" (v. 1). Keep your eyes on the crowd as we go through this chapter. They came so close the Lord had to leave the shore and teach them from a boat (vv. 2-3). After the teaching the Lord asked Peter to "put out into deep water and let down your nets for a catch" (v. 4). I imagine there was a cool poise in the Lord's voice, like it was nothing. Maybe there was a knowing twinkle in his eyes.

Peter's attitude is typical when we think a rookie is telling us how to do our business, isn't it (v. 5)? Peter is the experienced fisherman; Jesus is a handyman. Peter has been out all night; Jesus just got into the boat. Peter has not caught anything all night; Jesus thinks he knows the fish are biting. Peter is the one who has to row even though he is tired from working all night; Jesus sits in the stern of the boat. So you can imagine Peter's attitude. But Jesus is the rabbi, so Peter is going to humor him. He says, "If you say so, I'll let down the nets." Peter is basically passive-aggressive with a hint of self-righteousness.

Peter did not expect what we see in verses 6-7. They landed *two* boats full of fish, and they were sinking! Peter, James, and John were experienced fishermen, but they had *never* seen anything like this! They were all "amazed" (v. 9).

Something deeper happens to Peter. Something more profound enters his mind. When Jesus does this miracle, Peter glimpsed the Lord's glory and holiness. In the light of Jesus's holiness, Peter sees his own heart (v. 8). What about this miracle would cause Peter to fall before Jesus, confessing his sin? In this miracle Peter receives a glimpse of the glory, majesty, and holiness of Jesus Christ. Peter reminds us of the prophet Isaiah:

> *In the year that King Uzziah died, I saw the Lord seated on a high and lofty throne, and the hem of his robe filled the temple. Seraphim were standing above him; they each had six wings: with two they covered their faces, with two they covered their feet, and with two they flew. And one called to another:*
>
> > *Holy, holy, holy is the LORD of Armies;*
> > *his glory fills the whole earth.*

> *The foundations of the doorways shook at the sound of their*
> *voices, and the temple was filled with smoke. Then I said:*
>> *Woe is me for I am ruined*
>> *because I am a man of unclean lips*
>> *and live among a people of unclean lips,*
>> *and because my eyes have seen the King,*
>> *the* LORD *of Armies.* (Isa 6:1-5)

Seeing God in his holiness makes us aware of our sinfulness. John Calvin wrote in *The Institutes of Christian Religion*, "Man never attains to a true knowledge of himself until he has contemplated the face of God, and come down after such contemplation to look into himself" (37). That's what happens to Peter. He glimpses the face of God in Jesus Christ, and from that vision he comes down to see into himself. He finds in himself what we all find in ourselves: sin. Because he knows such a holy being as God should not be around a sinful man, Peter cries out, "Go away from me!" (v. 8).

Uniquely, here is a holiness that *comes to sinners*. Rather than going away, Jesus says, "Join me." Here is a holiness that uses a confessing sinner in its mission. Here is holiness that not only calls the sinner but *commissions the sinner* to become a fisher of men. Here is holiness so stunningly beautiful it causes a man to leave everything for its sake. It gives the former sinner a new purpose, direction, and call.

This is good news for us today. Romans 3:23 says, "All have sinned and fall short of the glory of God." So we all deserve God's going away from us. In fact, that is what hell is—the withdrawal of God's loving, kind presence from us. We all deserve hell because of our sin. It is the acknowledgment of our sinfulness that begins the goodness of the good news. For while we were still sinners, Christ died for us. God sent his Son to call us into his Son's holiness, where there is purpose and righteousness. We only need one thing to come to this holy Lord: to confess we are sinners and repent like Peter.

## Jesus Has a Holiness That Cleanses Us before God
### LUKE 5:12-16

It is one thing to expose our sin. It is another to make us clean in God's presence. What hope would there be if we only were brought to the knowledge of our sin? We need something or someone who cleanses us before God.

There are two eye-catching things in verse 12. First, the man has "leprosy all over him." "Leprosy" is any one of a number of skin diseases. It sometimes results in open sores and can be contagious. This man was covered with it. Second, this man was in a town around a lot of people. According to the law of God, he should have been quarantined outside the city or camp. He was to be treated as unclean before God. Leviticus 13:1-3 reads,

> *The LORD spoke to Moses and Aaron: "When a person has a swelling, scab, or spot on the skin of his body, and it may be a serious disease on the skin of his body, he is to be brought to the priest Aaron or to one of his sons, the priests. The priest will examine the sore on the skin of his body. If the hair in the sore has turned white and the sore appears to be deeper than the skin of his body, it is in fact a serious skin disease. After the priest examines him, he must pronounce him unclean."*

To be pronounced "unclean" meant a leper could not worship God. Leviticus 13:12-15 continues,

> *But if the skin disease breaks out all over the skin so that it covers all the skin of the stricken person from his head to his feet so far as the priest can see, the priest will look, and if the skin disease has covered his entire body, he is to pronounce the stricken person clean. Since he has turned totally white, he is clean. But whenever raw flesh appears on him, he will be unclean. When the priest examines the raw flesh, he must pronounce him unclean. Raw flesh is unclean; this is a serious skin disease.*

Our man in Luke 5 was "full of leprosy." He was likely "raw" from head to foot. So not only was he unclean; he was probably in constant pain and soreness. Leviticus 13:45-46 tells us how a leper was to act and be treated:

> *The person who has a case of serious skin disease is to have his clothes torn and his hair hanging loose, and he must cover his mouth and cry out, "Unclean, unclean!" He will remain unclean as long as he has the disease; he is unclean. He must live alone in a place outside the camp.*

The leprous man suffered a terrible condition. He suffered physical pain and social isolation. For as long as he had the disease, he was effectively shunned. He was cut off from God in worship and from Israel in community. He carried a heavy stigma because of his disease.

According to Leviticus 14, before a leprous person could be brought back into society, two things were necessary. First, the priest had to examine him to confirm the leprosy was clear. If so, the person would be considered clean again. Second, the man had to present an offering as atonement for sin. The priest would take the blood of the sacrifice and rub it on the right ear lobe, the right thumb, and the big toe of the right foot to symbolize his sin being atoned for or covered by the blood of the sacrifice. Then the leper could return to Israelite society.

The law and the priest could not *make* a man clean. They could only *determine* and declare whether he was clean or not. They had no remedy or power to change a person's standing before God. Atonement was necessary.

Here comes this man full of leprosy to Jesus in Luke 5. No one can touch him without becoming unclean and cut off from worship. To touch a leper was effectively to become a leper. The leprous man fell on his face and begged Jesus, "Lord, if you are willing, you can make me clean" (v. 12). It is not clear how he knew this about Jesus. He casts himself on God when he says, "Lord, if you are willing," and shows faith in Jesus's power when he says, "You can make me clean."

Here's the wonder about the holiness of Jesus. First, Jesus actually *touches* the unclean (v. 13). You can imagine the Jewish crowd holding its breath, leaning back, and inside screaming out, "Nooooo! Don't touch him! He will defile you!" But our Lord affirmed this man's humanity as he touched him. Second, Jesus healed him. Right away the leprosy departed! The Lord sent the man to the priests to keep the requirements of the law and prove he was now clean (v. 14).

Jesus possesses a holiness that is not defiled by touching the unclean, but with a touch he cleanses the unclean. Jesus possesses a holiness that produces what the law requires but cannot produce. "Sanctity [or holiness] is stronger than the whole of hell" (Merton, *Seven Storey*, 256).

Whom do we think of as "unclean"? This is an important question for us Christians to ask ourselves. The church has a Savior who cleanses the unclean, yet the church has a history of rejecting the unclean.

The church regarded persons with AIDS as unclean during the early days of that disease. Many Christians have thought of persons with same-sex desires as unclean. Drug addicts and drug sellers may get tagged with that label and stigma. Perhaps we view prostitutes, alcoholics, or the homeless as lepers in our day. We must reconsider whether we should regard people as unclean—especially if we are tempted to withdraw from them, for Jesus has a holiness that is not defiled by uncleanness but a holiness that cleanses by his touch!

We, in Christ, filled with his Spirit, can and should be around the "unclean" so we can tell them there is a way to be made clean before God. That way to cleanness is calling on the Lord to make them clean. He wills to do it for his people.

I believe the Lord wants us in our mission to our neighborhoods to have a special concern and love for the "unclean." That requires us to rethink our stigmas and attitudes. It requires us to rethink what makes a person clean. Jesus said in Matthew 15:11 that "it's not what goes into the mouth that defiles a person, but what comes out of the mouth—this defiles a person." It is the heart that defiles a person. Consequently, we cannot be defiled by our neighbors' actions. Christ has given us new hearts with his law written on them. With our new hearts and the gift of righteousness before God by faith in Christ, let us go to our neighbors and tell them that Christ cleanses sinners before God. We want to avoid the "holy huddle." We don't want to be plastic Christians. We want to feel ourselves thrust into the world with this good news, in full confidence that the Savior will cleanse everyone he touches through the gospel.

## Jesus Has a Holiness That Legitimately Forgives Sin
### LUKE 5:17-26

When we think of holiness, we rightly think of its incompatibility with sin. We are right to see that light and darkness do not mix; light chases away darkness.

Sometimes we go a step further. We think of the light *hating* darkness. We may think light crushes darkness. What if light does something else to darkness? What if holiness does something else to our sin?

The third scene is one of my favorite events in the Bible. It begins in verse 17, some days after Jesus cleanses the leper. The Lord is now teaching Pharisees and teachers of the law, or scribes. These are the "holy men" of Israel who lead Israel religiously. They've come from everywhere—even Jerusalem—to hear Jesus speak.

Luke gives us this juicy detail: "And the Lord's power to heal was in him" (v. 17). There's an extraordinary power with Jesus that day. We might call it an unction or anointing.

There is also an extraordinary demonstration of faith about to happen (vv. 18-19). I love this scene. Many people today get upset if someone spills a little something on their carpet or favorite tablecloth. Can you imagine someone coming through the roof of your house making a hole big enough to let a paralyzed grown man through? State Farm ain't covering that! Can you imagine the homeowner's reaction?

The act of letting their friend down through the roof was an unusual demonstration of faith. We know this because of what Jesus says next. "Seeing their faith he said, 'Friend, your sins are forgiven'" (v. 20). That stuns me. Jesus says *nothing* about the man's legs or paralysis. He focused on the man's *soul*. He forgives the man's *sins*. Listen, you can be paralyzed, unable to get around without your friends, lying motionless on your sickbed, and yet still be *full* of sin!

See how Jesus thinks. Our main need is not physical healing. Our main need is spiritual forgiveness. That why Jesus says things like,

> *If your hand or your foot causes you to fall away, cut it off and throw it away. It is better for you to enter life maimed or lame than to have two hands or two feet and be thrown into the eternal fire.* (Matt 18:8)

Better to limp into heaven than run into hell! Paralysis is nothing compared to God's punishment. Our main need is spiritual forgiveness. So Jesus forgives the man's sin.

## An Objection

The scribes and Pharisees, the "holy men" of Israel, have a theological objection (v. 21). They say Jesus blasphemes by claiming to do what only God can do. They have a proper theology of forgiveness—only God can ultimately forgive sins. That theology is correct as far as it goes. But they do not know God. They do not recognize the day of their visitation.

What they get wrong is not their assumption about God, forgiving sin. What they get wrong is their assumption that Jesus is not God.

## An Object Lesson

Pause for a moment. If you were Jesus, how would you answer their objection? Some few of us would call down thunder and lightning. It is good we are not Jesus. Most of us would likely give an argument of some sort. We would correct their theology with the use of words.

But that is not what Jesus does. In verses 22-24 our Lord responds to their objection with an object lesson, a parable by way of a miracle. He first raises the stakes in verse 23 with the question, "Which is easier . . . ?" It is easy for people to walk around just saying things like, "Your sins are forgiven." Anyone can do that. But then, so there is no argument about mere words, the Lord decides to *visibly demonstrate* that he is God who legitimately forgives sin. He proves that by doing the harder thing. He turns to the paralyzed man and says, "I tell you: Get up, take your stretcher, and go home" (v. 24). Immediately the paralyzed man obeys and begins to walk!

The phrase *I tell you* is emphatic. It stresses that Jesus is doing this miracle in his own authority. The religious leaders stumble at the notion that Jesus can do what God does in forgiving sin. The Lord essentially says, I will prove to you that I'm God by this miracle. Verse 25 provides miraculous proof that the Holy One of God can, in fact, do just that. The point was not ultimately the man miraculously walking but the Son forgiving sins.

In his holiness Christ does not chase away our sin. Nor does the Savior crush the sinner. The Lord of love does not hate the sinner. Instead, our holy Lord *forgives* the sinner. Forgiveness is one of the holiest acts of all.

Look at the people's reaction in verse 26. Do you know what I find extraordinary? They watched Jesus forgive a man's sin. Then they watched Jesus prove he could forgive sin by healing a paralyzed man. But not one of them then said to Jesus, "Since you can forgive sins, please forgive my sins, too!" They experienced general amazement and gave general praise to God, but they did not worship Jesus or seek forgiveness for their sin. That is amazing and tragic. Having eyes, they do not see. Having ears, they do not hear.

How often in our day is the gospel preached and sinners will not hear? How often do people say, "We heard a good sermon today," but no one says, "Forgive me my sins, Lord"?

Jesus Christ came into the world to save sinners. He lived in our flesh to offer God the righteous obedience we owed. He died in our place as an offering to satisfy the wrath of God against our sin. God raised him from the grave to *prove* his sacrifice was accepted. Now God calls men everywhere to repent of their sin and seek his forgiveness by placing their faith in Jesus Christ as Lord. All God requires is that we admit our sin and trust in Jesus. How often do men tragically turn away!

Beloved, I don't know what condition you are in. I don't know if you're a Christian with full assurance of faith who continually flees to Christ, if you've never heard that Jesus saves the unclean and the sinner, or if you've heard the message before and not yet believed. Oh, do not make the mistake of these persons in the Bible. Do not go away having heard the word of life only to leave it unaccepted. Today is the day of salvation. Do not harden your hearts. Confess your sins like Peter. Call on Jesus to cleanse you of your sin like the leper. Believe in Jesus and be saved.

Jesus makes things clear. He does not multiply words. He doesn't give verbal proofs. He does the harder thing, the greater thing. He *demonstrates* that he is the God who forgives sins—even a *holy* God who forgives sins.

## Applications

We could make at least three applications based on this text. First, vague notions of "God" and even being in "awe" of God are not the same thing as knowing God. These Jewish religious leaders have a good general theology, but they do not know Jesus. We meet people all the time who say, "I believe in God," but when you examine the claim, you find their understanding of God is murky and misty, and they do not know Jesus. John 17:3 tells us eternal life is knowing God and Jesus Christ whom he has sent.

Second, vague worship of God is not the same as worshiping God the way he requires us. God determines what is satisfactory worship from his followers. From accepting Abel's offering and rejecting Cain's, to the detailed law of the Old Testament, to his seeking those who will worship him in Spirit and in truth (John 4:24), *God* determines what worship pleases him and what does not.

Third, when people are confused about the true God and Jesus Christ, when gospel clarity is at stake, the proper response is plain statement of the truth (2 Cor 4:2). Our Lord does that here. The apostles leave us the same example. Since we live in a society increasingly confused about almost everything, it's important that Christians speak plainly and simply about the truth.

When we get to know Jesus as the holy One of God, his holiness exposes our sin to us, cleanses us before God, and brings forgiveness of sin.

## Jesus Has a Holiness That Calls Sinners to Repentance
### LUKE 5:27-32

Verse 27 begins with "after this." After the "holy men" failed to ask for forgiveness, Jesus saw a tax collector named Levi. In Jesus's day tax collectors were known sinners. They had a reputation for cheating people on their taxes. And remember for whom they collected taxes: Rome. So they were seen as oppressors of their own nation. People generally despised tax collectors.

Jesus sees Levi and calls Levi to follow him, to become one of his disciples. Levi does exactly that. Like Peter, Levi immediately leaves everything and follows Jesus (v. 28). Levi's response illustrates true repentance and entrance into discipleship.

When a man finds acceptance with the Lord, he naturally wants to celebrate. A person who finds acceptance with God wants his friends to find in Jesus what he found. So Levi throws a dinner party for "a large crowd of tax collectors and others" with Jesus as the featured guest (v. 29). Apparently Levi tries to reach his friends, and Jesus is willing to hang out with them.

But the Pharisees and scribes continue grumbling (v. 30). They apparently think eating with sinners is "unclean." They hold an idea of holiness that requires total separation from sinners. Also, they apparently think they themselves are not sinners! They ought to take a place at the table as sinners needing to be with Christ, but they remain blind to their own condition before God.

Religious people often struggle to know how to engage sinners. We ask, "Is it OK to go out with them after work? Can we go to their weddings? Can we have a drink with them? What about the club?" Those questions come from a good, godly concern for holiness and for Christian witness.

Our Lord's activities challenge our notions of holiness. If we think of holiness only or primarily as separation, we end up isolating ourselves from the people we hope to reach. We find ourselves at odds with Jesus's example here. And we find ourselves attempting something the Bible actually says is impossible. Do you remember how the Bible addresses this issue in 1 Corinthians 5:9-13?

The apostle Paul notes,

> *I wrote to you in a letter not to associate with sexually immoral people.*
> I did not mean *the immoral people of this world or the greedy and*
> *swindlers or idolaters; otherwise* you would have to leave the
> world. (emphasis added)

If we aim to separate ourselves completely from sinners, where will we go? We would have to start a colony on the moon—a colony of one because some other sinners are coming! To be holy by having no contact with sinners means we "would have to leave the world."

Then Paul continues,

> *But actually, I wrote you not to associate with anyone who claims to*
> *be a brother or sister and is sexually immoral or greedy, an idolater or*
> *verbally abusive, a drunkard or a swindler. Do not even eat with such*
> *a person. For what business is it of mine to judge outsiders? Don't*
> *you judge those who are inside? God judges outsiders. Remove the evil*
> *person from among you.* (1 Cor 5:11-13)

Do you see how the Bible says our instinct is upside down? The Christian church has too often been afraid to engage the lost world of sinners outside while being complacent about unrepentant sin on the inside! The Bible says to be concerned about "anyone who claims to be a brother or sister" but lives an unrepentant, immoral life. With that one, do not even eat; put him out of your fellowship. Practice church discipline. But regarding the outsiders, go to them; eat with them; drink with them, that you might be able to reach them. We cannot reach people with whom we have no contact.

Keep in mind the Lord's purpose in Luke 5. "Jesus replied to them, 'It is not those who are healthy who need a doctor, but those who are *sick*. I have not come to call the righteous, but *sinners* to repentance" (vv. 31-32; emphasis added).

We cannot call people to repentance if we are never with them. We cannot reach sinners without going where sinners are. They are not likely to come where we are. They find our parties boring. They find our fun boring. That's OK. We expect them to. They have tastes for *this* world while we have tastes for heaven. Those differing tastes are not easily joined together, so it creates a burden for us to cross a bridge to reach them without adopting their tastes.

That is what the Lord does here. The Lord Jesus attends Levi's party with the spiritual well-being of sinners in mind. The Lord does not sin with them; rather, he seeks to save them. We must follow his example while also remembering that we are not the Savior. We do not possess the Lord's invincible purity, so we need some safeguards:

1. Know your limits and temptations as you go into the world. If you are easily tempted with alcohol, you do *not* need to go with colleagues to the bar after work. You should *avoid* that setting. Give no room to the devil or make provision for the flesh. That means being honest about our temptations and the sins that so easily beset us.

2. Keep a redemptive purpose or goal in mind as you go into the world. We are not going into the world simply to hang out with the world. Sometimes Christians boast of their worldliness. That is immaturity and a bad example. We go not to boast of how liberal we are with the world but to seek their spiritual benefit and salvation.

3. Remember that Christ is our holiness (1 Cor 1:30). Colossians 2 tells us that multiplying rules is powerless to subdue the flesh. That kind of asceticism does not produce righteousness but produces hypocrites and Pharisees. Rather, we go into the world trying to fully embody life in Christ. We go declaring it is no longer we who live but Christ who lives in us (Gal 2:20). We go into those places and relationships with our hearts stocked with God's Word, hoping to insert it into conversations wherever we can.

The Lord Jesus has a preference among people. The Lord prefers those who know they are sick with sin. The righteous, those who think of themselves as "well," do not see their need of the Great Physician. In their self-righteousness they are blind. They imagine themselves to be good enough or holy enough for God to accept them like they are. Because they trust themselves, there is no room in their hearts to trust God's Son. Offer them salvation through faith in Christ, and they say, "No, I'm good."

John Calvin rightly observed,

> Such is our innate pride, we always seem to ourselves just, and upright, and wise, and holy, until we are convinced, by clear evidence, of our injustice, vileness, folly, and impurity. Convinced, however, we are not, if we look to ourselves only, and not to the Lord also—He being the only standard by the application of which this conviction can be produced. For, since we are all naturally prone to hypocrisy, any empty semblance of righteousness is quite enough to satisfy us instead of righteousness itself. (*Institutes*, 37)

The sick know they need the Lord's healing. The sick are closer to the kingdom of heaven. All they need in order to receive the kingdom of God is to hear the call to repent and believe in the Lord Jesus Christ. It's a call especially for sinners. The greater the sinner, the greater the Savior.

## Conclusion

As we close, consider what this text lays out before us. We get to know the holiness of Christ the Lord. It's a holiness that exposes our sin. It's a holiness that cleanses us before God. It's a holiness that legitimately forgives sin. It's a holiness especially for sinners who know their sinful state.

As we get to know Jesus in this passage, we learn something about how to respond to him. We should, like Peter, confess our sin. We should, like the leper, cry out to God to be made clean. We should, like the paralyzed man and his friends, put our faith in the Lord. We should, like Levi and the tax collectors, repent of our sin.

Notice something about the mass of people, the crowds in our text. The crowd presses in on the Lord so much they make it hard for him to carry on his ministry (v. 1). They make it hard for the paralyzed man and his friends to get to him. The crowds in Levi's house are amazed at the miracle but later grumble about Jesus. The crowds grumble about the Savior seeking to save sinners. Beloved, rarely do the crowds know the Lord or do the Lord's will. Rarely do crowds know the mind of the Lord. Rarely do the crowds follow Jesus.

So don't follow the crowd. Even if you must do it alone, drop everything and follow the Lord. If we would have eternal life in God's kingdom, we have to follow the one who knows the path to the kingdom. We have to forget the crowds and sing, "*I* have decided to follow Jesus."

Today is the day of salvation. Today the Lord calls sinners to repent. Forget about everyone else. Think of your own sins. Do you not need to be forgiven? Do you not need to be cleansed? If so, then you need to believe in Jesus and follow him as your Lord. Do it today. Decide to follow Jesus. Do not turn back.

## Reflect and Discuss

1. What do you think of when you think of holiness?
2. Consider Isaiah 6:1-5. What is the effect on us when we glimpse God's glory? Can you think of other biblical examples?
3. What hope would there be if God's holiness only exposed our sin?
4. Who do you think are the lepers and the unclean in our society today? What hope does Jesus offer them?
5. If you were talking with someone who said they feel unclean before God, what things about Jesus would you share with them? What aspect of his character or what story from the Gospels would you share with them?
6. Do you think there is a difference between truly knowing God through Jesus Christ and having a general belief in God? Why or why not?
7. Who gets to decide how God is worshiped? In what ways does our answer to that question affect our relationship with God?
8. In Luke 5:1-32 we see Jesus interacting with sinners in various settings. In what ways should Christians follow the Lord's example? In what ways or in what circumstances should Christians not follow this example?

# The Lord of Worship

LUKE 5:33–6:11

**Main Idea:** May the Lord himself cure the lurking Pharisee and scribe in us all.

---

I. **Should We Fast and Pray or Eat and Drink (5:33-39)?**
  A. The religion of the Pharisees denies pleasure (5:33).
  B. Faith in Jesus is all about joy (5:34-35)!
  C. Faith in Jesus begins a new era (5:36-39).
II. **Should We Serve the Law or Serve the Son (6:1-5)?**
  A. Jesus has not broken the law.
  B. Jesus owns the law.
III. **Should We Do Good and Save or Do Harm and Destroy (6:6-11)?**

---

Every Easter we Christians celebrate the resurrection of the Lord Jesus Christ. As surely as Easter comes every year, network television stations will broadcast special programs about Jesus. "Who is Jesus?" "Was Jesus actually the person most Christians believe him to be, or was he some other kind of figure?"

The speculations will not end with questions about Jesus's identity. They will continue with questions about what it "truly" means to follow Jesus. How you follow Jesus depends on what you think you know about him.

No doubt there will be rival interpretations of these questions. Some shows will do a better job than others at reporting the various points of view. One of the problems that comes with this treatment is that no point of view is dismissed as improbable, and some are privileged. Usually the privileged points of view have little to do with the Jesus we find in the Bible.

If we want to know Jesus, we must consider him as he reveals himself in the Gospels. We don't want to know Jesus as scholars or television producers present him. As we look to the Bible, we will discover that a clear understanding of who Jesus is profoundly affects how we worship him.

Two major sets of characters involved in our text are the Pharisees and scribes. These two parties in ancient Judaism were significant in shaping the worship of ancient Israel. The Pharisees were the "Bible guys." They were the ancient equivalent of the fundamentalists. They believed in the Bible. They believed in miracles. They were strict in their observance of biblical rules. In fact, they loved the law, or the rules of God. The scribes were the teachers of the law. They explained God's word to God's people.

Often we find the scribes and Pharisees in cahoots with one another. That fact prompted me to ask myself, *Why are the scribes and Pharisees so often mentioned in the Gospels?* They garner a lot of real estate in the Gospels. One answer is obvious: they are the major villains in the story. Their actions lead to the crucifixion of the Lord.

There may be a second reason the scribes and Pharisees are so often mentioned in the Gospels. The Pharisees and scribes are us—at least the temptation to become Pharisees is common to us all. That temptation first manifests itself in wrong thoughts about who Jesus is and how to follow him. The temptation prompts three questions on the nature of Christian worship:

## Should We Fast and Pray or Eat and Drink?
### LUKE 5:33-39

*The Religion of the Pharisees Denies Pleasure (5:33)*

Verse 33 continues with the scene started in verse 27. The Lord Jesus visits the house of a new disciple. Levi, a tax collector, calls together "a large company of tax collectors and others" (v. 29) for a dinner party with Jesus. Scribes and Pharisees visit Levi's home too, but they grumble and complain that Jesus eats with sinners (v. 30).

The conversation at the dinner party continues at verse 33. The scribes and Pharisees challenge the Lord by saying, "John's disciples fast often and say prayers, and those of the Pharisees do the same, but yours eat and drink." They continue to think that Jesus's attendance at a dinner party scandalizes religion.

The comment assumes that abstaining from eating and drinking is better than partaking. The comment illustrates that the scribes and Pharisees are religious ascetics, people who believe you must avoid all forms of pleasure or self-indulgence as an act of self-discipline for religious purpose. The ascetic believes abstaining makes you godlier and that it pleases God. They think the severe treatment of the body and avoiding pleasure leads to holiness (see Col 2:20-23).

In that way the Pharisees also seem to assume that religion is not about joy. They are suspicious of joy. Religion is not supposed to make you happy. Happiness, in their mind, gets in the way of religious devotion. For them, asceticism is better than joy.

But on what basis do they believe this? They rest their argument on the authority of their own example and tradition. They contend, "The Pharisees' disciples fast and pray. So why don't your disciples do it?" Their comment and their way of thinking are really self-righteousness. They cite their own authority not the Scriptures. They generalize from their example to everyone else.

The first step in becoming a self-righteous religious Pharisee is **using our personal religious example as a requirement for everyone else to obey**.

What does Jesus think about all of this? The Lord gives a two-part reply.

### Faith in Jesus Is All about Joy! (5:34-35)

Our Lord uses a wedding analogy. Ancient Jewish weddings had three basic phases. First there was the contract, when the parents of the bride and groom agreed their children would marry and a bride price was given to the father of the bride. That contract, according to Jewish law, effectively began a marriage, though the couple did not yet live together as husband and wife. Second came an indefinite period of time when the groom returned to his father's house to prepare a place for himself and his bride. Meanwhile, the bride was to watch for his return and ready herself for a marriage that could take place at any time. Not until everything was ready and her father gave him permission could the groom return to his bride for the actual wedding celebration. The wedding celebration marked the third phase. It was often a seven-day period full of dancing, music, food, and drink. Finally, after the celebration came the consummation, when husband and wife began to live together in marriage.

With the metaphor in verse 34, the Lord seems to be referring to the celebration. The bridegroom's coming was a time of joy and indulgence, not gloom and denial. No one during a wedding celebration would expect the guests to fast; it is time for rejoicing and thanksgiving. So it is with his disciples. They are the guests at the wedding. Jesus is the bridegroom, the one they have been waiting for. He is here to gather his bride. This is cause for rejoicing!

What Jesus says to those who have ears to hear is that following him is all about joy! It's about delight. It's about gladness. It's about feasting. It's about the great sumptuous meal the Savior spreads before us. To discover who Jesus is and to receive him as Lord and Savior is to find your greatest happiness. Finding Jesus is entering into a celebration far longer than seven days; it is an eternal joy.

In Matthew 13:44 Jesus uses a parable to describe the kingdom of heaven: "The kingdom of heaven is like treasure, buried in a field, that a man found and reburied. Then *in his joy* he goes and sells everything he has and buys that field" (emphasis added). The kingdom Jesus brings is so overwhelmingly wonderful that with joy we give up everything else in order to have this one treasure—namely Jesus himself. Christians are those who finally have discovered the fountain of joy in Christ! When we are with him, we celebrate.

### Faith in Jesus Begins a New Era (5:36-39)

The Lord compares this situation to a new garment and new wine. With this second parable the Lord teaches that a new era has arrived. There's a significant change in the administration of God's saving purposes in the world.

Imagine coming home from the mall with a new shirt or pants. Who takes that new shirt or pants, cuts off a piece, and then sews it onto some old ratty shirt or pants from college? Nobody does that. The Lord says, even if you did, the new piece will not match the old piece (v. 36).

Likewise, "no one puts new wine into old wineskins" (v. 37). The new wine will burst the old wineskins—wasting the skins and spilling the wine. It ruins everything. New wine and old wineskins are incompatible. You need supple wineskins that are appropriate for the new wine (v. 38). Also, if you have a taste for the old, you will not want the new (v. 39).

The old garment and old wineskins represent the old worship of Israel. Their view of fasting and their view of approaching God were part of the old covenant. But a new covenant was about to be offered in the blood and body of Christ. That's the new wine and new cloth. The old and the new do not mix or match. You cannot pour Christ into the old wineskins of the Mosaic law. He bursts those skins, and you lose Christ (Gal 5:1-6). You cannot attach Christ to the garment of the old system. He doesn't match, and trying to attach him will "tear the new" (v. 36) work of Christ apart. If you have been worshiping God in some old, man-made way, then the newness of the kingdom cannot be held in your wineskins.

We cannot have the gospel with just a little touch of law and legalism. We cannot have the law with just a few ounces of "Jesus" poured in. The gospel is an entirely different garment—a complete garment in itself. The gospel requires the fresh wineskins of New Testament Christianity for the fresh wine it brings. Those who drink the old religion of self-righteousness will not enjoy the new wine of the gospel (v. 39). There's something about legalism and self-righteousness that is natural to us. We are tempted to cling to it and to reject the new vintage that is altogether different.

Perhaps you have been thinking about God and how to worship him. Perhaps you have some ideas, maybe even some rules. If that is you, this text screams out to you, "Do not develop rules for self-righteousness! You will not earn your way to God's favor. You cannot pray enough, fast enough, or do any religious thing enough to satisfy God's righteousness." So do not hang on to self-righteousness. Even our best deeds have enough sin mixed with them to condemn us before a perfectly holy God.

Our righteousness must not be trusted. Our righteousness admits too many weaknesses and imperfections. It will never be sturdy enough to build a ladder to heaven. So we must repent before God of our righteousness. We must abandon *our righteousness* so that we can receive the *righteousness of another*—the perfect righteousness of Jesus Christ the Savior. He obeyed God perfectly where we failed. In obedience to the law in order to satisfy the law, Christ gave himself as a sacrifice for us to pay the penalty of our sins. In that penalty payment and through the righteousness of Christ, sinners are reconciled to God and forgiven. Through faith in Christ, we begin to follow Jesus in a way that God would recognize as worship.

Christian, be careful of holding others to your example rather than to the Scriptures rightly understood. It is easy to think an application appropriate to us, or a practice that seems to serve us, ought to be followed by everyone else. It is easy to slide over to the authority of our own example while thinking we stand on the authority of Scripture. We become Pharisees when we do that.

So let me offer a simple lesson on applying Scripture. There are *necessary* applications and *possible* applications. Necessary applications apply to all. They follow directly from the text of the Bible. For example, the command "Do not covet" (Exod 20:17) applies to us all and forbids any type of envy we can conceive. How we keep that command may vary. One person may say, "I will not watch commercials in order not to covet." That's great for you. That's one *possible* application, but it's not necessary for everyone to observe. The Pharisees take the *possible* and make it *necessary* for all people all the time. By doing so they effectively destroy Christian joy and Christian freedom. The Lord frees us from Pharisaism by binding our consciences to his Word, not to the preferences of men. Only the Word of God can legitimately bind the conscience.

That brings us to our second question.

## Should We Serve the Law or Serve the Son?
### LUKE 6:1-5

Pharisees don't give up easily. They tend to show up again and again, especially around religious times, like the Sabbath. Verse 1 says the disciples were going through "grainfields." This means they were in a rural area. They plucked enough grain to rub together in their hands. They were not exactly farming with large reapers. How did the Pharisees know that a few men walking in grainfields had rubbed a little grain in their hands? The Pharisees are all in the business. They are stalking Jesus. They spy on him and his disciples, looking for a way to trap him. You know you are being a Pharisee when you start inspecting grain!

They raise their concern in verse 2. They now switch from the authority of their own example to what they think is the authority of the Scriptures. God commanded Israel to observe the Sabbath and keep it holy by not working but resting. The Sabbath is patterned after the days of creation. God created the world in six days, and on the seventh day he rested. When God established a covenant with Israel, he commanded that Israel rest on the seventh day just as he did.

Breaking the Sabbath by working required the death penalty in ancient Israel. Because of this stiff penalty, we can well understand why faithful Israelites would want to understand exactly what is meant by "work" on the Sabbath. So they devised rules and lists for defining "work" on the Sabbath. You could not walk far, or it was considered work. You could not cook on the Sabbath. You could not light a fire. And on it went. Pretty soon, according to the Pharisees' rules, it became almost impossible to keep the Sabbath. So to the Pharisees, walking through a field and picking a handful of grain was profaning the Sabbath.

In verse 2 their question seems to spring from an assumption that keeping Sabbath regulations was more important than the needs of people—in this case, hunger. Because they elevate law over people, they become hard toward people and indifferent toward needs. They do not understand Hosea 6:6, which says, "I desire faithful love and not sacrifice." The Pharisees desire the opposite. They want sacrificial obedience to the law instead of loving mercy to fellow Israelites in need.

Here then is the second step in becoming a religious Pharisee: **Make our religious rules more important than Jesus himself.** They do this because they want Jesus to submit to their rules. They want Jesus under their law.

### Jesus Has Not Broken the Law

The Pharisees charge the Lord with breaking the law. The Lord's first reply is simple: he has done no such thing (vv. 3-5).

In fact, the Lord calls on another section of the Scripture, the history of Israel's greatest and most celebrated king, David. In 1 Samuel 21:1-6 David is not yet king. He is running from King Saul, who is trying to kill him because David is God's chosen king to replace Saul. While on the run, David and his men grow hungry. There's only one safe place they can go: the temple. In the temple there was always to be "the Bread of the Presence" (v. 6) kept before God as a memorial. The only people who could eat that bread at the end of the prescribed time were the priests. David and his men ate the bread with the priest's blessing. Yet nowhere does the Bible rebuke or condemn David for doing so.

Jesus reads the Old Testament narrative as applicable for his day and situation. Maybe the Pharisees object, "But David did not eat the bread on the Sabbath. It was a different day of the week and an extraordinary circumstance." When Matthew writes about this exchange between Jesus and the Pharisees, he adds an important detail. In Matthew 12:5-7 Jesus says,

> Or haven't you read in the law that on Sabbath days the priests in the temple violate the Sabbath and are innocent? I tell you that something greater than the temple is here. If you had known what this means, "I desire mercy and not sacrifice," you would not have condemned the innocent. (emphasis added)

Have you ever wondered to yourself, *If God forbids work on the Sabbath, how does he regard the priests who work on the Sabbath?* The priests are the holy representatives of God before the people. Each Sabbath is full of work for them, and yet God does not regard it as sin. This is the Lord's point. In Matthew's account the Lord adds, "I tell you that something greater than the temple is here" (Luke 6:5). In Luke's account that comment stands right next to Jesus saying, "The Son of Man is Lord of the Sabbath" (Matt 12:8).

### Jesus Owns the Law

What they do not yet see as they look to trap Jesus is that Jesus is greater than their law. He is not meant to submit to their law. He is Lord over the true law of God.

Luke 6:5 says, "The Son of Man is Lord of the Sabbath." As Lord of the Sabbath, he rules the Sabbath. He can only rule the Sabbath if, in fact, he owns it. He can only own it if he is the one who made it and gave it. The seventh day—like all days—is put beneath the Lord's feet. Verse 5 is a powerful statement from Jesus's own mouth that he is God. The Son of Man is Lord of the Sabbath, not servant to it, and he is guiltless before it.

When the scribes and Pharisees get legalistic about the Sabbath, they enslave men to the Sabbath as if the Sabbath were the greatest thing. But here before them is one greater than the temple, as Matthew tells us, and greater than the Sabbath. He is the Great Lawgiver who interprets the meaning of the law without any error.

Mark records this scene in his Gospel, too. Mark 2:27 adds one further thing. The Lord Jesus says there, "The Sabbath was made for man and not man for the Sabbath."

The Pharisees serve the law, but the law was meant to serve them. The law was intended to protect them from overwork and the idolatry of work. It was to protect them from the routine that regularly forgets God by reminding them for a full day at the least that God is their God and they are his people. God gave the Sabbath to refresh the souls and bodies of people by having them meet with the Lord. How kind of God to dedicate an entire day for us to do nothing but know him, meet with him, enjoy him, and find ourselves refreshed by him. This is why good worship never exhausts but fills, energizing and making ready.

This is why neglecting the Lord's Day brings such self-harm. We harm ourselves when we busy ourselves with the world's pursuits or the work we bring home. This may not be wrong in itself, but it's not the best thing. The best thing is what Mary discovered sitting at the Lord's feet, hearing his voice, enjoying the needful thing, being refreshed by his presence (Luke 10:39).

If we're going to worship in a manner that pleases God, we must serve the Son. When we serve the Son, we discover that the law was made for us, to bless us not to burden us. That's the case with all of God's Word, but it's especially the case with the law about keeping the Sabbath.

The Sabbath is a shrine in time. It's not a holy place but a holy period. It's time dedicated to rest and refreshment with the Lord. God made the Sabbath so that we would have a regular day for meeting with him and having our souls revived. The Sabbath was a gift to Israel, just as the Lord's Day (Sunday) is a gift to the church.

Jesus, the Lawgiver, has not come to demand that we obey the law. This is what makes Pharisaical religion so odious to God. Pharisees demand we keep the law when even the Lawgiver does not demand that for righteousness. We have already failed at keeping the law. The law requires that we die for that failure. But Jesus has come to perfectly fulfill the law (Matt 5:17) and to pay the penalty the law requires. Every demand God places on us, Jesus Christ has fulfilled—even the keeping of the Sabbath. That is why Jesus lives a perfect life in obedience to God: to offer to God the righteousness we do not have. And that is why Jesus voluntarily and lovingly sacrifices himself on the cross: to pay the penalty of death and to suffer God's condemnation in our place. All who believe in this Jesus stop trying to work their way to God; and, turning from any hopes of self-righteousness, they enter into the true rest, an unending Sabbath, based on faith.

That is why the writer of Hebrews tells us the real Sabbath is, first, ceasing from working to earn righteousness with God and, second, by faith in Christ entering the rest Jesus gives (Heb 4). The Sabbath, like all the law, prophesies about the coming of Christ and a coming rest. That rest is not merely the seventh day but eternity. We who believe have rested from our war with sin and have entered the rest Christ purchased by his blood. In that rest we flourish without effort. This is the true Sabbath, and all who believe in Christ live in it.

Should we serve the law or serve the Son? Oh, beloved, serve the Son and find rest for your souls.

## Should We Do Good and Save or Do Harm and Destroy?
### LUKE 6:6-11

Verses 6-11 provide us with another encounter between Jesus and the Pharisees "on another Sabbath" (v. 6). Jesus was teaching in the synagogue, and there's a man there "whose right hand has shriveled" (v. 6). The scribes and Pharisees are up to their old tricks. They "were watching [Jesus] closely, to see if he would heal on the Sabbath, so that they could find a charge against him" (v. 7).

Can I say a word to any skeptics among us? As a skeptic, you are doubtful about Jesus and the claims of Christianity. The scribes and Pharisees represent your position. I think God has kindly included them in the Gospel narratives so you can learn from their mistake. They watched Jesus, not to find evidence that would lead them to Jesus but to find something to accuse him with. They are in the synagogue on the day of worship hearing the Word of God taught, literally looking for a *miracle*—a miracle they know he can do and have seen before—*not so they can believe in him but so they can reject him.* In the social sciences we call this "confirmation bias." Confirmation bias happens when a person takes whatever evidence is contrary to their position and interprets it in a way that confirms their position. When we operate with a confirmation bias, we do not really adjust our thinking with the new evidence presented. We rearrange the evidence to leave our bias undisturbed. That is not honest thinking.

If you are skeptical of Jesus, beware this kind of confirmation bias. It will blind you just as it did the Pharisees and scribes. Do not repeat the Pharisees' mistake. See the evidence. Let it speak for itself. Then follow the evidence where it leads. Pay particular attention when the evidence feels most threatening or inconvenient to you. That is where your bias will be lurking.

The Lord has a wonderful sense of the dramatic. He calls the man to himself in front of them all and immediately heals the man's hand (v. 8). Our Lord knows what they think, so he's setting up a confrontation—not so much between himself and them but between what they are thinking and what they know is right. Our Lord publicly shames them by asking the powerful question of verse 9—"I ask you: Is it lawful to do good on the Sabbath or to do evil, to save life or to destroy it?"

It's like asking, Why would healing on the Sabbath be a problem? Healing is good. It relieves suffering. It restores the body. All of us would want to be healed were we sick. So Jesus effectively asks, "What is it about your understanding of the Sabbath, a holy day, that prevents people from doing holy and good things to bless others?"

The scribes and Pharisees seem to assume their religious rules for the Sabbath are more important than the need of the people worshiping on the Sabbath. That's the third step in becoming a religious Pharisee. **Their rules become more important than life itself.**

Our Lord's question adjusts their thinking and our thinking, doesn't it? Consider how Jesus thinks in verse 9. The question assumes (1) doing harm to anyone is not lawful; (2) destroying life is not lawful; and (3) it is always the right time to do good and save life. These simple statements seem obvious, don't they? But our religious rules and our biases can blind us to the obvious.

We might put it this way: To fail to do good or save life when you can is, in fact, to do harm and destroy life. There's no neutrality in the worship that Jesus teaches and models for us. We cannot pretend to worship Jesus if we refuse to help those in need

So, as Christians who follow the Lord, we cannot be silent about the plight of the unborn because we are on the way to worship—as if there exists a way to worship that calls a time out on saving life. As Christians we cannot avoid developing a Christian view of Black Lives Matter because black lives do matter. We cannot excuse ourselves from thinking this through because "it's time to preach the gospel"—as if the gospel has nothing to say about doing good and saving life. We cannot pit eternality against temporality. Sometimes you have to save a physical life in order to have an opportunity to save a soul.

We don't have to sign off on everything that comes under the banner of Black Lives Matter any more than we have to sign off on everything that comes under the banner of the pro-life movement. We do not endorse the shooting of abortion clinic doctors. We intend to save lives not take them. We do not endorse riots in the cause of protecting black lives. We are interested in the saving of life as a Christian obligation and responsibility as we follow our Lord and proclaim his gospel. There is no contradiction in these things.

The religious Pharisee in us would tempt us to think we cannot *both* proclaim the message of eternal life *and* defend the sanctity of all human life. We can do both things in the course of a sermon. So we must strive to do both things in the course of our daily lives.

Our worship must propel us to do good and to save lives. And it is always the right time to do what is right. That's our Savior's example here.

## Conclusion

Becoming Pharisees is easy. All we need to do is

- require everyone to follow our personal religious example and judge them when they fail;

- make our religious rules more important than Jesus himself; and
- make our religious rules more important than the well-being of others around us.

We might be surprised at how easily our hearts slide in this direction. But worship that pleases the Lord has a different character. God-pleasing worship

- emphasizes our joy not merely our duty;
- frees us to serve the Son rather than to attempt our own righteousness by the law; and
- frees us to do good and save life in the midst of worship as an act of worship.

Christ Jesus has come to save sinners so that we might truly worship. He is the Lord of worship and tells us what pleases him.

## Reflect and Discuss

1. Consider the Pharisees and scribes. The Pharisees emphasize rule keeping, and the scribes often denied fundamental truths of the faith. Which tendency do you most often notice in your life? In the church?
2. What do you think is the relationship between happiness and holiness? Can you think of any biblical passages to support your view?
3. Have you ever thought about the distinction between necessary and possible applications of the Bible? How does maintaining that distinction promote freedom in the Christian life?
4. How commonly do you think Christians hold others to their personal rules instead of to the necessary application of Scripture?
5. What would you say is the difference between obeying God's Word and creating religious rules that we try to hold others to? Do you think it's ever appropriate to treat our religious rules as more important than people? Why or why not?
6. Our Lord takes the opportunity to heal a person in the middle of religious worship. What does that teach us about true worship?
7. What good things do you feel the Lord calling you to do in the church and the community?

# A Great Moral Teacher?

## LUKE 6:12-49

**Main Idea:** Jesus *is* the good moral teacher, yet that means more than we can imagine or think!

---

I.   **Wealth without Jesus Is Doomed while Poverty with Jesus Is Blessed (6:20-26).**
   A.   Poverty with Jesus is blessed (6:20-23).
   B.   Wealth without Jesus is doomed (6:24-26).
   C.   The way Jesus thinks about value
II.  **Loving Our Enemies Is Rewarded while Loving Only Our Friends Is Worthless (6:27-36).**
   A.   Whom we are to love
   B.   How far we are to love our enemies
   C.   Why love this way?
III. **You *Can* Judge a Person's Heart, if You First Judge Your Own (6:37-45).**
   A.   Be generous to others (6:37-38).
   B.   Be careful whom you follow (6:39-40).
   C.   Deal with your own stuff (6:41-42).
   D.   Judge a person's heart (6:43-45).
IV.  **There's Only One Correct Way to Serve God and Live Safely; All Other Ways Lead to Ruin (6:46-49).**

---

Jesus was a great moral teacher." Many people believe that about Jesus, even if they do not believe he was God or the Son of God. Have you ever noticed that people who claim Jesus was a great moral teacher almost never go on to talk about his moral teaching? The phrase has a way of simultaneously communicating appreciation for Jesus while lowering the Christian estimation of Jesus. In fact, many will say, "Jesus was a great moral teacher" as a way of *denying* that he is the Son of God.

Christians traditionally respond to this claim by reasserting Jesus's deity. The famous Oxford professor C. S. Lewis argued that Jesus is either a liar, a lunatic, or Lord, but he cannot simply be a good moral teacher. Lewis took this position *because* of what Jesus teaches. Any man who claims to be the Savior of the world but knows he is not is, in fact, not a good teacher but a liar. Further, he tells a demonic lie that deceives people and leads them to hell. If any man says he is the Savior of the world and really believes it, yet is not the Savior, that man may be sincere, but he is crazy. He is a lunatic, to use Lewis's choice of terms. But if Jesus was telling the truth about himself and how we are saved, then he is Lord. C. S. Lewis argued that these are the only three options.

If Jesus was telling the truth, then his good moral teaching cannot simply be acknowledged like a "hat tip" on social media. His teaching actually has to be studied, accepted, and applied. Think about it: What good moral teacher should have their good moral teaching ignored? Shouldn't good moral teaching be embraced and followed by everyone—especially all those who think of themselves as good moral people?

Today's good moral people tend to believe four things.
1.  Poverty is a sin to be avoided, and riches are the goal of life.
2.  Love is the greatest virtue, and it justifies all our desires.
3.  You cannot judge someone else—ever. Period.
4.  There are many ways to serve God, and all of them are equally valid.

That is an interesting list of moral claims because nearly everyone takes these things to be basically true. Nearly everyone who tells you that Jesus was only "a good moral teacher" has failed to actually consider their moral claims in light of Jesus's good moral teaching. There's a reason for that.

When we consider the good moral teaching of Jesus, we find ourselves face-to-face with a way of being good unlike anything in this world. We find ourselves face-to-face with goodness itself. When we come face-to-face with morality as God defines it, we actually come face-to-face with our need for someone to rescue us from the demands of goodness. The British writer G. K. Chesterton once wrote, "The Christian ideal has not been tried and found wanting; it's been found difficult and left untried" (*What's Wrong*, 25–26).

Luke 6:12-49 features four teachings from Jesus that challenge our notions of goodness. In fact, these four teachings defy the commonly accepted virtues of our culture.

## Wealth without Jesus Is Doomed while Poverty with Jesus Is Blessed
### LUKE 6:20-26

Luke 6:12-19 sets the scene. In verses 12-16 the Lord holds an all-night prayer vigil. He prays in order to identify who among his disciples should be his apostles. An apostle is someone sent with a message. The twelve men listed in verses 14-16 would be the chief messengers of our Lord, and eleven of them would be the leaders of the early church. We will learn more about them as we study Luke's Gospel.

Verse 17 tells us that Jesus came down with his apostles to a meeting of "a large crowd of his disciples and a great number of people" from all over the region. They "came to hear him and to be healed of their diseases" (v. 18). Jesus did indeed heal people with unclean spirits, and "power was coming out from him and healing them all" (v. 19). What Luke wants the reader to understand is not the miracle of healing—he only gives us one sentence on that—but Jesus's *teaching*, which covers the rest of the chapter. Luke draws our attention to how Jesus's mind works regarding morality.

### Poverty with Jesus Is Blessed (6:20-23)

In verse 20 Jesus speaks to his disciples. *Disciple* means "student or follower." The Lord wants them to understand what life is like for those who follow him.

The word *blessed*, repeated four times in verses 20, 21, and 22, could be translated "happy." The Lord describes the happy or joyful life from a kingdom perspective. Notice whom he describes as happy: the poor (v. 20), those who are hungry now (v. 21), those who weep now (v. 21), and those who are hated, excluded, insulted, and slandered (v. 22). The poor, the hungry, the weeping, and the hated. When we follow Jesus and find ourselves in those conditions *because we follow him*, then we are "blessed" or "happy" from God's perspective.

Why? Verse 20 concludes, "The kingdom of God is yours." We may be **poor** and with no earthly kingdom, but the heavenly kingdom filled with glory belongs to those who follow Jesus. The kingdoms of this earth pass away, but the kingdom of God remains forever.

Not only that, but our **hunger now** will be traded for complete satisfaction. Our **weeping now** will be traded for laughter. When Matthew records his version of these beatitudes, he emphasizes them in a spiritual way. Matthew writes of the "poor *in spirit*" (5:3) and those who "hunger and thirst *for righteousness*" (v. 6; emphasis added). But Luke leaves us with a more literal meaning. Luke gives us a sense of the temporariness of hunger and weeping. They happen "now." Such temporal poverty, hunger, and thirst will barely be a memory in the kingdom of God. All of our longing, hunger, and poverty will be satiated with laughter and joy in the presence of God.

And when people **hate**, exclude, insult, and slander the disciple "because of the Son of Man" (v. 22), then our rejoicing reaches its highest level. When we suffer for our Savior's name, we receive a prophet's treatment and a *great* reward (v. 23). Jesus does not use adjectives superfluously. How does the Lord of heaven define "great"? How much reward will eternity provide in exchange for earth's sorrow? It is not what the world teaches us to expect, but these are the truly happy disciples.

### Wealth without Jesus Is Doomed (6:24-26)

Notice now the contrast. The Lord pronounces four "woes." In the Bible, when a prophet warned people of condemnation, he would often begin with the word "woe." Woe refers to unrelenting sorrow, pain, and agony, the kind that cannot be relieved. Woe crushes a person. And when prophets pronounce a "woe" against people, the woe comes at the hand of God's condemnation.

"Woe" comes to the rich (v. 24), the full now (v. 25), those laughing now (v. 25), and those who are popular in the world (v. 26). These persons appear to enjoy all the world has to offer, but there is no mention of the Lord in their life. In verse 22 Jesus says some disciples suffer in this world "because of the Son of Man." The rich, full, laughing, and popular do not suffer in this world, and there is no mention of the Son of Man. They live it up without Jesus. They receive a warm welcome from all those who enjoy false prophets (v. 26).

But they are doomed. The **rich** "have received" (v. 24) (past tense) their comfort. Their comfort was their money. When their lives end and their money is gone, there will be no comfort for them. They will outlive their money, and their money will outlive its usefulness. All that will be left apart from Jesus is woe.

The **now full** live high off the hog. They satisfy their desires now. They have refrigerators full and money to eat out. Now. But when judgment comes, they will be hungry. Hell for them will be a constant hungering, never being satisfied, a gnawing in their guts. Their worm will never die. They had it all in this life, and they will have nothing in the life to come because they did not have Christ.

Those who are **now laughing** will not laugh last. They "will mourn and weep" (v. 25). In fact, many places in the Bible describe judgment and hell as "weeping and gnashing of teeth." In the end they will be sorry they spent their lives laughing—laughing in worldly pleasures apart from Jesus.

The **popular**—those who knew what it meant to have "all people speak well of you"—will suffer woe too. Many people in Israel's history loved false teachers. They showered the false teachers with praise and rewards, but in the end the people and the false prophet perished in God's judgment. The people loved inviting preachers and teachers who would tell them all their itching ears wanted to hear. The true prophets they rejected, but the false prophets they loved. Beware platforms and popularity. Popularity is sometimes evidence of God's condemnation and a disciple's unfaithfulness rather than God's approval or favor.

A wealthy, well-liked person without Jesus is the most doomed person you will meet for as long as they are without Jesus. Everything about their life may look wonderful, but the Great Moral Teacher says, "They have no reward. Their future is full of woe."

The blessed or happy life is exactly the opposite of what most people think. There is greater, longer-lasting happiness with Jesus plus nothing than with everything minus Jesus. The happiness of "everything minus Jesus" is temporary. The joy of "Jesus plus nothing" is eternal.

The Great Moral Teacher *curses* what the world thinks is *good* and *blesses* what the world thinks is *bad*. Who do you think has it correct: the world or Jesus?

### The Way Jesus Thinks about Value

Jesus seems to envision a trade-off. On the one hand, you can choose him and the hardships of life that sometimes come with him and receive ultimate reward in glory. Or you can choose life without him and the pursuit of an earthly life of pleasure, only ultimately to suffer woe. The Lord teaches us in spiritual terms about delayed gratification and instant gratification. Instant gratification often ends in condemnation. As you give yourself to carnal desire, though you think you're having fun, you actually run straight for the guillotine of God's judgment. But when we avoid carnal desire by denying ourselves and carrying our cross, we then run toward genuine bliss in God's sight.

This is how Jesus thinks about value. He does not value what people value. He values himself above all things and blesses those who do the same. The Lord teaches this repeatedly. For example, the Lord asks questions like, "For what does it benefit someone if he gains the whole world, and yet loses or forfeits himself?" (9:25). Your one soul possesses infinitely more value than everything in the world *combined*. The value of the soul is kept when the soul is given to Christ.

Or the Lord says things like, "Watch out and be on guard against all greed, because one's life is not in the abundance of his possessions" (12:15). Abundant possessions do not determine the quality of our lives. Abundant life comes not from things but from Christ.

Or consider this challenging word from the Lord: "For it is easier for a camel to go through the eye of a needle than for a rich person to enter the kingdom of God" (18:25). The way the world values money and things is ultimately soul destroying. Jesus repeatedly teaches us the danger of riches. Luke 6 presents an exchange: Follow Jesus and suffer now, only to be greatly rewarded later. Or do not follow Jesus and seek pleasure now, only to suffer the "woe" of God's condemnation forever.

## Loving Our Enemies Is Rewarded while Loving Only Our Friends Is Worthless
### LUKE 6:27-36

Our world loves to talk about love. *Love* is a cheap word nowadays. Because love is so little understood, it is almost impossible to find. But "love" remains the justification for just about anything people wish to do. So people tell us that any two people who "love each other" should be able to marry—even if the two people are of the same sex. Their professed "love" for each other provides moral justification for their acts. "Love," we are told, "conquers all," and "love wins."

But here comes the Great Moral Teacher. And if Jesus taught anything, he taught us the truth about love. He showed us in his teaching and in his death on the cross the nature and scope of divine love. And the Lord calls his disciples to live out that love in two surprising ways.

### Whom We Are to Love

The first surprise concerns *whom* we are to love. Verse 27: "But I say to you who listen: Love your enemies."

Hatred for your enemies feels like the most natural thing in the world. It almost seems as if enemies were made for our hatred. They harm us, and we *at least* harden our hearts toward them. *At most*, we do them worse than they do us. We tell ourselves and others, "Retaliation is only right." An eye for an eye, a tooth for a tooth, we say. Is that not the way the world works? Is that not a morally acceptable way of thinking in our day? But heaven's morality differs radically. Our Lord says, "Love your *enemies.* "

Then he goes a step further. The Lord points out in verses 32-34 that our love for people like us is in one sense worthless in God's sight. Love for people like us does nothing to distinguish us from people who do not know God. There exists a kind of love completely natural to a fallen world. "Even sinners" (v. 32) love their friends and families, and they lend money to people they like. If we love those who love us, do good to those who do good to us, lend to those who can repay, then we really act out of self-interest rather than love. Jesus says, "Even sinners do that." In other words, people who do not know God and do not live for God demonstrate this kind of love all the time. There is nothing supernatural about it.

If we find that our love is limited to people like us—say, our skin color, our education level, our political party—and if we find ourselves doing good only for those who have done us some favor, then that may only be self-love spread over a slightly wider area. However, the love of God is not self-interested but selfless. It is sacrificial. Genuinely supernatural, Godlike love includes our enemies who wrong and abuse us. This is how Christian love surpasses the sinner's love. Christian love extends to enemies.

## How Far We Are to Love Our Enemies

That brings us to the second surprising thing Jesus teaches about love. Notice how far love goes.

> *"But I say to you who listen: Love your enemies, do what is good to those who hate you,* bless *those who curse you, pray for those who mistreat you. If anyone hits you on the cheek,* offer the other also. *And if anyone takes away your coat,* don't hold back your shirt either. *Give to everyone who asks you, and from someone who takes your things,* don't ask for them back." (Luke 6:27-30; emphasis added)

Love makes demands. Love cannot be shown with words only. We must love in word *and* in deed. Divine love returns good for evil. People hate us; we do them good. People curse us; we bless them. People abuse us; we pray for them.

Divine love calls us to lay down our lives for more abuse if necessary. They strike us on the cheek; we offer the other cheek also. They take away our coats; we give them the shirts off our backs too. They beg from us; we give to everyone who asks without requiring payback. When we walk down streets populated with beggars, we should reach the end of the street penniless. When we love our enemies, we give ourselves up for them.

The world's morality says, "Love your friends and hate your enemies." The Great Moral Teacher says, "Love your enemies and give them even more."

### Why Love This Way?

Why love this way? What's the rationale?

*First, we should love this way because it's how we would want to be treated.* "Just as you want others to do for you, do the same for them" (v. 31). Love puts us in the place of the mistreated, the oppressed, and the marginalized. It calls us to imagine that state for ourselves and then behave accordingly.

*Second, we should love this way to earn a great reward and prove we are God's children.* Jesus teaches this in verses 35-36. As Christians, we want the world to know that we serve the Most High God. We want the world to know we know him. The main way God intends the world to know this is by our love for one another (John 13:34-35) and our love for all others—including our enemies. When we love this way, we live out the family resemblance. When we act like our Father, it pleases him and he rewards us.

Loving our enemies seems utterly unnatural and impossible until we consider examples of it. Every January we celebrate the birth of Dr. Martin Luther King Jr. No social movement of recent history has embodied this sacrificial, redemptive view of love like the nonviolent protests of the Civil Rights Movement. People sometimes forget the Civil Rights Movement was a religious movement, a Christian movement. It was built on this call to love. Ordinary men and women willingly suffered at the hands of their enemies—at lunch counters, in jail cells, from dogs and water hoses, lynchings and beatings—all without retaliating, all returning love for brutality. Whatever else we may think of Dr. King, he surely understood and practiced love in a way that looks a lot like Jesus's teaching here. Dr. King and the ordinary persons who marched with him put most of us to shame when it comes to loving as Jesus commanded. We see the effect today. We could not imagine how different U.S. society would be right now if so many had not embraced the radical call to love. This kind of love transforms society. It changes the hearts of both the oppressed and the oppressor, the victim and the victimizer.

There remains an example of sacrificial love greater—much greater—than Dr. King's. That is the example of Jesus Christ himself. For whom did Jesus die? For whom did he suffer? The Lord was crucified at the hands of his enemies. The people who put him to death were the people he came to save. They mocked and abused him. Jesus prayed, "Father, forgive them, because they do not know not what they are doing" (23:34). They whipped and beat him. Jesus never said a mumbling word but gave his body to be broken for them and for us. They took his tunic and his robe, stripped him naked. He willingly allowed it. He did not demand his rights, repayment, or even an apology. The Son of God gave his life for sinners so that even though we were enemies of God, we might be made sons of God through faith in him.

When we were his enemies, Christ loved us. By so loving us, the Lord enables us to love him and love our enemies. We love God because he first loved us (1 John 4:19). Never underestimate the redemptive power of love.

The application for "love your enemies and do good to them" is pretty simple: Love your enemies and do good to them. Bless them. Pray for them. Endure their mistreatment. Give to your enemies and expect nothing back. So make a mental or an actual list of people you think of as enemies. Then do these things.

My friend, perhaps you are not a Christian. Reading this book, can you honestly say you love your enemies? Or do you show love mainly to those who treat you well and share your interests or background? It is good that you love those people, but can you see that Jesus defines that as a *sinner's* love? Such love will not make you right with God. It will not earn you forgiveness or cover over your sins. For forgiveness and atonement, you need a Savior. When we take Jesus's moral teaching seriously, it leads us to understand our need of rescue. We see the rightness of what he taught, and we see the wrongness of our hearts. If we are honest, we know we need someone to save us from our sinful selves. Only Jesus does that.

## You *Can* Judge a Person's Heart if You First Judge Your Own
### LUKE 6:37-45

Our culture insists we must not judge others. We are told that judging others is immoral. We are told that we cannot judge others because we do not know what is in another's heart. That has a certain appeal to it, doesn't it?

That's not how Jesus thinks about judgment. The Lord lays down four principles for righteous judgment.

### Be Generous to Others (6:37-38)

The first principle for righteous judgment is to be generous to others in our judgments. When it comes to our judgment and perception of others, what goes around, comes around. If we avoid judging and condemning, others will not generally judge and condemn us. If we forgive and give, others will generally forgive and give to us. In fact, our generosity toward others will generally produce an overflowing generosity toward us. That is the point of verse 38—which in context has nothing to do with how much you put in the offering on Sunday morning; it has to do with how we regard and treat other people. If we would be moral in our judgments, then we must be generous toward others. The first step in righteous judgment is acquiring the right posture of heart: generous, charitable judgment.

### Be Careful Whom You Follow (6:39-40)

The second principle for sound judgment is to be careful whom you follow. People become like their teachers. Whether in religious, business, or social settings, the people we look to as teachers will by their teaching and example press the pattern of their lives onto ours. Follow Jesus, and you become more like Jesus. If your leader is blind, then you will follow him into whatever pit or hole he walks into. If your leader sees with moral clarity, then you will follow him into righteousness and truth.

If we follow people who are hypercritical and condemning, sooner or later their manner becomes a part of our language and manner. If we follow someone who always builds others up, who shows kindness and humility, then we will likewise learn to be compassionate, patient, and tender.

### Deal with Your Own Stuff (6:41-42)

The third principle of sound judgment is to deal with your own stuff. We cannot deal with our neighbor's "splinter" while we have a "beam" in our own eye. That is hypocrisy. In verse 42 the Lord says, "First take the beam of wood out of your eye, and then you will see clearly to take out the splinter in your brother's eye." He does not say take the beam out of your eye and then do not worry about your brother. Morality requires we help each other with our failings. It is immoral to see a brother or sister in sin and not help (Gal 6:1-2). Yet it is hypocritical not to attend to our sins first. We cannot see to help others until we have helped ourselves.

If you have ever taken a flight on an airplane, you have heard an illustration of this point. Before takeoff, the attendant reviews the safety instructions, including instructions for putting on oxygen masks in case of an emergency. The attendant tells the passengers they must put on their own mask before helping those around them. So it is with our sin and the sins of others.

### Judge a Person's Heart (6:43-45)

After we have followed those three principles, then we are enabled by God's grace and Spirit to judge a person's heart morally and cor- rectly. Again our world tells us, "You cannot know someone's heart." The culture proclaims that "judging someone's heart" is about the most immoral thing we can attempt. Everyone says the heart is a secret place, closed off to the world, and no one must tell you what lies in your heart.

Consider what the Great Moral Teacher says. All of us are like fruit trees. We produce either good fruit or bad fruit. The fruit we produce actually comes from our hearts. The invisible things of the heart are revealed by the visible actions and audible words of a person. We do not see into another person's heart, but that does not mean the heart never reveals itself. The words and actions tell us what lies beyond natural sight in the heart.

In the end this means we cannot participate with people in our culture who love separating their actions from their hearts. Some people love justifying their wrong actions by appealing to "a good heart." Jesus, the Great Moral Teacher, rejects that tendency. If the habit of a person's life is sin, then that person is a sinner. If the habit of a person's life is righteousness, then that person is righteous. The fruit reveals the root.

We will not discern or judge the hearts of others with any kind of clarity or accuracy unless we are first generous in our posture toward them, are following sound teaching ourselves, and are eager to deal with our own stuff first. Until those things are true of us, we should not worry too much about others. Instead, we should fall to our knees before God asking for this kind of integrity and humility. A generous posture keeps us from being mean and stingy in our judgments. Following sound teaching helps us know what is and is not moral. Dealing with our own sin creates compassion and integrity.

That kind of person dispenses righteous judgment. We should ask God in prayer for this kind of people to serve as judges and lawyers in our court systems, officers on our police forces, and anyone with responsibility for deciding the outcome of people's lives. Such people are gifts to us—whether they are government officials or personal friends. They embody the moral vision of the kingdom of God. They promote that vision by speaking the truth to us in love. We want and need people like this in our lives. Moreover, we want to *be* these kinds of people through Christ.

So consider your friends. Are they the kind of people who can evaluate your heart because they are generous toward others, are careful about whom they follow, and first deal with their own sins? What about you and me? Can we accept their judgments when they give them to us? Or are we too proud? Are we the kind of people described in verses 37-45?

## There's Only One Correct Way to Serve God and Live Safely; All Other Ways Lead to Ruin
### LUKE 6:46-49

The Lord ends his sermon with a final challenge in verse 46: "Why do you call me 'Lord, Lord,' and don't do the things I say?" The Lord Jesus speaks this to his new apostles and his disciples. He also speaks this to us.

If we are disciples or students or followers of Jesus, then we must obey him. It is hypocritical to call ourselves Christians and not do what

Christ says. Worse than that: our disobedience proves we do not, in fact, love him. So Jesus says,

> *"If you love me, you will keep my commands."* (John 14:15)
> *"The one who has my commands and keeps them is the one who loves me."* (John 14:21)
> *"The one who doesn't love me will not keep my words."* (John 14:24)
> *"If you keep my commands you will remain in my love, just as I have kept my Father's commands and remain in his love."* (John 15:10)
> *"You are my friends if you do what I command you."* (John 15:14)

Obedience to Jesus's teaching is an essential requirement of Christian discipleship. Our obedience does not earn God's forgiveness or acceptance. No one will obey their way to heaven. God saves sinners by grace alone through faith alone. But saving faith is never alone; it is accompanied by an obedience that comes from faith (Rom 1:5). Forgiveness and acceptance come only by God's grace through faith in Jesus Christ. But if our faith is true, then our obedience must be real. He is our Lord, so he commands our lives. In our obedience we demonstrate our love for him, we prove ourselves to be friends with him, and his love and the Father's love rest on us.

To call him "Lord" and not do what he says is to make the word *Lord* meaningless. Years ago I heard a preacher illustrate this point by asking people to write two words on a note card. The two words were *No* and *Lord*. The preacher told us those two words could not stand side by side. We would have to cross one of the words out. He said, "If there is any area of your life where you say no to Jesus, then you must cross out the word *Lord*. But if you call him 'Lord' of your life, then you must forever cross out the word *no*." The only way to serve Jesus as Lord acceptably is to submit to his word in every area of life.

Obedience becomes a foundation for times of trial and storm. In the parable of verses 47-49, the obedient man lays a foundation on the rock, and though his house is battered by the rains, it stands to the end. The disobedient man builds his house on the sand. The storms of life destroy that house because he failed to build on the word of God. He did not obey the word of God, and so "the destruction of that house was great" (v. 49).

Ultimately, Jesus describes the difference between heaven and hell. Heaven belongs to those who believe the gospel and obey Jesus. Hell is the ruin that awaits those who reject the gospel and do not obey the Lord's words.

Is that moral? Our culture says you cannot force your morality on another. The world says it is bigoted and intolerant to require others to live by your standards.

But here is Jesus, the Great Moral Teacher, demanding that the entire world call him Lord and obey his commands. He forces his morality onto the world, threatens ruin to those who disobey, and promises safety to those who believe.

## Conclusion

In the end there are only two ways to live. We either obey the Lord and stand strong in his word, or we disobey the Lord and fall in ruin on judgment day. Obedience and blessing on the one hand; disobedience and ruin on the other. It all rides on whether you believe in and obey the Great Moral Teacher. You have to decide if Jesus is a liar, a lunatic, or your Lord. If he is telling the truth—and he is—then the only sane thing to do is accept him as Lord and follow his teachings all the days of your life.

## Reflect and Discuss

1. Think for a moment about our culture. What would you say are three or four cherished moral ideas in the culture? How do those ideas compare with the morality of Jesus?

2. Would you rather have wealth without Jesus or poverty with Jesus? Why?

3. The Lord Jesus calls his followers to love their enemies. How easy or difficult do you think it is to obey that command?

4. Can you think of a time when you were in conflict with someone and were enabled to love them, and it transformed your relationship?

5. What does Jesus think is more valuable: your soul or all the wealth of the world? Think about that for a moment. What are some ways you can practically show that your soul is worth more than everything in the world?

6. Is it a sin to judge the actions and motives of others? Why or why not?

7. In what ways does sinful judgment differ from righteous judgment?

# Friend of the "Nones"

## LUKE 7

**Main Idea:** Jesus is the best friend the "Nones" could ever have.

I.   Jesus Is a Lord Amazed by Faith (7:1-10).
II.  Jesus Is a Prophet Moved by Grief (7:11-17).
III. Jesus Is a Messiah Who Answers Our Doubt (7:18-23).
IV.  Jesus Is a King Who Exalts the Lowly (7:24-35).
V.   Jesus Is a Savior Who Forgives the Biggest Sinners (7:36-50).

Sociologists and scholars of religion are writing a lot these days about the rise of the "Nones." No, not the Roman Catholic ladies wearing their habits and rosary beads. These "Nones" are people who check the box "none" or "not religious" when asked about their religious life. They have no religious preference and are not active religiously.

The number of Nones are on the rise in America (Lipka, "Closer Look"; see also Smith and Cooperman, "Factors"). Scholars tell us that Nones now make up about 23 percent of adults in the United States— about one in four people you meet, or thirty-six million Americans. That is a sharp increase from 16 percent in 2007. Nones appear to be growing faster than other groups, especially among millennials, who make up 36 percent of all Nones. For every person who goes from not being religious to becoming a Christian, there are four people who say they grew up in Christian homes but are not now religious.

Nones tend to be younger than most other people in the country— about thirty-six years old. Sixty-two percent say they seldom or never pray. Though 61 percent say they believe in some kind of higher power or supreme bring, about the same percentage say religion is not important to them at all. In that way they consider themselves spiritual but not religious.

But here's the thing: Nones are not atheists. Only about 3 percent of people are atheists. Rather, Nones say they respect Jesus. They like the stories about him. They view Jesus as a champion for the poor who embraced the outcasts of society. Many Nones have friendly thoughts about Jesus; they simply do not believe in him as Lord.

What does such friendliness toward Jesus mean? Does it count for anything? If you admire Jesus but you do not follow him as Lord, what kind of person does that make you? Apparently, it makes you like a lot of other people. Thirty-six million Americans feel and think this way about Jesus. Here's the irony: Nones may feel friendly toward Jesus, but Jesus may not yet actually be their friend.

Luke 7 covers five scenes in the Savior's life. In these scenes we see the Lord interacting with humanity in the most profound and the most ordinary circumstances. We begin with the Lord going to the sickbed of a slave owned by a Roman centurion (7:1-10). Next we see the Lord meeting a funeral procession with a grieving widow who has lost her only son (vv. 11-17). Then the Lord receives a question from an imprisoned John the Baptist struggling with doubt (vv. 18-23; see Matt 11:2). The fourth scene features a conversation between the Lord and the crowds traveling with him (vv. 24-35). Then the chapter ends with the Lord visiting a Pharisee's house, where a sinful woman washes his feet with her hair and her tears (vv. 36-50).

These five scenes give us five windows onto who Jesus is. With each scene we also see the people's response to Jesus. What we will see in it all is that Jesus is the best friend the Nones could ever hope to have. He's more than a friend—Jesus is everything we need. In the text many Nones recognize something of the kindness and friendliness of the Lord.

## Jesus Is a Lord Amazed by Faith
### LUKE 7:1-10

In the first scene we find the Lord Jesus in his ministry headquarters in Capernaum. He's just finished teaching the people when the elders of the local Jewish synagogue come to him. A Roman centurion had sent these elders to Jesus for help.

A Roman centurion would have been a commander of about a hundred men. The Roman army was notorious for its use of force. Roman soldiers could be brutal. But this centurion was different. This commander was a loving man.

- He loved his slave. Verse 2: "A centurion's servant, *who was highly valued by him,* was sick and about to die" (emphasis added). Roman soldiers did not ordinarily value slaves—much less *highly* value them. But this man felt a great deal for his servant.

- He loved his subjects. Verses 4-5: "He is worthy for you to grant this, because he loves our nation and has built us a synagogue." The leaders of Israel testified to his generosity and love for Israel.
- He loved submission. Verses 8: "For I too am a man placed under authority, having soldiers under my command. I say to this one, 'Go,' and he goes; and to another, 'Come,' and he comes; and to my servant, 'Do this,' and he does it." Here's a man who understood and respected authority. He was a man of authority, and he embraced submission.

There's only one thing he did not love. He did not love himself. He was humble. Even though he was a man of authority and position, he did not let that go to his head. He remained humble. He didn't even think he was worthy to appear before Jesus or have Jesus in his home (vv. 6-7). He had immense respect for Jesus.

The centurion recognized something about Jesus that others—including the disciples—had not yet fully grasped. According to verse 6, the centurion recognized Jesus is Lord. Now others called Jesus "Lord" too, and I don't think the centurion knew fully what calling Jesus "Lord" would come to mean. But using that title shows he knew two things: He knew he was personally not worthy before the Lord, and he knew the power of Jesus's word.

Somehow this man grasped and believed the fact that Jesus was Lord over life and that Jesus showed he was Lord by his word: "But say the word, and my servant will be healed" (v. 7). The Roman centurion—not the Jewish elders or even the disciples—understood that part of what it meant to call Jesus Lord was to admit the authority of Jesus's word over life. If Christ would but "say the word" (v. 7), then he could do anything he willed to heal his servant.

What we need is faith. That's what amazes Jesus about this centurion. Yes, the centurion is a wonderful guy, but what Jesus notices is his faith. Jesus "was amazed" (v. 9).

That's a stunning statement on at least two levels. First, Jesus recognizes that the quality of this man's faith is extraordinary.

Second, Jesus recognizes that this man's faith surpasses the faith of all God's chosen people. This is all the more amazing when you read what Jesus asks about his followers in Luke 18:8: "When the Son of Man comes, will he find faith on earth?"

Faith is a wonderfully miraculous thing. The ability to believe ought not be taken for granted. It's amazing that anyone believes. And it's even more amazing that there are unbelievers with greater faith in Jesus than some believers. There are unbelievers who more firmly believe that Jesus is Lord of all than some believers who profess the same.

This first scene helps us get to know Jesus. While the Lord doesn't say much in the passage, we still learn a lot about him. First, that simple sentence in verse 6, "Jesus went with them," shows us the Lord is caring. Jesus doesn't know the centurion. He doesn't know the slave who's sick and dying. The elders of the synagogue are not his followers. Yet Jesus went with them to see about this sick and dying man. The Lord cares. He is sensitive to our needs.

Second, verse 10 teaches us that the Lord heals. Here's a God who uses his authority over life to give life. Really this miracle is a kind of brief commercial for what Jesus will do in the end: eradicate all disease, all sickness, and all pain. That's how he uses his authority—for our healing and blessing. With all of our Lord's authority, he is not too busy to visit the home of a sick slave. The Lord Jesus will not crush us. Instead, he uses his authority to heal. In the coming kingdom the Lord will make all things new and restore all that is broken.

Many of the so-called Nones have difficulty with the idea that there's a Supreme Being or God who has this kind of authority. Some Nones think this authority is dangerous and oppressive. They're troubled by the religious authority of institutions like the church. They are troubled by the idea that God should have authority over their lives. I get it. Men often abuse authority.

My friend, if you have never met Jesus, let me introduce you to him. He is the Lord of all power who compassionately heals the hurting. He is worthy of your trust and faith. The Roman centurion understood that. Do you?

Let me say a word to my fellow Christians for a moment. We have to stop looking for ways to prove that every Christian is a better person than every nonbeliever. We have this habit of seeing good things in the lives of people who do not profess to be Christians, and rather than commend them for it, we look to explain it away. We want to talk about why it doesn't "count" since they're not Christians.

That's not what Jesus does here. The Lord recognizes what's amazing in this man's imperfect faith. It's not saving faith. He is not professing repentance and faith, as we will understand by the end of the Gospel of Luke. But it is genuine trust that Jesus can heal his servant with a word. Many Christians do not trust Jesus in the same way.

Instead of trying to point out the failings in the Nones, we should invite them to an even deeper trust of Jesus as their personal Lord. People skeptical of God's authority need to know that his Son uses his authority to express his care. They should come to know that the Lord both cares and has power to show it. That kind of faith in Jesus amazes him.

## Jesus Is a Prophet Moved by Grief
### LUKE 7:11-17

The second thing we learn about our Lord is that Jesus is moved by grief. Verse 11 says that after the Lord heals the sick servant, he travels to a town called Nain. It's a small town not often mentioned in the Bible. Verse 12 gives us the scene.

All the details in this sentence matter. The funeral already approaches "the gate of the town." That means they're on their way to the tomb. Since it would have been unclean to leave a dead body in the city, it's likely this funeral is happening the day of the son's death. If that's correct, then they're in the height of a fresh grief.

The man is "his mother's only son." You can imagine the grief of burying your only child. No parent should have to outlive their children. And "she was a widow." She has already buried her husband. Perhaps the son's tone of voice, physical appearance, and gestures were reminders of her dearly departed spouse. So now all that existed of that former life heads to the grave. And, with no husband and no son, she had no way of providing for herself in that culture and time. She'll soon be alone. Perhaps that's why "a large crowd from the city was also with her." It's like the entire community knew what grief and difficulty lay ahead.

Verse 13 shows us what Jesus is like. The woman's grief moved the Lord. Her suffering touched him. He saw her and felt for her. He was not so smitten with popularity and adulation that he didn't have time to mourn with a widow.

Unlike the scene with the centurion, we're not told anything about this woman's faith. She doesn't request help. The woman doesn't even seem to notice him until the Lord says, "Don't weep." Now those words would be cruel and insensitive if they came from us in the middle of a funeral. "Don't cry" isn't really comfort if you can't change the situation.

Death is a situation ordinary human beings can't change. Death seems so final when it comes to our puny power.

But Jesus is not a normal human being. He is God. You can feel the eyes staring intently at the Lord as he approached and touched the casket (v. 14). Perhaps they were caught off guard or even offended that he would interrupt the funeral service. You can hear the questions exploding in heads when he says, "Get up!" But Jesus raised the dead! He spoke to a corpse, and a living man sat up! He spoke to a body wrapped in the prison of death's silence, and a son began to speak! He gave a crying mother the only thing that could fix her grief—her son back. That's how you stop a funeral!

We don't have to wonder about the people's reaction. The people are seized with fear (v. 16). You would be too. I wonder if they dropped the stretcher? I would've dropped it and run! This man was dead—prepared for the grave, on his way there, his mother and the whole town crying—and he sat up and started talking!

Jesus is not merely Lord over the living. He is also Lord over the dead! He has authority to reverse the power of death and to give life again. Raising this man from the dead is another commercial of what Jesus will do in the end. He himself would be raised from the dead for our justification, and in the end he will raise all men—the righteous to heaven and the wicked to hell.

The people declare that Jesus is a prophet. He is that, but he's so much more! They declare that "God has visited his people"—by which they mean a miracle has been done. But their words were truer than they knew. God was with them. True God from true God had just come to their town. Though they're amazed at the miracle, they're unaware of the Savior.

It is no honor to Jesus to ascribe to him some great title but treat him as something less than he really is. My Muslim friends make this mistake all the time. They say, "We honor Jesus as a great prophet who did great miracles." But they deny that Jesus is the Son of God. With that denial they actually dishonor the Lord. And there are many who say, "Jesus is a great moral teacher." That's true—yet that's not all that he is. In omitting the remainder of things that are true of Jesus, they actually miss him. Jesus did not come to be comfortably confined to our boxes. He has come to shatter this world with his glory, to make himself known in the fullness of his person. He is the one who entered space and time and with that entrance forever changed space and time itself. With his coming came also the kingdom of God, where life never ends and where God restores everything broken in the world.

An awakening of faith is happening in this section of Luke, but it's not quite saving faith. The people stop short and miss the whole picture. This is often the case with the Nones. They will acknowledge Jesus's compassion, for example, but they will not recognize him as God. But who else can raise the dead? And who else would do it—not as a magic trick, but as an act of compassion for a crying widow? Only God would be so tender and walk away without a further word. If it is a joy to awaken to a prophet, how much more wonderful will it be to awaken to the Son of God who defeats death for us?

## Jesus Is a Messiah Who Answers Our Doubt
### LUKE 7:18-23

The disciples of John the Baptist tell John about the things Jesus is doing. Matthew 11:2 tells us that John is in prison when he hears this report, and perhaps the despair of imprisonment begins to unsettle John. So in Luke 7:19 John sends two of his disciples to Jesus with a question. John wants to know if Jesus is truly the Messiah Israel has been awaiting.

John was dedicated to God from the womb. John had received prophetic visions from God. John preached the coming of the kingdom of God and prepared Israel to receive their Lord. He paved the way for Jesus; he even baptized Jesus. John spent his entire life looking for this moment and the Messiah. John was a great servant of God. John had a strong spiritual resume.

Yet John had a period of intense doubt while in prison. Faith and doubt can find room in the same heart. You can be a wonderful servant of God yet still have moments and seasons of intense doubt. If you struggle with doubt, know that you're not alone and you're not necessarily broken or wrong. Sometimes we treat doubt as though it's some really nasty evidence that someone does not truly trust Christ or is not a Christian. That's not necessarily so. We Christians may have to pray, "Lord, I believe; help my unbelief."

John's disciples deliver the question in verse 20. Jesus seems to perform the many miracles in verse 21 in order to send back concrete evidence for John's doubt in verse 22. He says, "Go and report to John *what you have seen and heard*" (emphasis added). These miracles signify that Jesus is the Messiah and that the kingdom of God is coming into the world. Jesus doesn't rebuke John for his doubt. He assures John with evidence. The Lord is tender and gentle with the weak and the doubting. Matthew 12:20 says, "He will not break a bruised reed, and he will not put out a smoldering wick."

Then the Lord adds this word of encouragement in Luke 7:23: "And blessed is the one who isn't offended by me." Or, as the New Living Translation puts it, "God blesses those who do not fall away because of me." In other words, "John, keep believing. In the end you will be blessed, made happy, by God. Don't fall away. Hold on to faith in me."

Jesus blesses those who continue to believe in him even if they experience some doubt along the way. What a tender and compassionate Lord! Do you have doubts? You can safely bring them to Jesus. Do you have questions? You can raise them in the Scriptures. I really dislike that strain of "Christian" teaching that demands we never doubt or question God. The Lord is the kind of Messiah that doesn't simply *talk* about being the Messiah; Jesus will *prove* it to you by raising the dead, giving sight to the blind, preaching the gospel to the poor, and giving evidence on which to base our faith.

Did you know that the majority of the thirty-six million Nones in the U.S. come from nominally Christian backgrounds? Only 9 percent of U.S. adults say they were raised without any kind of religious teaching. Most of the Nones are people like John, who began to doubt. The difference is, they didn't follow or have evidence for their faith, so they stopped following and began to say they had no religion. Based on Luke 7:23, Jesus would say they've chosen the cursed path rather than the blessed path. They've chosen what would end in sorrow rather than what would end in joy. Blessed is the one who is not offended by Jesus.

The way to happiness is not to give in to your doubt. The way to happiness is to answer your doubts with the evidence we have in Christ. Never treat your doubts with certainty. Always doubt your doubts. Never let your doubts have the last word. If they are truly doubts, then seek answers on which to stand. Find evidence. Follow the evidence to the truth and then build certainty with the truth. That's the life Jesus blesses.

Doubt makes us shortsighted. Faith gives us the long view. The Lord gives John evidence to answer his doubt, and he gives John a promise of joy to strengthen his faith. Jesus is a Messiah who answers our doubt.

## Jesus Is a King Who Exalts the Lowly
### LUKE 7:24-35

Verses 18-23 occur in the presence of a crowd. No doubt a lot of people overheard John's question and became aware of John's doubts. Some people were probably prepared to question the authenticity of John's faith. That's what many people do whenever they learn someone experiences doubt.

So it seems as if Jesus wants to prevent the crowd from reaching the wrong conclusions about John. The Lord anticipates our tendency to evaluate and criticize the faith of others.

The Lord asks a series of questions designed to help the crowd remember what they were seeking when they went to hear John preach. They weren't looking for some weak man. John was a powerful and fearless preacher who stood up to kings. They weren't looking for some fancy Dan "dressed in soft clothes" (v. 25). John was not a prosperity preacher in tailored six-button suits and crocodile loafers, living in a luxurious mansion. He was rough and lived a simple life.

They went to see a true prophet of God, and that's what they found. Jesus reminds them in verse 27 that John was unique among the prophets because John was the promised messenger whom Malachi 3:1 prophesied would prepare the way for the Messiah. The crowd needed to know they had seen the prophet whom Israel awaited before receiving the Messiah that God promised.

Jesus commends John in verse 28: "I tell you, among those born of women no one is greater than John." You can't get higher praise than that. This man, imprisoned and doubting, was the greatest man alive. The crowd needed to know and respect that.

Then Jesus says something surprising and pleasing to ordinary people. As great as John was among men, "the least" of men can be greater than John if they make it into the kingdom of God. The kingdom of God is a place where the lowly are exalted above the so-called great people of this world.

That's why "the people" and "the tax collectors" (v. 29) rejoiced when they heard this. The "average Joes" declared God just. They celebrated because God's kingdom does not work like man's kingdoms. The things men think make you great—power, position, money, etc.—don't count for anything in God's kingdom. In God's kingdom the first will be last and the last will be first.

While the "regular people" rejoice, the religious and cultural elites have the opposite response. God does not oppose people with position and power in this world. However, the elites of this world are often so proud they live as if they don't need God. That's the meaning of verse 30. The religious rulers didn't think they needed John's message of repentance and preparation for the kingdom. They assumed they were just fine the way they were. In the process they "rejected the plan of God for themselves" (v. 30).

Can you think of a more devastating statement than that? God had a plan for them, but they chose their own plans and purposes. Many people make that same tragic mistake every day. They become the kind of people Jesus describes in verses 31-34. It doesn't matter whether an evangelist comes in a happy, kind way with the message of the gospel or if a preacher comes in a stern, direct way. Either way they reject the message, just as these Pharisees did with John and Jesus. They become the kind of people who commit themselves to unbelief and doubt.

"Yet wisdom is vindicated by all her children" (v. 35). You can tell a wise decision by its results. The little people in this life who believe will be the great people in the kingdom of God. The big people in this life who disbelieve will not even enter the kingdom of God. Which, then, is wiser: unbelief or faith in Jesus Christ?

## Unbelief Is Not a Virtue

Many people make doubt a virtue. They think doubt somehow proves they have an open mind or that they're humble because religious certainty, they think, is a kind of pride. Some people are principally committed to uncertainty.

Clinging to doubt actually proves the opposite. Clinging to doubt closes the mind to actual evidence. Evidence is what Jesus gives John. The Lord gives John evidence not so John could remain doubtful or unbelieving but so John would become certain. It's as G. K. Chesterton put it: "The object of opening the mind, as of opening the mouth, is to shut it again on something solid" (*Autobiography*, 217). John is to close his mind onto the solid fact that Jesus Christ is the chosen Savior of God. That's where the evidence leads. That's what John is to believe. That's why Luke has written this account of Jesus's life: so that we may have certainty that what we have been taught is true (1:1-4).

This crowd all saw the same evidence and heard Jesus make the same promise. They were all required to believe as much as John. But they were a spiritual generation just like ours—skeptical, doubting, unbelieving—and willfully so, contrary to all the evidence.

Jesus is a King who exalts the lowly in his kingdom.

## Jesus Is a Savior Who Forgives the Biggest Sinners
### LUKE 7:36-50

Verses 36-38 describe our final scene. Put yourself in the place of the Pharisee. He's a religious man. He's serious about sin and holiness, morality and immorality. He doesn't have just anyone at his table. He's taking a risk having Jesus at his table because Jesus isn't like the Pharisees. But he's showing some level of hospitality. Then into his house—right up to his table—walks this woman known all around town as "a sinner" (v. 37).

Now put yourself in the place of the woman. She lives in that city, and she knows what Pharisees are like. Religious men. Often self-righteous. They make a big distinction between themselves and "sinners." They always reject "sinners" as unworthy. But Jesus is in the Pharisee's home, in her city, where she can reach him. What courage must it have taken for her to enter this Pharisee's home? What hope must have been in her heart when she gathered her most expensive possession, an alabaster flask of ointment? What brokenness must have rushed up in her heart and mind as she stood behind Jesus "weeping" (v. 38)? She knew she was a sinner better than anyone else did. There behind the Lord, at his feet, she knelt in a pool of her own tears.

Maybe she had planned to anoint his feet with the oil all along. Then she saw that the host had not washed the Savior's feet when he entered the home. Maybe she picked up on the minor insult, as washing a guest's feet was a common courtesy whenever anyone came to your home. Maybe she had been to homes and had not been given this common courtesy and knew the insult, or maybe she just loved Jesus. So she cried—so much that she could wipe the Savior's feet with her tears—and she took the tresses of her hair and wiped his feet. Then she kissed his feet in love and worship, and she anointed him with her oil.

It's a moving scene. In that dramatic moment we are not told what motivated this woman to behave this way, but we do receive a window into Simon's heart (v. 39). In the Pharisee's mind, holy men don't allow themselves to be touched by a sinner. And prophets can tell "what kind" of people they meet. She was that kind. Jesus must not be a prophet.

But Jesus knows what's in the Pharisee's mind. He knows what's in all of our minds. In verse 40 the Lord confronts the Pharisee about his thoughts. He tells the parable in verses 41-42. The punch line of the parable is the question, Who loves more—the one forgiven little or the one forgiven much? Simon answers correctly in verse 43—the one who has his larger debt cancelled.

See the scene in verse 44. Imagine the Lord's body language. "Turning to the woman" *but speaking to Simon*, Jesus said in verses 44-48,

> *"Do you see this woman? I entered your house; you gave me no water for my feet, but she, with her tears, has washed my feet and wiped them with her hair. You gave me no kiss, but she hasn't stopped kissing my feet since I came in. You didn't anoint my head with olive oil, but she has anointed my feet with perfume. Therefore I tell you, her many sins have been forgiven; that's why she loved much. But the one who is forgiven little, loves little." Then he said to her, "Your sins are forgiven."*

This is when we realize the woman's motivation for coming. She came to the house fully aware of her sin. She had a reputation in the town, but the town didn't know her failures as well as she did. She probably forgot more sins than they would ever be aware of. She knew the deep pain and brokenness of life apart from the mercy of God. She knew her debt before God—a debt she could not repay.

But she sensed something about Jesus. Jesus is a Savior who forgives the biggest sinners. She understood that Jesus could remove her guilt and shame, grant her a new heart, and give her a future. The more she remembers her sin, the greater Jesus appears. The more she weeps over her sin, the more she delights in the Savior. She knows she can rise up from that spot a new creature because Jesus makes things new. The biggest sinners who see and weep over their sin can come confidently to Jesus for forgiveness. The "little sinner" can come too. Both may be forgiven. But the big sinner has hope because Jesus is that kind of Savior.

To be a big sinner is not the worst thing; to not ask forgiveness through faith in Jesus is. You can recover from a sinful past—the church is full of people who have—but there is no recovery from God's judgment against sin.

You can't sin yourself out of the possibility of forgiveness. There's more grace and forgiveness in Jesus's little finger than there is sin in the vilest sinner.

I once shared the gospel with a woman who cut me off by saying, "Honey, God gave up on me a long time ago."

I said to her, "Honey, you don't know Jesus." There are many who believe like that woman: that God has given up on them. But if you would believe like this sinful woman—that Jesus is worthy of your love and that he will forgive your sins—then you may, like this woman, go away from Jesus forgiven and full of peace. Jesus is a Savior who forgives the biggest sinners.

He can do that because he's the Savior who takes the punishment for all of our sins—big and small, past and future, known and unknown. He did that when he was crucified on the cross. On the cross God the Father punished all of our sin by punishing Jesus Christ, who took our place. When God raised his Son from the grave three days later, he proved that Jesus's sacrifice was acceptable and we—even if we are the biggest sinners—can be righteous in God's sight by faith in God's Son.

Faith not only amazes Jesus; faith brings forgiveness from Jesus. Some like Simon the Pharisee miss out. Others like the sinner woman find it. Which are you? Will you believe and be forgiven? Or will you continue to check the box labeled "none" and have none of God's love and forgiveness? You must decide. Wisdom is justified by all her children.

## Reflect and Discuss

1. What do you think most people mean when they say, "Jesus was a good moral teacher"? What do you think would be the effect if people took that statement seriously?

2. Think about the culture where you live. What cultural values do you think people in your area cherish most? How would you compare those values to the priorities and values of the kingdom of God?

3. Why do you think the centurion's faith amazed Jesus? Does faith amaze you?

4. Do you think Jesus is moved by your grief and pain? What passages of Scripture help you believe or remember this?

5. What is doubt? Have you ever struggled with doubt? How have you handled it?

6. The woman who washed Jesus's feet with her tears was known as a sinner. Her reputation preceded her. How can a bad reputation keep us from seeking Jesus? What does Jesus do about the reputations and sins of the worst sinners? How might that affect how we view our sins?

# Sower of the Word

## LUKE 8

**Main Idea:** "Faith comes by hearing, and hearing by the word of God" (Rom 10:17 NKJV).

---

I. **Be Careful to Hear God's Word (8:1-33).**
   A. Those who hear the word should spread the word (8:1-3).
   B. God calls everyone to hear the word (8:4-8).
   C. Hearing the word of God is spiritual warfare (8:9-15).
   D. The more we hear, the more we receive; the less we hear, the more we lose (8:16-18).
   E. If we obey the word, it will change our loyalty (8:19-21).
   F. The word of God calms our fears (8:22-25).
   G. The word of God sets us free (8:26-33).
II. **Be Sure to Believe God's Word (8:34-56).**
   A. You cannot believe apart from God (8:10).
   B. Yet not believing is sin.
   C. Do not reject God's word (8:34-39).
   D. Your faith will make you well (8:40-56).

---

Over the last ten or fifteen years pastors have changed the way they refer to themselves. It used to be enough to simply have the title "pastor" or "reverend," but now such titles seem unpopular or insufficient. Now pastors are "motivational speakers" and "life coaches." Many pastors make a big deal of the fact that they are authors or speak at conferences. Before you ever get to the title of pastor, they list off their other accolades and roles—many of which seem to bear little relationship to the ministry of the word.

Over the same ten-to-fifteen-year period, there remain groups of people who are *not* ashamed to be called "pastor." However, they want bigger titles like "apostle."

What's happening in the minds of church leaders when they rest their identities on these titles? Titles have their place. We appropriately honor people for the roles they play in life. Titles often describe and honor those roles and the people in them. But how are we to understand a church leader grasping for a different way to be described or understood? Perhaps more to the point, how does craving such titles compare to the way Jesus describes himself? How does it compare to what Jesus makes primary in his own ministry?

Luke 8 divides into three scenes. The first scene begins in verse 1 when the Lord teaches three parables to his disciples. The second scene begins in verse 22, when Jesus and his disciples enter a boat to cross the Sea of Galilee and find themselves caught in an unexpected and violent storm. Then, while in Galilee, the third scene beings in verse 26, as the Lord performs four miracles: the calming of the storm, the healing of a demon-possessed man, the healing of a woman, and the raising of a little girl from death to life. Running through each scene—whether in Jesus's teaching or in the action portions of the chapter—is an emphasis on the word of God. Running through the chapter are various responses to the word of God. Each parable teaches us something about the nature of God's word. And each miracle teaches us something about how we must respond to God's word.

## Be Careful to Hear God's Word
### LUKE 8:1-33

Let me give you seven statements under this heading about the nature of God's word and why we need to be careful about how we hear it.

### Those Who Hear the Word Should Spread the Word (8:1-3)

These verses summarize Jesus's earthly ministry. He traveled "from one town and village to another, preaching and telling the good news of the kingdom of God" (v. 1). In other words, Jesus preached the gospel.

He wasn't alone. "The Twelve" refers to the twelve men Jesus called to be his apostles, the early leaders and teachers of the church. We're not surprised to see the men listed here, but then there are "some women" (v. 2) traveling with our Lord. That is surprising. Unlike every other rabbi of his day, the Lord Jesus included women in his ministry. They traveled with him. Not only that, but they were the supporters of his ministry (v. 3).

If Luke were alive today, he would use the hashtag #SayHerName because he notes three of the women in particular: Mary Magdalene, Joanna, and Susanna. We don't know much about Susanna apart from this verse. Joanna was apparently a woman of some status since her husband, Chuza, managed Herod's house. Mary Magdalene was at one point possessed by seven demons until Jesus delivered her. There are unnamed women, unknown women, women with a broken past, and women of position. All kinds of women served the Lord and supported his ministry.

The Christian church would never have gotten off the ground were it not for women. Churches around the world would have closed their doors generations ago if it were not for women. Luke affirms these women by naming them for us. If our Lord valued and included women in his ministry, then every church should include them in every way the Lord and his Word permits. In every way women are called and gifted to serve, we want to see them encouraged and flourishing in their service in accord with the Word of God so that the Word of God might be spread among us.

This was the pattern of Christian ministry from the start. It's a partnership to spread the word by those who heard the word. Some go preaching—Jesus and the apostles. Some give for preaching—Mary, Susanna, and Joanna. Everyone does one or the other or both. The entire aim is to spread the word of Christ to those who have not heard.

That's why the local church exists. Of all the things the Lord may call us to do, we must not fail to spread the word. We have a partnership in the gospel (Phil 1:6). That's our business. We do not look for government support or the resources of private foundations. We assume collective responsibility for supporting the ministry of the word in our neighborhood and beyond. Let us never forget or be distracted from this partnership. Those who hear the word should spread the word.

### God Calls Everyone to Hear the Word (8:4-8)

The sower sows his seed on four types of soil: the path, the rock, the thorns, and the good soil. The punch line of the parable is, "As he said this, he called out, 'Let anyone who has ears to hear listen'" (v. 8).

You often hear Jesus say, "Let anyone who has ears to hear listen." You might ask yourself the question, Who does not have ears? Nearly everyone does. But the saying suggests a person can have ears and *not* listen. That was my mom's most frequent complaint about my dad. She used to say, "Harvey hears what he wants to hear!" He had ears, but it was as if certain things just never entered them. My mom would say he didn't try to listen.

That's the thing about God's word: You must work to hear it. You have to tune your ear to God's word. You must train your appetite for it. There must be concentration in order to understand it. So Jesus calls his hearers to listen if they have ears. In other words, the Lord calls us to understand and obey—not merely register the sound of words.

Some Christians have grown accustomed to hearing sermons that entertain them. They like sermons with lots of stories and illustrations, with humor and the occasional clever twist. While preaching should be interesting and engaging, preaching is not entertainment. Preaching must be better than entertainment. In our culture entertainment is almost entirely passive, as people stare endlessly at screens. But with preaching, people must come to the Word of God fully awake and ready to do the work true hearing requires.

This is important because . . .

### Hearing the Word of God Is Spiritual Warfare (8:9-15)

The disciples ask the Lord to explain the meaning of the parable. They want to know what's up with the path and birds, the rock and withering away, the thorns that choke the seed, and the good soil that yields a crop. Hearing, they have not yet listened. So the Lord explains the parable.

Parables are not meant to be interpreted line by line. Parables have one major point that they make in a symbolic story. So the Lord explains the symbols. "The seed is the word of God" (v. 11). By implication, he and other preachers are the sowers. Then Jesus explains that there are three different ways to hear the word sown.

- Defenseless hearing (v. 12)
- Shallow hearing (v. 13)
- Distracted hearing (v. 14)

These first three soils remind us of the Christians' three enemies: the world, the flesh, and the devil. They all oppose God's word. That's why I say hearing the word of God is spiritual warfare.

The devil is mentioned in verse 12. He and his demons are real. The devil looks to snatch the seed before it can take root, like birds devouring seed. Christ spreads the seed generously, but Satan pecks it up from the human heart as quickly as he can. And why? A war is being fought on the soil of every human heart. The devil enters that war to prevent people from being saved. The ear is the gate to the heart. Satan steals the seed to kill the soul. Don't be defenseless. "Guard your heart above all else, for it is the source of life" (Prov 4:23). Guard the word that comes through your ear into your heart, for the word is able to save you.

The Lord alludes to the flesh in verse 13. Persecution or testing often arise because of the word. Though some people received the word joyfully, when trouble comes they "fall away." Apostasy is real. Do not faint or turn away in the day of testing. You will reap if you do not faint. To all those who overcome, the Lord will give the crown of life (Rev 2:10-11). When you suffer for the name of Christ and the gospel, you are being treated like the prophets, and your reward in heaven will be great! Do not fall away. Persevere.

The world is described in verse 14. The world chokes out the seed, so any early fruit does not mature. Do not let the world lure you away with its false and vanishing pleasures and riches. Many Christians have set out for the celestial city only to get snared in Vanity Fair. Too many Christians care too much for the ways of the world—about its power, its wealth, its beauty, its knowledge, its technology, its fashion, its cool. And the world keeps producing things for people to "get into." The world never encourages you to get into the Word of God. Never. It doesn't want the Word to produce fruit that remains in your life. It's warring against the maturing of your soul in Christ. Don't give in to it.

We are right now engaged in warfare. We are right now fighting against distraction from the world, the flesh, and the devil. When we listen to the preaching of God's Word, our thoughts travel to work on Monday morning, to lunch after church, and to the temperature of the room. Even trials that small will allure us from the Word of God. Some of us will face far more significant persecutions and trials. We will have to decide again and again whether we will hold onto God's Word or look away to something else. Satan and his minions fight to keep us distracted that they might destroy the power of God's Word in our lives.

A heart made of good soil provides the only antidote to the world, the flesh, and the devil. Verse 15 describes such hearts. We win the spiritual war of hearing when we hold on to the word like a soldier trained never to lose or surrender his weapon. We do that if our hearts are honest and good; in other words, if we receive the Word of God for what it truly is—the very Word of God. We don't receive it to justify ourselves. We don't cut out the difficult parts. We don't pick and choose what we will believe. We receive it all with a good heart—with an intention to do good and to believe what is taught. We win the war for the Word when we look to bear fruit with patience (Jas 1:2-4). We're not trying to rush into maturity or skip the things that produce growth. We just steadily read, believe, and apply the Bible, and let patience have its perfect work in our lives.

That's how we win. Hold fast. Have an honest heart. Bear fruit. Keep patient. Hearing the Word of God is spiritual warfare.

## The More We Hear, the More We Receive; the Less We Hear, the More We Lose (8:16-18)

That's the point of the second parable. The Lord compares the word of God to a light or candle. No one puts a lamp under a jar or under a bed. We don't hide light. We let it shine.

Verse 17 tells us why: the Word reveals everything. We can't hide things from God. God is light, and in him is no darkness at all. He sends his Word into the world, and it exposes the darkness. The Lord says,

> *"This is the judgment: The light has come into the world, and people loved darkness rather than the light because their deeds were evil. For everyone who does evil hates the light and avoids it, so that his deeds may not be exposed. But anyone who lives by the truth comes to the light, so that his works may be shown to be accomplished by God."*
> (John 3:19-21)

My mama would say, "It all comes out in the wash." Jesus says, "It all comes out in the light of God's Word."

The more of God's Word we hear, the more of it we receive. The more we neglect God's Word, the more of it we lose (v. 18). To hear more of God's Word is to receive more from God. To hear less of God's Word is to have what you had taken away.

It's not like we hear the Word at one time and can live on it for the rest of our lives. We have to keep replenishing the store, stocking the shelves of our heart so that we always have something to feed on. We're either going forward in the things of God, or we're going backward. There is no neutral ground. The more we hear the more we receive. The less we hear the more we lose.

I was convicted by these verses as I wrote this. I had slipped into a pattern of laziness when it came to my own personal study of the Scriptures. The Lord showed me that I wasn't sitting still in neutral. I was going backward. I needed to "take care" to "hear" well. Maybe that's you. Perhaps you need to take better care of how you hear God's

Word. This Bible containing God's promises is our life. We live by every word of it.

The second half of verse 18 promises that the word will be taken away from those who do not have it. I think this means that if we attempt to live on yesterday's quiet times today or last week's sermon for this week then we will find diminishing remembrance of God's Word. With our "little" we end up with "less" because Christians leak. Instead, we need to continually pour in the Word of God to keep our tanks filled. The more we receive God's Word, the more of it we get. The more we develop an appetite for Scripture, the more we hunger for it. The more we give ourselves, the more we receive. But the more we withhold, the more is taken away.

Isn't this a perfect description of how we sometimes find ourselves spiritually dry? We did not intentionally set out for a desert place. We woke up one morning a little late, running behind for work, so we skipped our quiet time. We could still smell the fumes from the gas of yesterday's quiet times, so we had a pretty good day despite not reading and pondering the Word that morning. The second morning we thought, *It went well yesterday, so I'll sleep in again.* On the third morning we felt a little guilty so we thought we'd at least get a little snippet of the Word into the morning. We rush our spiritual feeding like a man grabbing a piece of toast for breakfast as he runs out the door. The fourth day you have your quiet time, but it's less rewarding than it was last week. Now reading God's Word feels harder. Praying is more difficult. So you miss another day or two before trying to press your way back into the Bible. Before you know it, a couple of weeks have passed since you fruitfully received God's Word. You had just a little of the Bible, and more of it was taken away. You've been losing all the while, and now you're wondering, *How do I get it back?* The promise of the first half of verse 18 is that if you start with at least getting some of the Bible, then you will want more of the Bible. Water the dry places of your heart with the Scriptures, and the desert will bloom with truth. The more you water, the more you flower. The more you flower, the more you water.

Feed on God's written Word. Feed on it daily and several times a day. Let us not rest on sermons and studies from yesterday or last week or last year. Let us keep a fresh word in our hearts and minds by reading it and hearing it every day.

The result will be . . .

## If We Obey the Word, It Will Change Our Loyalty (8:19-21)

In verse 19 we transition from the Lord's teaching in parables to the action and miracles of the chapter. The Lord's earthly mother and brothers come to him. They can't reach him because of the crowds, but they get word to him that they're standing outside and want to see him (v. 20).

The Lord's response shocks us even today: "My mother and my brothers are those who hear and do the word of God" (v. 21). These words continue to astound readers who wonder if Jesus sinned against his mother by refusing to see them.

What we read in the Word of God redefines our relationships and our loyalty. The active obedience of the Christian to the Word of God actually creates in the Christian a higher loyalty than our closest earthly relationships. Our Lord is not diminishing or disrespecting parenthood. Instead, the Lord points us to the fact that there is a greater Father to whom we owe the highest loyalty. Our heavenly Father comes before our earthly mothers and brothers. The more we obey God's Word, the more we have in common with others who obey God's Word. We find ourselves closer to those who obey God's Word than we are to our blood relatives who do not believe.

I may never forget the year my wife and I realized that God's Word had done this in our lives. The girls were young, and our parents wanted us to come home for Christmas. That meant driving to both ends of North Carolina from the middle. But we made the journey—which also meant we weren't going to celebrate Christmas with our church family or in a way that fit our understanding of the Bible's priorities. At one point, while we were itching to get back to our home in Raleigh, one of our mothers said, "You guys love your church friends more than you do your own family." That rocked me a little. It wasn't that I loved my family less. It's that in Christ we now had a new family with whom we tried to live out God's Word. The Word of God forges new bonds and affections that natural families point to and symbolize.

You know God's Word is doing its work in your heart when you share a stronger bond with your brothers and sisters in the church than your blood relatives who do not believe. The Word creates family. This is wonderful because many of us don't have family or don't have good families. My father left the family when I was thirteen. Some of us have never met our fathers. Some of us grew up in homes where Mom and Dad were always fighting. Or perhaps you mourn the loss of a parent.

But the Word of God read and obeyed holds out the promise of a new and better family. We receive brothers and sisters, fathers and mothers one hundredfold through the Word of God. That's what the local church is to be—the family of God united by obedience to the Word. I praise God for the way he's been doing that in our lives already.

### The Word of God Calms Our Fears (8:22-25)

I can tell you that a storm on the Sea of Galilee is no joke. As verse 22 says, it's actually a large lake, but because the lake is below sea level, the winds that come down across it can cause it to act like a sea. That means big waves and storms can come up suddenly. That's what happened in verse 23. The Lord fell asleep in the boat, and a windstorm swept the lake.

These are professional fishermen. They know these waters, and they've likely been out in storms before. But this one is so violent that the boat starts to fill up with water and these grown fishermen start screaming, "Master, Master, we're going to die!" (v. 24a).

Now see the authority of God's word: "Then he got up and rebuked the wind and the raging waves. So they ceased, and there was a calm. They were fearful and amazed, asking one another, 'Who then is this? He commands even the winds and the waves, and they obey him!'" (24b-25). Winds and water do not have minds. Winds and water do not think. They do not have ears. Winds and water do not make decisions. Yet they obey the Lord at his word. Deaf creation may hear and obey better than smart people.

See the Lord's authority over creation. He exercises his authority through his word. The written Word, the Bible, is meant to have the same effect in our lives as it does to the winds and the waves. More so when you consider that we are made in God's image and made for fellowship with him. But since sin has come in the world, we find it difficult to obey God. The winds and the waves put us to shame. We have to look at unthinking things in order to know how we should think about God's Word and his authority.

### The Word of God Sets Us Free (8:26-33)

This is what we learn in the second miracle story when Jesus heals a man who was possessed by demons for years. This man was in rough shape (v. 27). Can you imagine him? This poor man has been devastated by these demons (v. 29).

When the demons encounter Jesus, they shout, "What do you have to do with me, Jesus, Son of the Most High God? I beg you, don't torment me!" (v. 28). The demons recognize Jesus, and they recognize who has the real authority. So they *beg* not to be tormented. There is not the slightest hint of "good vs. evil" in this passage, if you think evil has any chance against good. The demons know the moment they see Jesus that God has just stepped on the scene. They tremble in his presence.

The demons tremble at the Son's word (v. 29). The Lord controls their fate by his word. The demons can do nothing but submit to whatever Jesus commands. And there are *many* demons in this man—so many his name is "Legion" (v. 30). So it's not even a one-on-one battle. It's Jesus alone against a legion of demons! And they all must bow before the Lord and his command. They beg to go into pigs rather than to be sentenced to the abyss, which is the hell prepared for Satan and his demons.

The word of God controls the natural spiritual realms. The Lord rules things seen and unseen. Everything from demons and devils to waves and winds obey the word of God. By his word our Lord calms our fears, and by his word he sets the captives free.

- Those who hear the word must spread the word.
- Everyone must hear the word.
- Hearing the word is spiritual warfare.
- The more we hear it, the more we have of it.
- If we obey the word, it will place us in a new family.
- By his word, the Lord calms our fears.
- By his word, the Lord sets the captive free.

My friend, this is why we love the Bible. The Bible is the written Word of God, and God rules his world through his Word. And this is why Satan hates the Word. This is why our personal reading of the Bible and our listening to biblical sermons become so critical.

How do you respond to God's Word? What attention do you give to it? What habits do you build around it? When you hear it preached, do you *listen*?

## Be Sure to Believe God's Word
### LUKE 8:34-56

Jesus receives various responses as he sows the word. The responses teach us something about how we should respond. They teach us about the nature of faith or belief. I want to make four statements about faith.

## You Cannot Believe Apart from God (8:10)

No one can believe God's word or the gospel unless God gives us ears to hear. That's the point of verse 10, which quotes Isaiah 6:9-10. In Isaiah 6 God calls Isaiah to be a prophet and sends him to preach the word to Israel. But God tells Isaiah from the start that Israel will not believe or perceive. They will not believe because God will not give them faith. God promises to blind their eyes and stop up their ears so they will not believe.

Belief isn't something we work up or create on our own. Faith is a gift of grace (Eph 2:8-9). Knowledge of the secrets of the kingdom is given to some. Who does the giving? God does. Jesus prays in Matthew 11:25-27,

> *I praise you, Father, Lord of heaven and earth, because you have hidden these things from the wise and intelligent and revealed them to infants. Yes, Father, because this was your good pleasure. All things have been entrusted to me by my Father. No one knows the Son except the Father, and no one knows the Father except the Son and anyone to whom the Son desires to reveal him.*

Knowing the secrets of the kingdom, or knowing God the Father and God the Son, is a gift of God's gracious will. He makes it known to "infants." In other words, according to Jesus, God is in control even over who believes. If you have come to know Christ, it is because God has already changed your heart with the gift of faith.

## Yet Not Believing Is Sin

That's implied in verse 25 when the Lord asks the disciples during the storm, "Where is your faith?" We cannot create faith, but Jesus expects us to have faith. God expects us to trust him and believe in him. We cannot believe apart from God's giving us the gift of faith, yet it's sin not to believe. Romans 14:23 says, "Everything that is not from faith is sin."

So even our unbelief makes us guilty before God. So you may say, "Well, what should we do if we can't believe on our own, and we are guilty for not believing?" Good question.

You should call on God to give you the gift of faith. Pray with the sinner, "Lord, help my unbelief." Ask God to give you eyes to see and ears to hear. Ask him for an honest and good heart that patiently bears fruit in faith. What we *can* do is call on the name of the Lord with the promise of Romans 10:13 in mind: "Everyone who calls on the name of the Lord will be saved" (Rom 10:13). We should appeal to God's mercy, asking him to do even concerning faith what we cannot do for ourselves.

That really is the message of the gospel. Through Jesus Christ, God does everything we cannot do for ourselves. God provides righteousness for us through Jesus's perfect obedience. God provides payment for our sin through Jesus's death on the cross. God provides for us eternal life through raising Jesus from the grave three days later. Everything we need—from righteousness, to atonement, to new life—God provides through his Son; faith is no exception. By God's grace we come to believe. So what must we do? Simply ask, "Lord, give me this gift. Show me your mercy."

## Do Not Reject God's Word (8:34-39)

The Lord will give faith to those who are like little infants who receive his word with an honest and good heart (v. 15). Even if you don't understand it all, receive it. At the very least trust that it's God's word and then commit to growing in understanding.

Whatever you do, do not reject God's word. That's what the people do after Jesus heals the man with the many demons. Do you remember that in verses 34-39? They *see* the miracle. They *see* the man clothed and sane after he'd been running around naked and crazed for years. They *hear* how it had been done (v. 36). But they *do not receive* Christ or his word. Instead, they "asked him to leave" (v. 37).

Many people are like the people of the Gerasenes. When they visit a church, they see a room full of former sinners and reprobates. And they see how Christ has cleaned us up, has clothed us in our right mind, and has begun to renew our lives. They hear the explanation: "God loved the world in this way: He gave his one and only Son, so that everyone who believes in him will not perish but have eternal life" (John 3:16). They will hear people tell them that new and eternal life can be theirs through Jesus Christ. And do you know what they do? They effectively ask Jesus to leave. Or they themselves leave offended or afraid. They reject eternal life and the Savior.

This story is here to show us ourselves. The lesson is, do not refuse Jesus. Believe in him, and you will be saved from God's condemnation; he will clothe you in his righteousness and renew your mind. Look at how Jesus gives purpose to that formerly crazy man (vv. 38-39). Jesus made this man an evangelist and a preacher.

The demons begged to depart from Jesus. The man, when free of the demons, begged to go with Jesus. Don't let your response to Jesus be like the demons. Let it be like this man who became known throughout his town for praising God and telling others how much Jesus had done for him. You begin that new life by believing that Jesus died to pay for your sins, that he rose so you might live forever in his righteousness, and that he is coming again to receive all those who believe in him.

My plea to you if you're not a Christian is that you not respond like the demons. Respond like this man. Confess your sins. Beg to go with Christ. Beg that Christ would be to you a Savior and Lord. Beg that all Christ has done to turn away God's wrath against you and to reconcile you to God would be yours through faith.

### Your Faith Will Make You Well (8:40-56)

You may be wondering if believing in Jesus this way is worth it. What will you give up, and what will you gain? The last two miracles answer that question—if you have ears to hear.

In verses 41-42 a man named Jairus, a ruler of the synagogue, came to Jesus to heal his twelve-year-old daughter. I can tell you, a father of a twelve-year-old daughter will do almost anything to save his sick daughter's life. He'll go all John Q to save her. This man comes to Jesus.

As Jesus is going to see the daughter, a woman who has been bleeding for twelve years presses through the crowd to touch the hem of his garment. Verse 43 says she's spent all she had on doctors but couldn't be healed. A private medical savings account wasn't enough. Insurance wasn't enough. But she reasoned that just a touch of the Lord's garment would be enough. That's faith. Just as the father coming to Jesus was an act of faith.

She manages to press through the crowd and touch the Lord's garment, and power went out from the Lord (v. 46). When Jesus finds out she had touched him, the Lord said to her, "Daughter, your faith has saved you. Go in peace" (v. 48).

He says a similar thing when he arrives at Jairus's house. The people say the girl is dead; don't bother the teacher any more. They've given up and already begun their mourning. The crowd is more committed to the girl's death than the father is to the girl's life. But Jesus goes into Jairus's house with Peter, John, James, and her parents. He closes the door with everyone inside weeping and crying. The crowd laughs at him when he says the girl is not dead (v. 53). That's when Jesus does the miracle (vv. 54-55). In that moment Jairus's daughter becomes a fore-taste of the resurrection and the life to come.

## Conclusion

Did you notice how Jesus spoke to the woman and to Jairus? "Daughter, your faith has saved you. Go in peace" (v. 48). "Don't be afraid. Only believe, and she will be saved" (v. 50). From this we learn that faith in Christ makes the sin-sick sinner well. Faith in Christ raises the person dead in sin to newness of life.

Is faith worth it? Is living well and living forever worth it?

Faith comes by hearing and hearing by the word of God (see Rom 10:17). Salvation comes through our ears. Let us hear the word of God and believe. Christ is the sower of God's word. May the seed of the word find fertile soil in our hearts.

## Reflect and Discuss

1. What strategies have you found successful in helping you hear God's word?
2. As you think about your Christian life, in what ways has God's word changed you?
3. How can you spread God's word to someone before the day ends today or tomorrow?
4. Do you agree that hearing and obeying God's word is part of the spiritual warfare Christians face? Why or why not? If so, how do you fight the war?
5. Are there any parts of God's word you struggle to believe? Why or why not? How do you answer or work against your objections in order to fully accept God's word? Do you pray for God's help to receive and believe his word in those areas?

# The Chosen One of God

## LUKE 9:1-45

**Main Idea:** The way to get our deepest needs met in this world is to know and follow Jesus into the next world. This requires knowing Jesus personally and following Jesus closely.

---

I. **Who Is Jesus?**
   A. Herod with the crowd (9:7-9)
   B. Jesus with the disciples (9:18-22)
   C. The Father's testimony (9:28-36)
II. **What Can We Expect if We Follow Jesus?**
   A. Purpose and power (9:1-6)
   B. Supplies that satisfy (9:10-17)
   C. Cross then a crown (9:23-27)
   D. Triumph and truth (9:37-45)

---

We've embarked on this study of Luke's Gospel so that we might come to know more about our Lord and Savior. We want to know him better so we can follow him more closely.

Two dominant actions take place in Luke 9:1-45. We see Jesus training his apostles, and at the same time we see that many are beginning to ask, "Who is this Jesus?" The question has always been a challenging one. Perhaps it's a difficult question for you to answer. We pray the Lord would clearly answer that question for us.

## Who Is Jesus?
### LUKE 9:7-9,18-22,28-36

*Herod with the Crowd (9:7-9)*

After Herod the Great died, his son Herod Antipas became ruler of one-third of his father's kingdom, splitting it with his two brothers. He ruled from his father's death in 4 BC until AD 39. So Herod ruled Galilee and Perea for all of our Lord's lifetime. The question "Who is Jesus?" is first asked by Herod the tetrarch in verses 7-9.

Herod hears "about everything that was going on" (v. 7). No doubt as a ruler he would express keen interest in reports of mass healings, the dead being raised, and miracles being performed by a new leader and his followers. Herod hears about Jesus, so he asks about Jesus. But he is "perplexed." He's confused. The crowds give him conflicting reports (vv. 7-8). Everyone has a theory about Jesus's identity. The crowd's theories have three things in common:

- All the responses are religious theories. They're certain Jesus is a prophet of some sort.
- All their theories are supernatural. Each of these suggestions requires either a resurrection (John or an old prophet) or a miraculous return of Elijah, who was raptured to be with God and was prophesied to return before the Messiah.
- Each theory is wrong. Crowds rarely answer important questions correctly. Crowds are almost always divided and wrong. Do not put your confidence in the opinions of crowds for anything.

So Herod is perplexed because of the conflicting reports. But there's another reason. He tells us in verse 9, "I beheaded John." That took place between Luke 3 and this text. Herod stole his brother Philip's wife. John called them both out on it. Herodias asked for John's head on a platter, and Herod delivered. This is a wicked man. It's chilling how he so matter-of-factly says, "I beheaded John." He publicly admits to killing a prophet and doesn't even blink. He just goes on to ask, "But who is this I hear such things about?" (v. 9).

Luke tells us one other tragic and chilling thing about Herod when he writes, "And he wanted to see [Jesus]" (v. 9). Kings in Jesus's day could do almost anything they desired. If they ordered someone to appear before them, that someone would appear. If they wished to visit someone with an army of soldiers, they could make such a visit happen. But Herod only *tried* to see Jesus. We have to ask ourselves: What could stop a ruler from seeing anyone he wanted to, if he really wanted to? I think Herod remained satisfied with being perplexed. He did not press forward to get an actual answer.

You don't get any points, praise, or rewards for asking about Jesus while never going to see or getting to know Jesus for yourself. It is a tragic mistake leaving the question "Who is Jesus?" unanswered. We must all answer that question. We should not rest until we answer the question biblically, factually, and clearly.

*Jesus with the Disciples (9:18-22)*

The second time the question appears, Jesus himself asks it of his disciples: "Who do the crowds say that I am?" (v. 18).

The disciples initially respond the same way the crowd does. They just give Jesus the results from the latest public opinion poll (v. 19). Some say John; some say Elijah; some say a prophet of old.

In reply, Jesus presses the question beyond the opinion of crowds. He makes it personal in verse 20: "But *you*, . . . who do *you* say that I am?" (emphasis added). The "you" is emphatic. The question "Who is Jesus?" has to be settled by every individual person—young or old, rich or poor, male or female, ruler or citizen. We cannot avoid, duck, or put off the question. The Lord of lords asks us all. Heaven has a one-question pop quiz for all of humanity: "Who do *you* say Jesus is?"

There are people in the world we will never know, and it will not cost us a thing. There are people our friends and families know well but we've never met, and that will not change eternity. But Jesus we must all know. Don't be like Herod and leave the question unanswered. Know the answer for yourself.

In verse 19, "They [all] answered" when talking about what the crowds think. Some professing Christians can be experts on all kinds of opinions other people have about Jesus but know little about him for themselves. When Jesus makes the question personal in verse 20, only one man answers. Peter says, "God's Messiah."

Peter knows Jesus better than the crowds. Two things need to be added here:

- Peter didn't come up with this by himself. In Matthew 16:17 Jesus says to Peter after this confession, "Blessed are you, Simon son of Jonah, because flesh and blood did not reveal this to you, but my Father in heaven." We cannot get to know Jesus listening to men. *God* must teach us by his Spirit through his Word.
- Though Peter knew Jesus was the Christ, Peter didn't yet know everything that confession involved. His answer to the exam was partially correct. We cannot think we know *everything* about Jesus once we know *one* thing about Jesus. The Lord is infinite and inexhaustible. Even when we know him well we only partially know him. We will be getting to know Jesus our entire lifetime and indeed for all eternity. We have to grow in our knowledge of the Lord.

This is why Jesus responds the way he does: "He strictly warned and instructed them to tell this to no one" (v. 21). Verse 22 defines what it means to call Jesus "Messiah" or "the Christ" or "Chosen One." In answering the question "Who is Jesus?" the first thing we learn is that Jesus is the Messiah, which means God chose him to die for sin and rise for eternal life to rescue men from the coming judgment of God against sin. He does this so that we might never die but live with God forgiven, counted as righteous, and adopted into God's family.

This truth is what everyone in the chapter continues to miss. So Jesus warns them against sharing this truth because (a) they don't understand it yet and (b) he hadn't finished his mission yet. But this is who the Lord is: the Chosen One who dies and rises for sinners.

Here's the question: Do you believe this? At this point are you Herod who doesn't even meet Jesus, the disciples who stick with what they've heard about Jesus, or Peter who begins to see but not yet fully? Is Christ Jesus your personal Savior and Lord? If not, he can be. Confess your sins. Put your trust in him as the atonement for your sin and the Lord of your life. Start with what you do know. Put your faith in Jesus. He will teach you more.

### The Father's Testimony (9:28-36)

The crowds get it twisted. Herod remained confused. Peter is only partially correct. God the Father settles the matter.

Jesus again goes to pray with three of his disciples—Peter, John, and James. As Jesus prays, something extraordinary happens.

> *As he was praying, the appearance of his face changed, and his clothes became dazzling white. Suddenly, two men were talking with him—Moses and Elijah. They appeared in glory and were speaking of his departure, which he was about to accomplish in Jerusalem.* (9:29-31)

Now I think we're meant to see in this scene a parallel between Moses on Mount Sinai in Exodus 34 and Jesus on the Mount of Transfiguration. Both went up on the mount. Both talked with God. Both had their faces changed. But there are significant differences, too.

- Moses's face shone with God's glory, but Jesus's entire appearance changed in a flash to radiate glory.
- Moses was alone; Elijah and Moses appear with Jesus.

- Moses received the law; Jesus discusses the gospel.
- Israel, apart from a mediator, wanted to hide from God's glory; Peter, James, and John see Jesus's glory and want to worship (v. 32).

The biggest difference between Moses and Jesus is that God speaks to the disciples to answer the question "Who is Jesus?" "Then a voice came from the cloud, saying: 'This is my Son, the Chosen One; listen to him!'" (v. 35). When the Father speaks, we learn two further facts. First, Jesus is God's Son. Jesus shares deity with the Father. He is God. Second, Jesus is God's spokesperson. Do you want to know what God thinks about something? Listen to the teaching of Jesus. Do you want to know what's on the mind of the Father? Read what Jesus speaks in the Gospels.

We are to listen to Jesus for the final word on salvation, not Elijah and Moses or any other prophet from old. The New Testament never looks favorably on Christians turning back to the law or to Judaism. Those things belong to the former time. In these last days God has spoken to us by his Son (Heb 1:1-3). We are to listen to Jesus alone. When the cloud disappears, only Jesus remains. He is greater than Moses and all the other prophets.

> *For Jesus is considered worthy of more glory than Moses, just as the builder has more honor than the house. Now every house is built by someone, but the one who built everything is God. Moses was faithful as a servant in all God's household, as a testimony to what would be said in the future. But Christ was faithful as a Son over his household. And we are that household if we hold on to our confidence and the hope in which we boast.* (Heb 3:3-6)

When God finally grades the one-question exam, we need to demonstrate that we know Jesus is the one God chose to die and rise from the grave to save us from our sin, that he is God's Son and is Master of God's house. We need to demonstrate that we have heard and understood this message and that we have put our hope in its truth.

When it comes to the question "Who is Jesus?" who are you listening to? The crowds? Your own incomplete knowledge? Or God who reveals his Son most clearly and fully? To get to know Jesus, we have to listen to Jesus.

# What Can We Expect if We Follow Jesus?
## LUKE 9:1-6,10-17,23-27,37-45

This question takes us to the other major thread woven into this chapter. It takes us to those scenes where Jesus trains his disciples. We discover that if we get to know Jesus, Jesus will be our great Provider. The better we get to know Jesus, the more we see his provision for us. The Lord provides us with four resources and rewards.

### Purpose and Power (9:1-6)

If we follow Jesus, our lives will have purpose and power. The purpose will be to spread the gospel of the kingdom to every nation (v. 2). The power will be the authority and power of Jesus himself (v. 1). Everyone who follows Jesus as Lord receives this same purpose and power from the Holy Spirit (see Acts 1:8).

If we follow Jesus, we receive meaning not only for this life but for all of eternity. He gives us not only a purpose but also power to fulfill the purpose. How many of you are now experiencing or have experienced purposelessness? Perhaps you feel every day bleeds together with other days; and, though you try, you can't find an interest or pursuit for your life. The lack of meaning can become a thick smoke that suffocates and chokes us. But the Lord blows the smoke away, clears our vision, and gives us meaning connected to God's purpose for the entire world. The Lord changes the world and impacts eternity through us when we believe and follow him. When we embrace the Lord's purpose and power for us, it redefines our entire life and reason for being. We no longer live for career, houses, cars, clothes, and the like. Those things fade into the background; and in the foreground appear the Lord Jesus, the cross, and the salvation of the world. Then the entire world becomes our theater for acting out the drama God plans for our lives. The gospel not only saves a soul but gives purpose and power to a soul.

As the Twelve live in Jesus's power and purpose, they are to learn to depend completely and solely on Jesus (v. 3). Moreover, as the disciples live in Jesus's power and purpose, they are to expect opposition. But they are not to be discouraged by opposition. In fact, they are to stand as witnesses against such people and places (v. 5). Jesus's power and purpose motivate them to keep moving and to keep preaching.

Luke 9:1-6 involved "the Twelve." Those are the twelve disciples who would become apostles of our Lord. This is a historical event that applied to the apostles uniquely. It's not a pattern for all times. We need to see that, lest we get distracted by things like driving out demons, curing diseases, and going on mission trips without any luggage. This was a short-term trip that was not a pattern for all time. It was for while Jesus was on earth. We know this because of Luke 22:35-36. When Jesus approaches his betrayal and crucifixion, he says,

> *"When I sent you out without money-bag, traveling bag, or sandals, did you lack anything?"*
>
> *"Not a thing," they said.*
>
> *Then he said to them, "But now, whoever has a money-bag should take it, and also a traveling bag. And whoever doesn't have a sword should sell his robe and buy one."*

Luke 22:35-36 becomes the pattern for all disciples. And according to Matthew 28:18-20 and Acts 1:8, we have the same purpose but now have a greater power than the disciples in Luke 9—the gift of the Holy Spirit.

I point this out because sometimes, if we're not careful, we can covet what belonged to the apostles in the Gospels before the crucifixion and resurrection so much that we miss the fact that what belongs to us after the resurrection is so much greater. We can so busily chase supernatural healings that we miss the Holy Spirit himself.

Jesus provides his disciples power and purpose.

### Supplies That Satisfy (9:10-17)

Here's another passage where Jesus appears as a greater prophet than Moses. Each time someone says Jesus might be Moses, we get a scene where Jesus seems to be contrasted with Moses. God repeatedly proves his Son is greater than Moses.

Jesus and the disciples go to Bethsaida (v. 10), a wilderness place. Crowds come out to Jesus where he welcomes them, heals them, and teaches them about the kingdom (v. 11). Apparently they stay out there all day, and now it's growing late and the people haven't had dinner (v. 12).

All of this reminds us of Moses's wandering with Israel in the wilderness for forty years. Do you remember what God did for Israel's hunger in the wilderness? He showered them with manna and quail. God supplied their needs, but Israel grumbled; they were not satisfied.

Jesus teaches his disciples a valuable lesson: unlike Moses, Jesus will supply *and satisfy* their needs. I don't know how this miracle worked. Did fish and loaves keep miraculously filling their baskets? Did the fish and loaves all appear at once? Did they fall from the sky? I really don't know. And how did these fishermen react to all of this? Did they wonder, "How in the world did we get fresh fish in a desert wilderness?" I don't even know how a person would process an event like this.

But I do know this: Jesus had a point to make. It's a point everyone who follows him needs to hear. When the Twelve fed five thousand men in one hundred groups of fifty, over and over again they could see Jesus meeting their physical needs. When each of the disciples walked away with a basket of leftovers, it was a clear way of saying, "I supply for you. Trust me." That's the message every disciple needs to hold on to.

Jesus supplies. And he also satisfies. "Everyone ate and was filled" (v. 17). They were satisfied. I believe they enjoyed the taste. I believe the fish was delicious. Jesus wouldn't perform a miraculous fish fry and burn the fish. This fish was cooked in heaven. It was delicious, just like the water turned to wine at the wedding in Cana was the most delicious wine the people had ever tasted.

Jesus supplies and satisfies. His promise to supply and satisfy our needs runs throughout the Bible.

> *"Come, everyone who is thirsty, come to the water; and you without silver, come, buy, and eat! Come, buy wine and milk without silver and without cost! Why do you spend silver on what is not food, and your wages on what does not satisfy? Listen carefully to me, and eat what is good, and you will enjoy the choicest of foods."* (Isa 55:1-2)

> *"But seek first the kingdom of God and his righteousness, and all these things will be provided for you."* (Matt 6:33)

> *The Lord is my shepherd; I have what I need.* (Ps 23:1)

> *And God is able to make every grace overflow to you, so that in every way, always having everything you need, you may excel in every good work.* (2 Cor 9:8)

Do you believe Jesus will supply and satisfy? Are you listening to Jesus? Then expect the Lord to supply and satisfy as he meets your needs.

### Cross Then a Crown (9:23-27)

Jesus provides purpose and power, supplies that satisfy, and third, a cross followed by a crown. When Peter confesses that Jesus is the Christ, Jesus explains what that means in terms of his betrayal, crucifixion, and resurrection. Then Jesus teaches the disciples that following him as their Christ has a requirement, a reason, and a reward.

Discipleship **requires** a cross. Don't let Twitter and Facebook define "following" Jesus for you. If following Jesus only meant clicking a button, then everybody would do it. "If anyone wants to follow after me, let him deny himself, take up his cross daily, and follow me" (v. 23). Jesus goes to a cross, so we who follow him must go to a cross too. He dies *for* us, and we die *with* him. The cross of suffering and death comes first in the Christian life. As Dietrich Bonhoeffer once put it, "When Christ bids a man to follow him, he bids that man to come and die" (*Cost*, 89). That's the requirement.

This cross is necessary. As the hymn writer puts it, "There is no other way than to trust and obey." We can't follow a crucified Savior without a cross of our own. Some people say, "Yes, Christ is up front carrying the cross, and we are to follow." But they think Christ is up front carrying his cross while we are in a parade behind him, riding floats and waving at the crowds like the queen. We are in a parade, but it's a long parade of men and women, boys and girls, walking—not floating—each hunched over carrying the tool of their own death. This cross-carrying is necessary.

This cross-carrying is humbling, too. "Let him deny himself." We can't follow Jesus and at the same time come first. We have to deny ourselves: say no to our desires so we can say yes to Jesus. He is King; we are servants—slaves of Christ.

This cross-carrying is daily. "Let him . . . take up his cross daily." No vacation. No holidays. No sick days. No summer breaks. Every morning we wake, we must say, "Good morning, my cross." (Now don't say that while you're facing your spouse! Even if your spouse is part of your cross.) Every morning we wake to die to self and the world so we can follow Jesus.

What does this look like, this carrying our cross daily?

*I have been crucified with Christ, and I no longer live, but Christ lives in me. The life I now live in the body, I live by faith in the Son of God, who loved me and gave himself for me.* (Gal 2:20)

*Now those who belong to Christ Jesus have crucified the flesh with its passions and desires.* (Gal 5:24)

*But as for me, I will never boast about anything except the cross of our Lord Jesus Christ. The world has been crucified to me through the cross, and I to the world.* (Gal 6:14)

What's the **reason** we carry our cross? We are required to carry our cross because life lies on the other side of it (v. 24). The death in discipleship is the door to eternal life. Broad is the way that leads to destruction; narrow is the way that leads to life. Nothing in the world—not even the entire world itself—is worth our souls (v. 25). The world is a soulless and soul-destroying system, so we are required to abandon the world to save our souls.

What then is the **reward** for accepting the cross? In the Christian life, first comes the cross, then comes the crown. The reward is a crown, a kingdom. This kingdom is a share in God's glory (v. 26). The kingdom of God is a kingdom of glory. Our blessed hope is the glorious appearing of our Savior from heaven. When that happens, we will see his glory and be transformed into his glory (see 2 Cor 3:18). For all the self-denial and suffering of the cross in this life, those who follow Jesus will receive unending glory and joy in the life to come. Don't be ashamed; look to his glorious coming. This is what makes it wise to die daily in order to live forever. This is why it makes sense to forsake the world in order to gain glory.

For our encouragement and hope, Jesus allowed some to see that glory even before he or they died. That's why in verse 28 Luke flashes forward eight days. He joins the transfiguration to the promise of verse 27 because the transfiguration is a foretaste of the glory that is to come. This glory, this kingdom, this crown is what Jesus provides for all those who take up their cross.

He provides purpose and power, supply and satisfaction, a cross then a crown, and finally . . .

### Triumph and Truth (9:37-45)

There are things we cannot do in the Christian life. Some things are beyond our ability. The disciples in verses 37-40 could not cast the demon out of this man's son. They tried and failed—even though they had been given authority to do so.

The problem apparently was their unbelief. They doubted. That's why Jesus says what he says (v. 41). Some things only come out by prayer and fasting—which are disciplines for the believing. Some things we cannot do in our own strength, and nothing is safe to do in our own strength.

Here's the lesson to learn: our triumph over evil is won by Jesus (v. 42). He defeats all our enemies. Our task is to stand by faith in the victory he has already won. That's what we read in Ephesians 6:10-13:

*Finally, be strengthened by the Lord and by his vast strength. Put on the full armor of God so that you can stand against the schemes of the devil. For our struggle is not against flesh and blood, but against the rulers, against the authorities, against the cosmic powers of this darkness, against evil, spiritual forces in the heavens. For this reason take up the full armor of God, so that you may be able to resist in the evil day, and having prepared everything, to take your stand.*

That's how we triumph—by taking our stand by faith with Christ. That's how we escape being a part of an "unbelieving and perverse generation" (v. 41).

If we triumph with Christ, then Christ will give us his truth. Notice the difference between the disciples and the crowds in verses 43-45. "And they [the crowd] were all astonished at the greatness of God." Now watch this: "While everyone was amazed at all the things he was doing, he told his disciples, 'Let these words sink in: The Son of Man is about to be betrayed into the hands of men.'"

The priceless thing in the text is not the casting out of the demon. The greatest thing about Jesus isn't his miracle-working power. The greatest thing about Jesus is his cross and resurrection. That's the main thing. The crowd missed it because they were dazzled by the exorcism. The crowd is amazed, but belief is more than astonishment. Belief requires revelation from God. True belief requires truth to believe (v. 45). That's what Jesus gives the disciples in verse 44. If we have ears to hear, then we marvel at the truth that Christ died for us.

But the disciples still don't get it (v. 45). They've heard it at least three times in the last couple of weeks—at a prayer meeting with Jesus (v. 18), on the Mount of Transfiguration (v. 31), and here after a miraculous healing. But they don't yet get it. And, tragically, they're too afraid to ask.

My Christian friend, when we walk with Christ, we will see triumph, but the greater thing will be the truths we gather from him. We all need to grow in our knowledge of Jesus. No one's knowledge of the Lord is complete. We're like these disciples, and that's not a wicked thing. We just need to apply ourselves to learning Christ. Sometimes we get to playing church and we get afraid to say we don't understand or know something. That's the mistake these disciples make. We should learn from their mistake. We should not be afraid of the one who died to save us. We should ask that we may know him better.

My non-Christian friend, you've heard this message about Jesus's death, burial, and resurrection to save sinners several times now. Is it still hidden from you? If it is, it's because God has hidden it from you or Satan has snatched away the seed of God's word from your heart. Are you afraid to ask God to protect you from Satan and show you the truth? Don't be afraid. He delights to do it.

> *Now if any of you lacks wisdom, he should ask God—who gives to all generously and ungrudgingly—and it will be given to him. But let him ask in faith without doubting. For the doubter is like the surging sea, driven and tossed by the wind. That person should not expect to receive anything from the Lord, being double-minded and unstable in all his ways.* (Jas 1:5-8)

## Conclusion

Just as in verse 11 with the crowd, Jesus will welcome you and teach you about his kingdom if you ask. Don't be like Herod. Don't be like the disciples who were afraid. Do two things. (1) Ask the Father to show you Jesus so you will know him as Savior and Lord. (2) Ask your Christian friend to explain more about what it means to be a Christian. Don't stop until you have done what is necessary to settle the question, "Who is Jesus?" When you've settled the question, don't stop following him but trust him to provide for you in every way.

The only way to get our deepest needs met in this world is to follow Jesus into the next.

## Reflect and Discuss

1. What do you think about heaven?
2. In your own words, "Who is Jesus?" What things about Jesus do you most treasure? What things about Jesus would you like to understand better?
3. In what ways is Jesus a "greater Moses"?
4. What would you say is your purpose in life? How would that compare to God's purpose for you?
5. Do you believe Jesus will satisfy your needs? Why or why not?
6. How does knowing that the cross comes before the crown help us in our suffering and difficulties as Christians?

# The Great Apostle

## LUKE 9:46–10:24

**Main Idea:** May the Lord of the harvest make us better evangelists.

---

I. **Four Attitude Adjustments for Reaching Others (9:46-62)**
   A. He turns us from pride to humility (9:46-48).
   B. He turns us from tribalism to cooperation (9:49-50).
   C. He turns us from vengeance to mercy (9:51-56).
   D. He turns us from security to sacrifice (9:57-62).
II. **Five Action Items for Reaching Others (10:1-24)**
   A. Pray earnestly (10:1-2).
   B. Go meekly (10:3-4).
   C. Seek peace (10:5-8).
   D. Preach boldly (10:9-16).
   E. Rejoice greatly (10:17-24).
III. **One Aim in Reaching Others (9:48; 10:16)**

---

When the Lord began to give us vision and a hope for Anacostia River Church, he led us to meditate on the book of Titus. And in that book he gave us five *M* objectives to focus on:

- Spreading the *message* of the gospel
- Showing *mercy* to our neighbors
- Supporting the *maturity* of our members
- *Multiplying* church plants and Christian leaders
- Sending international *missionaries*

We reasoned from Scripture that if we could pursue those five objectives, then we would, by God's grace, be a church that follows the Bible and we would, by his grace, reach many of our neighbors for Jesus.

Today's text helps us think about a couple of our *M*s: spreading the message and sending missionaries. In Luke 9–10 that's what we see the Lord Jesus Christ doing. He's training the first disciples to approach people with the message of Christianity. He addresses three things: their attitude, their actions, and their aim.

## Four Attitude Adjustments for Reaching Others
### LUKE 9:46-62

*He Turns Us from Pride to Humility (9:46-48)*

The first attitude adjustment Jesus teaches his followers is to turn them from pride to humility. This lesson comes on the heels of verses 44-45, where Jesus for the second time teaches his disciples that he must be betrayed, crucified, and killed. While Jesus talks about his death, the disciples in verse 46 argue about who is the greatest among them! Everybody wants to be Muhammad Ali. Everybody shouts, "I am the greatest! I am the greatest! I am a baaad man!"

Now what must be in our hearts to even argue with others that we are the greatest? To even enter that argument, a person must have some level of pride. That person must feel pretty good about himself—too good, given that we are all sinners. When you imagine the scene, it all looks rather childish.

Jesus knows their hearts. Almost as if to say, "This is childish," the Lord places a child by his side. A child in that culture was not greatly valued. Children occupied the lowest place in society. So Jesus makes a powerful point by putting this child at his side and saying, in effect, the least of persons in society are greater than you. It's a humbling thing.

More than that, the Lord teaches why being like children makes you greatest in the kingdom. Do you see the logic in verse 48? Jesus means the message is greater than the messenger. Even if the message comes from a little child, the Lord offers *himself* to the world *in the message.* The Christ preached is greater than the preacher of Christ. What makes the child so great in this verse is that the child brings Jesus with him. Why is that so great? It's because in receiving Jesus you also receive God the Father. Which is greater? The child or God? For this reason the messenger is always lower than the message. The main thing is not the *giver* of the message but the *God* in the message.

We need to know this in a day when preachers, their gifts, and their platforms are so widely idolized. Knowing that the message is greater than the messenger keeps us from fighting about who the "great preachers" are. It keeps us from saying as they did in Corinth, "I belong to Paul. I belong to Apollos." Do you remember what Paul said to that? He asked, "What then is Apollos? What is Paul? They are *servants* through whom you believed" (1 Cor 3:4-5; emphasis added). The preacher serves the message. The truly great preachers do not boast in their preaching ability or verbal prowess. The truly great preachers boast in the Lord! There should be no famous preachers—only a famous Savior.

The Lord checks their pride because the message will be lost in their arguing about who is "greatest." If their argument continues unchecked, they will offer the world more of themselves rather than more of Jesus. Sometimes fallen men love themselves too much and exalt Christ too little.

### He Turns Us from Tribalism to Cooperation (9:49-50)

The disciples *see* a man casting out demons (v. 49). This wasn't a rumor or report. They are eyewitnesses to a miracle. This man does the right thing with the right motive. He is "driving out demons in [Jesus's] name." He's doing the work of the Lord.

So we might ask, "Why did they try to stop him?" Why would you stop someone from doing an obviously good thing for an obviously good reason? Why would you stop someone from doing the work of the Lord?

They give us the answer in verse 49: "Because he does not follow us." Their opposition boils down to one fact: he was not in their clique, their group, their little tribe. So they tried to shut him down. They raised their group above the mission itself. That, friends, is tribalism, not Christian ministry.

Tribalism will make you crazy. Here are disciples on their first training mission—they're just *trainees* trying to learn how to do something—and they attempt to stop somebody from *doing* what they're being trained to do. What they attempt to stop isn't error or falsehood. They're trying to stop the work of God. Why? Because the worker wasn't from their tribe.

You know, we have a lot of ways of being tribal, don't we?

- Black vs. white (ethnic tribalism)
- Male vs. female (gender tribalism)
- Reformed vs. Arminian (theological tribalism)
- Young vs. old (generational tribalism)
- Urban vs. suburban (community tribalism)
- Rich vs. middle class vs. poor (class tribalism)
- Republican vs. Democrat (political tribalism)

We could go on. We even combine them to make even smaller tribes: someone might say, "I am a black, male, Reformed, urban, Democrat." We place ourselves in social cliques and act as if no one outside that clique really knows God or really is faithful to do God's work. Then we create shibboleths for testing whether someone really belongs to our tribe. The main thing becomes whether they are "with us" rather than whether they are with Jesus. That's crazy!

Don't get me wrong. There are good and necessary distinctions to be made in life. There is such a thing as truth and falsehood, good and evil, and so on. There is such a thing as a true gospel and false gospels. Regarding those things we do not hesitate to draw and defend lines. But tribalism occurs among people who all name Christ as Lord and believe the same gospel. Because they are not "with us," we are not with them. That attitude is to our shame.

The Lord checks our tribal attitudes and demands an attitude of cooperation (v. 50). If a person isn't against you in God's work but is doing God's work, then that person is *for* you. Tribal people can't see who is actually for them in the gospel. Only cooperative people can see that.

But our Lord's words are a two-edged sword. We may be comfortable saying, "If they are not against us, then they are for us," as long as we assume *we* are the standard and others have to come to us. But can we embrace the statement in the other direction? Can we joyfully conclude, "If we are not against them, then we are for them"? If we cannot, then tribalism probably remains in our hearts and will likely get in the way of our seeing the work of God being done by others. What a tragedy that would be because it will push us into smaller and smaller tribes of isolation and make us doubt that God is at work in the world.

### He Turns Us from Vengeance to Mercy (9:51-56)

Tribalism merely aggravates and inconveniences when it exists by itself. When you add power and anger to tribalism, a destructive potential results.

The Jewish people of Jesus's day had nothing to do with Samaritans. The Samaritans were a people who were part Jewish and part Gentile. So we are surprised to read that Jesus instructed his disciples to enter this village and make preparations to stay there (v. 52).

The Samaritans returned the favor to their Jewish neighbors. They had nothing to do with Jewish people. The situation is rife with ethnic prejudice. When the Samaritans learned that Jesus and his disciples were headed to Jerusalem, they refused to receive the Lord (v. 53). Their prejudice came out. They were nativists. They wanted Samaria for Samaritans. They wanted the foreigners out.

Now the Samaritan attitude is wrong—they opposed the Lord—but the attitude that most needed adjustment was the disciples'. They wanted to call down fire from heaven to consume or kill the people (v. 54). They wished to punish the Samaritans. They were impatient and merciless. Tribalism married to power and vengeance is deadly.

So the Lord rebuked them (v. 55). Some manuscripts record the Lord saying to them, "You do not know what manner of spirit you are of. For the Son of Man did not come to destroy men's lives but to save them" (vv. 55-56 NKJV). We are reminded of James 1:20—"The anger of man does not produce the righteousness of God" (ESV). In sinful, fallen anger the disciples want to call down judgment on people who have refused Jesus. That is not the Christian spirit, beloved. If people in the community reject Christ and us, we should not call for judgment. Judgment will come soon enough. That will be a great and terrible day. While it's still day, our job is to announce the good news: there is a way to escape the coming judgment through repentance and faith in Christ.

If they will not hear the good news, then in mercy we simply keep moving. Luke says, "They went to another village" (v. 55). They didn't argue with the Samaritans. They didn't look to destroy them. They left town. That was the merciful thing to do. The proud would argue. The tribalist would shut them down. The vengeful would destroy them. But the disciple would leave, hoping the Lord might have mercy on them later.

Pride and tribalism in combination with the power to exact vengeance is deadly. If you bolster that with religious zeal, then the deadly force is almost unstoppable. Isn't that what we are witnessing with ISIS? May it never be so among Christ's people. Before we can be of any use to our cities, neighborhoods, and neighbors, we must temper justice with mercy. Otherwise the gospel will not ring true.

This observation applies to at least three situations:

- *Evangelism*: We warn of judgment to come, but we don't call it down. Judgment will come soon enough. We should seek mercy and time for people to eventually hear.
- *Gentrification*: Some community activists sound like Samaritans rejecting strangers. Christians should fight for justice, but that can't look like racializing places in a way that forbids freedom.
- *Political candidates*: Some of our candidates sound like the Samaritans in their immigration policy. Christians should reject any appeal to nativism and vengeance against those who aren't "one of us."

The Lord turns us from pride to humility, from tribalism to cooperation, and from vengeance to mercy.

## He Turns Us from Security to Sacrifice (9:57-62)

In one way or another, each of the three persons in this passage saying they would follow Jesus wanted to do so with the guarantee of security and comfort. Apparently the first person thought he would follow Jesus to some comfortable home, but Jesus says, "The Son of Man has no place to lay his head" (v. 58). The Creator of the universe was homeless in his own creation. That's humility and sacrifice. He divested himself of all the glories and privileges of heaven to enter creation homeless. To follow this Lord means following him into the life he lives. Christ did not come to lead us into riches and mansions in this life. If we would follow him, we will have to sometimes give up home and the safety of home—just as many of you have moved into this neighborhood, forsaking more comfortable and secure places for the sake of Jesus's mission.

The second person wanted to wait and collect the inheritance after his father's death (v. 59). Perhaps he heard Jesus say to the first person that he had no place to live. So he decided first to secure some money of his own so he wouldn't have to follow Jesus poor.

The third person wanted to have more time with his family. He wanted to say his good-byes (v. 61).

Each of these is a failure to commit to Christ at the cost of comfort. The proclamation of the kingdom is at stake in all of this. That's why the Lord tells one person, "Let the dead bury their own dead, but you go and spread the news of the kingdom of God" (v. 60). The Lord tells another, "No one who puts his hand to the plow and looks back is fit for the kingdom of God" (v. 62). Our desire for comfort and security often hinders our obedience to the Great Commission.

Do you remember the parable of the sower in Luke 8? Do you remember how some seed fell among the thorns, which was a symbol for how the word of God is "choked with worries, riches, and pleasures of life, and produce no mature fruit" (8:14)? Isn't that what's happening here? Don't a lot of people find it difficult to follow Jesus because they love the world?

Security smothers sacrifice. That's tragic when the kingdom of God is at stake. Beloved, we want to have a sacrificial attitude because time is short, hell is real, and souls are at stake.

My Christian friend, what are we unwilling to sacrifice so that people may hear of the kingdom and be saved? Which of these attitude adjustments are most necessary in your life? The best gospel work begins in our own hearts before it can reach our neighbors.

To my friends who are not yet Christians, the message we bring we're willing to bring to you in humility, in cooperation, in mercy, and at great sacrifice. Do you think we would go through all of that to bring you something that would hurt you? Do you think the Lord Jesus would require it of us only to abuse you? Certainly not! We recognize we have sometimes failed to have these positive attitudes when speaking to you of Jesus—please forgive us for those failures—but do not let Christians keep you from Christ. Consider the gospel fairly.

The Lord offers you forgiveness and eternal life through faith in him. He died on the cross to pay for your sins. He lived a sinless life to provide your righteousness before God. He was resurrected from the grave as proof that God accepted his sacrifice on your behalf. Now God calls you to repent of your sin and to place your trust and hope of eternal life in Jesus as your personal Lord and Savior. Do not allow God's love to pass you by. Receive it through faith in Christ.

## Five Action Items for Reaching Others
### LUKE 10:1-24

If Luke 9:46-62 was Jesus preparing the disciples for action, then 10:1-24 is Jesus sending them out to do the work. In this work we see five actions the disciples are to take. This is their strategy for reaching their cities and towns.

### Pray Earnestly (10:1-2)

The first great work of Christian evangelism is done on our knees in prayer. We must earnestly seek the Lord to supply laborers. The problem is not that there is no harvest. The problem is that there are too few laborers, too few Christians doing the work of telling people about Jesus. This is why I find the Saturday evangelism teams and stories of workplace evangelism so encouraging. You are doing the work of evangelism. But we need more laborers, for the fields continue to be plentiful.

The Lord commands the disciples to pray. In the following verses he sends them out to do the work. In a real sense they were the answers to their own prayers for laborers. So it is with us. We must pray earnestly, which means we must be prepared to be the answer to the prayers. We cannot be faithful Christians without at least being stumbling evangelists. We don't need to be perfect evangelists with all the answers delivered smoothly from the top of our heads. Remember the example Jesus used of "the great evangelist" (see p. 168). It was a child. Surely all of us can be like children, trusting the Lord, unworried about what we don't know but really consumed with what we do know, telling others in the power that comes from prayer.

Let us be people of earnest prayer so that the plentiful harvest might actually be brought in and the storehouses of God's kingdom filled to overflow with the saved.

### Go Meekly (10:3-4)

The attitude adjustments are crystalized in these two verses. Lambs in the midst of wolves is a picture of danger. Wolves snarl, bare their fangs, circle around, ready to tear into defenseless lambs. Everything that is a predator is stronger than the lamb.

Christ sends his people not into a safe house or monastery but right into the midst of wolves and dangers. He calls the disciples to go without supplies because he will supply for them. He commits to guarding them in the midst of danger and supplying for them in the midst of want.

When we come to Luke 22:35, the Lord nears his death and ascension. Then he instructs them to take their knapsacks and materials as their supply. So now we cooperate together as a church. We combine our resources—which we received from Christ—to carry on the mission of our Lord. This is why we give and then use those resources to buy Bibles and tracts, help in benevolence, and assist community organizations.

The "go" of Luke gets echoed at the end of his Gospel and in the Great Commission. This command applies to every Christian. There is no way to be a Christian and not be a goer—at least across the street or to your child's bedroom. We must meekly go and bear witness to Christ's love.

### Seek Peace (10:5-8)

As ambassadors of peace, we are to seek the people of peace. Our Savior is the Prince of Peace. Sometimes we may meet those who do not return peace. We are to keep moving in such cases. Other times we will meet those who receive us and receive our message. When that happens, we are to share in all good things together. We let our peace rest on them.

We are instructed not to move from house to house. I think the Lord tells his disciples this so they do not develop a reputation for "mooching" off those to whom they must give the gospel. Even today many people think, "The church only wants my money." Beloved, we do not want your money. That is too little a sum in light of eternity. What we want is your soul, and there is nothing you can give in exchange for your soul. The gospel is about whether you spend eternity in hell or heaven, in condemnation or in love. Don't give your money to a church if that's a concern for you. But do give your heart, soul, and life to Christ. Everything else will follow. We do not want what you have; we want you to have our Savior.

## Preach Boldly (10:9-16)

Jesus determines what is preached: "The kingdom of God has come near you" (v. 9). The preacher does not determine the message. A faithful preacher only delivers what Christ has said. By the preaching of the gospel, the kingdom of God comes to men.

Do you see the boldness of this message? Even if rejected, we must proclaim the message in the city streets! We must pronounce the "woe" of God on those who reject his King (vv. 10-15). That warning is an act of mercy. There's nothing more merciful than warning a person to flee a burning building. It requires boldness and love.

We must tell the truth that God is angry about sin. His judgment is near. So is his kingdom.

Some of the most popular preachers today make a big deal of never talking about sin and judgment. Any person who will not speak plainly with you about the state of your soul is not your friend. These people make themselves an enemy of your soul. Any people who will not tell you about the real dangers of a real hell and a coming judgment prove they care nothing about you—even if they tell you smooth things about how wonderful you are and how great you can be. Do not believe them, beloved.

For the message about Jesus to be good news, we must understand the bad news. The bad news is, God is a God of condemnation. The good news is, we can escape his condemnation through faith in his Son. When a preacher says "woe to you" for sexual immorality, laziness, anger, stealing, abandoning your kids, or disobeying your parents or your boss, then that preacher is being a friend to you. Any one of those things and a thousand more are enough to condemn us to hell. If we break one law, then we break all of God's law. God will not wink at sin or turn a blind eye. He will simply ask if we have trusted his Son who takes away wrath by becoming our sin bearer or if we have rejected him and remain in our sin. That is the choice. Receive Christ; believe in him and be saved.

Christian, let us preach this message boldly to all. The message does not change based on the audience's response. Whether the people receive us or reject us, the message remains the same: the kingdom of heaven is near. This means we don't have to worry about what to say. We simply need to know the gospel. If we know the gospel, then we know everything we need to know in order to see our neighbors saved. Preach that message boldly. And remember that what looks like opposition in the beginning ends with a melted heart and sincere faith in the end. Preach boldly.

## Rejoice Greatly (10:17-24)

The seventy-two return with joy that even demons obeyed them in Christ's name. They go from opposing the other man who cast out demons to now being happy to have the same ability. The Lord replies by pointing to Satan's fall from heaven and the power he has delegated to them. However, that's not the basis for their rejoicing. Instead, they should rejoice that their "names are written in heaven" (v. 20). That is a far greater cause for rejoicing than even the ability to cast out demons. We should always rejoice that we are not among those cities and people condemned in God's judgment. We are citizens in the kingdom of heaven. That's been accomplished at great cost and great love—the blood of Christ. No matter what happens in life, we have reason to rejoice if our names are written in heaven!

Second, we should rejoice that God has revealed the truth to us. Verse 22 startles some people. They do not like the idea that God reveals himself to some and not others. I understand. It's alarming. But the burden of the text is verse 21. We are to rejoice in the things that Jesus rejoices in. Our Lord rejoices that God has made the gospel known to those who believe. It's as if God with his own fingers has opened our eyelids and given us sight. He opened our eyes to see Jesus. He removed the scales and glaucoma that blocked our sight of Christ. He touched us and caused us to see. We were once blind and now we see. What made the difference? God revealed himself to us through his Son, and the Son showed us the Father. If you can see God through faith, you ought to rejoice. The most significant spiritual problem in the world today is spiritual blindness. Men don't see this glorious truth, but that's not a reason to think hard thoughts against God. That's a reason to fall on our faces in gratitude for God's kindness to us! Rejoice because you can see!

Third, rejoice as Jesus does because we live in an era that the prophets looked forward to (vv. 23-24). We have the privilege of living in the fulfillment of what they hoped for. They looked forward with fragmentary vision. We look backward to the cross and the full revelation of God in Jesus Christ. We see more than the prophets did because all of the revelation of God is complete and has been given to us. We can know the mind of the Lord through his Word. We have received insider knowledge. We've been pulled aside privately by the Lord and given the glories of the gospel, so we would rejoice and be glad in Christ.

## One Aim in Reaching Others
### LUKE 9:48; 10:16

Perhaps you saw the aim of this passage repeated in the text. We see it in 9:48 and 10:16:

> *Whoever welcomes this little child in my name welcomes me. And whoever welcomes me welcomes him who sent me.*
>     *Whoever listens to you listens to me. Whoever rejects you rejects me. And whoever rejects me rejects the one who sent me.*

These two statements give us the aim in both positive and negative statements. There are only two ways to live. We either receive the messenger and the Savior offered in the message, or we reject the messenger and the message and the God offered in the message. Those are the only two options.

The aim, beloved, is that all people might receive Jesus as he offers himself in the gospel. Once again, if you are not a Christian, we beg you to receive Jesus. Consider Jesus. Consider your sin and the corruption of your heart. Is not sin real? Can you not discern it in your own heart? Do not thoughts of sin travel through your own mind? Do you even need to look beyond your own thoughts to know the reality of sin? Then we open the paper and watch the news where we see sin displayed around the world. Someone once said, "The only doctrine of Christianity for which we have empirical evidence is sin." Isn't that true?

Ask yourself, "Why am I bothered by my sin?" Oh, I know that we are not always bothered. But ask yourself, "Don't I see how I work to not be bothered? How I press down the sense of guilt and shame in order to pursue the sin?" Aren't we bothered because at some deep level we know that our sin is wrong—and "wrong" means something to us? Even if we don't know how we came to know it's wrong, we know that it *is* wrong and we shouldn't do it or desire it. When we let ourselves think about our sin, we feel bad about ourselves and what we've done. Do you know what that's called? It's called "conviction."

Do not push conviction aside. Conviction is a gift of God's grace. It's how God tells us personally that our sins displease him and we should escape them. Let conviction work in your heart and mind. Be convinced of what you already know—that your sin is shameful and wrong. It makes us guilty before God. The answer is not to suppress the knowledge of our sin but to ask, "What can we do about it?"

Perhaps you've asked that question and you've begun to see something more troubling: You've not been able to escape your sin. Everywhere you go, there your sin is with you. You've set out to establish new habits. You've read self-improvement books. You've talked with friends about breaking these patterns. Finally, you've become aware that your sin is stronger than you are and it won't leave you alone just because you ask and try.

I want to offer you something. It's a way to be free of the power and guilt of sin and to be increasingly victorious over sin. One day you will be absolutely free from sin. The offer is this: If you let Christ pay the penalty of your sin and allow Christ to provide a perfect righteousness to God that you cannot provide, and if you put your faith in him and follow him, then he will increasingly free you from sin and make you new. That's what God offers you, and God never makes a promise he does not keep. If you desire to be free from sin, then do not reject Christ. Receive him, and he will make you new.

## Reflect and Discuss

1. Which of the attitude adjustments do you think you need most?
2. Which of the attitude adjustments do you think the Christian church needs most? Why?
3. Luke 10:1-24 provides five action items for reaching others for Christ. Which of these are strengths for you? Which are weaknesses?
4. Do you have a specific plan for praying for workers to enter the harvest? If not, talk with others about how they organize their prayer lives to pray for the nations and for Christian workers.

# Daily Life in the Kingdom

## LUKE 10:25–11:13

**Main Idea:** To sit at the Lord's feet and learn from him and to persist in prayer until filled with the Spirit describes the victorious life God offers to his children.

---

I. **The Inheritance God Gives Cannot Be Earned (10:25-37).**
II. **The Inheritance God Gives Cannot Be Taken Away (10:38-42).**
III. **The Inheritance God Gives Cannot Be Imagined (11:1-13).**
  A. He explains the pattern of prayer (11:2-4).
  B. He emphasizes persistence in prayer (11:5-10).
  C. We expect provision from prayer (11:11-13).

---

What is Easter about? Is it about pretty dresses and new suits? Is Easter about egg hunts and baskets with surprises? Or is Easter only about another day off work? Perhaps time with family?

Theories and ideas about Easter show up everywhere. Some people think Easter is actually a pagan holiday based on worshiping the sun. Others tell us that Easter is about Jesus and what his early followers thought of him, but they quickly tell us that those first followers were wrong about the resurrection. They tell us the early disciples were so stricken with grief over the crucifixion that they made up the story to feel better or to make some spiritual point. Some say the resurrection was a mass delusion caused by the trauma of the crucifixion.

It's amazing how many ways there are to *not* celebrate Easter. There are a variety of ways to twist its meaning. People seem to invent ways to be religious at Easter without really enjoying Jesus.

Luke 10:25–11:13 carries the burden of helping us understand that the greatest thing in the world is to know and enjoy Jesus. In one sense, knowing and enjoying Jesus is precisely what Easter is about—God's doing everything he needs to do to bring creatures separated from him because of sin back to him. We celebrate the resurrection because without it there is no good news. We would still be in our sin separated from God. But we also celebrate the resurrection because through it we get to know and enjoy Christ as our living Lord.

The major idea of "inheritance" runs through this section of Scripture. We see it in 10:25. We see it in another way in 10:42 ("choice"). We see the entire idea reflected in 11:1-13 in the Father's giving good gifts. The text reminds us that there is something we are meant to possess and enjoy as a gift from God.

Three major comments regarding this inheritance run through this section:

> *"You've answered correctly. Do this and* you will live." (10:28; emphasis added)

> *"Martha, Martha, you are worried and upset about many things, but one thing is necessary. Mary has made* the right choice, *and it will not be taken away from her."* (10:41-42; emphasis added)

> *"If you then, who are evil, know how to give good gifts to your children, how much more will the heavenly Father* give the Holy Spirit *to those who ask him?"* (11:13; emphasis added)

## The Inheritance God Gives Cannot Be Earned
### LUKE 10:25-37

That's the major point from the discussion between the lawyer and the Lord Jesus. The lawyer is not sincere. He "stood up to test [Jesus]" (v. 25). This lawyer thinks he's smart. But here's a tip for us all: If you're ever going to test Jesus, do it sitting down. You won't have as far to fall when you fail!

Here's a second tip: Don't play games with the most important question in the universe. Do you see what the lawyer asks as a test? "Teacher, what must I do to inherit eternal life?" (v. 25). That's an incredibly important question. There's never been a more important question.

"Eternal life" is what many people think of when we use the term *heaven*. The word *eternal* means "forever." This life is forever-life with God as it was meant to be with God. Eternal life is life to the fullest extent possible. That's what the lawyer asks about. And that's the question that should be on the mind of every person who will one day die.

Before we think about Jesus's answer, notice that the man assumes there is something he can or must *do* to earn eternal life. It seems natural to think that way, doesn't it? Most people in the world think there's something they must do or stop doing to earn God's approval. But watch how this unfolds.

The man is a lawyer. In ancient Israel the lawyers or scribes studied God's law and interpreted it for the people. So Jesus turns the lawyer's attention to the law (v. 26). When we are getting to know Jesus, it's helpful to recognize that Jesus believes the Bible to be God's word. He believes the law to have been given by God to Israel. Jesus thinks the place to find the most important answer to the most important question ever asked is in the most important book ever written. The answer cannot be found in philosophy books. The answer cannot be found in self-help books. The answer cannot be discovered in other religious books. The answer to the question of eternal life lies in God's law, the Old Testament, the Bible. If Jesus trusts the Bible, then we should trust the Bible.

This man is a good lawyer. He understands what he has been studying. In response to Jesus's question, he summarizes the whole law: "Love the Lord your God with all your heart, with all your soul, with all your strength, and with all your mind; and your neighbor as yourself" (v. 27). The lawyer quotes the *shema* of Deuteronomy 6:5 and Leviticus 19:18. Jesus confirms that his answer is spot on (v. 28).

Then comes the twist. Then comes the sharp point the lawyer wasn't ready for. The Lord goes on to say, "Do this, and you will live" (v. 28). In other words, obey God's commandments *perfectly*, and you will have eternal life. Perfect obedience to God's command to love him and love our neighbors is one way to gain eternal life.

But we *can't* perfectly do all that God commands. We have not done it. If perfect obedience to the law is one way to live forever, then all of us are going to die guilty. That's the hook. That's the twist. If we have to *do* something, then we're doomed to hell. There remains a massive difference between answering correctly *theologically* and living perfectly *practically*. The lawyer knows in his head what is the correct answer, but he cannot do with his life what is the correct answer. This exchange illustrates the Bible's teaching that the law was not given to us for righteousness but to expose our sin and lead us to a Savior.

I believe this lawyer felt guilty in that moment. When the Lord told the lawyer his answer was correct and he needed to *do* it, that lawyer immediately began searching for an excuse. He saw that *perfectly* loving God and loving neighbor was impossible. I bet you he remembered in that moment or felt in his soul the ways and times he'd failed at this. He was guilty, and he knew it.

That's why the scribe replies as he does in verse 29. He was guilty, but he wanted to justify himself, to find a way to be right in his own sight, a way to say, "I am a good guy." He couldn't do that by obeying God perfectly. None of us can. The only way to do that is to fudge on the law. He had to somehow lower the requirements to a point where he could do it. So he asked, "Who is my neighbor?"

That's what people often do when they see that they've broken God's law. They look for a way out, an excuse, a loophole, some way to say that they're not that bad and God should cut them some slack. Do you think a holy, sinless God will cut an unholy, sinful person some slack? "Do not be deceived; God is not mocked" (Gal 6:7 ESV). Rather than loosen the definition of "neighbor," Jesus radically expands it. The Lord tells the story of the good Samaritan (vv. 30-35), a story that blows all the categories of the day. The story

- features the brokenness of this sinful world (v. 30),
- exposes the emptiness of religion without love (vv. 31-32),
- challenges the racism and prejudice we all can feel (v. 33), and
- requires sacrifice and risk (vv. 34-35).

When Jesus asks, "Which of these three do you think proved to be a neighbor to the man who fell into the hands of the robbers?" he radically redefines *neighbor* and practically demonstrates what it looks like to love God and neighbor. That lawyer never in his wildest dreams thought God would define his neighbor as a *hurting man* in a *rough part of town* from a *different ethnic group* who *needed his compassion.*

The lawyer also never thought that God the Son would come into the world to be this kind of neighbor to him. He had no idea that he was at that moment speaking to the true Neighbor that the Samaritan only symbolized. The Lord Jesus does everything the Samaritan did and more when he suffers crucifixion in our place and is raised from the grave for our justification and eternal life.

- The Lord Jesus sees our brokenness in sin and comes to us in compassion.
- Jesus demonstrates God's love for us in this: while we were still sinners, Jesus Christ died for us on the cross (Rom 5:8).
- Jesus brings an end to racism. He reconciles us to God and to one another through his body on the tree (Gal 3:28; Eph 2:14).
- Jesus pays the cost for our salvation by shedding his blood.
- Jesus is coming again to receive us into eternal life and a never-ending kingdom.

The Lord Jesus Christ does for us everything we could not do when it comes to obeying God and paying the penalty for our sin. We were left for dead in our sin; but Christ rescues us, heals us, and pays for our needs by his grace. He freely gives to us what we could never earn. He gives to the world the hope of eternal life based on his perfect obedience to God and sacrifice of his life. So those who repent of their sins and trust in him receive as a gift eternal life from God. What the Lord Jesus gives we cannot earn.

### Race, Class, and Samaritan Concern

The call in the story of the good Samaritan applies to all of us. This text motivates our living and witness in the community. We hope to be a church that lives in the community and for the community so we might be a blessing to the community. We want to be those like the good Samaritan who welcome inconvenience and lay down our lives for those in need.

I love the church I serve. I love the way it models the ethics of the good Samaritan so well. A good number of the members are crossing ethnic and cultural lines to lay down their lives to minister to those from different backgrounds in our community. We have white, Hispanic, and Asian brothers and sisters among us. They now live in a community that remains about 90 percent African-American. They now struggle with some things many of us have experienced when we have been in predominantly white settings. This congregation recalls the cost that was paid to be in those settings. We remember the insecurity we sometimes felt or how we pushed back feelings of uncertainty about whether we were welcome. We now have white, Hispanic, and Asian brethren feeling the same things. It is our task and privilege as Samaritans to cross the bridge to assure them, encourage them, and love them just as it was their task to cross the bridge with the gospel into a community not their own. We must meet one another on that bridge, bringing grace and mercy to one another.

We have in my church family homeless persons and persons who are K Street lawyers. God by sovereign design has sent us people from every point on the economic and class spectrum. As James 2 instructs, we must not show favoritism but have an equal concern for each member of the body (see also 1 Cor 12:24-25). We must cross the class divide. The world would separate us along those lines, but Christ in his body has transcended those barriers to make us one. We do this to make the mercy and inclusion of God known to our neighbors.

For those of us who have received eternal life, we must now prove ourselves to be true neighbors (v. 37). We exist as a church in this community to "go and do the same" individually and collectively with our neighbors.

## The Inheritance God Gives Cannot Be Taken Away
### LUKE 10:38-42

This is a well-known passage in the Christian world. Jesus visits the home of a woman named Martha. Now that doesn't sound like much in our day. But in Jesus's day, a Jewish rabbi or religious leader would never receive hospitality by a woman this way. If the parable of the good Samaritan exposes racism and ethnic prejudice as anti-Christian, then this story exposes sexism as anti-Christian. Our Lord, from the beginning, loves and includes women among his disciples and in his fellowship.

He visits Martha's house. Martha's sister, Mary, "sat at the Lord's feet and was listening to what he said" (v. 39). Meanwhile, "Martha was distracted by her many tasks" (v. 40). This is a real-life circumstance. I watch my daughters argue almost every day about whose turn it is to load the dishwasher, who put up the dishes last, and on and on. By the time they finish arguing, they could've washed all the dishes! Mary and Martha have something like that going on.

Martha "came up and asked, 'Lord, don't you care that my sister has left me to serve alone?'" (v. 40). Martha's comment strikes me for all kinds of reasons. First, you've probably met a Martha before. She is happy to serve, but somehow her serving makes her sour. She's a little bossy. "Tell her to give me a hand." She's a little impatient with people she thinks aren't helping enough. Churches can be full of Marthas. Second, Martha is bold, isn't she? She's in the Lord's grill. She's got a rag in one hand and the other hand on her hip. Third, Martha accuses the Lord of not caring about her serving alone. Now how many women have felt something like that? You serve your family every day, but there doesn't seem to be a lot of thanks. You wonder if what you do as a wife, mother, or woman matters in the Lord's sight. You quietly ask, "Does anybody notice? Does God care?"

The routine never ends early. She rises before everyone else in the home. The husband still snores. The children turn in their beds. She gets little help and little thanks. Kids must be prepared for school.

Breakfast has to be put on the table. Book bags have to be inspected. Then there's the drive to school. It all has to happen with enough time to get yourself together and get to work. Then you've got to hustle after school to pick up the kids, get dinner on the table, check homework, and squeeze in discipline, correction, or instruction with the kids. You feel as if you're the only one doing anything. He hasn't helped nearly enough or said thanks. No one seems to notice, and you're exhausted.

My wife describes housework as constantly putting pearls on a necklace with no knot at the end of the string. There's a futility in the beauty of it all. The sense that life as a woman, a mother, or a wife "doesn't count" haunts a lot of women. Maybe that sense that there's too much to do as a woman keeps creeping in on you.

Judith Warner, a sociologist, has captured this feeling in her book, *Perfect Madness: Motherhood in the Age of Anxiety*:

> This book is an exploration of a feeling. That caught-by-the-throat feeling so many mothers have today of always doing something wrong. And it's about a conviction I have that this feeling—this widespread, choking cocktail of guilt and anxiety and resentment and regret—is poisoning motherhood for American women today. Lowering our horizons and limiting our minds. Sapping energy that we should have for ourselves and our children. And drowning out thoughts that might lead us, collectively, to formulate solutions.
>
> The feeling has many faces, but it doesn't really have a name. It's not depression. It's not oppression. It's a mix of things, a kind of too-muchness. An existential discomfort. A mess. (Warner, *Perfect Madness*, 3–4)

I think she perfectly describes the "too-muchness" and messiness a lot of women face. What's the answer to that "too-muchness"? Martha thinks the answer is to get more help.

Jesus gives a different answer. Jesus says to Martha and women (and men) everywhere: In all your busyness don't forget that only one thing is necessary. That one thing is not the next task on your to-do list. That one thing is not serving others. The one necessary thing is enjoying the Lord himself.

That's what Mary chose. The Lord calls it "the right choice." And it "will not be taken away from her" (v. 42). The use of the word *choice* is interesting. It's related to the lawyer's use of the word *inherit* in verse

25. Throughout the Bible, God says that he himself is the "portion" or "inheritance" of his people.

> *Who do I have in heaven but you? And I desire nothing on earth but you. My flesh and my heart may fail, but God is the strength of my heart, my* portion *forever.* (Ps 73:25-26; emphasis added)

> *Because of the LORD's faithful love we do not perish, for his mercies never end. They are new every morning; great is your faithfulness! I say, "The LORD is my* portion, *therefore I will put my hope in him."* (Lam 3:22-24; emphasis added)

The purpose of eternal life is enjoying the Lord as your portion. The reason we are saved is to enjoy God. To sit with him. To listen to him. To talk with him. To treasure him as our inheritance. The Lord Jesus is the good portion we should choose before or instead of being busy with all kinds of acts of service.

And not only is the Lord our portion, but we are his portion, too. Deuteronomy 32:9 says, "The LORD's portion is his people." We inherit him, and he inherits us. And here's the wonderful promise: When Jesus is your portion, he "will not be taken away from" you. The Lord is forever ours. We are forever his. Nothing will ever separate us from his love. No one will ever pluck us from his hand. Never will he leave us; never will he forsake us. The Lord is our portion and inheritance forever. That's why Mary has chosen the one necessary thing: sitting at Jesus's feet in the fellowship of his word.

Here's what I had to ask myself writing this: If the Lord is my portion and he is never taken away from me, how much of my day is he sitting, waiting for me to notice he is the one necessary thing? Far too often I tragically miss out on sitting at his feet, pushing back on the busyness of the world, to savor the love of the Lord. Let us repent together of this and be a people who enjoy the salvation the Lord purchased for us. Let us go to Christ with the comforting promise, "It will not be taken away from us."

Husbands, one of the best ways you can love your wife is to make sure she has time to meet with the Lord. Rearrange the family schedule. Take on more of the household responsibilities. Rescue her from the children. Do whatever is necessary for her to have adequate time to sit like Mary at the Lord's feet. It's an everyday expression of love that will bless her soul immensely.

Practicing a benign neglect of things that can be neglected in order to commune with Christ is a great privilege to the Christian.

## The Inheritance God Gives Cannot Be Imagined
### LUKE 11:1-13

Jesus "was praying in a certain place" (v. 1). A disciple saw him and asked, "Lord, teach us to pray" (v. 1). That request means prayer is not something learned automatically. Prayer is not natural. Effective prayer has to be taught and learned. There's no shame in not knowing how to pray or feeling uncomfortable in prayer. There's only shame if we don't ask to be taught and as a result spend years of our Christian lives ineffective in prayer.

In response to their request, Jesus shows them three things about prayer.

*He Explains the Pattern of Prayer (11:2-4)*

First, Jesus explains the pattern of prayer. We see this in Luke's abbreviated version of the Lord's Prayer. He doesn't mean their prayers should be limited to these exact words. He means that these are the kinds of priorities that should shape their prayer lives. It's a kind of template.

They are to address God as "Father" (v. 2). Prayer is something that happens between the Father and his children. It's a family conversation. There is to be intimacy in it.

They are to ask for two things related to God: (1) that his name be honored and (2) that his kingdom come. They are to pray that God's name would be "holy" (v. 2) and revered. To honor God's name is to respect God's person. They're praying for the fear of the Lord to grip the hearts of men. To pray for his kingdom to come is to pray for the eternal life the lawyer asked about. It's to pray for the Lord to return, to resurrect the dead, and to bring in eternity where sickness and death are no more, only love and joy with him. Their prayer ought to begin with God and focus them on the kingdom.

Then they are to ask three things for themselves: (1) daily bread, (2) forgiveness of sins, and (3) protection from temptation. They are to depend on God for all their daily needs, including the daily need for forgiveness and victory over temptation. And just as disciples have received forgiveness, they are also to give forgiveness.

That's the pattern: first pray for God's kingdom, then for man's needs. This pattern keeps us from wandering all over the place in prayer or from simply praying the same things. This structure gives us direction.

## He Emphasizes Persistence in Prayer (11:5-10)

Just having a pattern of prayer won't make us prayer warriors. We also need determination. To truly pray, Jesus wants us to understand that we must persist in prayer. We can't ask for something one time then go off as if we never asked anything of the Lord. It's persistence that gets the results.

Maybe we're helped to understand this story if we bring it up to our day. Imagine you receive a phone call at midnight. What's the first thing you think? *Who's calling at this time of the night?* They call again. This time you might check the caller ID. But you don't answer the phone, do you? You say to yourself? *I wonder what they want?* Nevertheless, you roll over saying, "It can wait 'til morning." Then the phone rings again, and you think, *She isn't going to leave me alone. I better answer the phone!*

It's the caller's persistence that gets the assistance. So Jesus says in verses 9-10, "Ask . . . seek . . . knock." Those are continuous verbs. These are actions we're supposed to start and not stop.

The pattern of verses 2-4 plus the persistence of verses 5-10 equals effective prayer.

## We Expect Provision from Prayer (11:11-13)

No good father would answer his child's request with an evil substitute (vv. 11-12). If an evil man gives good answers to his children's requests, how much more will our heavenly Father give us his best?

Matthew 7:11 ends this same saying of Jesus with "How much more will your Father in heaven give good things to those who ask him." Luke gets more specific: "How much more will the heavenly Father give *the Holy Spirit* to those who ask him?"

God gives his children the best answers to their prayers. He gives himself. He gave his Son to us on the cross, and he gives his Spirit to us for daily living. He who did not spare his own Son but gave him up for us all, how will he not along with him give us every good thing?

We can live in daily dependence on God because our Father will give us the one necessary thing: the Holy Spirit. Through the Spirit, God provides all we truly need to defeat temptation, forgive sin, and find daily bread.

## Conclusion

Many Christians are *almost* following Jesus.

- They believe they love God, but they do not show compassion to their neighbors.
- They are busy doing acts of service, but they do not sit at Jesus's feet.
- They offer up prayers, but they do not persist until they receive the Spirit in power.

They are *almost* living a victorious Christian life. But "almost" only counts in horseshoes and hand grenades. We don't want to settle for an almost Christian life. We want to enter into the eternal life Christ has purchased for us. We want to sit at the Lord's feet to learn his ways. We want to persist in prayer as the children of God until filled with the Spirit. That's the life the Lord gives all who believe in him. It's the best life possible. Live this life today and each day.

## Reflect and Discuss

1. Why do people seem to naturally think gaining eternal life is a matter of what we do?
2. What are ways you can "go and do likewise" following the Samaritan's example? In your church? In your community?
3. How does the parable of the good Samaritan show us Jesus is the true neighbor?
4. Do you identify most with Martha or Mary? If Martha, how will you become less busy and more often at his feet?
5. How can the Lord's teaching about prayer help you abide at his feet?

# The Only Way

## LUKE 11:14–12:12

**Main Idea:** Jesus is the only way to God.

---

I. **The Only Way to Be on God's Side Is to Join Jesus in His Work (11:14-26).**
   A. A divided kingdom cannot stand (11:17-19).
   B. The kingdom of God is here (11:20-22).
   C. Don't be recaptured by Satan's kingdom (11:23-26).
II. **The Only Way to Have Light in Our Hearts Is to Obey Jesus's Word (11:27-36).**
   A. Don't miss the greater sign (11:29-32).
   B. Don't suffer the more severe condemnation (11:33-36).
   C. Don't reject the gospel.
III. **The Only Way to Be Clean before God Is to Offer Jesus Our Souls (11:37-54).**
   A. First point: Pharisees are hypocrites (11:39-41).
   B. Second point: The Pharisees will be condemned (11:42-44).
   C. Third point: Scribes are hypocrites to be condemned too (11:45-52)!
   D. Main point: Give your soul to the Lord if you would be clean (11:41).
IV. **The Only Way to Be Safe before God Is to Acknowledge Jesus before Men (12:1-12).**
   A. Fear the coming judgment (12:1-3).
   B. Fear the Father (12:4-7).
   C. Fear the Son (12:8-9).
   D. Fear the Holy Spirit (12:10-12).

---

One objection many people have to Christians and Christianity is that they think we are narrow-minded for insisting that Jesus is the only way to God or to heaven. They ask, "What about the billions of people on earth who are not Christians and who are good people? Will they fail to reach heaven just because they don't believe in Jesus or have never heard of him?"

Many people think all roads lead to God. What matters, they say, is being sincere. If you're a person of sincere belief, whatever the belief, then your religious approach is as good as any other, and people shouldn't condemn you for it. They reject the exclusive claims of Christianity.

We can understand those views. If all religions *are* equally true or equally false, then it wouldn't matter much. We'd simply have to make our choice and go happily on our way. It *would* be arrogant and narrow-minded to insist on one way if all the ways were equal.

But what if they are *not* equally true or false? What if some religious views are false or incomplete? What if the idea that Jesus is the only way was not something his followers made up? What if that was actually what Jesus himself thought and taught?

Inside the DNA of Christianity is a claim Jesus himself made. It remains an exclusive claim.

## The Only Way to Be on God's Side Is to Join Jesus in His Work
### LUKE 11:14-26

Verse 14 opens with Jesus casting out a demon. It's a simple but profound scene. Jesus drives out the demon. The demon that caused the man's muteness leaves. The man speaks. But these simple actions reveal profound truths.

- Demons are real. Their activity in the New Testament seems to cluster around the earthly ministry of our Lord.
- Demons sometimes afflict people.
- Jesus rules over and casts out demons.

The crowds "were amazed" (v. 14). But two groups of people respond in two different ways. The **slanderers** say, "He drives out demons by Beelzebul, the ruler of the demons" (v. 15). And the **skeptics**, "as a test, were demanding of him a sign from heaven" (v. 16).

The Lord addresses the first group in verses 17-26. He gives us some teaching on spiritual warfare. Then the Lord ends his sermon by dividing the world into two groups: those who are with him and those who are against him.

## A Divided Kingdom Cannot Stand (11:17-19)

No group will last long if it's fighting itself. It will fall. So Jesus says that the idea that he casts out Satan by satanic power makes no sense whatsoever (vv. 17-18). Why would Beelzebul fight against Beelzebul? He'd be destroying his own kingdom.

Apparently there were Jewish exorcists at the time. So Jesus asks about their own sons who cast out demons (v. 19). Are they under Beelzebul's power as well? The Lord points out the hypocrisy of the slanderers.

## The Kingdom of God Is Here (11:20-22)

If a divided kingdom cannot stand, then that must mean a new kingdom has come. Jesus tells the crowds that he drives out demons "by the finger of God" (v. 20). That's a wonderful phrase. It takes us back to two amazing scenes in the book of Exodus. In Exodus 8:19 Moses struck Egypt with the plague of gnats. Pharaoh wanted his magicians to copy the plague in order to discredit Moses, but the magicians couldn't do it. They turned to Pharaoh and said, "This is the finger of God." In other words, this is genuine power from God, not witchcraft or trickery. In Exodus 31:18, when God finished giving Moses the Ten Commandments on two stone tablets, the Bible says the tablets were "inscribed by the finger of God." The phrase shows up in the Bible when God's power and revelation in redemption advances in a new way.

When Jesus says he casts out demons by the finger of God, it's a way of referring to the direct power and action of God in the situation. Our Lord is the strong man of verses 21-22. He overpowers Satan's house and takes away the spoils. But some in the crowd could not see it. They missed the kingdom of God among them.

## Don't Be Recaptured by Satan's Kingdom (11:23-26)

So Jesus warns the crowd not to be recaptured by Satan's kingdom. Unless Christ cleans a person like a house and then lives in him, that person will be indwelt by demons. People are in danger of being overcome again if they don't come into God's realm. If Israel rejects their Messiah, then their end will be worse than their beginning (v. 26). We do not get better by rejecting the gospel. We do not grow in health, strength, and prosperity by hearing the word of God and rejecting it.

The way to spiritual soundness cannot be found by rejecting the power of God.

There are only two sides in this warfare: "Anyone who is not with me is against me, and anyone who does not gather with me scatters" (v. 23). Our Lord makes this exclusive claim about himself. Jesus puts himself forward as the only way to do the work of God. He basically says a person is either with him or against him in doing or failing to do God's work. There are no other options. There is no neutral ground, no Switzerland. The way we know which side we're on is by whether we gather with him or scatter against him. In other words, do we try to gather people through sharing the good news about Jesus, or do we scatter them by failing to share the good news?

Perhaps you are not yet a Christian. Have you ever thought of yourself as being against God? Most people do not. These religious Jewish people did not think of themselves that way either. Yet here they are opposing the Son of God. I wonder if you see that there is no middle ground. In the warfare for your own soul, you are not neutral. You had better not try to be neutral. You had better be for the betterment of your soul. The only way to do that is to be with Jesus. He is the only way to enter into the work and kingdom of God. All of us not with Jesus are against him and against ourselves by not being with him.

When we say Jesus is the only way, it's not a matter of Christians being proud, feeling themselves superior to others. We did not assert this simply because we are Christians and boastful. That's not what is going on at all. Actually, we are saying the kingdom of God has come into the world through a person, Jesus Christ the Son of God. We're saying Jesus is the only door through which you can enter. So we point to him that you might know the one way in. All the other doors lead to destruction, but Christ leads to the kingdom and power of God.

## The Only Way to Have Light in Our Hearts Is to Obey Jesus's Word
### LUKE 11:27-36

You know, it's funny. You never know where your "amen" is going to come from. The crowds don't always say "amen" at the right time. A woman in the crowd gets a little happy. So she yells out, "Blessed is the womb that bore you and the one who nursed you!" It's a curious thing to shout, but she's trying to "amen" the Lord.

The Lord replies, "Rather, blessed are those who hear the word of God and keep it" (v. 28). With those words the Lord redirects the woman. There is no hint of the Roman Catholic idea of the veneration of Mary. If ever there were a place for our Lord to teach such a thing, it would be here in this context. He would only need to "amen" her blessing. Instead, the Lord turns the woman's attention and our attention away from Mary to God's Word.

There is promise and warning in verse 28. The thing that counts is obeying the Word of God. That is the "blessed" or "happy" way of life. That's the promise. The Lord has a conception of blessedness that includes all those who keep God's Word. The related warning is this: it's possible to hear the Word of God but not obey it.

### Don't Miss the Greater Sign (11:29-32)

Verses 29-32 illustrate how this happens. Here Jesus answers the skeptics from verse 16. Some people in the crowd demanded a sign from heaven. Jesus responds that the only sign this evil generation will receive is "the sign of Jonah" (v. 29).

Jesus has just said you have to obey the Word of God; now he is referring to it. The Lord compares himself to the prophet Jonah. God recruited Jonah to go to the wicked people of Nineveh. But Jonah disobeyed and tried to run the other way. God prepared a great fish that swallowed Jonah and spat him up on the shores of Nineveh where God originally told him to go. Jonah was in the belly of the fish three days and three nights (see Matt 12:40). The Lord says those three days and three nights were "the sign of Jonah." In other words, those three days, like all signs, pointed forward to something greater. The Lord says that he is the greater Jonah. He will be dead in the belly of the earth for three days, but then he will be resurrected. That's a far greater miracle than Jonah's.

With these words Jesus teaches that if we read our Bibles well, then we are reading about him. He sees in the story of Jonah a pointer to his own passion and resurrection.

Then the Lord looks back in the Scriptures to the account of the "queen of the south" (v. 31), likely Ethiopia, who comes to seek wisdom from King Solomon. The Lord declares that anyone who knows the

Scriptures would know that he is Wisdom personified. The wisdom of Solomon was simply a foretaste of the Wisdom of God (1 Cor 1:30; Col 2:2-3). He explains that one greater than Solomon is standing before them.

### Don't Suffer the More Severe Condemnation (11:33-36)

Yet the people of Jesus's day miss the sign. That's the point of this parable. Their eyes are bad, which means they focus on evil rather than light. Their sight is darkened, and so their entire bodies are darkened.

Their condemnation will be more severe than the judgment against the queen of the south—even though she was a Gentile—because she pursued and acknowledged God's wisdom. Their condemnation will be worse than the people of Nineveh—even though those people were Gentiles—because Nineveh repented at Jonah's preaching.

Jesus takes an ancient prophet from the Bible and the events from that prophet's life, and he says those things were really signs about him. Two things should be evident: The only way to read the Bible properly is to read it understanding that it is ultimately about Jesus. And Jesus sees himself as central to God's work of salvation.

### Don't Reject the Gospel

The only way to enter the kingdom is to hear God's Word and recognize the sign of the cross and the empty tomb. The only way is by hearing and obeying the Word of God, beginning with the gospel. It is by believing the gospel that light enters our souls.

> *For the time has come for judgment to begin with God's household, and if it begins with us, what will the outcome be for those who disobey the gospel of God?* (1 Pet 4:17)

> *[God will afflict the ungodly when Jesus] takes vengeance with flaming fire on those who don't know God and on those who don't obey the gospel of our Lord Jesus. They will pay the penalty of eternal destruction from the Lord's presence and from his glorious strength.* (2 Thess 1:8-9)

*The finger of God points you to the kingdom of God through faith in the Son of God so you might escape the wrath of God.* The people in Jesus's day missed it and were condemned. Will you miss it, or will you obey? Will you repent and believe? Or will you suffer condemnation forever?

## The Only Way to Be Clean before God
## Is to Offer Jesus Our Souls
### LUKE 11:37-54

When the crowd questions him, Jesus the preacher shows no fear of the people in public. The scene changes: Jesus no longer hangs out with the crowds. He now sits as invited guest in the private home of an unnamed Pharisee. Apparently there are also other guests there. Verse 45 mentions "one of the experts in the law." It seems to be a private gathering of some major Jewish religious leaders—Pharisees and scribes.

The Pharisees are upset because Jesus didn't wash his hands according to their custom (vv. 37-38). The issue was not Jesus's cleanliness; the issue was the Pharisees' traditions. They want Jesus to show respect for their religious customs even though their customs really have nothing to do with God's commands.

So what does the Lord Jesus do? He preaches another sermon *in the Pharisee's home*. We might call this sermon "The Problem with Legalists." It goes something like this:

### First Point: Pharisees Are Hypocrites (11:39-41)

The Pharisees are so worried about outward appearances that they have neglected the state of their hearts. What matters most is not outward obedience alone. What matters is *both* outward behavior *and* inwardly clean hearts.

Might I remind you that Jesus is saying these things to his host? He shows no fear, and he is not done.

### Second Point: The Pharisees Will Be Condemned (11:42-44)

A message of "woe" was designed to make the people go, "Whoa!" Here Jesus pronounces three woes on the Pharisees, each revealing why they are unclean.

*You don't love justice or love God* (v. 42). They were specific about giving a tenth of their mint and herbs, but they were specious about God. I was never more convinced than I am now that the Pharisees are not only an ancient Jewish sect but are alive and well today. To meet one, all you need to do is speak of "justice" as a Christian and they come out in force. Just the mention of the word angers them. The insinuation that there is some injustice in the world for us to confront causes them to gnash their teeth and sharpen their pencils so they can detail the exact rules of "Christian engagement," so they can dot all their theological i's and cross all their theological t's while neglecting true justice, compassion, and the love of God. Jesus thinks the Pharisees' approach is not what it means to follow him—to do the first (tithe) and neglect the second (justice, mercy, love). The Lord would indeed have us be scrupulous about the small things but to then go on to complete the larger matters of the law (Matt 23:23). We cannot neglect the love of God and love of neighbor when the whole law is summed up in these points.

*You do love yourselves* (v. 43). They want applause and popularity, not God. They want to *be* worshiped, not *offer* worship. They think little of God but much of themselves. It's possible to use religion for popularity and privilege. That's the Pharisees.

*You lay traps for others* (v. 44). In Judaism touching a grave made a person unclean. Jesus says to this Pharisee that following him is like walking across an unmarked grave. Men walk right into the unclean grave of hypocrisy without even knowing it.

That's the problem with Pharisees, and they are sternly judged for it.

### Third Point: Scribes Are Hypocrites to Be Condemned, Too! (11:45-52)

Now this is funny. Just as Jesus finishes rebuking the Pharisee, a scribe speaks up in verse 45. He says, "Teacher, when you say these things you insult us too." Jesus responds, "Woe also to you experts in the law!" (v. 46). Jesus turns to the scribes and pronounces three woes against them, too!

*You burden the people with the law without helping them* (v. 46). Jesus does his work by the finger of God, but these people will not lift a finger to relieve others.

*You bury the prophets like your ancestors did without seeing the condemnation* (vv. 47-51). The Lord tells them the fruit doesn't fall far from the tree. They are just like their fathers before them.

*You block the path to salvation without entering it* (v. 52). What a devastating condemnation of these religious leaders. Perhaps the hottest parts of hell are reserved for such religious leaders, who knowing the gospel will not preach it, who knowing the entrance to heaven will not point it out, who will not enter that blessed kingdom themselves and forbid others also.

The Lord tells them that their guilt remains on their hands. They are not saved and keep others from being saved. These are *not* the kind of preachers you want for your soul. The agony of their condemnation will be terrible.

## Main Point: Give Your Soul to the Lord if You Would Be Clean (11:41)

"But give *from what is within* to the poor, and then everything is clean for you" (emphasis added). The Lord offers this gospel to those who know that their lives are messed up because of sin and that they need a Savior. They know their need for repentance, and they delight to turn to the Lord from sin for his salvation. Those sinners who turn and trust are cleansed by Christ. If you would offer your entire self to Christ, to be his servant, to follow him, he will cleanse you, make you new, wash you. Feel dirty? Feel soiled and unclean? Come to the one who washes souls. Feel broken and torn apart? Come to the one who will heal and mend you, who will take the pieces of your life and make you whole. Come to Christ.

*Preachers, be sure your souls are secure in the salvation of Christ.* The Puritan pastor Richard Baxter offers sober words for preachers of God's Word:

> Take heed to yourselves lest you should be void of that saving grace of God which you offer to others, and be strangers to the effectual working of that gospel which you preach; and lest, while you proclaim the necessity of a Saviour to the world, your hearts should neglect him, and you should miss of an interest in him and his saving benefits. Take heed to yourselves, lest you perish while you call upon others to take heed of perishing, and lest you famish yourselves while you prepare their food. . . . Many men have warned others that they come not to the place of torment, which yet they hasted to themselves; many a preacher is now in hell, that hath an hundred times called upon his hearers to use the utmost care and diligence to escape it. (*Reformed Pastor,* 53)

*Church, be careful how you hear the Word of God.* We know what we prefer by whether we accept the hard truth gladly or become enemies of the truth teller. When a hard truth hits a hard heart, you get sparks and resistance. But you can't soften the truth, or it ceases to be the truth. A hard heart must be broken. Jeremiah 23:28-29 says,

> *"The prophet who has only a dream should recount the dream, but the one who has my word should speak my word truthfully, for what is straw compared to grain?"—this is the LORD's declaration. "Is not my word like fire"—this is the LORD's declaration—"and like a hammer that pulverizes rock?"*

God expects his word to fall like a hammer and break up the rocky heart.

A good preacher never shades or softens the truth. He never preaches the truth unlovingly, but he does preach it unflinchingly. That's how our Lord preached in this passage.

It's the hearer's responsibility to keep a soft heart. A soft heart is like a fluffy pillow. When the word falls into a soft heart, it rests gently and comfortably in that heart. That's the hearer's responsibility.

How do you keep a soft heart toward God and his Word?

- *Pray* for a soft heart. If ever you notice hardness in the heart, pray for a fresh softening.
- *Read* and meditate on God's Word daily. By the Word our hearts are changed and made glad before God.
- *Receive* God's Word in faith. Do not receive it as cold and dead. The Word is alive and active, so take it into your heart.
- *Apply* God's Word and obey it. If we read the Bible, God will speak to us; but we will receive more from his voice in the Bible if we commit ourselves to obeying it.
- *Expect* God's blessings in righteousness and growth.

## The Only Way to Be Safe before God Is to Acknowledge Jesus before Men
### LUKE 12:1-12

Chapter 12 begins the third sermon. In this scene "a crowd of many thousands came together." Most Christian leaders and Christian churches would say, "That's success!" We love to measure ministry effectiveness by numbers. The fear of man often expresses itself in love of crowds.

But Jesus is not impressed with numbers. We know this because the Lord never preaches to please crowds, and he often leaves the crowds to be with his small group of disciples. That's what Jesus does here. His third sermon—for his disciples—might be titled, "Fear God

Always." It's a sermon on how to cultivate the fear of the Lord. He has four points:

### Fear the Coming Judgment (12:1-3)

The main problem with the Pharisees was their hypocrisy. It's also the main problem of too many professing Christians today. Hypocrisy is saying one thing but doing another. It's living a double life. Hypocrisy is moral inconsistency. It's when people praise God with their lips, but their hearts are far from him.

The problem with hypocrisy is that it spreads. Jesus says it's like yeast. Yeast is that leavening ingredient in bread that spreads throughout the entire loaf. In the Bible it's often used as a symbol for sin. The Bible says, "A little leaven leavens the whole batch of dough" (1 Cor 5:6). That's why our Lord tells his disciples to beware, or "be on your guard against the leaven of . . . hypocrisy" (v. 1). For not only does it spread, it also condemns. It will be exposed in the judgment of God (vv. 2-3).

One day our lives will be shown on the big screen of God's judgment. It will be a split screen. On one side will be the life we showed the world. On the other side will be the life we tried to hide. If they're the same, then we have integrity. We are true disciples—true to God, true to self, and true to others. But if the two screens show different pictures, then we will be condemned as hypocrites. It will be shouted from the rooftop of heaven.

So we have to ask ourselves—every one of us who claims to be a disciple: Am I a hypocrite? Do I fear God's judgment? Fearing the searching, all-seeing judgment of God is the first step in cultivating the fear of the Lord.

### Fear the Father (12:4-7)

We have to embrace and respect two aspects of God's character—his terrifying power on the one hand and his trustworthy love on the other.

Jesus speaks of God's terrifying power to destroy the soul in hell:

> "I say to you, my friends, don't fear those who kill the body, and after that can do nothing more. But I will show you the one to fear: Fear him who has authority to throw people into hell after death. Yes, I say to you, this is the one to fear!" (vv. 4-5)

When we think of what other human beings can do to us rather than of what God can do to us, we are guilty of the fear of man rather than the fear of God.

Jesus seems to have in mind the reality of his disciples' being persecuted. He pictures men killing his disciples. He says, don't fear them; fear God instead. Jesus pushes us to see beyond the body to the soul. That's why twice he tells us to fear God. Tremble in God's presence. Tremble at his judgment. For God deals with body and soul. Hell is far more serious a problem than physical death! Our bodies cease to exist, but our souls don't. Physical pain may be great, but it's temporary. The agony of souls in hell is eternal! We had better fear God's judgment much more than man's.

There's another side to learning to fear God's very person: we must learn to love and appreciate God's goodness. The life of sparrows isn't worth much in the eyes of men; in Jesus's day you could buy five for two pennies. But the sparrow's life is precious in God's sight; he does not forget one of them. If God cares that way for sparrows, how much does he care for his people? God's care for Christ's disciples is so particular it includes the number of hairs on our heads! Because of this, Jesus says, "Don't be afraid" (v. 7) of God.

Do you see the tension? We are to fear God's judgment (v. 5). But we are not to be afraid of God in his love (v. 7). That's what holy reverence or the fear of the Lord consists of: trembling before his holiness and rejoicing in his love.

My daughter has a classmate in school. I've seen him a couple times at her performances and school events. He's got a pretty nice voice for singing and the like. My daughter told him that I said he has a nice voice. The young man said, "Your dad seems like he's real cool, but I am still afraid of him sometimes." Yeah. That's how I want them—trembling to shake my hand and smiling with the hopes I'll be kind! Something like that is the Christian's fear of the Lord. We tremble at the thought of him lifting his hand in judgment, but we run to his hand for his love.

We must cultivate fear for God's coming judgment. We must cultivate fear of God's person.

### Fear the Son (12:8-9)

Here's where we see Jesus's thoughts about himself most clearly. Here is where he clearly tells us that he is the only way to God. Jesus says to his disciples and says to us,

> *And I say to you, anyone who acknowledges me before others, the*
> *Son of Man will also acknowledge him before the angels of God, but*
> *whoever denies me before others will be denied before the angels of God.*

This is a stunning sentence. Jesus presents himself as standing between man and God. The key factor in whether we have Jesus's approval before the court of heaven is whether we remained loyal to Jesus before the courts of earth. If we continue to acknowledge Jesus as Lord and God, then we have an advocate before the angels of God. But if we disown Jesus before men, he will disown us before the angels.

This means following Jesus is not a matter of our convenience, popularity, or man's approval. We're to follow Jesus no matter the cost and trust that he will reward us when men reject us.

We had a wonderful example of this a couple of years ago. Perhaps you followed the story of Meriem Ibrahim. She was the pregnant Sudanese woman imprisoned for professing faith in Christ. She was nine months pregnant and had her twenty-two-month-old son imprisoned with her. The penalty was to be one hundred lashes and death if she did not disown Jesus to the Muslim authorities. This pregnant, frail woman, whose husband is wheelchair bound with muscular dystrophy, never disowned Jesus. She feared the Son of God more than she feared men.

I think her reward in the kingdom of heaven will be great. I believe Jesus said to all the heavenly hosts, "Do you see my daughter? She belongs to me. She will be honored in all of heaven for all of time, for she did not reject me and I will never reject her!"

So it should be with everyone who follows Jesus as Lord. Let us fear the Son, lest we perish. Let us acknowledge him at all times before all men so that he will never be ashamed of us.

## Fear the Holy Spirit (12:10-12)

Jesus warns that we can be forgiven of blaspheming, or slandering, him. There's pardon for slandering the Son, but there can be no forgiveness or pardon for blaspheming the Holy Spirit.

These words take us back to where we began. Do you remember those who said Jesus cast out demons by Beelzebul? They were slandering the work of God. They were slandering the Holy Spirit. They were hardening their hearts in unbelief. That slander and hardening, ultimately, is blasphemy of the Holy Spirit.

But those who truly believe trust the Holy Spirit. Even in times of persecution, they rely on the Spirit's power. Verses 11-12 tell us that the Spirit will speak through the apostles and for us on the day of our earthly trial. We do not worry about defending ourselves. The Lord the Spirit will argue our case. So rather than blaspheme the Spirit of God, we trust him.

## Conclusion

Ecclesiastes 12:13 says, "When all has been heard, the conclusion of the matter is this: fear God and keep his commands, because this is for all humanity."

In all of this, Jesus teaches us what it means to fear God. It is to

- recognize the finger of God,
- obey his Word,
- fear his judgment, and
- fear Father, Son, and Spirit.

Do you fear God? The fear of God is the beginning of wisdom, knowledge, and eternal life. That fear points out to us the one way to heaven itself. We only need one way. Truth be told, if there were many ways we would take none in our confusion. God has been merciful in giving us one way, marking it clearly, and calling us to it. Seek the Lord Jesus Christ while he may be found. Seek him and live.

## Reflect and Discuss

1. Do you think there's only one way to God? Why or why not?
2. How would you respond to a neighbor who says, "All roads lead to God"?
3. What is the relationship between spiritual light and God's Word?
4. Jesus claims the Old Testament is about him. Is that an exclusive claim? How can we know it is true?
5. Have you ever faced the fear of man? What was the situation, and how did you respond to it?
6. How does fearing God displace the fear of man?

# The Author of Life

## LUKE 12:13–13:9

**Main Idea:** The Lord Jesus himself is the answer to all of these questions, and it is Jesus who gets us through this life and into the next life.

---

I. **What Is Life (12:13-34)?**
   - A. Life is not defined by a lot of stuff (12:15-21).
   - B. Life is more than food and clothes (12:22-24).
   - C. Life is wasted by worry (12:25-28).
   - D. Life is for seeking God and his kingdom (12:29-31).
   - E. Life follows treasure (12:32-34).

II. **How Should We Live Life (12:35-48)?**
   - A. Stay woke (12:35-40).
   - B. Stay on our grind (12:41-48).

III. **What Will We Face in Life (12:49–13:9)?**
   - A. Distress (12:49-53)
   - B. Hypocrisy (12:54-56)
   - C. Strife (12:57-59)
   - D. Disaster (13:1-5)
   - E. Fruitlessness (13:6-9)

---

I am one of those people who was rocked when I heard Prince died. Prince was my dude growing up. He could rock high-heeled boots, a blousy shirt with lace, and a killer perm while *still* being the manliest dude in the coliseum. He was a musical genius—flat out. I know some of you liked Michael Jackson, but MJ was number two.

If you are under forty and you had good home training, you've probably never heard much of Prince's music. I'm not recommending his music; it will hinder your sanctification. But if you're over forty and you were in the world, like me, then there's a good chance Prince was your sound track growing up. He had this way of making you both celebrate and rejoice in life but also sometimes think about life. That's what good artists do.

In the well-known opening words of one of his many hits, "Let's Go Crazy," he points out that we're all trying to make it through life and that there's something beyond life: the afterworld. That's not a bad start to a popular rock song. Forget the flamboyant outfits, the stunning guitar riffs, and the steady stream of women. Prince was like everybody else in the world: struggling to make his way through life while pondering eternity.

In a real sense that's what our text is about: getting through life. It's a section that starts with Jesus's being asked a question. But the Lord's answer is deeper than the question. What we learn is how Jesus views life and how we are to view it, too.

## What Is Life?
### LUKE 12:13-34

A recurring word through the first half of the chapter is *life*. The second half of the chapter presses the question of whether we will be ready for eternal life when Jesus comes. So it's appropriate that we begin with the question, What is life?

"Someone from the crowd said to him, 'Teacher, tell my brother to divide the inheritance with me'" (v. 13). Now that's an interesting thing to just yell out in a crowd. That's really something to work out inside the family. If there is an inheritance to be divided, that means there is a death to be mourned. One of your parents has died, probably this person's father, and he doesn't seem interested to find help with mourning or grief. The man is not at the funeral. He's not talking with his brother. He's trying to find someone with authority to tell his brother to split the money.

However, the Lord Jesus will not get entangled in petty family disputes. The Lord declines to stoop to petty conflict about material possessions (v. 14). His agenda focuses on life and the state of our hearts. Still, what the Lord does say reveals five important facts about life.

### Life Is Not Defined by a Lot of Stuff (12:15-21)

Greed means wanting what doesn't belong to you. The Ten Commandments forbid it. It's a kind of possessive jealousy. It's a sin of the heart that leads to many other sins like stealing and adultery. The Lord says to this man and he says to us, "Watch out and be on guard against all greed." Here's why: "Because one's life is not in the abundance of his possessions" (v. 15).

Think of how many scams are effective because people are greedy. If we watch against greed, we can protect ourselves from so many things—from get-rich-quick schemes, prosperity gospels, pyramid schemes, and coveting. The only reason prosperity preachers and Internet scam artists and everyday hustlers can run their game is because so many people are greedy and think life is defined by what they have. Storage businesses are one of the fastest growing businesses in the country because we covet and hoard, then we buy more space so we can continue coveting and hoarding.

But the Lord says that way of thinking is foolish. That's why he tells the story of the man building a bigger barn to hold all his stuff. Some people think the good life is relaxing, eating, drinking, and being merry (v. 19). But before we know it, God will call us all to the judgment seat. He will require our souls of us, and we must give an account for how we lived. The people who defined life by what they possessed and enjoyed will be called fools! It is foolish to think our lives will not end. It is foolish to think our lives are defined by what we have. There is a way to be rich toward ourselves and stingy toward God (v. 21), and God calls that foolish.

### Life Is More Than Food and Clothes (12:22-24)

Verse 22 says, "Don't worry about your life"—what you will eat, your body, your wardrobe. Don't worry about those needs because your needs are not your life. In fact, your life is *more* than those things. Life is not defined by the things we have; life is worth more than all our things.

The Lord gives an illustration. The reason you shouldn't worry about your needs, and the reason your life is worth more than your needs, is that you and I are worth far more to God than ravens. If God cares and provides for ravens, then he will care and provide for us!

Do you believe that? Do you believe you're worth more to God than birds? Do you believe God will provide for you because you're worth so much to him?

It's wrong to think that if you don't have anything then you are worth nothing. When the Lord says, "Aren't you worth much more than the birds?" (v. 24), he is asking a rhetorical question with an obvious answer: Of course you're worth more than birds! This is a fact! Never judge your life or God's care for you by your possessions. You are worth far more than your needs, and your life is not determined by your possessions.

## Life Is Wasted by Worry (12:25-28)

Perhaps the people were saying to themselves, "Jesus, that's fine, but I still have to eat. How am I going to get through this thing called 'life'?" So the Lord says, "Can any of you add one moment to his life-span by worrying? If then you're not able to do even a little thing, why worry about the rest?" (v. 25).

The world is full of worry. We're tempted to think that worrying is the same thing as thinking or planning or even protecting ourselves. But worry is completely useless and ineffective when it comes to adding to our life. We can't even add one minute by worrying. The Lord calls adding a minute to our lives a little thing! So if we can't add a minute to our lives by worry, why do we think things like protecting our children, getting good jobs, ending war, or making our neighborhoods safe will be done by worry? These are all good things but not things that can be addressed by worry.

We're not to worry. We are to trust God. In fact, every place where we experience worry, God is inviting us to depend on him. Look at verses 27-28 again. God dresses grass better than kings! "If that's how God clothes the grass, which is in the field today and is thrown into the furnace tomorrow, how much more will he do for you—you of little faith?"

The Lord is saying, "When it comes to life, God's got you. He will supply your needs. You need evidence? Just look at the beauty he places on flowers and short-lived grass!" Does God not provide for all his creation? He will certainly provide for those who bear his image and likeness. It is for us to believe.

## Life Is for Seeking God and His Kingdom (12:29-31)

I love following our church Google group sometimes. Sometimes a note goes out with a need or request. The need can be kind of "out there" sometimes. I read those emails and I think to myself, *Not sure anybody's gonna help with that.* Then moments later the person making the request sends another email saying, "Need met!" It's the most wonderful thing! People seek help, and needs get met.

That's perhaps a small picture of verses 29-31. When people seek God's kingdom, God meets their needs in life. In fact, life is meant to be lived seeking God and his kingdom. The natural consequence of doing that is God taking care of those seeking him.

There is something unchristian and worldly about seeking things and needs apart from God and with worry. All the unbelieving, sinful nations do that. Instead, we are to remember our "Father knows that you need them" (vv. 29-30). We are to "seek his kingdom, and these things will be provided for you" (v. 31). Our Father knows what we need.

My father left home when I was thirteen. He moved across town, but from time to time I would see him. We would have superficial conversations that usually ended with him asking, "Do you need anything?" On some level he wanted to supply my needs. But my father didn't know my needs in advance. His asking always revealed a poverty in our relationship: he didn't know me well, and my telling him what I needed only reminded me of that. It is not like that with God. Long before we pray and ask, even before we know what our needs are, our Father in heaven sees and knows. He never leaves us or forsakes us. He's never caught off guard by our needs. And there's no need our heavenly Father cannot supply.

The purpose of life is to seek God and his kingdom, not things and our needs. The mystery of life is that when we seek God and his kingdom he provides our needs. We receive a kingdom in exchange for worry.

Why does it work this way? Well, the neediest people in the world are those who do not have the kingdom of God. That's our greatest need. When we seek God and his kingdom, we not only have our greatest need met, but we also have our lesser needs met. We must get this in our minds and in our souls because we can have everything in the world, but without the kingdom of God, we are broke!

Are we using our lives to seek God and his kingdom or to seek the things we think we need? Life is not a lot of stuff. Yet life is *more* than food and clothes. Life is wasted by worrying. Instead, the reason we have been given life is to seek God and his kingdom.

### Life Follows Treasure (12:32-34)

What an encouragement verse 32 is! The kingdom of God is not like an Easter egg hunt. You don't search for it wondering if you will find it. It's not hidden so that you miss it. "Your Father delights to give you the kingdom." Hallelujah! It delights the Father to give his children his royal possession. He does not resent giving it to us. He need not apologize for lacking anything we need. Instead, it pleases God to give to his children. If we ask anything according to his will, he hears us, and we have our request (John 14:14; 1 John 5:14).

When we realize this, then the world's possessions and our needs lose their grip on us. That's why the Lord gives us applications in verse 33. We can use this life's possessions to bless the needy because we know the Father gives us a kingdom and a treasure that cannot be taken away, stolen, or decay.

Show me a person who cannot give to others, and I'll show you a person who does not believe the Father gives to him. Show me a person who cannot lend, and I'll show you're a person who doubts she has greater riches in the kingdom of heaven. Show me a person who cannot part with his things, and I'll show you a person who does not believe the treasures of heaven are better. It's that simple. Our life follows our treasure (v. 34).

The key to life is to have "treasure in heaven" (v. 33) or to be "rich toward God" (v. 21). We do not live life for ourselves and what may be gained on this earthen ball. We have life to seek and know God.

I think Prince had it correct: we all struggle to make our way through life, and we all wonder about the afterworld. In Christian speak, the afterworld is the kingdom of God. That is the something else for which life was created: to find and enter the kingdom. How do you do that? Not by listening to Prince's songs. We enter God's kingdom by repenting of our sin and believing on his Son as our Lord and Savior. God's giving to us begins with his giving us his Son. He sent his Son into the world to save us from the judgment to come by making atonement for our sins on the cross and rising from the grave for our justification. Christ Jesus takes our place in righteousness and in sin bearing. By his active and passive righteousness we are reconciled to God, and we enter that life that really is life. This is the gift of God given to everyone who believes.

## How Should We Live Life?
### LUKE 12:35-48

All of this brings us to a second question: How should we live life? Let's assume we are citizens in the kingdom of God through faith in Jesus Christ. Now what? We're not yet in heaven. How are we to live? The Lord provides us two lessons.

### Stay Woke (12:35-40)

#StayWoke is a slogan and a hash tag. The phrase refers to what we used to call "consciousness." It means to be aware of the cultural, racial, ethnic, and political realities of our time.

Our Lord teaches us to "stay woke" in a different, more important sense. Here, staying awake refers to being ready for the Master's return (v. 35). Those who are awake when the Lord returns are the "blessed" or happy ones (v. 37). The master "will get ready, have them [the woke servants] recline at the table, then come and serve them" (v. 37). Isn't that amazing? In the parable the master serves the servants!

This parable is really about "the Son of Man" coming back at an unexpected time (v. 40). The Lord Jesus will come again. He returns to get his servants and take them to his kingdom. He comes back to condemn those who do not trust and follow him. No man knows the day or the hour of his return, but when he comes, the Lord of lords will in some indescribable sense serve the servants who have been awake and waiting for his return.

To "stay woke" in the Christian sense means to actively watch and wait for our Lord's second coming. Titus 2:13 calls the appearing of the glory of our great God and Savior Jesus Christ "the blessed hope." The promise of the Lord's coming is our happy hope.

For those experiencing unhappiness right now, what are you hoping will make you happy? Where are you seeking happiness? Jesus just told us life does not consist in the abundance of possessions, life is worth more than our possessions, and worrying does not add to our life. Instead, God intends us to use our life to seek his kingdom. In that kingdom God has stored our happiness. This is why the New Testament so often tells us that our joy is connected to Christ's coming. If we only live for joy on this earth, then we find ourselves perpetually unhappy.

Why should we live this life in anticipation of that day? Second Timothy 4:8 tells us, "There is reserved for me the crown of righteousness, which the Lord, the righteous Judge, will give me on that day, and not only to me, but to all those who have loved his appearing." If we love his appearing and look for that day, then when he comes, he will reward us with the crown of righteousness, and joy will flood our souls. The happy ones are those who are waiting for Christ, watching for the Master's arrival with diligence.

### Stay on Our Grind (12:41-48)

When we say, "Stay woke," we don't mean sit around daydreaming, looking at the stars, and zoning out. While we watch and wait for the Lord's coming, we must also "stay on our grind." That means we must do the work the Lord has given us.

The key verses are 43-44. The Lord's teaching just keeps getting better and better, doesn't it? When Jesus comes and finds us being faithful stewards doing his will, then he will set us over all his possessions. If we are found faithful with the little of this world and life, then he will make us faithful with the many things in the next world and life (Matt 25:21). But the unfaithful steward will be condemned (vv. 45-47). We can't think we're Christ's servants while refusing to do Christ's work. God's condemnation of that servant will be severe.

There's a difference between an unfaithful servant and an ignorant servant (v. 48). The ignorant still receives a beating, a "light beating" compared to what the unfaithful servant receives, but it's still a beating.

Here's the principle: the knowledge of God's will is a trust, a stewardship. The more you know of God's will, the more you are required to do (v. 48). This suggests we must listen to God's Word eagerly. We must listen actively and expectantly. We do not wish to be like the man James describes, the man who looks into the mirror of God's Word then turns away forgetting what he saw, failing to do what he heard (Jas 1:23). We wish to be hearers and doers of the Word. We do not wish to be stony-ground hearers or hearers from whom ravens snatch the Word of God from our hearts. So we must obediently apply God's Word in our lives.

What has God taught you about his will for you? What has the Lord called you to do? Are you doing it? Are you doing it knowing that he is coming again and he is bringing his reward with him?

So in this life we must not only stay woke; we must also stay on our grind. We must pray, "Command what you will, Lord, and grant what you command."

## What Will We Face in Life?
### LUKE 12:49–13:9

We've considered two questions so far: What is life? How should we live life? This brings us to our final question: What will we face in life? That's a critical question. Many people don't live life as they ought because they're overwhelmed, surprised, or preoccupied with the things they face in life. They get caught up, caught off guard, or caught sleeping.

The Lord turns his attention to describing the times. He was, of course, describing his own time, but not much has really changed since then. These words apply to our time as well. The Lord warns us about these trials so we are not overwhelmed, distracted, or discouraged by them.

### Distress (12:49-53)

The first trial we will face is distress. The Lord spoke of *his own* distress in verses 49-50. He's referring to the fire and baptism of the cross and all the suffering that goes with it. That's why he was distressed: death was closing in on him.

But he also warns of *our* distress (vv. 51-53). If we follow the Lord Jesus, we may find ourselves divided from loved ones who don't follow him. In that sense the Lord brings a sword of division. Following Jesus may cost you your family. That is distressing, but it's worth it.

### Hypocrisy (12:54-56)

The second trial we will face is hypocrisy. The Lord preached to religious people who could look at the sky and tell you the weather, but they could not look at their present times or at Jesus and tell you what God was doing. Jesus rebukes them as "hypocrites" (v. 56).

Why call them "hypocrites"? A hypocrite is someone who pretends to have religious belief and virtue but doesn't. The fact they didn't know the will and work of God proved they didn't know God himself.

Right now there are many professing pastors who can tell you all kinds of things about business, psychology, politics, and so on, but they can't tell you where to find John 3:16 even when you say, "John 3:16." And there are a lot of professing Christians who claim to know God but can't tell you much about Jesus or what he demands. Our challenge is to avoid being one of them. We must inspect our hearts for any measure of hypocrisy. We should ask the Lord to prevent us from praising him with our lips while our hearts are far from him. Let us ask him for grace to praise him with our hearts first and also with the fruit of our lips.

### Strife (12:57-59)

A third trial we will face is strife inside the church. That's what we see with the lawsuits in verses 57-59. In our strife we're tempted to appeal to secular and ungodly authority rather than judge righteously among ourselves. Paul addressed the same problem with the Corinthians (1 Cor 6:1-7).

Haven't some people turned away from the local church and away from Christ because they've experienced strife in the church? They tell you of their hurts. They tell you of their difficulty trusting. My point isn't to deny that such hurts take place. They do happen, and they really hurt. My point is that, by telling you of such strife, we won't be surprised when it happens. And because you're not surprised, you won't be so offended that you stop waiting and working with Christ's return in mind. When strife comes, may we leave our gifts at the altar and pursue reconciliation (see Matt 5:23-24).

### Disaster (13:1-5)

Then, fourth, we will face disasters. In Luke 13:1 some people asked Jesus about the Galileans who were killed by Pilate and had their blood mingled with their sacrifices. In verse 4 Jesus mentions the eighteen who were killed by a tower that fell in Siloam.

It's easy to look at tragedy and doubt God's goodness, to see tragedy as absurd. It doesn't make sense to us. If we're not watching, waiting, and working, we could be overwhelmed.

But in verses 3 and 5 the Lord gives us one purpose of disaster. It's not the only purpose, but it's an important one for survivors. The Lord allows these tragedies as a reminder to repent. The natural disaster communicates a spiritual demand: repent or perish. We could all die in an unexpected instant just as these people did. The only way to be prepared for that possibility is to be repentant before the Lord. Why think that only sufferers need to repent? Survivors need to as well. Martin Luther wrote that when Jesus said "Repent," he meant repent and keep on repenting. We need to constantly turn from the brokenness of a sin-stricken world to our sin-atoning Lord. Suffering and tragedy invite us to come to the Lord.

### Fruitlessness (13:6-9)

Finally, while we stay woke and stay on our grind, we will face judgment. The parable of the fig tree symbolizes religious people in Jesus's day. They were given opportunity to produce fruit. They were only worth something if they did produce fruit. A good tree produces good fruit, but if it doesn't, it will be cut down.

The Lord is being patient. He gives more time. He waits for his servants to bear fruit. But he will not always wait. He will not always be patient. One day he will inspect us for fruit. The question is: Will we be fruit bearing, or will we be fruitless?

## Conclusion

The life we have been given is not that long. It's really a commercial spot for the life that is to come. The life we've been given is a stewardship entrusted to us. We should not use this life to store up treasure in this world, but instead we should send treasure ahead to glory. We are to be rich toward God in our service to him and to one another. That's what life is for. That is how we get through this thing called life. It's how we lay hold of that life that really is life.

## Reflect and Discuss

1. How would you define "life"?
2. What would you say life is for? How does your answer compare to what Jesus teaches in this section of Luke's Gospel?
3. How can love for things ruin rather than enrich life?
4. Of the trials we will likely face as we follow Jesus, which concerns you most? Does it worry you? How does Jesus expect you to respond to this worry?

# The Evangelist

**Main Idea:** Jesus models evangelism by urgently, boldly, and compassionately preaching the reality of the kingdom of God.

---

I. **The Lord Announces the Kingdom of God (13:10-21).**
   A. The Lord announces the kingdom of God with a miracle (13:10-17).
   B. The Lord announces the kingdom of God with two parables (13:18-21).
   C. The kingdom of God is not always recognized or accepted.

II. **The Lord Urges People to Enter the Kingdom of God (13:22-30).**
   A. You strive to enter.
   B. You hurry before it's too late.
   C. You better know God for real.
   D. Everybody talkin' 'bout heaven ain't goin'.
   E. Create an honest urgency.

III. **The Lord Looks at People with a Bold Brokenness (13:31-35).**
   A. Boldness (13:31-33)
   B. Brokenness (13:34-35)

IV. **The Lord Challenges People Personally (14:1-24).**
   A. The religious (14:2-6)
   B. The proud (14:7-11)
   C. The wealthy (14:12-14)
   D. The presuming (14:15-24)

V. **The Lord Is Up Front about the Cost of Discipleship (14:25-35).**

---

The local church exists to glorify God by making disciples of Jesus Christ from the four corners of the block to the four corners of the globe. To do that, we must first do the work of evangelism. Evangelism is telling the story of Jesus's life, death, resurrection, and second coming with the goal of persuading people to repent of their sin, follow Jesus as Lord, and rely on him to save them from God's condemnation. The Lord promises that everyone who trusts Jesus as Savior receives eternal life, fellowship in God's love, and a place in God's kingdom.

To fulfill our mission, we must learn effective evangelism. There's no better person to learn evangelism from than the Lord Jesus Christ himself. Our text divides into five sections illustrating how our Lord did evangelism.

## Introduction

Our text moves through four scenes.

- In 13:10 we begin with Jesus "teaching in one of the synagogues on the Sabbath."
- Then in 13:22 "He went through one town and village after another, teaching and making his way to Jerusalem."
- In 14:1 we fast-forward to another Sabbath when we find Jesus "went in to eat at the house of one of the leading Pharisees."
- Finally, in 14:25 the Lord is outside again with "great crowds."

The thread that stitches all these scenes together is the idea of the kingdom of God, which is mentioned several times throughout.

- We see the kingdom of God described in parables in 13:18 and 20.
- In 13:28 the kingdom of God refers to that place where the forefathers of faithful Israel have gone after death.
- In 13:29 the kingdom of God is where all the faithful from all over the world "share the banquet."
- In 14:15 the kingdom of God is a place of special blessedness for those who enter it.

So we're not surprised that Jesus the Evangelist begins his evangelism by announcing the arrival of the kingdom of God.

## The Lord Announces the Kingdom of God
### LUKE 13:10-21

This is scene 1 in the synagogue on the Sabbath (v. 10). Jesus announces the kingdom of God in two ways.

*The Lord Announces the Kingdom of God with a Miracle (13:10-17)*

Verse 11 introduces us to "a woman was there who had been disabled by a spirit for over eighteen years. She was bent over and could not straighten up at all." This is more than back problems in old age. Her problem was not physical but spiritual. This is nothing less than satanic bondage. Look down in verse 16: "Satan has bound this woman . . . for eighteen years." There she was in the synagogue on the Sabbath. What do you think she was looking for? No doubt she was hoping God would remember her and deliver her.

Verses 12-13 say, "When Jesus saw her, he called out to her, 'Woman, you are free of your disability.' Then he laid his hands on her, and instantly she was restored and began to glorify God." The kingdom of God sets people free from the bondage of devils. Wherever the kingdom comes, it breaks the rule and power of Satan. There will be no disability in the kingdom of God. Everything that's crooked—including the backs bent from a devil's riding—will be straightened and Satan thrown off and glory given to God!

### The Lord Announces the Kingdom of God with Two Parables (13:18-21)

The first parable (v. 19) teaches that the kingdom of God grows *outward and upward.* It starts small—like a mustard seed—but it grows and stretches like a mighty tree with birds nesting in its branches.

The second parable (v. 21) teaches that the kingdom of God grows *inward and through.* It's like yeast. You can't see it, but it works its way through the entire batch of bread dough.

The kingdom of God grows in *visible and invisible* ways.

> *Being asked by the Pharisees when the kingdom of God would come, he answered them, "The kingdom of God is not coming with something observable; no one will say, 'See here!' or 'There!' For you see, the kingdom of God is in your midst."* (17:20-21)

Strictly speaking, the kingdom is not a piece of real estate. Because of this, Christians are not hung up on what happens in Israel as a nation-state. What the kingdom of God brings is not of this world. It is something that exists in us. When Jesus preaches the gospel of the kingdom, he has in mind the reign and rule of God that breaks into the world and breaks the power of Satan. It frees all who had been held hostage by the devil's power and breaks into believers' very being, setting them free.

When the Lord does evangelism, he doesn't simply talk about forgiveness and atonement. The Lord teaches us of a reality, a world that's much larger than his sacrifice. There is no kingdom apart from his sacrifice, but because of his sacrifice, so much more is opened to those who believe.

## The Kingdom of God Is Not Always Recognized or Accepted

Not everyone welcomes or recognizes the kingdom of God when it comes. In verse 14 "the leader of the synagogue" gets "indignant because Jesus had healed on the Sabbath." He demands that people get healed on the other six days—as if he were healing people like this all week—but not on the Sabbath. He knows the religious rules but not what they point to. Jesus calls him a "hypocrite" (v. 15). A hypocrite is someone who pretends to be religious and holy but isn't. He's the kind of man who would give water to an ox or a donkey on the Sabbath but would not stand to see a woman of faith ("daughter of Abraham," v. 16) freed from Satan's torment and healed on the Sabbath.

Jesus calls him out and puts all of them to shame. The greatest shame is this: hypocrites will not recognize the kingdom of God when it comes.

## Applications

How do we apply this in evangelism?

*Preach the kingdom.* It's good to share the gospel in terms of the death, burial, and resurrection of Jesus Christ. But don't forget that the gospel work of Christ brings an entire kingdom. It's a kingdom where the rule of Satan is broken and the work of God spreads outwardly and inwardly. Christ renews all things. His sacrifice not only saves sinners; it also renews the cosmos. Sometimes in our evangelism we need to teach people an even bigger part of the story. That part of the story answers some pastoral questions that the death, burial, and resurrection does not.

For example, think of those people who have a hard time believing in God when they see people suffering around them. Here's a scene with a woman suffering for eighteen years! What does Jesus have to say to that woman and thus to all who suffer? "You are free from your disability." "You are free from your suffering." The Lord says, "The devil came to steal, kill, and destroy, but I have come that you might have life and have it to the full" (see John 10:10). When we find different ways of getting into the gospel, we may find ourselves making contact with people's objections from fresh perspectives.

*Be confident.* Let us also be confident when we evangelize. Those two parables of the kingdom give us a picture of the kingdom's spread. It's growing—sometimes visibly and sometimes invisibly. That's so wonderful. It means we shouldn't measure our success by what we see. The Lord may give us great numbers in a great harvest, or he may be kneading yeast into the dough in ways we cannot see. It also means we will one day see all the branching success of God's kingdom. We can do the work of evangelists with faith and confidence because we know the kingdom grows even if we can't see it yet.

Further, we are not in a losing struggle. The devil has no power to challenge Christ. The Christian view is not a dualistic philosophy with equal rival powers tugging it out. No. Christ comes into the world to break the back of Satan's schemes. In Christ we are winning the battle. Let us take heart and do the work of evangelism with confident joy!

## The Lord Urges People to Enter the Kingdom of God
### LUKE 13:22-30

The Lord not only announces the kingdom of God, he also urges people to enter it.

The Lord has left the synagogue, and he is now in the towns and villages. He's making his way to Jerusalem, where he knows he will be crucified, but he still stops off in the little towns and hamlets on the way. I love that. The Lord is never too busy for "the little guy." Even when the Lord has the most important assignment of the universe—to go to the cross to atone for our sins—he has time for ordinary people in small towns.

In the village someone asks the Lord a good question. This man wants to know if there will be "few" or many who are saved (v. 22). To be "saved" is to be rescued and kept. We need to be *rescued from God's judgment* against sinners, and we need to be *kept for God's love* and fellowship. This person seems to understand that people need saving.

However, the person might be making an assumption in the question. Perhaps he thinks he is safely in the kingdom, saved from God's wrath, so the question applies to other people, not him. I say this because of the way the Lord answers the person. The Lord doesn't talk conceptually about the "few" or the "many." The Lord basically says three things:

### You Strive to Enter

The subject is an understood "you." "*You* make every effort to enter." "Worry about yourself! Make sure *you* get saved!" "Forget about everybody else. You be sure *you* get in." Can you sense Jesus's tone? He's urgent. He's emphatic. He's blood serious. Why?

## You Hurry before It's Too Late

The Lord urges this person because some people will start looking for the door when it's too late. That's the meaning of the story Jesus tells in verses 25-29. Once the door on this life is closed, there is no other chance. Time will be up. Remember: No one knows when the master of the house is coming, but when he comes, the kingdom will be shut and locked. It'll be too late to enter. There will be no way of sneaking in, no windows to crawl through, nobody to wake up to unlock the door for you. You will be either in or out. The Lord says to that person and says to us, "You'd better hurry." The night is coming when no man can work. Today is the day of salvation. Christ is coming on a day and hour no man knows. So we had better hurry to enter the kingdom. Jesus urges us to believe *now*.

## You'd Better Know God for Real

It will not matter that they heard some preaching once before. It will not matter that they saw some man of God before. That's what they say in verse 26—"We heard you preach and used to see you around town. We ate and drank together." The Lord responds in verse 27, "But he will say, 'I tell you, I don't know you or where you're from. Get away from me, all you evildoers!'" *A passing acquaintance with God is not the same as knowing God.* You can't stop at a few facts and the odd sermon or two. You can't settle for having gone to some special church service with your mama or your grandma. John 17:3 says, "This is eternal life: that they may know you, the only true God, and the one you have sent—Jesus Christ." Life is in the Son of God. "The one who has the Son has life. The one who does not have the Son of God does not have life" (1 John 5:12). You must really know God in order to be saved. The only way to know God is to know his Son, Jesus Christ. No one comes to the Father except through Jesus, the Son (John 14:6).

## Everybody Talkin' 'bout Heaven Ain't Goin'

Some will be "thrown out" of the kingdom of God. They will be the ones in the beginning of verse 28 weeping and gnashing teeth. While they are going through such sorrow and pain, they will "see Abraham, Isaac, Jacob, and all the prophets in the kingdom of God" (v. 28). Can you imagine the scene? How will it feel to be cast out of the kingdom while you watch all the heroes of the faith inside the kingdom? Not only that, but in verse 29 an untold number are gathered from east, west, north, and south to "share the banquet in the kingdom of God." What will it be like to watch those millions and millions stream into God's kingdom while God locks the door and throws out others?

You strive. You hurry. You be sure you know Christ.

### Application: Create an Honest Urgency

Our evangelism should create an honest urgency. Too many people act as if hell is only a conceptual problem. They act as if hell is not real. They act as if there's no kingdom to gain or to lose.

Pastor Lon Solomon at McLean Bible Church once had his Jewish rabbi say to him, "Hell is a Gentile problem." So he stopped going to synagogue and started living a hellish life. That must have been something of the attitude of this Jewish man in Jesus's day.

I was once in the Middle East sharing the gospel with a group of Muslim men. We'd been at it for about an hour when one of the men, the quietest of the bunch, looked at me and said, "Do you mean to say I could go to hell?" I told him, "Yes." He stroked his beard, leaned back in his chair, and as if to correct my misunderstanding said, "Don't you know I am an *Arab* Muslim?" He emphasized "Arab" as if to say hell is a non-Arab problem.

Many people go through life as if hell is not their problem. Beloved, I am here to tell you, our evangelism should shake a comfortable man into terror. We know "it is a terrifying thing to fall into the hands of the living God" (Heb 10:31). Our evangelism should communicate that fear. "Therefore, since we know the fear of the Lord, we try to persuade people" (2 Cor 5:11). We must be convinced of the terror of God's judgment so we can persuade as we ought.

No one outside of Christ should ever ask the question, "Are only a few people going to be saved?" without trembling in horror that they may not be in the number.

## The Lord Looks at People with a Bold Brokenness
### LUKE 13:31-35

While Jesus is in the towns and villages, some Pharisees warn him that Herod is out to kill him. That's interesting, isn't it? The Pharisees want to kill Jesus too, but these Pharisees warn the Lord. Somehow they know that Herod wants the Lord dead as well. In that day if a king wanted you dead, there was not much you could do about it, so the threat is real and serious.

### Boldness (13:31-33)

But the Lord is bold as an evangelist. *First, he is bold in the face of threats.* "He said to them, 'Go tell that fox, "Look, I'm driving out demons and performing healings today and tomorrow, and on the third day I will complete my work"'" (v. 32). In other words, "I'll leave town when I am ready." Most of us would hear the threat and think, *Well, I guess the door is closed to the gospel here. This is a "closed country." I guess we should move on.* We would cloak our fear in religious language, but not our Lord. He does not wilt in the face of threats. Truthfully, there would be no closed countries if we had more of the Lord's boldness in the face of danger.

*Second, the Lord is bold in the face of his hearers.* He says to his Jewish audience, "Behold, your house is forsaken" (v. 35 ESV). Today it's popular for preachers to tell their hearers that God has a big house for them. Some people dedicate themselves exclusively to a message of positivity and prosperity. That's not how Jesus evangelizes. He tells his audience that they are about to be cast out of the kingdom of God. Their place in God's plan of redemption is in danger. They are about to be forsaken. The Lord is bold.

### Brokenness (13:34-35)

But the Lord is also broken. He knows that death awaits him in Jerusalem (v. 33). Yet the Lord weeps not for himself but for Jerusalem, the forsaken house (v. 34). It breaks the Savior's heart that his people refuse to be saved. In 19:41, when Jesus finally reaches the city, he weeps over it. He wept over such hardness of heart that would refuse the free offer of an eternal kingdom.

### Application

The Lord is bold, but he is also broken. When we evangelize, we often have one but not both attitudes. We can be "bold" but uncaring. Or we can be "broken"—tender toward people—but fearful of man to the point of not telling them the truth. We want enough boldness to risk ourselves as the Lord does, but we also want enough brokenness to weep when people refuse to repent.

We cannot shrink away from hard truth if we are to be faithful evangelists. That's unloving and untruthful. But we ought never speak hard truth with a hard heart. That's unloving and misrepresents the truth. We are most ready to evangelize when we have both boldness and brokenness. Let us be that kind of church, marked by genuine zeal to tell people the good news, and as we go, we leave a trail of tears, weeping over the lost. We need Jeremiahs among us—weeping prophets. We ought to ask the Lord to examine our hearts to see if we are either too hard and uncaring or too brash in a worldly boldness. May the Lord by his Spirit give us the correct temper of brokenness and boldness to declare the gospel.

## The Lord Challenges People Personally
### LUKE 14:1-24

Fourth, the Lord challenges people directly and personally. Luke 14:1 moves us to the third scene in our text. It's another Sabbath. This time the Lord appears at a dinner party "at the house of one of the leading Pharisees." This party includes all the important people of religious society. It's not a friendly dinner party. "They were watching him closely." They hoped to trap him.

The Lord is not seeking the approval of anyone there. He's not trying to fit in, to schmooze, or to shape his message so people feel more comfortable. In fact, the Lord is in everybody's face. As an evangelist, Jesus challenges people in every situation.

### The Religious (14:2-6)

The Lord heals a man who had dropsy. He knows they're watching him, and he knows it's the Sabbath. It sure does seem like the Pharisees start a lot of conflict on the day of rest! This issue of the Sabbath just keeps coming up. Apparently you can't change a Pharisee in one conversation. Religious hypocrisy is stubborn.

Jesus heals this man right in from of them. But before he does, he asks the lawyers and Pharisees if it's lawful to do so (v. 3). And after the Lord heals the man, he asks them if they wouldn't do the same for a son or an ox (v. 5). Jesus designs the question to provoke compassion in them and to convict them with regard to the man with dropsy.

Jesus performs the miracle *right before their eyes,* and their hearts do not soften one bit. No one's mind is changed. No one's heart is changed. When we pray for evangelism and the work of God, let us not be like those Christians more concerned for miracles than the message itself. To a hard heart, miracles are no more compelling than words. No one is saved simply by witnessing miraculous events (see 16:30-31). Let us be more concerned that the Lord give our *words* power. The Lord may send miracles if he wants, but let us not trust in miracles but in the power of the gospel itself.

Jesus heals the man, and "they could find no answer to these things" (v. 6). But they did not need to give an answer to these things, to refute them. They needed to humble themselves and submit to the Lord. These scribes and Pharisees are just like the ones earlier in our text. They're hypocrites. The Lord effectively says so to their face at a dinner party.

### The Proud (14:7-11)

The Lord addresses the entire room now because he notices everyone attempting to sit next to the host. The Lord tells a story about sitting at the head of the table and getting bumped down to the bottom. It's a story about pride and seeking prominence. Verse 11 delivers the punch line: "For everyone who exalts himself will be humbled, and the one who humbles himself will be exalted." The way to be exalted is to seek humility. It is better to start low and allow others to exalt you than to start high and have others demote you. This is the way of the gospel and the kingdom: those who seek humility find that God exalts them.

### The Wealthy (14:12-14)

Then Jesus speaks to the wealthy. He tells them not to throw banquets for their rich family and friends. Instead, they should give a feast for the poor, the maimed, the lame, and the blind. That's how they will be blessed—by showing generosity to those who cannot repay them and waiting for their reward in the resurrection. I'll bet you that room full of rich and powerful people fell quiet. There were no poor, broken, or lame people there because there was no concern for the kingdom there. But our Lord wasn't finished.

## The Presuming (14:15-24)

The Lord addresses those who seem to presume they're going to heaven (vv. 15-24). Someone at the table said, "Blessed is the one who will eat bread in the kingdom of God!" (v. 15). Maybe he was like the man who asked whether there would only be a few in the kingdom because Jesus answers him similarly. Perhaps he assumed the wealthy would surely enter the kingdom. The Lord relates a story about a man who gave "a large banquet and invited many" (v. 16), but all the folks on his first list made excuses and said they couldn't come. One person said he had to look after his newly purchased field (v. 18). Another person said he had cattle to tend to (v. 19). Someone else said he was on his honeymoon (v. 20). They all probably think they are in good standing with the man who invited them and can presume upon their position with him.

So the man tells his servant to go into the streets and alleys of the city and "bring in here the poor, maimed, blind, and lame" (v. 21). When there's still more room, the man says, "Go out into the highways and hedges and make them come in, so that my house may be filled" (v. 23). If the kingdom is taken away from the worldly wise and powerful, it's given to the poor and marginalized. That truth runs throughout this passage and Luke's Gospel. We see it in verses 2, 13, and 21. The man in the story symbolized God. God has an underlying and continuing concern for the poor, the broken, and the mistreated of society. God fills his house with such people. "For I tell you, not one of those people who were invited will enjoy my banquet" (v. 24). The broken enter the kingdom, not the healthy. The more we admit our brokenness and need, the closer we get to the kingdom of God. The more we deny our brokenness and need, the further away we get from the kingdom of God.

When Jesus addresses the religious, the proud, the wealthy, and the presuming, he is not simply shaming people over small sins. Each of those attitudes is a major, damnable sin.

- The hypocrite—the Lord hates hypocrisy. "Woe to you, scribes and Pharisees, hypocrites! You shut the door of the kingdom of heaven in people's faces. For you don't go in, and you don't allow those entering to go in" (Matt 23:13).
- The proud—God hates pride. "God resists the proud, but gives grace to the humble" (Jas 4:6).

- The wealthy—money can be an idol. God hates idols. "No servant can serve two masters, since either he will hate one and love the other, or he will be devoted to one and despise the other. You cannot serve both God and money" (Luke 16:13).
- The presuming—without repentance you cannot enter the kingdom. "Therefore produce fruit consistent with repentance. And don't presume to say to yourselves, 'We have Abraham as our father'" (Matt 3:8-9).

God shows kindness to sinners so that they might recognize his kindness and come to him. All of these sins are, in fact, major sins that keep men from the forgiveness and love of God. That is why the Lord addresses them directly and personally—even at a dinner party.

## Application

Let us redefine the term *hard to reach*. We often talk about "tough neighborhoods" and "poor neighborhoods" being "hard to reach." But in Luke's Gospel the poor and the broken flock to Jesus. Those who trust in their riches, who seek power among men, who make religion a show are "hard to reach." Those are the ones who have their houses forsaken, who get cast out.

Jesus tells these same types of people that "tax collectors and prostitutes are entering the kingdom of God before you" (Matt 21:31). That is a real check on religious hypocrisy and pride.

The Lord says, "It is easier for a camel to go through the eye of a needle than for a rich person to enter the kingdom of God" (Luke 18:25). It seems God thinks the wealthy are "hard to reach," and the poor should be invited to come into his kingdom.

When we get this backward, we think we need the favor of the rich while we hesitate to reach the poor. In the Bible Christ gives the kingdom to the poor and condemns the rich who trust their riches. If the area of D.C. east of the Anacostia River is known for its poverty and crime, we should rejoice! The Lord has a people here who will believe the gospel and enter the kingdom of God long before many people in suits on Capitol Hill.

God will fill his house (v. 23). He will compel people to come. The gospel is compelling, beloved. And our neighbors will fill the halls of heaven!

## The Lord Is Up Front about the Cost of Discipleship
### LUKE 14:25-35

Finally, the Lord tells people up front what it will cost to follow him.

It's the fourth scene. "Great crowds were traveling with him" (v. 25). But a crowd is not the same thing as a church. You can gather a crowd through a lot of methods. You can only gather a church through evangelism and discipleship. So the Lord turned and began to address the crowd. He wants to be crystal clear about what it means to follow him.

Following Jesus requires four significant costs: (1) "Hate" our family and our lives (v. 26). (2) Bear our own cross (v. 27). (3) Count the costs (vv. 28-32). (4) Renounce all that we have (v. 33).

By **"hate" your family**, the Lord does not mean carnal hatred. "Hate" is metaphorical. We know that because almost everywhere the Lord commands his people to love. By "hate" he means to make them such a distant second in priority relative to him that it seems you hate them by comparison. In other words, for the Christian the family cannot be an idol. We care for our family, yes. We provide for them as a demonstration of faith (1 Tim 5:8). But discipleship will call you to leave family and to reprioritize them in ways completely contrary to the world's system. We must count that cost.

By **bear your own cross**, Jesus means we must join him in suffering. Every disciple has a cross to bear. We must pick it up and carry it daily. That cross is our dying. It's our self-denial. It's joining the Savior in his suffering so that we advance his kingdom. Jesus teaches that cross-carrying is essential—not incidental—to the Christian life. Our crosses look different. For one it's family persecution. For another it's remaining sexually pure while single. For another it's refusing corruption. They differ, but we all have one. To be disciples, we must each carry our cross.

**Counting the costs** means considering what the Lord requires of you so you don't turn back when you are forced to pay up. We must look squarely at the costs of following Jesus and then commit ourselves with that knowledge. Do you have enough to complete the tower or go to war? Will you persevere until the end no matter what? Will you deny yourself in order to serve him? Will you serve him no matter the family pressure? Will you endure hardship like a good soldier for the sake of knowing him? Or will you let those things make you ashamed and turn back? The point is not to count the costs and turn away if it's too costly; it is to count the costs and embrace them because it is worth it. As someone has said, "Salvation is free, but it will cost you everything." If we continue, then we are his disciples. If we turn back, then we never knew him.

In summary, following Jesus requires we **renounce everything** we have: our relationships, our desires, our lives, our possessions, everything. None of it will have a hold on us—only Christ. None of it will command our top loyalty—only Christ. None of it will keep us from serving Christ. Our death in discipleship is really our life in Christ. To follow Jesus as a disciple means we exchange the entire world for that kingdom to come.

- Am I willing to hate all other relationships to receive the love of God in Jesus Christ?
- Am I willing to die to my own desires and plans to live by God's will for me?
- Am I willing to surrender all my possessions to receive God's kingdom?

Consider the alternative. If we reject our Lord's cross and our cross, we become as worthless as ruined salt. In the ancient world salt was used as currency and as a preservative. But ruined salt had no value; neither does a "Christian" without a cross. We are properly tossed to the manure pile. The wasted life is the life that's jealously grasped and forgets the cross. So the Lord asks, "For what will it benefit someone if he gains the whole world yet loses his life? Or what will anyone give in exchange for his life?" (Matt 16:26).

## Conclusion

The blessed life is the life gladly surrendered and found again in Christ. That can be you today. You have a decision to make between life and death, blessing and cursing, between the kingdom of God and an everlasting hell. You may have life, blessing, and a kingdom that cannot be shaken or ruined or lost. You may have a life that truly is life, abundant and everlasting. Or you may have a death that is not "sleep" but torment, that is not a moment but everlasting, that is not quiet but agonizing. Hell is no vacation for the cool people of this world. Hell is not a place of partying but of suffering.

Christ has come into the world to save you from hell and to keep you for heaven. He lived in our place to provide our righteousness. He died in our place to atone for our sin. In his resurrection he proves he has defeated death and the devil. In his resurrection he proves there is acceptance with God and a life with God that will not end. He offers that life to all who will repent of sin, believe in him, take up their cross, and follow him. Today is the day of salvation. Hurry. One day the door to the kingdom will be closed. Do not delay.

## Reflect and Discuss

1. On a scale of 1 to 10, how would you rate yourself as an evangelist?
2. When was the last time you spoke to someone about Jesus? How did it go?
3. How would you rate your brokenness and boldness as an evangelist? Spend some time praying for God's grace in this area.
4. When you hear the phrase "hard to reach," who comes to mind? Who are the "hard to reach" in this section of Luke's Gospel? How does your answer compare to Luke's?
5. Why do you think people tend to regard the poor as "hard to reach" and not the wealthy?
6. Consider the marks of Christian discipleship in Luke 14:25-35. Do you think most people think of these marks when they think of being a Christian? Why or why not? What difference would these marks make on Christian life and ministry if they were remembered and more tightly applied?

# The Great Shepherd

## LUKE 15

**Main Idea:** Repentance (turning around) is how God finds sinners and brings us home with joy.

---

I.   **Six Reasons to Confess Our Sin and Repent (15:3-24)**
  A.   Repent because we are of great worth in God's sight (15:3-7).
  B.   Repent because our repentance brings joy to God (15:8-10).
  C.   Repent because sin destroys our lives (15:11-16).
  D.   Repent because sin is a kind of insanity (15:17-20).
  E.   Repent because God will still be a loving Father to us (15:22-23).
  F.   Repent because repentance reflects the miracle of the new birth (15:24).

II.  **One Reason Not to Continue without Repentance (15:25-30)**

---

I am like most male drivers: I don't stop for directions. Ever. It's in *The Real Man's Handbook*, chapter 3. "Never stop for directions" is part of what it means to be a man. The "ask for directions" gene is on that second X chromosome that men are missing.

Most men think getting from A to B is simply a matter of confidence. If we believe in ourselves hard enough, then we can get anywhere. It's navigation by confidence. And the worst thing that can happen to a male driver like me is when I actually do "figure out" where I am or where I went wrong. Every time we "figure out" our way, it reinforces our confidence. It grows our sense of direction.

The only thing that can undermine a man's confidence in driving is a woman in the car. You can fill a car with men who don't know where they're going. Do you know what they do? They "figure it out" together. They share their confidence with one another until everyone is sure they know the way.

But put a woman in the car, and the first thing she says is, "Do you know where you're going?" "I think we're lost." "I've seen that house before." They say, "Pull over and ask him for directions," and it can be some guy who's clearly as lost and aimless as you! You think you can figure out any misdirection, and a woman thinks anybody *but you* can do it!

Let me set the record straight. I have never been lost. If I had, I wouldn't be here now. All the previous episodes of misdirection were resolved by me "figuring it out." That's why I am here. I figured it out. I made a turn, or I turned around, and presto: I am here, and I know exactly where I am.

I don't know why men think turning around or asking for direction is such a bad thing, but I do know this: if we try to live our spiritual lives by being confident, going our own way, figuring it out, never turning around, then we are truly lost. We will never find our way home to heaven like that. One essential thing about the spiritual life is that it requires turning around ("repentance") to find God. In order to find God, we actually have to look behind ourselves. We have to forsake the path we've been on in order to find the path we've been missing.

## Introduction

Verses 1-2 set the context for our chapter. We are told, "All the tax collectors and sinners were approaching to listen to him" (v. 1). What an amazing sentence! Since Adam and Eve in the garden, men in their sin have sewn fig leaves and hidden themselves from God. Isaiah tells us,

> He was despised and rejected by men,
> a man of suffering who knew what sickness was.
> He was like someone people turned away from;
> he was despised, and we didn't value him. (Isa 53:3)

But here the people approach him. "Tax collectors" were reviled much the way IRS agents are today. Ancient Jews despised them as traitors to the nation and supporters of their oppressors. "Sinners" refers to all types of immoral people living contrary to God's Word. These despised and immoral people want to hear Jesus. A revival breaks out.

Verse 2 alerts us to a problem: "The Pharisees and scribes were complaining, 'This man welcomes sinners and eats with them.'" The meaning you get from a sentence depends, in part, on the tone you associate with the words. For example, the Pharisees' and scribes' words could be read with wonder: "This man (a holy God) welcomes and eats with sinners!" There should be a sense of awe in these words. God in the flesh has come into the world and receives outcasts and sinners! He eats with them! This is what Jesus is like—near to the broken and contrite. He draws near to people in his humility and kindness. A world of wonder should inhabit their words.

However, they uttered these words as a complaint. Awe is not their tone; grumbling is. What the Pharisees *think* they see disturbs them. All they see are sinners. All they can think of is how unclean these sinners are and how inappropriate it is that a rabbi, a holy man, should dirty himself with their presence. They say, "This man welcomes sinners," and that's *bad* news to them. They utter the most precious words imaginable—"Jesus welcomes sinners"—not to commend Jesus but to condemn him. This raises the question, What do we see when we look at Jesus? Do we regard him with grumbling or with wonder? Do we think the Lord hard or tender?

Do you remember what Jesus says of people like this in 11:52? "You have taken away the key to knowledge. You didn't go in yourselves, and you hindered those who were trying to go in." Here they are wishing to hinder sinners from coming to Jesus. The single biggest reason the Gospel writers depict the Pharisees as the bad guys in the Gospels is that they don't see with true spiritual sight. They're willfully and spiritually blind to the realities of heaven. As someone said on Twitter recently, "Satan's true masterpiece is the Pharisee, not the prostitute." Their grumbling provides the context for the three parables in Luke 15.

## Six Reasons to Confess Our Sin and Repent
### LUKE 15:3-24

These six reasons are motivations to repent—either for the first time unto salvation or as a lifetime of turning to God in fellowship.

Repentance isn't merely a duty that people perform. Repentance isn't merely the "hard part." Repentance is not just the leaving behind of things we once enjoyed. Repentance is not just the unpleasant conversation that saints must have with sinners in evangelism. No! Repentance is a fountain of joy in heaven! Nothing prompts a party in heaven like the turning of a soul from sin to the Savior!

### Repent Because We Are of Great Worth in God's Sight (15:3-7)

Do you think the Pharisees really valued the people who were coming to Jesus? No. As far as the Pharisees were concerned, there were already enough people in their religious club—the right kind of people.

Churches have to be careful never to assume that they're big enough or that enough people are already Christians. We have to ask ourselves, Why doesn't God relax and settle for the great numbers he already has in his possession? Why doesn't he look at the ninety-nine and feel satisfied? Why doesn't he clutch the nine coins and shrug off the one? Why carry out such a diligent search? Why go to such lengths and take such risks to secure just one more sheep or coin?

Is it not because God places such high value on the soul that belongs to him? These are sheep and coins with *owners*. This one wandering lamb belongs to a shepherd. This one missing coin belongs to a woman. They are *owned* so they are *valued*.

A poverty comes to their owner when they are missing. There is a wanting in the owner's heart. The owner feels their absence. That's why he can't remain with the ninety-nine but must go after that solitary sheep. That's why she can't sit comfortably in the house but must ransack it until she has the coin. They *feel* the loss.

Verse 7 teaches that ninety-nine righteous people cannot produce more happiness in heaven than just one sinner who turns from sin toward God! Keep our Lord's audience in mind: the self-righteous Pharisees are the ninety-nine, and the sinners and tax collectors are the one sheep. The Lord tells the audience that the one sinner's repentance pleases God more than the self-deceiving self-righteousness of ninety-nine Pharisees.

When the unrepentant are found and recovered by the Owner of their souls, their worth and value are once again felt and affirmed by God. Heaven rejoices over every repentant sinner because the sinner is of great worth to God. The worst thing in the world is not to be a sinner but to be a sinner who thinks God does not value you. The value God attaches to the sinner's soul is seen in the cross and the blood of the Son of God. If we turn to God, we discover that God was not out to crush us but to save us and make us his own.

### Repent Because Our Repentance Brings Joy to God (15:8-10)

Joy is all over this chapter, isn't it?

- Verses 5-6: "When he has found it, he *joyfully* puts it on his shoulders, and coming home, he calls his friends and neighbors together, saying to them, '*Rejoice* with me, because I have found my lost sheep!'" (emphasis added).
- Verse 9: "When she finds it, she calls her friends and neighbors together, saying, '*Rejoice* with me, because I have found the silver coin I lost!'" (emphasis added).
- Verse 10: Angels *sing* and *celebrate* over a single soul who repents.

- Verse 23: The father says to his servants, "Let's *celebrate* with a feast" (emphasis added).

The celebration grows as each individual sinner is brought safely home in repentance. Friends, neighbors (vv. 6,9), and angels (v. 10) are called together to share the joy. Heaven rejoices at finding even one lost soul.

Who are these friends and neighbors? It must be the Christian, the evangelist. Christians are not only the *means* of bringing heaven joy through evangelism but also the *invited guests* who share in that joy! Our God will one day call us into the halls of his banquet and bid us delight in the miracle of those once-lost, now-found repentant sinners brought home on the shoulders of Christ Jesus. *If heaven is happy at the repentance of sinners, Christians will share in that happiness too.* We will experience this rejoicing for all the unending days of glory!

There is perhaps something Jewish about verse 10's reference to the angels. Rather than use the name of God and risk taking it in vain, faithful Jewish persons would often use the throne of God or the angels as a reference to God himself and all those in his presence. Angels reflect the heart of God himself.

False humility claims not to be worthy of God's seeking and saving us. False humility keeps us from repentance. But verse 10's emphasis on *only one* repenting shatters such false humility. God takes time to pursue every individual. When that individual repents, God takes time to celebrate, and he invites all heaven to celebrate with him. This speaks volumes about the value of every individual in God's sight.

Heaven rejoices over every repentant sinner. Christians do too. Pharisees don't.

## Repent Because Sin Destroys Our Lives (15:11-16)

Sin is a destroyer. Satan is a devourer. Consider the younger son's steady decline into sin and squalor in verses 11-16.

In this third story the Lord slows down the film. The first two parables by comparison are short and focus on God's action in granting us repentance. In this third parable the Lord slows down to show us what takes place in our lives when we descend into sin and later repent.

As a member of his father's home, the young man starts with everything. But he's ungrateful and impatient, so he makes himself *fatherless* (v. 12). Because he wants to gratify his sinful desires, he also makes himself *homeless* by going to "a distant country" (v. 13). Without self-control or delayed gratification, he ends up *penniless* (v. 14). In the end he is *friendless and foodless* (vv. 15-16). He wallows in the pigpen with what Jewish persons considered disgustingly unclean animals.

A sinful life is a riches-to-rags story. His life slides deep into squalor and loneliness. If you live *for* yourself, you'll soon live *by* yourself. He doesn't have a friend in the world to help him (v. 16).

This is what living apart from Christ looks like from the vantage point of heaven. God the Father watches his rich but rebellious children squander his love and his riches as they run from him to the far country of sin. Sinners want all the goodness of God's creation and all the enjoyment of God's blessings, but they do not want God himself. They do not understand his fatherhood. They refuse to return his love. Unless God restrains the sinner, they squander their lives and waste away as they chase every desire of the flesh.

"Life" apart from God is really a slow death. Apart from God we are living to die. But repentance is dying to live. It is dying to self that allows us to find life in the Lord Jesus Christ.

### Repent Because Sin Is a Kind of Insanity (15:17-20)

Three adjustments come to the son's life. First comes a *recognition*. "When he came to his senses" (v. 17) suggests he had been out of his mind in rebellion and sin. He lived a nightmare but called it a dream for a season. But something snapped back into place. All of a sudden he came to his senses and began to recognize something.

He recognized the goodness of God. He's a servant in fields begging for the pods that swine eat, but in his father's house the hired servants have more than enough bread! Unlike the master in the far country, the younger son's father is generous toward those who serve him. A man cannot repent until he sees the insanity of sin in light of God's goodness. Living apart from God and God's gracious rule amounts to craziness, depravity.

Second comes *a resolution*. The son decides his place is with his father. More than that, he decides to make one of the greatest confessions in the Bible. He confesses his sin against heaven (God) as well as his father. "He was aware of a holy God and a broken Law" (Chantry, *Today's Gospel*, 48). As Terry Johnson puts it,

> He confesses without conditions and without qualifications.
> He makes no excuses. He offers no explanations. He had

sinned. Period. The problem with most confessions is that they primarily express regret for the consequences of sin rather than regret for sin itself. (*Parables*, 286)

That's the difference between worldly sorrow and godly repentance (2 Cor 7:10).

Third comes *a resignation.* He sees himself and his sins in light of God's goodness and greatness. He knows his depravity, so he resigns any thoughts of sonship. He would settle to be a servant in his father's house. Given his sin, he can't claim to be a son; he can only hope to serve.

Charles Spurgeon comments:

The prodigal, when he said, "I will arise and go to my father," became in a measure reformed from that very moment. How, say you? Why, he left the swine-trough: more, he left the wine cup, and he left the harlots. He did not go with the harlot on his arm, and the wine cup in his hand, and say, "I will take these with me, and go to my father." It could not be. These were all left, and though he had no goodness to bring, yet he did not try to keep his sins and come to Christ. ("Number One Thousand," 340)

So it is with true repentance. Those who turn to God begin to see God as they never have before. They begin to recognize the greatness of God's love. They begin to see his generous character. They understand the holiness of God and the wretchedness of sin. They're brought low. They're humbled. They know God is generous so they come to him. But they know their sins are great so they make no demands on God. The humility of repentance does not set its gaze on much, just the hope of inclusion. Repentant people plead only for a servant's place, and they would leave all their sins for the lowest place in the kingdom of heaven (see Ps 84:10).

Repentance is beautiful because it finds God beautiful, just as this young son now sees his own father as wonderful. Heaven rejoices when God is valued.

## Repent Because God Will Still Be a Loving Father to Us (15:22-23)

Sure enough, the son returns to the father and makes his confession in verse 21. He's no doubt filthy and ragged. He was once finely manicured, a prince at the party, but now he returns a pauper, thinking himself orphaned by his sin. He has no claim to the family. He prematurely requested and then subsequently wasted his inheritance, his share in the family. He does not expect to be treated as a son.

But his repentance creates a theater for the display of God's rich grace. See how the father responds to the lost son.

> *"So he got up and went to his father. But while the son was still a long way off, his father saw him and was filled with compassion. He ran, threw his arms around his neck, and kissed him. . . .*
>
> *"But the father told his servants, 'Quick! Bring out the best robe and put it on him; put a ring on his finger and sandals on his feet. Then bring the fattened calf and slaughter it, and let's celebrate with a feast.'"* (vv. 20,22-23)

See the excellent qualities that shine forth from the father. The father recognized the son's sin and destruction long before the young man did. He saw the folly coming. He also saw his son coming home from a distance (v. 20). There is compassion. There is tenderness in his embrace and his kisses. There is adoption and generosity. The father receives his son *as a son.* He places a robe and ring on him, signs of his sonship (v. 22). And there is that joy again—kill the fatted calf and let's celebrate!

Here's where the gospel defies every human expectation. We think the son might be chastised. We think the father would have been generous simply to allow the son back as a servant. We think the son could and perhaps should have been cut off. He has spent his inheritance; how can he come back asking for anything?

But the father in the story, a reflection (although faint) of God the Father, pours out the storehouses of his grace and mercy at the faraway sign of his son's repentance! The distant sighting of a sinner's return elicits the fountain of God's love! The sinner who turns finds that he turns right into the waiting arms of his God. God receives the penitent with the riches of heaven: the robes of Christ, the signet of sonship, the banquet of salvation! A kingdom for a beggar—that's what heaven is! It makes the riches of God's grace all the more glorious.

My friend, if you've wasted your life in sin, turn to the merciful arms of God the Father. The Father will be tender and compassionate. You may come to him without fear. He will receive you.

*Repent Because Repentance Reflects*
*the Miracle of the New Birth (15:24)*

"This son of mine was dead and is alive again; he was lost and is found!" (v. 24). When we see a repentant man, we know a resurrection has happened. The one who was dead in trespasses and sins in which he once walked has been made alive again through Christ!

The lostness wasn't just a misplacement; it was death. The son had been dead to the father. But in the miracle of repentance, he has been raised to newness of life. He has been brought back—not as a corpse for a funeral but as a living soul for a banquet.

Heaven finds repentance beautiful because it brings back to life those whom sin had killed. There is never any downside to repentance. We may sometimes feel our confessions and repentance will result in our loss, more pain, or something worse. These parables challenge us not to think that way. Though we find ourselves in the pig trough, the reward of coming back to God will be far and away greater than anything we risk losing from that trough! If we repent, God will be our Father. And unlike our human fathers, who have sometimes failed us, God will be the perfect Father who will never fail us, never forsake us, never punish us for his own convenience, but clothe us, love us, and rejoice over us. There's no father like this Father. So come to God ready to be loved!

## One Reason Not to Continue without Repentance
### LUKE 15:25-30

There's one final reason heaven finds repentance beautiful: the repentance of one sinner exposes the lack of repentance and the self-righteousness of others.

The second son, the older brother, comes into the picture. He hears the party (v. 25) and seeks an explanation (v. 26). When he hears the brother has returned and the fattened calf killed because his brother is "safe and sound," he loses it. "Then he became angry and didn't want to go in. So his father came out and pleaded with him" (v. 28). In this refusal the older brother dishonors his father every bit as much as the younger brother. He refuses to share in his father's happiness. Further, in requiring his father to come out to him, he causes the father a second indignity; he fails to honor his dad as he should have.

Though his father entreats him gently, all the older son can see is his own righteousness. Leon Morris writes, "The proud and self-righteous always feel that they are not treated as well as they deserve" (*Luke*, 267). So the elder brother makes his case with his father (vv. 29-30). The older son feels self-righteous: "I have never disobeyed your orders" (v. 29). He feels a scandalous amount of disdain about the entire situation. See how he refers to "this son of yours" (v. 30) rather than to his brother. He recounts the younger brother's sins. Pharisees are expert at confessing the sins of others. He is exasperated to the point of dishonoring everyone.

Pride, entitlement, and self-righteousness keep him from repenting. If we think we have something to boast about before God, then we won't see our need for turning to God in repentance. This man thinks his obedience justifies him before his father just as the Pharisees through their self-righteousness made them right before God.

How many of us have a difficult time detecting the fault in the older son's thinking? How many of us sympathize with him? The Pharisees certainly did. In fact, Leon Morris writes, "We can easily imagine the elder brother saying of his father, 'This man receives sinners and eats with them'" (*Luke*, 267).

The father's response reveals the son's blindness. The elder son did not know what he had: "He said to him, 'you are always with me, and everything I have is yours'" (v. 31). Again, to quote Leon Morris: "He did not really understand what being a son means. That is perhaps why he didn't understand what being a father means. He could not see why his father should be so full of joy at the return of the prodigal" (*Luke*, 267). He could not see that celebration is necessary. The father says, "But we had to celebrate and rejoice, because this brother of yours was dead and is alive again; he was lost and is found" (v. 32).

The sinner's repentance exposes the hardness of the self-righteous. A sinner's repentance should be good for a saint's heart. Though we like to imagine ourselves to be the younger brother, many of us are actually the older brother. In our self-righteousness we tend to think that self-help is how we made it. We tend to think those broken by sin ought to go on and mend themselves and mend their ways in order to become the "deserving spiritual poor." Then maybe—just maybe—we will celebrate at their repentance.

But in God's sight, the first sign of repentance requires a celebration by the godly. Repentance is for the joy of the church. It's for our revival and celebration.

## Conclusion

There are five things I am fighting to remember as an evangelist as a consequence of studying and now preaching Luke 15.

*Repentance is for the joy of heaven, the joy of the church, and the joy of the sinner.* When we call a man to repent, we call him to his joy. We need never be embarrassed about calling people to an eternal joy that satisfies every party concerned.

*Calling people to repent of sin is calling them to recognize their worth in God's sight.* Sin has been destroying their dignity and value as beings made in the image of God. Repentance restores that value.

*What we are calling people to in repentance isn't merely to give up this life's pleasures; it is to gain heaven's greater pleasures.* In the presence of the Lord is pleasure forevermore. Repentance returns a lost man to the presence and pleasures of the Lord.

*Our emphasis on repentance isn't so much an emphasis on dos and don'ts in the Christian life. It is more fundamentally an emphasis on seeing life as it really is—including God.* Christianity and moralism are two different religions. While the Christian subscribes to high morality, his morality is not what makes him a Christian. His unique covenant relationship with God wherein he comes to enjoy God forever makes him a Christian. Repentance opens his eyes to see and savor God.

*When we call a person to repent, we're calling him into what God finds beautiful.*

## Reflect and Discuss

1. When did you first repent of sin?
2. When did you last repent of sin? Is repentance common practice for you, or do you resent, avoid, or fear repenting?
3. Of the six reasons to repent, which one most encourages you and why?
4. What do you learn about the character and actions of God in the parables of Luke 15? Can you think of other places in the Bible where those traditions are taught?
5. Would you say you celebrate and rejoice when you hear of or see others repenting? Do you think your heart most resembles the father, the prodigal son, or the older brother?

# The Master of the House

## LUKE 16

**Main Idea:** The good steward who is shrewd, faithful, and obedient will receive the reward of God.

---

I. **God's Stewards Must Be Shrewd (16:1-9).**
II. **God's Stewards Must Be Faithful (16:10-13).**
    A. The character (16:10)
    B. The consequences (16:11-12)
    C. The challenge (16:13)
III. **God's Stewards Must Be Obedient (16:14-18).**
    A. You can't fool God (16:15a).
    B. God doesn't love what you love (16:15b).
    C. God's commands are what stand (16:16-17).
    D. God must be obeyed (16:18).
IV. **God's Stewards Will Be Rewarded (16:19-31).**
    A. Two persons (16:19-21)
    B. Two places (16:22-23)
    C. Two petitions (16:24,27-28)
    D. Two problems (16:25-26,29-31)

---

We don't read our Bibles just to gain Bible facts. The main aim of reading the Bible is to get to know the Lord. God reveals himself most clearly and most reliably in the Bible through his Son, Jesus Christ. In the Bible God speaks to us and reveals himself to us.

Because the Lord is wise, he may speak to us in various ways about his character and actions in the world. Sometimes he simply states things about himself or the world in simple facts or propositions. But often the Lord teaches us what he and the Father are like by using pictures, symbols, and images in stories. In John 10 he tells us that he is "the good shepherd." In John 6 the Lord says he is "the bread of life." In John 15 he portrays himself as "the true vine."

In all these images we learn not only what the Lord is like but also what our relationship with God is like. As the shepherd he cares for us.

As the bread of life he feeds and nourishes us. As the true vine he supports our branches and gives us sap for life.

One image that's not as popular as the good shepherd, the bread of life, or the true vine is the "master of the house." Luke uses that image multiple times in his Gospel. This image teaches us that the Lord owns a house and all that's in it. We find the image in 12:35-40, where Jesus tells a story about a master of the house who goes away for a while and will return at a day and time no one knows. The Lord uses the master-of-the-house image again in Luke 14:16-24, where he tells the story of an owner of a house who throws a great banquet but no one comes.

In these stories Christ is the owner of the house and all that's in it. The writer of Hebrews compares the Lord to the prophet Moses:

> *Moses was faithful as a servant in all God's household, as a testimony to what would be said in the future. But Christ was faithful as a Son over his household. And we are that household if we hold on to our confidence and the hope in which we boast.* (Heb 3:5-6)

So not only does the image of master of the house teach us about the Lord's ownership; it also teaches us about our stewardship. Those who serve God are stewards or servants in the house, not owners.

That idea of stewardship runs throughout Luke 16. The Lord's ownership is assumed. We relate to him as servants relate to the owner of a mansion. Luke 12:42 asks, "Who then is the faithful and sensible manager [or steward] his master will put in charge of his household servants to give them their allotted food at the proper time?" The Lord Jesus gives an answer in Luke 16.

## God's Stewards Must Be Shrewd
### LUKE 16:1-9

Jesus tells a story to his disciples (v. 1). A disciple is one who follows Jesus and lives by Jesus's teaching. God is "the rich man" in this story. The "manager" or steward represents the disciples.

Parables are stories intended to teach one main point. Here's the point of the parable: God's stewards must be shrewd. We must be shrewd in a certain way: by using the wealth of this world to get a home in the world to come. Let's look at the parable together. Consider the flow of the story.

*First, there's the screwup* (v. 1-2). The steward faces the charge of wasting the rich man's possessions. In fact, the steward has failed to properly manage two things: (1) the rich man's possessions as well as (2) his own reputation as a steward. In verse 2 the rich man "called the manager in and asked, 'What is this *I hear* about you?'" That's the steward's reputation. He was known to mismanage the rich man's possessions. He has screwed up.

*Second, there's the "hook up."* What does the steward do? He's gotten too soft in his stewardship (v. 3). He's "not strong enough to dig; [he's] ashamed to beg." He's the kind of man with manicured hands, too good to work and too proud to panhandle. He apparently used his master's wealth to indulge his own appetites. Verse 4 gives us his goal: He's trying to figure out a way to live at other people's expense. He's a freeloader. So he hooks up the people who are in debt to the rich man so they'll hook him up when he gets fired. He discounts their debt so they are in debt to him.

*Third, there's the "big ups."* Verse 8 can be a confusing verse. The rich man actually *praises* the "unrighteous manager" for being shrewd. He gives him "big ups." Why does the owner praise this dishonest servant?

In the second part of verse 8, the Lord steps out of the story to interpret it for us. The rich man praised the dishonest manager because "the children of this age are more shrewd than the children of light in dealing with their own people." The "children of this age" refers to people who are not disciples, who are not Christians. "The children of light" refers to Christian disciples. When it comes to worldly things, the world tends to be wiser about being the world than the Christian does. The world does worldliness far better than the saints. Which, incidentally, is why the church should never attract the world using worldly methods. We look like poor imitations of something we do not understand. So the parable, in praising the steward, does not encourage us to mimic the world in its worldliness.

Verse 9 gives us the punch line. Here's what the Christian disciple or the steward of God's possessions needs to do. We need to use "worldly wealth"—the money and possessions of the world—to make friends. The wealth is going to fail. Our money will fail us; it is not an adequate god to worship. So we need friends who outlive our wealth. In fact, we need friends who outlive our world. These need to be friends who can "welcome you into eternal dwellings." These need to be friends who can give us homes with them that last forever.

What friends can do that? Only God the Father, God the Son, and God the Holy Spirit. Any man who has God for a friend has a home without end. The Christian who stewards this world's wealth to do God's work God's way will have God as a friend and heaven as home. Money in *this* world is for getting a home in the *next* world.

We are not good stewards if we cannot see beyond earthly dwellings and possessions to the home that is coming in the kingdom. So we must ask ourselves some questions. Do we recognize that all we have belongs to God? He is the owner; we are merely the stewards, the caretakers. Do we use what we have in a way that pleases God or cheats God? Are we storing up for ourselves treasures in heaven, or are we trusting the world's riches that will surely fail?

God's stewards must be shrewd in how we handle his possessions. We need to handle them in a way that gets us an eternal home.

## God's Stewards Must Be Faithful
### LUKE 16:10-13

You can be wise and still be unfaithful. That was the problem with the dishonest manager in the parable. He was crafty, he was shrewd, but he wasn't faithful or true. He didn't handle his master's business correctly. So here the Lord emphasizes faithfulness.

### The Character (16:10)

We discern the difference between the faithful steward and the unrighteous steward by considering what they do with "very little." We can predict what people will do with great responsibilities by looking at how they handle small responsibilities (v. 10). Faithful in little, faithful in much. Unrighteous in little, unrighteous in much.

This isn't simply a matter of ability; it's a matter of character. That's why the terms "faithful" and "unrighteous" are used. We're looking at the *character* of the disciple. Character separates the good steward from the bad one. The Lord doesn't say in verse 10 "unskilled in little"; the Lord says "*unrighteous* in little." When the disciple fails to be a good steward, it is like promising God to take care of his things but then not doing it. It's cheating the Lord.

### The Consequences (16:11-12)

Verse 11 relates the consequences of this difference in character. If we can't be trusted to be honest and faithful with "worldly wealth," we can't be trusted with "genuine" riches. The genuine riches are the treasures and glories of heaven. How we manage money in this life determines whether we receive the blessings or riches of the life to come.

If we can't manage someone else's property, why will the Lord trust us with our own property in heaven? That's the point of verse 12. In heaven we move from being stewards to being owners together with God. We become heirs and coheirs with Christ (Rom 8:17), owners together of a kingdom God has promised to us. But we can't be good owners if we can't first be good stewards.

### The Challenge (16:13)

Now here's the real challenge: We cannot serve two masters. We cannot worship two gods. We must make up our minds. Will we serve the false god of money and possessions—which is idolatry—or will we serve the one living and true God who owns all things?

That's really what determines whether we're faithful or dishonest stewards. Whom are we serving—God or money? We cannot be devoted to both. To be devoted to one is to hate the other. There are no two ways about it. Stewardship is worship. We declare who our God is every time we make a money decision. Either our money is Lord or Christ is Lord.

God's steward must be faithful. Verses 10-13 define "faithful" as keeping good character, keeping consequences in mind, and keeping God first and only as Lord.

While I was writing this, the Lord began to address me about my own stewardship. He exposed weaknesses in my own thinking and behavior as a disciple. It left me with questions I'll now share with you.

- Where would you say you're strongest as a steward: in character, in considering consequences, or in worshiping God alone?
- Where would you say you need to ask God for more grace and sanctification: character, consequences, or the challenge to worship God alone?
- Practically speaking, what decisions about money and possessions do you need to make differently in order to demonstrate your devotion to God?

The Lord's teaching about discipleship as stewardship brings our faith down to real life. The rubber of discipleship meets the road of practical decisions about money and possessions. The Lord teaches us that we display our relationship with God in our decisions and actions as caretakers of his possessions.

## God's Stewards Must Be Obedient
### LUKE 16:14-18

Verse 1 says Jesus began telling these stories to his disciples, but verse 14 tells us the audience changed. When it says, "The Pharisees . . . were lovers of money," it means they did not love and serve God (see v. 13). Money was their master, not God. They were devoted to riches and possessions, not God's will. When they heard Jesus teaching stewardship, they rejected his teaching, and they scoffed at him. They made fun of the God who came to save them.

The Lord says four things to these religious people who did not truly love God.

### You Can't Fool God (16:15a)

The Pharisees were good at convincing people that they were holy, that they were God's people. They were good at convincing people that they were the ones who truly obeyed God's law. They were so good at convincing people that they eventually brought people under the yoke of their traditions. They emphasized their outward show of piety and religiosity. They seem to have reached the point where they believed their own hype.

Here's the difference between the Pharisees, the people, and God—"Humans do not see what the LORD sees, for humans see what is visible, but the LORD sees the heart" (1 Sam 16:7). They could fool men, but they couldn't fool God. God knows their hearts.

What's striking about verse 15 is how often you hear people saying "God knows my heart" as a way of *excusing* their sin. It's their way of saying, "God will be OK with me. God understands and accepts my sin." But when Jesus talks about God knowing our hearts, it's to make it plain that we can't fool God. His judgment will be perfect. He will see our thoughts, our motives, our desires, our feelings, and everything else that is under the surface of all our pretending. We should tremble when we read, "God knows your hearts." It's the knowledge of our hearts that creates the crisis with God! This is why we don't want to treat our hearts as the best guide to life. Our problem *is* our heart. As Jeremiah 17:9 says, "The heart is more deceitful than anything else, and incurable—who can understand it?" We may fool ourselves and others, but we will not fool God. God knows who we are all the way down to the bottom of our souls. How foolish it is, then, to risk heaven and hell with a weak appeal to "God knows my heart."

## God Doesn't Love What You Love (16:15b)

"For what is highly admired by people is revolting in God's sight."
People tend to think others love what they love. We should not make
the mistake of thinking God values something because we value it.
God's ways and thoughts are not like ours; his ways and thoughts are
higher (Isa 55:8-9).

If we love a thing like money to the point that it rivals God, then it
becomes an idol. If we should not trust our hearts, then we should not
trust our loves either. We should test our loves by God's Word as well. We
must be careful to ensure we love what God loves and that the things we
love are not revolting in his sight.

Men have a tendency to worship their possessions. That's what's
going on with these Pharisees. They're like the rich young ruler.
That's the man who went away from Jesus sad because Jesus told him
to sell all he had and give to the poor (18:18-23). The man had a lot
of things, and those things had a hold on his heart. Whenever we
exalt things before God, God calls them revolting! God hates idols. He
views them as unclean. The heart that loves money loves an abomina-
tion that God hates.

## God's Commands Are What Stand (16:16-17)

The Pharisees preferred their own way of life based on the love of
money. They rejected the teaching of Jesus and laughed at it. When
they did that, they were rejecting the commands of God. That's why our
Lord says about the Bible in verses 16-17,

> "The Law and the Prophets [the Old Testament] were until John
> [the beginning of the new covenant]; since then, the good news
> of the kingdom of God has been proclaimed, and everyone is urgently
> invited to enter it. But it is easier for heaven and earth to pass away
> than for one stroke of a letter in the law to drop out."

Nothing God has ever said and written in his Word has an expiration
date. No requirement of God for his people has "void" written on it as if
it were a cancelled check.

God's Word continues in force. Christ fulfills it, but that does not
give us warrant to conclude, "That's the Old Testament; it does not
apply." Or, "That's something in New Testament times, and times have
changed, so we don't have to obey it." Those are terrible ways of looking

at God's Word. God's Word will stand—every jot and tittle—until it is all fulfilled and Christ returns. The Word of God obligates us until the return of Christ. By the Word of God, we come to understand how Christians should manage God's house as stewards.

### God Must Be Obeyed (16:18)

This seems like it comes out of nowhere. How does Jesus go from discussing stewardship and possessions to talking about divorce and adultery?

Think about where your thoughts have gone while reading this. Chances are, at the mention of "stewardship," you began to think about your own money and spending decisions. Then there's a good chance you began to think not just about yourself but about your family—their needs, limitations, and desires. So eventually the mind focuses on our relationships. Here the Lord calls to mind the most intimate and fundamental of relationships. He views marriage as a stewardship. How we manage or care for that relationship matters to God.

So in the context of obedient stewardship as required by God's Word, it makes perfect sense that Jesus should speak against adultery to a religious people who believed you could get a divorce for almost any reason. Some rabbis in ancient Judaism supported divorce for "offenses" as minor as a woman burning her husband's food or the husband simply finding her displeasing in some way. Sinful humanity has had a low view of marriage from the time Adam blamed Eve for eating the fruit down to our day of no-fault divorce.

Jesus speaks into that culture to remind us that we don't steward only possessions, but we steward relationships as well. Though we live in a fallen world where marriages end for all kinds of reasons—sometimes good ones and sometimes despite the best effort of one spouse—God intends our marriages to be lifelong. He intends us to steward that relationship until the end, the way Christ cares for his bride until the end. If we won't steward the blessing of marriage but live adulterously, then we shouldn't think we can steward the blessing of riches and live faithfully. We should not convince ourselves that we will be faithful to our covenant with God if we express covenant disloyalty in relationship with our spouse.

We can't fool God. God doesn't love what we love. His Word stands forever. So all who call themselves "Christians," "disciples," or "stewards" must obey God.

Is there any area of your life where you trick others into thinking you're religious but the truth is something different? Have you soberly considered that God knows your heart and can't be fooled? Is there an area of our life where we think God must be pleased with us or with something we're doing simply because it pleases us? Have we considered that that area or thing, if it's contrary to God's Word, is revolting in God's sight? Have we been thinking God's commands no longer apply to our life or that we do not have to obey God? Let us be suspicious of any notion that it's OK to disobey God. Finally, how are you stewarding your relationships in your home, in the church, and in the community? Do we manage our relationships in a way that demonstrates we are God's servants?

## God's Stewards Will Be Rewarded
### LUKE 16:19-31

### Two Persons (16:19-21)

The story features a "rich man" and "a poor man named Lazarus" (vv. 19-20). The rich man remains anonymous, but the poor man is named, perhaps a hint at God's particular care for the poor and oppressed. The rich man was clothed in "purple and fine linen"; Lazarus was "covered with sores." The rich man was "feasting lavishly"; Lazarus begged to be fed with crumbs from the rich man's table. The lives of these two persons couldn't have been more different.

### Two Places (16:22-23)

Both the rich man and the poor man die (v. 22), but they go to two different places. "The poor man died and was carried away by the angels to Abraham's side"—which is a way of referring to heaven. The rich man "was buried. And being in torment in Hades." Hades refers to hell. The Lord tells us here that his people are often and more likely the poor and outcast rather than those who live for riches. If we're getting to know Jesus, we must recognize that Jesus believes in a real heaven and a real hell. The person who dies will go to one of these two places. There is no in-between, no purgatory, no do-overs or mulligans. God appoints a person to die once, and after that comes judgment (Heb 9:27).

## Two Petitions (16:24,27-28)

Lazarus never speaks in this story. He is named, but he is silent. The rich man speaks twice. He pleads with Abraham for two things. First, he is in hell crying out for mercy. He wants just a drop of water to cool his tongue because he is "in agony in [the] flame" of hell. He's gone from feasting sumptuously to thirsting in anguish. Verse 24 gives us a picture of the desperation of hell, of the agony of conscious torment in God's condemnation.

Second, the rich man pleads for his family—but only after he pleads for himself. Sinners remain selfish even in hell. "'Father,' he said, 'then I beg you to send him to my father's house—because I have five brothers—to warn them, so they won't also come to this place of torment'" (v. 27). Even in hell, this rich man thinks Lazarus should serve him. He's unrepentant of his selfishness and his lack of love for the poor.

The rich man remains fully conscious of his suffering and torment. Hell is not a dream or a place without feeling. The Bible does not present the afterlife as sleep or as annihilation without suffering. It's a place of intense suffering because God has removed even that common grace that we so much enjoyed in this life even if we are not Christians. Being utterly removed from grace leaves only misery and sorrow. We cannot imagine what horrible, horrible suffering is the removal of God's love and mercy.

The rich man does not want those he loves to join him in Hades. If our loved ones who died apart from Jesus could speak to us, they would tell us to repent, follow Jesus, and not come to hell. Many are tempted to leave the faith or reject Christianity because they cannot stomach the doctrine of hell. The sad irony is they would be doing the opposite of what their loved ones in misery would encourage them to do!

When I think of the doctrine of hell, I can't help but think of my father. Unless my father repented and placed his faith in Christ at a time I'm unaware of, he is now the rich man in Hades. He would, because he loved me, urge me not to turn from Christ. He would warn me against coming there. He would tell me not to be troubled by him but to rest in Christ. Certainly don't flee the only path of salvation, which is faith in the Son of God crucified, buried, and resurrected to rob hell of its victims. He would call me to be wiser, humbler, and more clear-eyed than him by trusting Christ as Lord and Savior.

Beloved, perhaps you have a loved one who died apart from Christ and it troubles your soul. I understand that pain. But your loved ones would not have their departure keep you from heaven and the love of God. They would have you confess your sins to God, turn away from sin, and trust in Christ as your Savior.

### Two Problems (16:25-26,29-31)

But there are two problems. Lazarus had a lifetime of suffering (v. 25). Now it's his turn to enjoy the comfort of being with God. All our suffering will be turned to comfort in the presence of God. Suffering will give way to glory. The first will be last, and the last will be first. No one who trusts Christ will face shame in eternity. Lazarus sits with Abraham—a picture of fellowship with God—and it will never be taken from him.

There will be no changing things after we die. There's a great chasm firmly in place so that no one can pass from hell to heaven or from heaven to hell. Once you're in heaven, you're in heaven. Once you're in hell, you're in hell. There can be no change of address.

There's a second problem. People who will not believe God's Word will not believe even a great miracle like someone coming back from the dead (vv. 29-31). The Old Testament ("Moses and the prophets") is enough to get someone saved from hell and into heaven, provided they believe it. The rich man's family had enough gospel in those Scriptures to come to God and be saved. A person who will not believe the Bible and repent of sin will not believe and repent even with a resurrection. How many mock the good news of the resurrection!

There are some who hear "the good news of the kingdom of God" proclaimed and urgently "enter it" (v. 16). This urgency begins with turning away from sin, away from their desires, and away from the world in order to follow Jesus wherever he leads as Lord and Savior. This urgency to enter the kingdom continues with obedience to Christ and growing in holiness. The reward will be the comfort and joy of being with God in glory.

Don't be like this rich man. The Lord said in verse 9 that riches will fail. It's certain. This man discovered that, didn't he? He lived a great life with fancy clothes and lavish feasting, but his money couldn't buy him heaven. He could not escape hell once there. He couldn't even warn others. The gospel is only good news to us if we respond in time. We must repent and believe before we die so that we might have Christ as our friend and an eternal dwelling with him.

## Conclusion

How will you steward your one soul? How will you steward the good news of Jesus Christ? Will you use this life to take hold of eternal life, or will you waste this life and suffer forever in hell? Be a good steward. Use what you have heard to gain what you have not yet seen.

Christian, what a great stewardship we have. What an amazing thing God has done in making even our ordinary stewardship decisions foretastes of the faithful reward we will receive from God. We are but stewards now; but if we prove faithful, we will be coheirs of all in the kingdom, and our hearts will be filled with his glory.

## Reflect and Discuss

1. Do we recognize that all we have belongs to God?
2. Do we use what we have in a way that pleases God or cheats God?
3. Are we storing up for ourselves treasures in heaven, or are we trusting the world's riches that will fail?
4. Where would you say you're strongest as a steward: in character, in considering consequences, or in worshiping God alone?
5. Where would you say you need to ask God for more grace and sanctification: character, consequences, or the challenge to worship God alone?
6. Very practically: What decisions about money and possessions do you need to make differently in order to demonstrate your devotion to God?
7. Is there any area of your life where you trick others into thinking you're religious but the truth is something different? Have you considered that God knows your heart?
8. Is there an area of our life where we think God must be pleased with us or something we're doing simply because it pleases us? Have we considered that area or thing might be revolting in God's sight?
9. Have we been thinking God's commands no longer apply to our life or that we do not have to obey God?
10. How do you feel about the doctrine and reality of hell? How does the rich man's testimony from Hades affect your understanding of hell and what those there would desire for those still living?

# The Humble King

## LUKE 17

**Main Idea:** Jesus teaches the values and ethics of the kingdom of God.

---

I. **Jesus Commands Us to Forgive (17:1-10).**
   - A. Offense: you must forgive (17:1-4).
   - B. Unbelief: you must have faith (17:5-6).
   - C. Pride: you must obey (17:7-10).

II. **Jesus Expects Us to Be Thankful (17:11-19).**
   - A. Sick men's request (17:12-13)
   - B. The Savior's merciful reply (17:14)
   - C. The Samaritan's return (17:15-16)
   - D. The Savior's final response (17:17-19)

III. **Jesus Is Coming in His Kingdom (17:20-37).**
   - A. The Pharisees can't see it (17:20-21).
   - B. The disciples can't miss it (17:22-25).
   - C. The world won't expect it (17:26-30).
   - D. Only the self-denying will find it (17:31-33).
   - E. Those who miss it will perish (17:34-37).

---

Luke 17 opens with the Lord Jesus Christ headed to Jerusalem. He is going to Jerusalem to give his life as a ransom for sinners. Three times Jesus has already predicted his trial, conviction, crucifixion, and resurrection in Jerusalem.

In this section of travel to Jerusalem, we find Jesus doing the things he customarily does: teaching people about the kingdom of God and performing miracles that authenticate his teaching. The chapter divides into three scenes. The first scene begins in verse 1 where the Lord Jesus teaches his disciples. The second scene begins in verse 11 where the Lord passes between two largely Gentile regions of Samaria and Galilee. There the Lord performs a miracle. The third scene begins in verse 20 where the Pharisees ask Jesus a question about when the kingdom of God is to come.

# Jesus Commands Us to Forgive
## LUKE 17:1-10

*Offense: You Must Forgive (17:1-4)*

The first scene in our chapter opens with Jesus speaking to his disciples. In verse 1 the Lord gives the disciples two facts of life.

Fact 1: "Offenses will certainly come" ( v. 1). An "offense" is a stumbling block, something that might cause a person to fall into sin—a temptation. Make no mistake about it. Every living person will face temptation to sin. If you have never been tempted, then either you are very young or you are oblivious. Temptations are a fact of life. Now, being tempted is not the same thing as sin itself. A temptation is a pull, an influence, an enticement to do wrong. Being or feeling tempted is not itself sin. Temptation gives birth to sin when we give in to it (Jas 1:14-15). Jesus reminds us that we live in a world where we will feel or experience the influence of temptation.

Fact 2: "But woe to the one through whom they come!" (v. 1). In other words, there's something worse than feeling tempted to stumble. It's worse to be the one who brings the offense, who does the tempting. A tempter's life resembles the life of the first tempter, Satan. The one facing temptation may escape sin, but the one tempting others will not escape judgment. Jesus says, "Woe" on them. That "woe" means the ones who tempt others will surely and seriously be condemned.

Arguing from the lesser to the greater, the Lord illustrates how serious and inescapable that condemnation is (v. 2). Drowning with a millstone anchored to our necks is the lesser thing! Far worse is the greater thing of God's condemnation!

Let that word picture play out in your mind. An ancient millstone weighed quite a bit. Though women often used millstones in Israel, it sometimes took several men to move one from its place. These large stones carved in circles usually had a hollow center, like a huge, stone donut. The Lord asks us to imagine a rope tied around a millstone through that center and tied on the other end around the tempter's neck. I imagine the tempter and the millstone are somehow in a seagoing vessel when the stone is thrown overboard. First the rope would snap taught as the weight of the stone sent it diving toward the bottom of the sea. Then would come the violet snap of the rope at the tempter's neck as it pulls him overboard into the ocean. The tempter splashes into the water—not upright as if to dog paddle or horizontally as if to swim—but head first with feet thrashing overhead. You're wrestling with the taught rope, wanting to scream except there's water all around. You feel the salt water rushing into your eyes and nose. Finally, unable to hold your breath any longer, your mouth flies open and water floods into your mouth and eventually your lungs. While conscious, you fight in terror, upside down in the sea, struggling against an invincible weight and desperate for life's necessary air.

It would be better to suffer that way than to suffer the "woe" of God against sin and the tempter.

Because temptation and sin are facts of life, the Lord tells us, "Be on your guard" (v. 3). In other words, watch out for yourself and one another. As our church covenant requires, we are to "exercise a watchful and affectionate care for each other." In particular, we must pay attention to this matter of rebuking and forgiving. "If your brother sins, rebuke him, and if he repents, forgive him" (v. 3). A church is a collection of people receiving and giving correction as we avoid temptation while living for Christ.

One temptation we can face is to be all rebuking and no forgiving. If you are excited about the prospect of rebuking someone, you're probably tempted toward being harsh. On the other hand, someone may gravitate toward being forgiving and never seeing the need to rebuke others. If you are glad to forgive, failing to offer a correcting word when it's needed may be your temptation. Such a failure is not more loving than being harsh. The Lord gives us a balanced instruction that includes both rebuking for sin and forgiving for repentance.

"And if he sins against you seven times in a day, and comes back to you seven times, saying, 'I repent,' you must forgive him" (v. 4). Every act of repentance requires an act of forgiveness. The Lord's words are strong: "You must forgive him." It's a command. In Matthew 6:13-15 Jesus says,

> "And do not bring us into temptation,
>     but deliver us from the evil one.
>     "For if you forgive others their offenses, your heavenly Father will forgive you as well. But if you don't forgive others, your Father will not forgive your offenses."

Forgiving others is so important that God won't forgive us unless we forgive others.

At this point we could have two wrong responses to this teaching.

## Unbelief: You Must Have Faith (17:5-6)

The first wrong response is unbelief. That must have been what some of the disciples felt. "The apostles said to the Lord, 'Increase our faith!'" (v. 5). Maybe you read verse 4 and thought something similar: "The Lord will have to help me with that one. I don't know if I can forgive all like that."

Well, it is easier to say, "You must forgive" (v. 4), than it is to actually forgive in some cases. That's true. But remember in verse 1 the Lord said that stumbling blocks "will certainly come." Unforgiveness is one such temptation to stumble into sin. We don't want to give in and sin by refusing to forgive our confessing brother or sister.

When we feel tempted to not forgive, we need to remember verse 6. We can stagger at those words if we only think about the fact that we've never seen a tree literally move at a human's command. If we read or hear the words that way, then we are likely driven deeper into unbelief. So we must ask ourselves, "What is the Lord's pastoral point with this saying? What does he want us to take away from these words?" The Lord pushes against unbelief, so going deeper into it must not be his aim.

I don't think the Lord's statement in verse 6 is meant to be taken literally. It's hyperbole. He's exaggerating to make a point. He's saying a small amount of faith can move a tree into the ocean. Surely with even smaller faith you can forgive your brothers and sisters who sin against you. Which is harder? To command a tree to move into the ocean or to forgive our brothers and sisters when they sin against us? If with a little faith we can move trees, then with tiny faith we can forgive.

## Pride: You Must Obey (17:7-10)

But now there's an opposite problem. Some people may be tempted to stumble into sin when they face the challenge of forgiving others, but other people may face the temptation of pride when they do forgive others. We can feel like we should get a medal and a parade when we forgive. That's why the Lord tells the short parable of verses 7-10.

The rhetorical questions in this parable underscore the nature of the master-servant relationship. A *servant* does *not* take a seat beside his master and eat with him right out of the field. The master does *not* thank the servant for doing what he was told to do. The same is true when Jesus commands us forgive (v. 10). Forgiveness is our duty as servants. Forgiving others is not a reason to boast. We are not to feel entitled to a thank-you from the Lord or a seat at the table beside him.

We have only done our duty. Remembering this keeps us from the temptation to pride.

### Application

The necessity of forgiveness becomes even clearer when we learn in Matthew 6:14-15 that we will not be forgiven by God if we do not forgive others. Our duty to forgive is bound together with whether we have been forgiven ourselves. Not only do hurt people hurt people, but forgiven people forgive people.

The question is, Is there any brother or sister you must forgive? Ask the Lord for faith; then go obey as a faithful servant.

## Jesus Expects Us to Be Thankful
### LUKE 17:11-19

In verse 11 the scene switches to Jesus "traveling to Jerusalem . . . between Samaria and Galilee." Samaria and Galilee were both heavily Gentile areas. The people there would have been regarded as outsiders, foreigners to the covenant of God.

### Sick Men's Request (17:12-13)

"As he entered a village, ten men with leprosy met him. They stood at a distance and raised their voices, saying, 'Jesus, Master, have mercy on us!'" (vv. 12-13). Leprosy was a skin disease. The disease, sometimes contagious, made them "unclean" according to Jewish law, so they had to be isolated from the city and from people. Wherever lepers traveled, they were to call out, "Unclean! Unclean!" as a warning to others to stay away from them. How difficult it must have been to be required to be the prophet of your own uncleanness, the herald of your own unworthiness before God. Imagine the burden of having to tell everyone you encountered that you were "unclean."

Imagining such a life helps us understand why they call out for mercy. In our sin we differ very little from these lepers. Our sins make us all unclean. We should all cry out to God for mercy.

### The Savior's Merciful Reply (17:14)

In sending them to see the priests (v. 14), Jesus was obeying the Word of God. Before a leper could be declared clean and brought back into the camp, a priest had to examine him. Even more wonderful than our

Lord's simple obedience to God's word is his mercy to these men. "While they were going, they were cleansed." In the act of turning to obey Jesus, the Lord took away their disease. With a word from a distance, the Lord answered their prayers for mercy. He heard their humble cries. He healed them. A prayer for mercy is the prayer Jesus always answers in the Gospels.

I love the way Jesus loves lepers. I love the way the Master gives attention to the unclean. Before him is the most important task in the universe—the cross. He has fixed his face like flint to go to Jerusalem. But on the way some nameless lepers on an isolated hill call out to him, and the Savior of the universe takes time to show mercy! Is this not a beautiful God? Some people worship cruel gods who crush their worshipers, but the one true and living God does not crush us in our weakness or finally cast us out in our uncleanness. When we cry for mercy, he answers our prayer!

### The Samaritan's Return (17:15-16)

One of the men saw that he was healed. When he saw it, he "returned and, with a loud voice, gave glory to God," and "he fell facedown at [Jesus's] feet, thanking him." He had been a leper separated by the law and social distance, but in mercy Christ eliminated the distance between the leper and God. Now he's a healed, clean man right at the feet of Christ. That's reason to give thanks!

Now you'd think everyone who was healed would have given thanks to God. You'd think the other nine, when they heard this man "with a loud voice" praising God, would have turned back to see what he was saying. You'd think the most thankful would have been the Jewish persons in the text. But it was the *Samaritan* who turned back (v. 16).

Perhaps two things should happen with each of us every morning when we wake. If nothing else, we should first say to the Lord, "Thank you for waking me this morning." Then, second, we should pray, "Lord, have mercy."

### The Savior's Final Response (17:17-19)

The Lord wonders, "Were not *ten* cleansed? Where are the *nine*? Didn't any return to give glory to God except this foreigner?" (vv. 17-18; emphasis added).

When the Lord answers our prayers, the only appropriate response is thanksgiving. From the moment we're children, our parents teach us to say "Thank you" when someone gives us something. How much more should we do that when God answers our prayers for mercy?

And how much more should it be the case when the people of God receive mercy? We're supposed to recognize the irony here: It's the Samaritan foreigner who returns with thanks—not the nine Jewish people. God's people take him for granted and don't even give thanks, but this man outside the covenant of Israel recognizes what has happened and falls down in worship.

Here's another reason I love Jesus: almost no one reading this would even hope to know God if the Lord had not determined, before the world was created, to establish Israel as his chosen people but then to send the Messiah to justify Gentiles as well (Gal 3:8). If the Lord had not appointed "foreigners" to eternal life, none of us would have a prospect for salvation. But the Lord determined to take a people who were not his people and make them his people (Rom 9:25-26), one new man, Jew and Gentile (Eph 2:11-22), known by his name. We would all be lost if our merciful Lord had not thought from eternity past to include us.

It's to this foreign man that Jesus says, "Get up and go on your way. Your faith has saved you" (v. 19). The gospel says to the unclean foreigner, "Come to your Lord's feet and receive his mercy."

## Application

We should never forget the Lord's love and concern for the lepers of society. The Lord loves those who have been cast out of the community. He loves those who are thought of as "unclean." He hears their prayers for mercy. He heals them. He accepts their worship and their thanksgiving. In the Bible it's not the religious Jews who get praise for their religious attitudes and actions. In the Bible, especially the Gospels, it's the social rejects who receive the most praise for coming to the Lord in faith.

## Jesus Is Coming in His Kingdom
### LUKE 17:20-37

Our third and final scene begins in verse 20. Verses 1-19 give us commercials for the kingdom of God. The kingdom of God produces a community of people who repent and forgive. The church is meant to practice these graces constantly until Christ comes to perfect his bride. The kingdom breaks into the world with healing and restoration, which points to the ultimate healing and restoration when all imperfections and distortions of beauty are fixed.

These "commercials" prompt the Pharisees to inquire of Jesus "when the kingdom of God would come" (v. 20). Though the Pharisees asked the question, the Lord's answer addresses several groups.

## The Pharisees Can't See It (17:20-21)

The Pharisees expected a literal physical kingdom on earth. They wanted an earthly ruler. They didn't understand the nature of God's kingdom. It's not a kingdom you can mark with borders or establish with war. It's a spiritual kingdom that was already in their midst. Everywhere the gospel goes and people respond to it in faith, there you have an expression of the kingdom. The rule of God had already begun and was spreading, but they couldn't see it. They didn't have spiritual eyes to see it though it was in their midst. They had asked the question of the King of the kingdom because they missed it!

If you are not a Christian, you do not have to search in far-off places to find the kingdom of God. It is in your midst. It can even be *in you* if you would put your trust in Jesus Christ.

## The Disciples Can't Miss It (17:22-25)

While the Pharisees couldn't see the kingdom, the disciples couldn't miss it. The Lord turns to talk with his disciples in verse 22. He says essentially three things to them.

*Do not believe it when people tell you they know where the kingdom is* (vv. 22-23). Don't follow them. Think of how many cult tragedies would never have happened if people would take seriously these two verses. There would be no Jim Jones at Jonestown. There would be no David Koresh and the Branch Davidians in Waco. There'd be no Heaven's Gate cult massacre. All of these people died because they listened to someone say, "The kingdom is over there!" or "Look! There's the messiah!" If someone tells you they know the secret path to the kingdom, point to Luke 17:22 and refuse to believe them or give them a hearing.

*The coming of the kingdom will be like lightning that fills the entire sky* (v. 24). The disciples can't miss it. It's unmistakable. You won't need someone to point you to it. It'll be plain for all the disciples to see. Christ's coming will be so glorious and obvious it will petrify the world. The world will stand still in awe of the brilliance and glory of the coming of the Son of God. His coming is the blessed hope of the church (Titus 2:13). If you have this hope in you, it will be fulfilled.

*There's only one event before the coming* (v. 25). A lot of Christian theology presents the Lord's second coming in elaborate schemes and charts.

But notice how Jesus puts it. Verse 25: "But *first* it is necessary that he suffer many things and be rejected by this generation" (emphasis added). In other words, first the Lord must make it to Jerusalem where he will be mocked, rejected, tried, and crucified. In Jerusalem the Lord Jesus will die for the sins of the world and be resurrected three days later to save all those who believe in him. That's first. But no "second" is mentioned. After the Lord's death, burial, and resurrection, the coming of the kingdom could happen at any time.

### The World Won't Expect It (17:26-30)

The world will continue with its business. That's what the world was doing "in the days of Noah" (v. 26). That's what the world was doing "in the days of Lot" (v. 27). The world was going to work, partying, marrying, eating and drinking, starting businesses, planting gardens, and so on. Life continued as it had always happened. The righteous Noah warned his generation, but no one believed him. Lot attempted to warn his sons-in-law, but no one believed him. And in a moment—as the world continued on without expecting—the floods began in Noah's day and fire began falling from the sky in Lot's day. When the rain and the fire came in those two judgments, it was already too late for those who thought life would continue as usual. So, captivated with the hum of a busy world, they failed to consider the announcement of God's salvation from God's judgment. The judgment of God came against the world and against Sodom, and there was no escape. God "destroyed them all" (vv. 27,29). God's judgment against sin is so complete and perfect there will be no escape unless we escape through Jesus Christ.

God's judgment is real, and it is coming. God's salvation is free, and it is for you. Through the atonement of Christ for your sin and his resurrection for your justification, God freely offers to you his escape from wrath and his invitation to his love. Repent of your sin and believe on Christ before the judgment of God comes!

### Only the Self-Denying Will Find It (17:31-33)

When the day of the Lord comes, it will not be a time for getting your possessions and going back to your homes. Those three simple words of verse 32 are poignant: "Remember Lot's wife!" When the Lord destroyed Sodom and Gomorrah, he sent angels to rescue Lot and his family. But Lot's wife loved that wicked city. While they were fleeing, she looked back with longing and was turned to a pillar of salt. She nearly escaped the judgment, but while running away, she broke God's command to not look back. She paid the price. The day of the Lord will be like that. Those who look back with fondness for this world will perish.

But the ones who lose their lives will keep them. The Lord is fond of this saying; he uses it at different times in the Gospel. Verse 33 captures the counterintuitive nature of the kingdom. We don't save our lives by tightly grasping them in this world. We die to ourselves. We deny ourselves. We lay down our lives in faith in order to live for Christ. Everyone who does that will keep his or her life forever in God's kingdom. We can't live for God until we die to ourselves.

### Those Who Miss It Will Perish (17:34-37)

That's the sad truth. "Where the corpse is, there also the vultures will be gathered" (v. 37) is not heaven. Everything in heaven is alive. There are no corpses, no carrion. A corpse is a dead, lifeless body. Vultures are birds that eat dead things. There is no rapture to be with Christ from that place. This is a final judgment, a picture of death.

There are only two ways to live. We may sleep peacefully and work joyfully knowing we have a place in the kingdom of God through faith in Jesus Christ. Or we may be taken suddenly and carried to the place of death because we never repented and believed in Christ. If those are the only two ways to live, then surely the choice is clear. Believe in Christ and enter his kingdom.

## Reflect and Discuss

1. Do you find forgiving others difficult? Why or why not?
2. Do you find asking for forgiveness difficult? Why or why not?
3. What kinds of things have made extending and seeking forgiveness more doable? How has God helped you as you have stepped out in faith to forgive or seek forgiveness?
4. Is there any brother or sister you need to forgive or from whom you need to seek forgiveness?
5. Can you recall a time when God showed you mercy? Did you give thanks to the Lord for it?
6. With pencil and paper, spend some time listing all the reasons you can think of for giving God thanks.
7. How often do you think about the coming of our Lord? Is it your "blessed hope" (Titus 2:13)? What difference does remembering the second coming make in your daily life?

# The Rewarder of the Faithful

## LUKE 18

**Main Idea:** God rewards those who seek him.

---

I.  **God Rewards the Elect with Justice (18:1-8).**
    A. The goal of the parable (18:1)
    B. The independent judge (18:2)
    C. The persistent widow (18:3-5)
    D. Interpretation (18:6-8)
    E. Dr. King and the Civil Rights Movement
II. **God Rewards the Sinner with Mercy (18:9-14).**
    A. Audience (18:9)
    B. Parable (18:10-13)
    C. Interpretation (18:14)
III. **God Rewards the Humble with His Kingdom (18:15-17).**
    A. The scene (18:15)
    B. Jesus's reply (18:16-17)
IV. **God Rewards the Self-Denying with Eternal Life (18:18-30).**
    A. The ruler's question (18:18)
    B. Jesus's call for clarity (18:19-22)
    C. The ruler's response (18:23)
    D. Jesus's perspective on wealth and salvation (18:24-27)
    E. It's worth it (18:28-30)!
V.  **God Rewards the Blind with Sight (18:31-43).**
    A. Jesus's instruction about his crucifixion (18:31-34)
    B. A blind beggar's call for mercy (18:35-39)
    C. Jesus's response (18:40-43)

---

We are consumed with getting to know Jesus because Jesus is God. In getting to know Jesus, we get to know what the Father is like, what to expect of him, and how to come to God through Jesus his Son.

For example, we learn that our approach must involve faith but also knowledge of God's character. As we read in Hebrews 11:6, "Now without faith it is impossible to please God, since the one who draws near to him must believe that he exists and that he rewards those who seek him." So approaching God requires two things: faith in his existence and an expectation of his reward for seeking him.

Hebrews 11:6 is Luke 18 in a nutshell. The chapter features five people who want to draw near to God. In each case they come to Jesus with a question, need, or desire. In four of the five cases, we see Jesus reward these seekers. The Lord responds to them in answer to their prayer with an act of mercy. In verse 1 the Lord tells a parable to "them," meaning his disciples. In verse 9 the Lord tells another parable to "some who trusted in themselves that they were righteous." Verse 15 features a group of parents bringing their infants to Jesus and the disciples. "A ruler" approaches Jesus with a question in verse 18. Finally, the Lord addresses the Twelve in verse 31 and a blind man in verse 35.

## God Rewards the Elect with Justice
### LUKE 18:1-8

### The Goal of the Parable (18:1)

The Lord wants to teach the disciples to persevere in prayer. He's concerned they may lose heart, which is easy to do, especially when it seems an answer isn't coming or coming soon enough. We falter and quit, assuming God must not be listening or will not give us what we seek. Indeed, the spirit is willing, but the flesh is week.

### The Independent Judge (18:2)

The judge of verse 2 does not fear God or man. He will not respond to anything outside himself. In the parable the judge is unrighteous, but ultimately the judge represents God. God is not moved by anything outside himself. Theologians refer to this truth about God as his aseity. God exists and works in the world without dependence on any of his creatures. Nothing outside of God constrains him. In this way God rules as the perfect impartial Judge.

### The Persistent Widow (18:3-5)

A certain widow calls out for justice against her adversary. In our Lord's day a widow lived in near complete dependence on others. She had no family and likely no income. The parable implies that she has at least one enemy who opposes her. She appeals to the judge for justice.

Though the judge initially wants nothing to do with the woman, he cannot withstand her persistence. He fears she may drive him crazy with her constant and repeated requests for justice, so he relents and gives her justice.

### Interpretation (18:6-8)

If an unrighteous judge who fears no one is eventually moved by persistent pleading, how much more does a righteous God, moved by compassion, goodness, mercy, and faith, hear the prayers of his people who pray night and day (v. 6)? Contrary to the human judge's slowness, God gives justice *"swiftly"* (v. 8; emphasis added).

Do not grow weary in prayer because a good God is listening who does not fear man and will respond out of his goodness to provide for his people. That is the point the Lord wants his disciples to hear. If we come to him in prayer seeking him in faith, then he will reward us with the justice we seek.

The parable repeatedly mentions justice. For several years we have heard so much about justice. We have witnessed so many pleas and demonstrations for justice. Our text reveals the connection between the prayers of the elect and the answer of justice from God. The surest way to get justice in this world for God's people is not by marching, though marching may have its place. The surest way to achieve justice in this world is not by protest signs, though those also may be appropriate. The surest way to find justice is never by rioting and burning down your own neighborhood. Justice comes most surely by falling on our knees with our heads bowed. When God's justice comes, it will be perfect, proportionate, and balanced.

### Dr. King and the Civil Rights Movement

Many people regard the Black Lives Matter movement as a continuation of the Civil Rights Movement. There are ways that's true, but there are also ways the two movements differ significantly. The differing approaches to prayer reflect one such difference. The Civil Rights Movement of the 1950s and 1960s was a *religious* movement. The foot soldiers of the Civil Rights Movement were Christians, and so were the leaders. Before Dr. King and the leaders of the Civil Rights Movement ever conducted a protest, they committed themselves to doing their homework on the issues involved to be sure their cause was just. That's really important. Once they decided a cause was just, Dr. King emphasized spiritual preparation for the protest. He called the people to seasons of fasting and prayer. I have to think the prayers of the people brought forth God's justice in what was really a short period of time. If we want justice, let us be a praying people who seek a God who himself loves justice and rewards those who seek him.

### Application

Pray for justice. We do more on our knees with our voices lifted in prayer than we do on our feet marching with our voices lifted in protest. We ought to protest in righteous causes that demand it, but we ought never to protest without praying before, during, and after. Do we have the persistent widow's kind of faith in seeking God?

## God Rewards the Sinner with Mercy
### LUKE 18:9-14

The scene in verses 1-8 and the scene in verses 9-14 both include a parable featuring prayer.

### Audience (18:9)

The Lord told this parable to "some who trusted in themselves that they were righteous, and looked down on everyone else" (v. 9). It's amazing how often self-righteousness and looking down on others come in a package.

### Parable (18:10-13)

The parable represents their self-righteousness in a Pharisee whose pride and contempt are exhibited even in prayer to God. He stands by himself. He's so righteous and holy no one can come next to him even in prayer. He rehearses his spiritual resume and contempt even in prayer (vv. 11-12). He depends on his religious exercises for righteousness before God. He doesn't think he's like other sinners. Perhaps he has not committed the particular sins of others, but in fact he is a sinner like other men. He reveals his sin even in his prayer. He *stands* in God's presence as if he need not bow even to God. He stands as if his life makes him acceptable before God. He's spiritually blind.

Contrast the Pharisee to the tax collector. Everything about them strikes us as different. Tax collectors were social outcasts in Israel and were seen as those who aided Israel's oppressors, the Roman government.

People viewed them as thieves who extorted regular citizens. However, the tax collector emerges as the hero in this parable. The tax collector stands far off. He does not rush into God's presence, assuming he has a righteousness all his own. He strikes us as humble. He bows his head in prayer, not even feeling good enough to lift his head toward heaven. He remains aware of his sin, so he prays, "Have mercy on me a sinner." He offers no defense, no rationalization, and no justification. He simply admits he is a sinner and needs mercy.

### Interpretation (18:14)

The Lord interprets the parable by simply noting the tax collector "went down to his house justified rather than the other." The word *justified* means "righteous or in right standing with God." He is not justified by anything he has done; all he could do was confess his sin. He goes home justified because he has confessed and has thrown himself on the mercy of God's court. That's the only way any sinner can come to God: casting himself on God's mercy through Jesus Christ.

The self-righteous Pharisee goes home deceived, believing himself justified, yet unrighteous and unknowing. It is a terrible thing to think you are right before God when you are not. It is foolish to try basing your righteousness with God on the things you do. Our goodness falls far too short. But it is wonderful to be a sinner, head bowed, pleading for mercy, and being rewarded with that mercy through faith in Jesus Christ.

The tax collector went to the temple broken and bowed, but he likely left with a light step and glad heart because he had found God's mercy. There's a profound and counterintuitive reason the tax collector left justified: "Everyone who exalts himself will be humbled, but the one who humbles himself will be exalted." The Lord rewarded his humiliation with a gracious exaltation.

### Application

We have no case for our own righteousness. All of us are sinners. However well dressed we are on the outside or messed up on the inside, we all need God's mercy because of our sin.

Since we are all sinners, none of us should look down on others because of their sin. If we look down on others, that itself is a sin that God hates.

Let us seek mercy and humility as a way of life. We do not give up with our sins still intact since we have a God who forgives sin. We don't settle for our brokenness since we have a God who heals. We don't quit with our heads hung low; our God lifts our heads and gives light to our eyes. Let us be constant in going to him when we see our sin. The smallest glimpse of our sin may humble us like the tax collector, and we may feel far off. Let us not linger far off. Close the distance with God by going to the Father through the sacrifice of Christ. Let us go confidently because God rewards those who seek him, even sinners needing mercy.

## God Rewards the Humble with His Kingdom
### LUKE 18:15-17

Verse 14 ends with the picture of the humble tax collector who was exalted by Christ. Verses 15-17 pick up on the theme of humility.

### The Scene (18:15)

Parents come to Jesus with hope for their children. They want the bless-ing of Christ on them. Christening ceremonies and baby dedications are modern-day equivalents of bringing your child to Christ.

However, the disciples rebuke the parents for doing so. The dis-ciples seem to share the culture's attitude toward children, who had little value or status in society. The disciples aren't any more enlight-ened than the rest of the culture. And this child-dismissing attitude can be true of society and even the Christian church today.

However, the disciples' attitude isn't solely about children. It also reveals who they think can come to Jesus. Who is worthy to approach the Lord? The disciples say, "Not children." They seem to think certain per-sons are worthy of the Lord's time and attention while others are not.

### Jesus's Reply (18:16-17)

The Lord Jesus calls the children to himself. He then explains that the kingdom belongs to those who are like children, those who are valued little in society. I love our Lord's habit of taking the marginal-ized and dignifying them as examples and symbols of everything that's great about God's kingdom. So any who would enter the kingdom must receive the kingdom like children, not like the disciples. All who would enter God's kingdom and truly know God must enter with a childlike humility and faith.

Our Lord's statement to the disciples challenges us. Are we like these little children—humble, dependent, trusting? Even in a worship service we can see children looking to their parents. Perhaps they are fidgety and look to their parents for approval. They look to Mom and Dad, perhaps feeling a twinge of hunger and trusting their parents to provide for them. In just a little while they will look to Mom and Dad to strap them into their car seats and keep them safe on the drive home. This constant looking up to Mom and Dad in dependence, trust, hope, and humility is what God calls us to as we look to him as our Father. God promises to give an infinite, unshakeable kingdom to those who seek him that way. In that kingdom we will reign with him.

From infancy to eternity, we were made for more than the paltry pleasures of this life. When our God made us and sent us into the world, he did not intend that we find satisfaction with the baubles and trinkets of this life. He certainly did not send us into this world that we might be satisfied with those thieving pleasures of sin. The Father did not intend that we would waste ourselves on things that break us and destroy us. He created us to be with him and find our joy in him. We were made for infinite pleasure and joy, for a kingdom and a King who brings us into his glory.

## God Rewards the Self-Denying with Eternal Life
### LUKE 18:18-30

### The Ruler's Question (18:18)

This famous passage of the Gospel focuses us on the major question of existence: "What must I do to inherit eternal life?" No more important question could ever be considered. John 17:3 defines eternal life as knowing the one true God and Jesus Christ whom God has sent. Eternal life is personal knowledge of God through his Son, Jesus Christ. This man comes to the right place with the right question.

### Jesus's Call for Clarity (18:19-22)

Our Lord responds by pointing the man to life. Jesus says he must be clear on three things. First, the man must be clear on who Jesus is (v. 19). When the Lord asks, "Why do you call me good? No one is good except God alone," he does not deny that he is God. He attempts to lead the man to the logical conclusion of his assumption: If Jesus is truly good, then he is also God. He wants to know if the man himself has come to the point of confessing Christ as Lord.

Second, the man must clearly understand what God requires of him (v. 20). We must keep the law. However, we must not keep the law in our own strength. The man doesn't yet understand this. He claims to have kept the second table of the law since his youth. However, he doesn't notice that Jesus temporarily omits the first table of the law that records those duties we owe to God. We must have no god but God. So the Lord calls the man to practically demonstrate he has no other gods but God by selling his possessions and giving to the poor. The Lord promises the man treasures in heaven if he forsakes treasures on earth and follows him. What a promise!

The man went away sad. He not only had wealth; his wealth had him. He was rich in material possessions but spiritually impoverished. Christ was calling the man to show the kind of faith that relinquishes this life in exchange for eternal life. The Lord required the man to lay down the things of this world so that he might have Christ. Christ is too big a God to have him in our hands and hold on to the world as well. Christ displaces all the world's treasures so that he alone will be adored, trusted, and obeyed.

This man speaks with the living Lord but does not recognize it. He hears an answer to the most important question in the universe, but he cannot receive it. The deceitfulness of riches blinds him. He looks at Jesus and then his things, and he chooses his things over Jesus.

## The Ruler's Response (18:23)

He kept what he had, losing nothing, but he goes away "sad." Beloved, this man's reaction dramatizes the life choice of so many people today who look at their possessions, look at Jesus, and choose their possessions. They walk away with an inexplicable sadness. Their possessions do not satisfy them anymore, but they cannot let them go—which is how we know their possessions have become idols. They are sad with it, but they must have it! So many people waste away like Gollum from *Lord of the Rings*, stroking their "Precious" and dying from it!

## Jesus's Perspective on Wealth and Salvation (18:24-27)

The man walks away sad, and Jesus feels sad for him. The Lord does not thunder condemnation from heaven. He points out how difficult it is for rich people to enter the kingdom (vv. 24-25). Riches strangle the spirit in many. The Lord laments what created things do to immortal souls.

Again the disciples think like the world (v. 26). Because the rich have access and ease in this world, they assume the rich will have access and ease with God. They think riches in this life indicate God's pleasure with a person. They even go so far as to suggest that if the rich can't gain eternal life then nobody can! They have not yet come to understand how the kingdom works.

Jesus explains that with man it's impossible for a camel to travel through the eye of a sewing needle, and it's even harder for a rich man to come to saving faith. But nothing is too hard for God—even putting a camel through the eye of a needle! God can save a rich man, but it will be an act of God, not a result of wealth. No one is beyond the reach of God's salvation.

### It's Worth It! (18:28-30)

Peter begins to understand. He mentions the things the disciples have left (v. 28). The Lord assures the disciples that no one making this sacrifice will go unrewarded (v. 29). We must forsake our lives if we are to gain our lives. When we deny ourselves, then we find ourselves and the kingdom of God and eternal life! There is a way to have your cake and eat it too—it's by coming to Christ. If your "cake" includes the things of this world, you will have to let it go, but Christ promises a better "cake"—a better feast, in fact. You will have to forsake all things to follow Christ, but it's worth it!

Ultimately the rich young ruler is a bad businessman. He was offered ultimate profit in a kingdom of glory, and he turned it down. He made a bad trade. A healthy sense of self-interest and a healthy desire for sustained pleasure ought to lead every person to trade this world for the eternal world to come. Christ will certainly make demands on our lives. He will demand our entire lives. He will rearrange our lives. He will remove us from relationships and circumstances that we love but that are not pleasing to him. He will cause us to make stands, even against our loved ones, where he is concerned. He will call us to make stands that may cost us greatly—like our spiritual brethren in Muslim and Hindu lands who lose their families, homes, and churches in persecution. He will call us to do all of these costly things, but he will reward us with an everlasting kingdom and eternal life.

Only one person in Luke 18 went away from Jesus without a reward—the man who would not deny himself. He trusted his treasures rather than Christ. Do not make this man's mistake.

## God Rewards the Blind with Sight
### LUKE 18:31-43

*Jesus's Instruction about His Crucifixion (18:31-34)*

Luke orders this section intentionally. In verses 31-34 the Lord meets privately with the disciples to relate the events about to take place in Jerusalem. He prophesies the facts of his passion and resurrection. But the disciples understood none of these things (v. 34). Hearing, they did not understand. It's as though a veil lay over their eyes.

*A Blind Beggar's Call for Mercy (18:35-39)*

Contrast the disciples with the blind beggar we meet in verse 35. Because of his blindness the man is reduced to begging in order to survive. He sits near the city gate when the crowd passes in commotion. He calls out to understand what is happening. When he learns Jesus is passing by, he springs to his feet and repeatedly calls out to Jesus using an Old Testament messianic title: "Son of David." The Son of David was prophesied to be the descendant of David who would rule on David's throne forever (2 Sam 7). The Scriptures prophesied that the Son of David would fulfill all God's plans for his people. Though the beggar cannot see and has not met the Lord before, this man knows the Lord's true identity.

The blind man discovers more riches in Christ than the rich man had without Christ. The blind man sees more in Jesus than the disciples with their sight. The beggar was not present in the private meeting Jesus held with the disciples (vv. 31-34), so he did not know Jesus had used another messianic title, "Son of Man" (v. 31), from Daniel 7. The disciples with the private study could not see it while the blind man sitting by the streets saw perfectly. He prays, "Jesus, Son of David, have mercy on me!" (v. 38).

As a young boy I grew accustomed to hearing older persons in my family and community say, "Lord, have mercy." The words ran together in a southern twang, "Ham-mercy." The older saints would use that phrase with variable tones and richer meaning than I could grasp at the time. Now that I'm older, I'm beginning to understand a little more. This blind man by the city gate shared a lot in common with my grandmother as she cried out or whispered the same prayer, "Lord, have mercy."

He sees with the eyes of faith. He believes that if he seeks Jesus, the Lord will reward him. He's hoping for the blessings prophesied in the Old Testament. He will not be silenced, even though the crowds insist that Jesus does not have time for blind beggars (v. 39). This man will not let the crowds keep him from Christ. The crowds of religious people do not always value what is in fact good and true.

### Jesus's Response (18:40-43)

The Lord calls the man to himself and asks, "What do you want me to do for you?" (v. 41). The Lord gives the blind man a blank check in prayer! It's the same blank check he gives us. He asks us each day, "What would you have me do for you?" The Father has given us his Son. How will he not, along with Christ, give us all things (Rom 8:32)?

The man asks to recover his sight. He wants to see again, to behold colors. He perhaps wants to again see the faces of his wife and children—not by slowly fading memory but with his own eyes. He wants to behold trees swaying in the breeze and blades of grass bending beneath his feet. He wants to behold life again.

I love the story of Fanny Crosby, the great hymn writer who was blind from a young age. A well-meaning visitor one day lamented her blindness and told her he wished she had her sight. He said he was sure that she too wished she could see. Fanny Crosby said to him, "Oh, no." She said she trusted Christ with her life. "Blindness," she wrote in later life, "cannot keep the sunlight of hope from the trustful soul." She maintained a wonderfully joyful perspective on her life. She wrote,

> It seemed intended by the blessed providence of God
> that I should be blind all my life, and I thank him for the
> dispensation. If perfect earthly sight were offered me
> tomorrow I would not accept it. I might not have sung hymns
> to the praise of God if I had been distracted by the beautiful
> and interesting things about me. ("Fanny Crosby")

But the most remarkable insight, in my opinion, came from her longing for heaven. She expressed it with these words:

> If at my birth, I had been able to make one petition to my
> creator, it would have been that I should be made blind. . . .
> Because, when I get to heaven, the first face that shall ever
> gladden my sight will be that of my Saviour. (Moseley H.
> Williams, "The Man Born Blind," 302)

This man comes to Jesus asking for his sight. Jesus replied, "Receive your sight. Your faith has saved you" (v. 42). Then the first thing that floods this man's renewed vision is the face of the Savior!

As the hymn writer puts it, "Oh, I want to see him, look upon his face." His is a face so full of glory that when our eyes open on the day he comes we will be transformed into the glory we see in him. To see him will be the highest happiness of heaven. Of all that's promised in the kingdom, of all the rewards, of all the treasures of infinite worth, none will compare to that moment when we lock our eyes on the face of Christ. Then, beloved, we will be satisfied (Ps 17:15)! Then we will be glad for sight. We will no longer take seeing for granted. We will see with perfect vision the perfect glory of our Lord's perfect face. All that we see will make glad the weary heart, will strengthen the tired soul, will replace all of our struggle with infinite joy.

Perhaps that's why the text ends by saying the once-blind man praised God. When we see him, we will praise him too.

## Conclusion

Ultimately, the Lord rewards us with himself. In all of his giving and answering of prayer, in the end we will receive Christ, and Christ will be the greater part.

In verse 8 the Lord asked, "When the Son of Man comes, will he find faith on earth?" That's the question that comes to us now. Are we people who believe? Are we people who trust in him? When the Savior comes, I think he will find faith because he gives faith. Those of us who receive the gift of faith may now rejoice in him.

Will you be found in faith when the Lord comes? If you are not now in the faith, consider what you have gotten to know about Jesus from this passage. He rewards those who seek him. Call on his name while you may be saved. Call out for mercy. He will answer you. Ask for the gifts of repentance and faith. Consider his love for you, proven through the crucifixion of his Son. Meditate on the righteousness God offers through Jesus's resurrection. Then ask for saving faith so that you would be found in Christ on the day of his coming. Confess your sin, repent, and believe, and the hope of seeing Jesus will be yours.

## Reflect and Discuss

1. Justice, mercy, the kingdom, eternal life, and sight—among these, which do you think is the most precious gift in this chapter?
2. What do we learn in this chapter about Jesus's attitude toward marginalized people? What do we learn about the tendency of disciples and crowds to keep marginalized people away from Jesus? How would Jesus have us act in these situations?
3. Consider the instances of prayer in this chapter. What do we learn about the Lord's response to prayer? What ideas from the chapter encourage you in your prayer life?
4. Do you think riches and material possessions are a significant hindrance to eternal life for some people? If so, why do you think some people choose their possessions rather than Christ? What is it about riches or about people that gives money this power?
5. What do you think it will be like when we finally see Jesus?

# The Savior of the Lost

## LUKE 19:1-27

**Main Idea:** Jesus came to seek and to save the lost. Now we join him in that mission.

---

I.  **Do Everything You Can to See Jesus (19:1-10).**
    A.  Zacchaeus tries to see Jesus (19:2-4).
    B.  The people grumble against Zacchaeus and Jesus (19:5-7).
    C.  Zacchaeus repents and is saved (19:8-10).
II. **Do Everything You Can to Serve Jesus (19:11-27).**
    A.  The people in the parable (19:12-14)
    B.  The problem in the parable (19:15-24)
    C.  The philosophy of the parable (19:25-27)

---

As we look into God's Word and see God revealed in the person of his Son, we have the privilege of getting to know God himself. We find ourselves drawn into the presence of his love. Luke 19 teaches us that Jesus is the Savior of the lost. Because the Lord Jesus, the Son of God, is the Savior of the world, he certainly finds whomever he searches for. Since he finds the ones he seeks, the Lord leaves us with two things: an imperative to do everything to see Jesus and, if we have seen him and love him, to do everything to serve Jesus.

## Do Everything You Can to See Jesus
### LUKE 19:1-10

We begin with a well-known story in the Christian world. We even have a children's song about it.

> Zacchaeus was a wee little man, a wee little man was he;
> He climbed up in a sycamore tree, for the Lord he wanted to see.

Luke 19:1-10 is a good part of Scripture to turn into a children's song because it teaches us tremendous things about Jesus and about why we should seek him.

After traveling for the last few chapters, Jesus finally enters Jericho (v. 1). It's the last major city the Lord visits before entering Jerusalem. He has prophesied several times that when he reaches Jerusalem he will be betrayed, tried by sinful men, beaten and mocked, killed, and then raised from the grave three days later. Verse 1 reminds us of what fast approaches.

### Zacchaeus Tries to See Jesus (19:2-4)

It's in that context that Zacchaeus tries to see the Lord Jesus Christ. Verses 2-4 introduce us to Zacchaeus and record the effort he went through. Verse 2 says he was "a chief tax collector" and "was rich." Both of those descriptions tell us something about Zacchaeus's spiritual life.

Regular tax collectors were hated in Israel because they worked for the Roman government that oppressed the Jewish people. Zacchaeus was a *chief* tax collector. In all likelihood he did not receive that position by working hard. He probably rose to that rank by being more crooked than other tax collectors, who often cheated people out of their earnings.

Also, Zacchaeus was "rich." Do you remember what our Lord says about rich people in the previous chapter?

> *How hard it is for those who have wealth to enter the kingdom of God!*
> *For it is easier for a camel to go through the eye of a needle than for a*
> *rich person to enter the kingdom of God.* (18:24-25)

Zacchaeus is a sinner, and he's rich. He's the kind of guy you wouldn't expect to make it into the kingdom, according to Jesus.

But verse 3 says, "He was trying to see who Jesus was." I think this sentence is pregnant with meaning. They didn't know each other, but perhaps the crowd piqued his interest. Perhaps he'd heard something about this new rabbi who did miracles, astounded people with his teaching, and even accepted outcasts. He's looking for Jesus, but there's a problem. Zacchaeus was a short man and couldn't see over the people (v. 3).

So this rich man, who likely oppressed people and might have been accustomed to others deferring to him out of fear, ran ahead and climbed up into a sycamore tree to see Jesus. We might expect to see children climbing trees and sitting on branches with their legs dangling over limbs. One of the great growing-up pastimes is climbing trees. But we do not expect to see among any children in the tree a grown man in an expensive robe hugging a tree trunk and looking into the crowd.

Zacchaeus has put himself where he can *physically* see the Lord.

## The People Grumble Against Zacchaeus and Jesus (19:5-7)

Jesus saw Zacchaeus in the tree and called him by name. They'd never met before, but the Lord knew Zacchaeus before Zacchaeus knew the Lord. That's the case with us all. The Lord says, "Zacchaeus, hurry and come down because today it is necessary for me to stay at your house."

By putting himself in position to see Jesus physically, Zacchaeus has now also put himself in position to see Jesus personally and socially. He receives Jesus's instruction and invitation. He does so "joyfully," which is the only way to respond when the Son of God calls you by name. No doubt some of you have been hearing the Lord call you to come to him. You should, like Zacchaeus, hurry to meet the Lord. Zacchaeus has gone from trying to see who Jesus was to hurrying to have Jesus over for dinner. He's doing everything he can to know the Lord.

But verse 7 presents a problem. Crowds have mood swings. They had been traveling excitedly with Jesus, but now they see Jesus calling down Zacchaeus to eat with him, and they all "began to complain." They said, "He's gone to stay with a sinful man." The crowd seems to think that holiness means separating from sinners and shunning them. They seem to think that if Jesus were really a prophet or a rabbi, then he should have nothing to do with the likes of Zacchaeus, a known sinner.

Let us be careful of ever daring to assess whether someone is worthy of meeting God. When we feel someone is unworthy of God, we actually insult that person and God. When we think someone is unworthy of God, we throw that person away long before God ever would. At the same time, should God welcome them, then we put ourselves in a position, like the crowd, of questioning God. We ought to concern ourselves with our own unworthiness if we find ourselves condemning others. What's true of Zacchaeus is true of us all: we're all sinners who have fallen short of the glory of God (Rom 3:23).

A grumbling crowd is a dangerous crowd; it turns on you. A grumbling crowd is a sinful crowd, since grumbling against the Lord is a sin in itself. Just as when Israel grumbled against God in the wilderness (Exod 16:8; Num 14:27; Jas 5:9; Jude 1:16), the crowd proves its own sinfulness as they grumble because of Zacchaeus's sin.

Not everyone will be happy when you fellowship with Jesus, even among the crowds that follow Jesus. A godly person would rejoice to see you turn from sin and follow the Lord; but not everyone in the crowd, though religious, knows the Lord personally. It can be difficult to live down your sinful past when the crowds know who you were or what you did. But never let the crowds keep you from Jesus. Never let grumbling people interrupt the chance you have of getting to know Jesus.

### Zacchaeus Repents and Is Saved (19:8-10)

God saved Zacchaeus after he put himself in position to see and know the Lord. Zacchaeus repents of his sin by giving half of his possessions to the poor and returning four times as much to anyone he has extorted from or defrauded. Zacchaeus forsakes stinginess and greediness and turns to the poor in generosity. In a world where riches choke out the word and strangle faith, to give to others signifies genuine repentance. Zacchaeus also turns back to his victims to return to them fourfold what he has taken. In this way he turns back to God's law to submit to the Bible's vision of justice and restoration for wrong. He demonstrates newfound obedience to God. Zacchaeus provides us a marvelous picture of repentance.

He also provides us a marvelous picture of Luke 18:27. Here God demonstrates the "possible" salvation in a rich man's life. God can call people from all their idols, a lifetime of sin, and the habit of abusing privilege, position, and others, and turn such persons to himself, making them new.

Zacchaeus is not buying his salvation. No amount of money can buy salvation. No, he's showing by his giving the change of heart he's had. When a person is truly repentant, it affects how they view and use money. At the very least, money is no longer their god—Jesus Christ is. They don't look to *cheat* people *for* money; instead they look to *bless* people *with* their money. They become givers rather than takers because they've been set free from greed and idolatry. A converted man is a generous man.

That's why the Lord proclaims in verse 9: "Today salvation has come to this house, because he too is a son of Abraham." Zacchaeus was saved from God's judgment against sin on that very day. He was saved because he became that day a true "son of Abraham." Abraham believed God's promise, and God counted Abraham as righteous because of his belief (Gen 15:6). The same has happened here with Zacchaeus. He has believed the promise of God and has become a "son of Abraham," a person of faith.

Conversion is the heart of Jesus's mission in the world. So the Lord says in verse 10, "For the Son of Man has come to seek and to save the lost." If someone ever asks you, "Why did Jesus come?" here's the perfect answer from Jesus himself. He came to seek and to save the lost.

Jesus came looking for "lost" people. What does it mean to be "lost"? We know when we are lost, but we usually don't know it until we are lost. It's like a driver speeding along to his favorite song. He enjoys the music and impresses himself with "the good time he is making," and he never notices he missed the turn or exit. At some point he recognizes he doesn't know where he is. He didn't start out uncertain; he started with confidence. But now he doesn't know where he is or how to get where he wants to be—even back to where he started. He cannot go forward or backward with any confidence that he's going in the right direction. Lostness disorients us. Then his pride kicks in as he refuses to stop for directions or accept help from his wife. He clenches his teeth and presses further into his lost state.

That's what it is to be "lost." Spiritually, we are all lost apart from Christ. We cannot determine how we got where we are or how to get back where we've been. We are surprised at our spiritual location. And it may be that we've been lost so long that we don't know where home is. We can be so separated from God that we forget we were made to be with God in his kingdom, face-to-face in his love.

Lost people are people who cannot find their way to God because of sin. They have lost their way, and they are lost to God. But the Father sent his Son to find them—not only to seek them but also to rescue them and bring them back safely home.

## Applications

*Gospel appeal.* Sinner, Jesus is looking for you. He still seeks and saves the lost. Don't let the crowds keep you from him. Do everything you can to see him. Don't let your pride drive you deeper into lostness. Instead, receive the love of God through Jesus Christ his Son. The Son gave his life on the cross to pay the penalty of your sins. Three days later God raised him from the dead for your justification. Now home lies the way of the cross. Put your faith in Christ, repent of sin, and follow the Lord home to glory.

*Evangelism.* Like Zacchaeus, who was a sinful tax collector and hardened to God because he was rich, God's people are sometimes camouflaged as sinners. So they must be sought. This is the work and goal of evangelism. Many people think of their neighborhood as "tough" or "distressed," but every neighborhood is filled with people who are destined to be God's people through faith in Christ. We are to go seek them and tell them the way of salvation. If it was "necessary" (v. 5) for Jesus to go to Zacchaeus's home, then a necessity falls on us to go into the world to seek and save the lost.

We exist to make disciples from the four corners of the block to the four corners of the world. If we are not going to go to our neighbors with the good news, then we don't need to be in the neighborhood where God has placed us. If we wish to reduce Christianity to a preaching point one morning a week, then we may as well locate ourselves in the most convenient place and be sure to drive traffic to our website. If we do not want to risk anything in meeting our neighbors and building relationships, then let's move to the suburbs and enjoy manicured lawns. No, God has placed us where we are to make real-life contact with people made in the image of God to tell them how to get home. We *must* do this, and it's our *privilege* to do it.

*Justice.* A converted man is a just man. We see two forms of justice in verse 8. First, there is justice in the form of **redistribution** of wealth. Zacchaeus gives half his goods to the poor. This deed is free and voluntary. It's the opposite of the rich man in Luke 18. Not everyone everywhere is commanded to do exactly as Zacchaeus does here. But it's a mighty fine example. Some people somewhere sometimes ought to do this because it's how God cares for the poor—through the just redistribution of wealth that we call giving, charity, or alms. Genuine conversion produces generosity in the converted.

There's another kind of justice here too. It's **restitution** to the victim. When Zacchaeus says he will give fourfold to anyone he has defrauded, he goes from lawbreaker to lawkeeper. He seeks to do justice for those he has wronged. Repentance isn't complete until there is justice given to those we've sinned against. We cannot say we are repentant and following Christ if we intend to leave unaddressed and unchanged the wrongs we have committed against others. Repentance includes restitution and reconciliation.

We talk a lot about justice in our day, but the surest way to see justice among men is to see men converted and to teach them to live as God requires. In the words of Micah 6:8,

> *Mankind, he has told each of you what is good*
> *and what it is the LORD requires of you:*
> *to act justly,*
> *to love faithfulness,*
> *and to walk humbly with your God.*

Zacchaeus does everything he can to see Jesus. When he meets with the Lord, he actually becomes a brand-new man, born again through faith in Jesus Christ.

## Do Everything You Can to Serve Jesus
### LUKE 19:11-27

Verse 11 tells us that the people "were listening to this." When they heard these things, they made two mistakes in their thinking. (1) They forgot they were on the way to Jerusalem. (2) All the talk of salvation coming to Zacchaeus's house *on that day* had them thinking "the kingdom of God was going to appear right away."

They were ready to skip the cross and go straight to the kingdom. That's a mistake people make all the time, but the truth is, there is no kingdom unless there is first the cross. First comes suffering; then comes glory. That's why Jesus tells them this parable. He's trying to fix the two mistakes they're making in their thinking.

### The People in the Parable (19:12-14)

The parable has three sets of characters in it. There is the **nobleman** who goes into a far country to receive for himself a kingdom and then return (v. 12). That nobleman represents Jesus. He goes to Jerusalem where he would be killed. He would rise three days later and then ascend into heaven. That's the far country where the Lord receives his kingdom. He's going away for a time.

Then there are the ten servants in verse 13. Those are Jesus's followers or **disciples**. They receive ten minas or coins. They're supposed to engage in business until the nobleman returns. In other words, the servants or disciples are to be good stewards for the Lord, serving him until he returns.

Finally, there are the **citizens** in verse 14. They "hated him and sent a delegation after him, saying, 'We don't want this man to rule over us.'" These citizens represent the lost sinners who reject Jesus Christ. In their sin they attempt to be their own lords.

### The Problem in the Parable (19:15-24)

Verse 15 flashes forward to when the nobleman returns from the far country and has "received the authority to be king." So Jesus is looking down the tunnel of time to his second coming. Despite the servants' protests, the nobleman does in fact return with his kingdom intact. So, too, will Jesus. The first thing the nobleman does is call his servants to him to give an account for how they conducted his business. The parable illustrates what 1 Peter 4:17 says: "The time has come for judgment to begin with God's household." The first people called before King Jesus are those of us who follow him.

We all must give an account for what we do with our "minas" or coins, which symbolize our whole selves. In what way are we stewarding all that we have to complete our Master's business of seeking and saving the lost?

We get a report on three of the ten servants. The first servant (vv. 16-17) turned his one mina into eleven, and because of that he rules over ten cities. The second servant (vv. 18-19) turns his mina into six and rules over five cities. Ruling over cities represents our reign with Christ in his kingdom. The reward is proportional to the return on investment. A life of serving Christ is an eternally rewarded life!

Then you get to "another" servant in verse 20. That servant came with excuses rather than profit. He had put the money in a handkerchief and buried it. Verse 21 says this servant did that because he was afraid of the nobleman. He thought the nobleman was "harsh." The servant thought the nobleman reaped or received where he did not sow or work. This servant thought hard thoughts toward his lord, and in his fear he thought his excuse might be enough to justify his failure to use what the nobleman had given him.

The problem is, he didn't act on what he knew about the nobleman. In verses 22-23 the nobleman uses his own words against him. He says, basically, if you knew those things about me, then you should have used what I gave you to make more. The nobleman points out that this man does not live by his theology. He confesses something about his lord but does not live in light of the confession. Even with his partial knowledge, the servant should have acted. Why didn't he even make a safe investment, like depositing the money in the bank to earn interest?

God expects us to use what he gives us to make more for his kingdom. God expects us to use our theology to motivate our actions. We should act on what we know about God. There's no acceptable excuse for not acting on the truth we know about God. That very truth will condemn us. It's not that we are responsible for the truths we *don't* know. It's what we do with what we *do* know.

Someone once said, "I am not troubled by the parts of the Bible I don't understand. I am troubled by the parts of the Bible I do understand."

That person knew some things were clear in the Bible. The clear things of the Scriptures make us accountable to God. Whatever truth we know *about* God, we are responsible for that truth *before* God. Even if we—like this servant—don't like the truth or it seems unpleasant to us, we must steward it by acting on it to make a profit for the kingdom.

Instead of inheriting cities to rule, the third servant loses the cities, and he loses his stewardship. He himself is not lost, but all that he could have had as a reward in the new kingdom is taken away. Live for the reward of heaven. Live for the promise of glory. God calls us to live for a reward we cannot imagine. What will it be like to rule with Christ, to sit on thrones ruling over cities? How sublime will it be to share in the glory of Christ when he is eternally enthroned? We should serve Jesus until we see Jesus, when we hear the "well done" and share his reward.

Do you need a reason to get out of bed tomorrow? How about the promise of an eternal kingdom with Christ?

### The Philosophy of the Parable (19:25-27)

In his kingdom God rewards faithfulness. That's what the Lord means by "everyone who has" (19:26). Each of the servants had one mina, but one was unfaithful; he didn't multiply it. So his share was given to the faithful who had a one thousand percent return on his stewardship.

We often refer to the poor as the "have nots." But that's not what Jesus has in mind in verse 26. The "one who does not have" refers to the unfaithful. Though he had a mina, he didn't steward it well. So when he buried it, it's as if he didn't have it.

The faithful are rewarded.

The wicked are condemned. Verse 27 comes back to the citizens. Do you remember them? They were those who hated the nobleman and protested against his rule.

They are not forgotten. When the judgment of his servants is complete, then the judgment of the haters begins. Haters gon' hate. But haters gon' be judged too. They are slaughtered before the king. That is a violent image, but it does not even compare to the condemnation of the wicked in hell. The Lord reaches for a graphic image to help us understand how terrible the consequence of lostness is. Those in hell wish they could be slaughtered and have it over with. However, they have sinned against an infinite God and pay an infinite penalty. If nothing else, the constant reminder of Jesus's kingship and rule will be agony to their souls.

There is no good reason to rebel against Jesus. Can you think of a good reason to rebel against a God who loves you and gave his life to save you from hell and to love you forever? I can't. Rebellion only ends in destruction.

There is every reason to believe in him and to follow him and to serve him. Faith ends in eternal life and ruling with Christ in an everlasting kingdom.

Be like Zacchaeus: repent of sin. Believe in Christ as your Lord. Be faithful to serve Christ all your life. Then receive glory and honor as you reign with him. That's the philosophy of this chapter. That's the philosophy of the Christian life. There's no better way to live. This is the only way that can properly be called "living." Everything else is a kind of death. Believe on the Lord Jesus Christ and you will live.

## Reflect and Discuss

1. How well positioned are you to see Jesus? Do you need to move in some way (physically, socially, spiritually) in order to get a clearer sight of the Lord?

2. What evidences of repentance do we see in Zacchaeus? What evidences of repentance were present at your conversion?

3. The crowds disapprove of Jesus's fellowship with Zacchaeus, yet Zacchaeus comes to faith in the Lord. How commonly do you think Christians resemble the attitudes of the crowds who did not think Zacchaeus was worthy to be with Jesus? How can we better spot those attitudes and root them out?

4. Do you think Christians give appropriate emphasis to justice in our Christian lives? Why or why not?

5. What does Jesus seem to think about hell based on this passage? How should the horror of hell factor into how we steward the gospel?

6. What do we learn about the sovereignty of Christ and the certainty of his kingdom from this passage? Do these things give you hope?

# The King of Peace

## LUKE 19:28-48

**Main Idea:** God offers true and lasting peace when we praise, seek, and listen.

---

I.   **Peace Is a Person (19:28-40).**
   A.   Jerusalem, the city of peace (19:28)
   B.   Riding on a colt (19:29-35)
   C.   Praise for peace (19:36-40)
II.  **Peace Is Elusive (19:41-44).**
   A.   Not knowing what makes for peace (19:42)
   B.   Not knowing that God is with us (19:43-44)
III. **Peace Requires Maintenance (19:45-48).**
   A.   We maintain peace by speaking to God (19:45-46).
   B.   We maintain peace by listening to God (19:47-48).

---

Few things are more fragile than peace. You can break windows with a stone, but you can break peace with as little as a look or a word.

Entire nations have not known peace for generations. We think of Israel's conflict with the Palestinians, the long civil war in Sudan, and the "troubles" in Ireland.

Local communities sometimes long for peace. The great city of Chicago sees so much violence on its south side some now call it "Chiraq." The streets where I live in Washington, D.C., lack peace.

A lack of peace affects families and individuals, too. Marriages fill with strife. Parents and children argue. We may lack peace within ourselves. We may be unsettled, uncertain, conflicted. One moment we are angry. The next we are sad. Then all of a sudden we are happy—without ever knowing exactly why we feel any of those things.

We simply know we need peace. Indeed, we need peace with men and we need peace within.

Do you have peace? Where did you get it? Do you know where to find peace or how to keep it? Do you know what makes for peace? Would you recognize peace if it were offered to you? Would you know what to do with it if you had it?

Our text lies between two great conversation partners—the Old Testament prophet Zechariah and the New Testament apostle Paul. This text, with its simple action, fulfills profound prophecy and can only be explained in light of the finished work of the Lord Jesus Christ. As we examine Luke 19:28-48, from time to time we want to bring Zechariah in to speak with us. And from time to time we want to bring the apostle Paul in to share an insight so that we might understand this text as fully as possible.

Luke 19:28-48 holds out to us a rare thing: a true and lasting peace. The world cannot give us the peace of Luke 19, and the world cannot take it away. Do we want this kind of peace?

## Peace Is a Person
### LUKE 19:28-40

Since Luke 9:44, the Lord had been predicting his death. "When the days were coming to a close for him to be taken up, he determined to journey to Jerusalem" (9:51). From that point the entire Gospel builds to Luke 19:28. Now, finally, the Lord arrives at the holy city. In Jerusalem Luke reveals that Jesus is the King of peace. Luke makes the revelation in three ways.

### Jerusalem, the City of Peace (19:28)

First, we get a hint at the theme of peace in the city name, "Jerusalem." Sometimes cities have nicknames for themselves. Philadelphia is the "City of Brotherly Love"—which you cannot tell from its sports fans! Pittsburgh boasts that it is "Steel City." Detroit is known as "Motor City." Kristie and I lived for years in Raleigh, North Carolina—the "City of Oaks." The name *Jerusalem* literally means "Foundation of Peace."

### Riding on a Colt (19:29-35)

The Lord's kingship of peace is alluded to in a second way. In verses 29-35 the Lord instructs his disciples to enter a nearby village. They will find a never-ridden colt there. He tells them to untie the colt and bring it to him. If anybody asks, "Why are you untying it," they are to answer, "The Lord needs it" (vv. 33-34).

Zechariah helps us understand the business with the colt that had never been ridden.

*Rejoice greatly, Daughter Zion!*
*Shout in triumph, Daughter Jerusalem!*
*Look, your King is coming to you;*
*he is righteous and victorious,*
*humble and riding on a donkey,*
*on a colt, the foal of a donkey.* (Zech 9:9)

Zechariah predicted that the true king of Israel would come to Jerusalem on a young, unused colt. When kings came to cities in times of war, they came on mighty warhorses, terrible steeds. But when kings came on a donkey, it meant they were coming in peace.

Perhaps this is why the people simply allow the disciples to take the donkey. It's a peculiar scene. The disciples find the colt just as Jesus prophesied. As far as we know, the disciples are strangers to the colt's owner. Can you hear the owners speak up, "Uh . . . what are you doing, bro? You just gon' take m' donkey?" Then the disciples say, "The Lord needs it." And the owners are like, "Oh, OK, then. Go ahead." Where does *that* happen? Perhaps the owners of the colt were expecting the Lord, just as Zechariah prophesied.

## Praise for Peace (19:36-40)

If Zechariah's prophecy and Jesus's riding on a donkey were too subtle, notice what the crowds say. A praise parade breaks out in verse 37. The crowds seem also to fulfill Zechariah's prophecy as they "rejoice greatly, Daughter Zion." They proclaim "Hosanna!" (Matt 21:9) and lay their cloaks before the Lord. Having witnessed Jesus do great things amplified the praise of the crowds. They discern that the Lord's coming has something to do with peace. "Peace in heaven and glory in the highest heaven," they proclaim (v. 38). Their words in verse 38 hark back to Luke 2:14, where our Savior's birth took place. The angels cried, "Glory to God in the highest heaven, and peace on earth to people he favors!"

Wherever Jesus goes, he brings peace. When he was born and came to earth, the angels cried, "Peace on earth." When the Lord was about to be crucified and ascend to God, then men cried out, "Peace in heaven." Here is the King of peace entering the city of peace on a beast of peace.

## Application

Do you know where to find peace with God? We find it with God's Son, Jesus Christ. "He himself is our peace" (Eph 2:14 ESV). We will not have peace with God, peace with men, or peace within until Jesus Christ becomes our peace.

What is this peace? It is wholeness or wellness. It is a kind of integrity that puts the soul at rest. Everything has a place and is in its place. No matter what happens in the rest of the world, there's a stillness, a quiet and confident certitude that you're going to be all right.

When Christ comes to us, he comes to give us this peace. Sinners though we are, rebels though we have been, though far from the will of God we have strayed, he comes to bring us back to God that we might have peace with God. He not only brings us peace with God but reconciles us with one another. So the New Testament church becomes a community of peace where people are stilled, quieted, and calmed. Christ has joined each of us to himself, and in joining us to himself has joined us to one another in peace.

Whoever knows Jesus and has seen his mighty works cannot help but praise him. The Pharisees want Jesus to rebuke his disciples because of this praise (v. 39). They think the crowd has gone too far. They don't like to see Jesus praised as king. They don't like this talk of glory where Jesus is concerned. They want this ended.

Our Lord's response is famous in every expressive church and among those who love to praise God. God *will* be praised by his creation, even if inanimate rocks must give voice to his greatness (v. 40). The rocks will cry out. The trees will clap (Isa 55:12). The mountains will skip and sing (Ps 114:4,6; Isa 55:12). The sky will proclaim his handiwork (Ps 19:1). Everything that has breath will praise the Lord (Ps 150:6).

Do not let anyone stop you from praising Jesus, including outwardly religious folks. Do not be afraid to express yourself when you praise him. He is worthy! If Christ brings you peace, then bring him praise!

## Peace Is Elusive
### LUKE 19:41-44

The Lord finally catches sight of Jerusalem itself (v. 41). The Prince of Peace also weeps. You can have peace in yourself and weep over your city. Jesus does. Perhaps there's something wrong with someone who claims to have the peace of Christ but never seems to have the tears of Christ. That may not be peace but indifference and hard-heartedness.

Our Lord looks on the city he loves, and his heart melts. Perhaps you have not thought about this at any length, but *God cries.* Here the Son of God with all power and glory looks on the city of sinful man. Thunder does not rumble, and lightning does not flash in divine curses. The earth does not quake in destruction. Instead, rivulets of tears flow down the Savior's face. He weeps for the city, for entire cities and entire communities and entire nations. He weeps because what he has come to bring has somehow escaped them. It eluded them.

## Not Knowing What Makes for Peace (19:42)

Peace is elusive. First, peace eludes people when they don't know what makes for peace (v. 42). The Lord wishes Jerusalem knew the key to peace. He wishes Jerusalem knew what would settle their hearts and minds. He wishes they knew what would heal their relationships, what would give them a settled confidence before God.

Even today cities are full of people who do not know what things produce *shalom,* peace. People try all kinds of things. We pass people along the way who are medicating themselves with drugs and alcohol. We see people trying to calm their raging hearts with sex and relationships, money and power. There are those seeking peace with God in false religions and cults. If you ask them why, they tell you that they are looking for peace.

Peace substitutes will not fulfill or last. But Jesus has come to give us this peace. In some ways Jesus's mission may be summed up in that one idea (1:76-79). When someone comes to guide you to Christ and into the knowledge of his salvation, forgiveness of sin, and the righteousness of God, they come guiding you into peace.

## Not Knowing That God Is with Us (19:43-44)

Jerusalem will one day be surrounded and besieged by enemies. Those enemies will reduce the city to rubble and tear families apart because they did not know the day or recognize the moment of the visitation, when God came to them.

Peace is a difficult thing to find if you do not know that God is present with you. All that Jesus prophesies in verse 43 comes to pass. In AD 70 the Romans occupied and destroyed Jerusalem along with the temple. No stone was left on another. What had been known of that great city was obliterated. Our Lord effectively says, "It would have been different for you if you had known I had come to visit you."

Have you ever thought about how many of our problems come from a failure to recognize God's presence with us? That was true in Jerusalem, and it is true today as well.

Yet Christ has fulfilled God's law by sacrificing himself on the cross. His act of self-giving made peace—peace between men, peace within, and peace with God. When Christ died on the cross for our sins, he ended the strife so characteristic of a fallen world. So whether we are Jews or Gentiles, by the preaching of Jesus Christ crucified, buried, and resurrected, we have peace. By faith in the Son of God, we receive reconciliation with God. We stop trying to earn God's approval by our good works. We stop trying to please men. Instead, we begin to live to please God who accepts us in his Son.

We worry no more about God's acceptance because Christ has become our righteousness (1 Cor 1:30). We worry no more about God's justice because Christ has been condemned for us. He was punished in our place. All the anger of God toward the sin of men is satisfied in the Son of God. There is peace with God—a quiet mind and confident assurance that in believing and following Jesus we are reconciled to our Father in heaven and to our brethren on earth.

Do not let little church squabbles fool you, beloved. Oh, we may have our periods of disagreement. Some of those may be sharp. We may think differently on things. But such struggles should never rob us of peace as the people of God. For our peace remains in Christ who has reconciled us to himself, to one another, and to the Father. Nothing in this world can destroy that peace.

## Peace Requires Maintenance
### LUKE 19:45-48

Not only is peace elusive; it also requires we maintain it once we have it. Keeping peace differs little from grass that needs to be mowed, exercise that needs to be monitored, or a relationship that needs repeated investment. In fact, since peace is most fundamentally a relationship with Christ, we should not be surprised if, like all relationships, we must give peace with Christ constant attention.

### We Maintain Peace by Speaking to God (19:45-46)

First, once Jesus enters Jerusalem, he purges the temple and restores prayer. Sinful men have always made religion big business. People have always attempted to make money off of their gods. Such people are not true worshipers or teachers. These are the false teachers who worship mammon.

In Jesus's day the money changers set up shop right in the temple. They sold the animals and things people needed to make offerings to God. They did so for a profit rather than for genuine religious motive. The temple became a den of robbers.

Sometimes maintaining peace requires confrontation. So the Lord Jesus made a whip and drove them out. To say Jesus is the King of peace does not mean he is soft. The Lord can be angered just as he can weep—especially when predators corrupt his worship.

We are God's temple (1 Cor 3:16; 6:19). We are also his priesthood. So we ought to be a people of prayer. We can never pray enough if we want to maintain the peace of God. God will "keep the mind that is dependent on [him] in perfect peace" (Isa 26:3). So do you pray as you should? What robs you of prayer and peace? Is there anything you should drive out? If so, do it before Christ makes a whip and cleanses you, his temple.

### We Maintain Peace by Listening to God (19:47-48)

Once the Lord cleansed the temple, he went back to teaching the people. Jesus loves to teach. "*Every day* he was teaching in the temple" (v. 47). How important must the Lord's teaching be if near the end of his life he did it every day?

"The chief priests, the scribes, and the leaders of the people were looking for a way to kill him." However, "They could not find a way to do it" (v. 48). Why could they do nothing? "All the people were captivated by what they heard." There were too many people peacefully listening to Jesus's words, so conflict could not advance. They hung on his words. All around them conflict and violent rage surged, but they sat listening to Jesus. They were content. They were filled with peace. The remedy to blindness, ignorance, and disquieting anger is listening to God's word.

What will we do with seasons of peace when the Lord gives them to us? We should be captivated by Jesus's every word.

God's people don't always have this peace and quiet. In a few days the calm of this scene will be shattered by the crucifixion. The peace that comes before the storm suggests we may better survive suffering and disappointment by using seasons of peace to store up our Lord's word. Later the disciples remembered what the Lord taught while he was with them. By remembering his teaching, they regained and maintained peace. By remembering the teaching they had received in seasons of peace, they were able to correctly interpret and understand the horror that befell them on Calvary.

How about us? How are we doing at being captivated by the Lord's words? Are we more focused on the chaos around us or on Christ's word?

## Conclusion

Praise God for his peace. Seek God for his peace. Listen to God for his peace. Praise, seek, and listen, and peace will be yours. The world cannot give and cannot take away the peace the Savior gives (John 14:27; 16:33).

## Reflect and Discuss

1. Where do you think most people search for peace?
2. Why do you think some people easily believe peace apart from God is possible while peace through a relationship with God seems unreal?
3. What has God done to provide mankind peace?
4. Would you say you are in a season of peace or of turmoil? How might getting to know Jesus better increase your peace?
5. The Lord promises that the world cannot take away the peace he gives (John 14:27; 16:33), but we see Christians who lack peace and face trouble. How do we reconcile those two things?
6. What are you doing to maintain peace with God? How can you help others find greater peace in Christ?

# David's True Son

## LUKE 20

**Main Idea:** We are likely to wrestle with authority and its abuse until we see Jesus in all his perfect use of authority.

---

I. **You Cannot Question His Authority (20:1-8).**
   A. The challenge (20:1-2)
   B. The clap back (20:3-7)
   C. The conclusion (20:8)
II. **You Cannot Refuse His Authority (20:9-18).**
   A. The parable
   B. The point
   C. The privileged
   D. The point, again
III. **You Cannot Trump His Authority (20:19-26).**
   A. The plot (20:19-20)
   B. The pretense (20:21-22)
   C. The perceptiveness (20:23-26)
IV. **You Cannot Trivialize His Authority (20:27-44).**
   A. The Sadducees' scenario (20:27-33)
   B. They don't understand the ages (20:34-36).
   C. They don't understand the resurrection (20:37-40).
   D. They don't understand David's Son (20:41-44).
V. **You Cannot Avoid His Authority (20:45-47).**

---

Authority. Most people want it. Few people want to be under it.

We are suspicious of authority. We don't trust claims to power and control. And sometimes we have reason. We've seen all kinds of authority abused. We've seen parents mistreat their children. We've seen bosses terrorize their employees. We've seen government leaders become dictators. We've even seen church leaders prey on the people they were meant to shepherd.

With so much misuse of authority, it's no wonder many people withdraw from it. Since at least the 1960s, American society has questioned, challenged, opposed, and even ridiculed authority. Rebels are seen as heroes. Mavericks are thought to be independent. "Sticking it to the man" has become a pastime, even when you're not sure who "the man" is.

But no matter our attitude, the world remains filled with authority. Individuals and institutions control our lives. We still report to bosses. We still pull over when officers turn on their sirens. We still obey our parents. We still submit to our government and its laws. We even submit to religious leaders in voluntary religious organizations like the church.

Why do we submit to authority? Why do we sometimes want it when we don't have it? Why do we question those in authority and mistrust it?

## You Cannot Question His Authority
### LUKE 20:1-8

Verse 1 takes us back to the last few days before Jesus's death. The Lord has finally entered Jerusalem, where he will be tried, crucified, and resurrected. Luke casually tells us that it was just "one day." It's almost as if this day began just like any other day. "One day." And what do we find the Lord doing? It cannot be stressed or highlighted enough that Jesus preached the gospel. How important is the gospel? Well, the Lord Jesus Christ proclaimed it up until his death! Until he died, the Lord told people why he came to die. If the good news is that important in the Lord's sight, then it must be about the most important thing imaginable!

What was the good news Jesus preached? It was simple, but it was and is the most important news ever. You can summarize this good news in four sentences:

- The only true, living, and holy God made all of mankind in his image and likeness so that all people could know him and enjoy him forever.
- People have broken their relationship with God through sin and now deserve God's righteous condemnation in hell.
- To rescue mankind from his condemnation and to bring us back to his love and acceptance forever, God made up for our sin by sending his Son Jesus to suffer condemnation in our place on the cross and to defeat death in the resurrection.
- To receive that new life and to be brought back to God in righteousness, God requires all people everywhere to confess their sin, turn away from it, and follow Jesus as their Savior and God.

That's the good news. That's what Jesus was proclaiming on that day. That's what we're preaching today. And we want you to believe, to put your trust in Jesus, and to rely on him to rescue you from hell.

### The Challenge (20:1-2)

As Jesus was preaching the gospel—the most important message in the universe—some religious people interrupted him. "The chief priests and the scribes, with the elders, came and said to him: 'Tell us, by what authority are you doing these things? Who is it who gave you this authority?'" These people make up the entire religious authority of the Jewish people in Jesus's day. They controlled worship and spiritual life in Israel and in the temple where Jesus was preaching. These are the conservative religious folks. They believe the Scripture, so they say. They believe in obeying the law. In a way they take religious authority and faith seriously.

But they challenge Jesus's authority. They know they had not granted Jesus authority to teach and preach in the temple. And while they didn't recognize Jesus's authority, they sure did want to hold on to their own. So they challenged the Lord by questioning his authority.

### The Clap Back (20:3-7)

The Lord has a little clap back of his own. He answers their question with a question in verse 4: "Was the baptism of John from heaven or of human origin?" They didn't expect that. So they did what religiously conservative people do when they have a question—they held a conference (v. 5). They formed a little holy huddle. You could see them with bowed heads talking and looking up at Jesus every once in a while.

After their discussion, all they could come up with was a Washington, D.C., answer we hear a lot during election season: "We don't know." They don't know because they don't want to know. They don't want to say John's baptism was from heaven because they rejected John. They don't want to say it was from man because all the people recognized John as a prophet from God. They were stuck between conviction and cowardice. They're trying to control the spin.

But, beloved, sometimes the simple admission of wrong is the most freeing thing in the world.

*The Conclusion (20:8)*

When they said that "they did not know its origin" (v. 7), the Lord answered them, "Neither will I tell you by what authority I do these things."

Beloved, this is a stunning scene. With one question the Lord Jesus Christ exposed the spiritual emptiness of Israel's religious authorities. If you don't know where authority comes from, then you can't truly have it yourself.

By that one question the Lord demonstrated that all of Israel's religious authorities were unqualified to question his authority. If they couldn't tell the difference between a prophet and a mere man, how could they judge the Son of God when he came?

When we meet Jesus, we meet a person with unquestionable authority. Mere men cannot challenge the Lord's right and ability to teach and to rule.

Do you question or do you recognize Jesus's authority in your life?

## You Cannot Refuse His Authority
### LUKE 20:9-18

If the Lord's authority cannot be questioned or challenged, that means his rule cannot ultimately be refused.

*The Parable*

The Lord turns from the religious leaders to address the people. He tells a story about a man who planted a vineyard and then rented it out to tenants. When the man wanted some of the fruit of the vineyard, he sent servants to collect. Each time the tenants beat the servants, treated them shamefully, and sent them back empty-handed. Finally, the man sent his son, and the tenants killed him.

The **man** in the story symbolizes God the Father. The Father owns the vineyard, which represents his kingdom and the rewards of his covenant. The **tenants** represent the religious leaders of Israel. They were not owners of God's kingdom and covenant; they were merely stewards who were to give God what was his when he asked for it. The three **servants** that were sent were prophets God sent to Israel. Israel had a long, long history of rejecting God's prophets and mistreating them. The **son** in the story represents the Son of God, Jesus himself.

## The Point

Verse 13 portrays God as the owner asking himself after all the servants have been abused, "What should I do?" Now don't misunderstand that. The story is not picturing God as confused about things or out of ideas. That question has the ring of something like this: "How much more can I do? What greater step should I take?" The image is of an owner God who continues to pursue what is his, including the tenants. So the owner decides to send the dearest thing in the world to him—his son. And when the son is sent, the tenants decide to murder him with the hopes of taking the vineyard once and for all (v. 14).

These fools are crazy. How was that supposed to work? Let's kill the son, and then we can have his inheritance. What father do you know who will give his wealth to his son's murderers?

In rejecting the son, they rejected the owner's highest expression of love. So now we need to feel the question of verse 15: "What then will the owner of the vineyard do to them?" Doesn't verse 16 make perfect sense in this story? "He will come and kill those farmers and give the vineyard to others."

No one can safely reject the Father's prophets or the Father's Son, Jesus Christ. "How will we escape if we neglect such a great salvation?" (Heb 2:3). We will not. We will be destroyed.

## The Privileged

If you understand that these tenants deserve this judgment, then you understand something about the justice of God in condemning sinners. But not everybody will admit this so clearly. The people said, "That must never happen!" (v. 15). It's as if they understand the point of the parable but refuse to accept it. The moral logic of the parable is clear, but they try to refuse it.

Why would someone *not* believe this? It is entitlement and privilege right there! They think the kingdom is their right and not a gift. They still can't see how much like the tenants they really are. They are *right then* denying the King's authority over them and over his kingdom.

## The Point, Again

I love what verse 17 teaches us about the boldness and seriousness of our Lord when it says he looked at them. You get the sense that the Son of God is not playing any games. In an authority contest the Lord does not back down. He leans in and locks eyes.

This time, rather than tell a parable, the Lord quotes the Scriptures. "The stone that the builders rejected has become the cornerstone" (v. 17). He asks them if they know the meaning of this text found in Isaiah 28 and Psalm 118. A cornerstone is used in constructing a building to make sure the foundation is square and level. If the cornerstone is off, the entire building will be off, so this one stone is essential to the entire structure.

The Lord Jesus was speaking of himself. Acts 4:11 says, "This Jesus is the stone rejected by you builders, which has become the cornerstone." The entire building of God's kingdom is built on the Lord Jesus Christ. If we fall on that stone (by rejecting him) or that stone falls on us (in condemnation), then we will be "broken to pieces" or it "will shatter" us (v. 18). If we reject Jesus Christ when he offers himself to us in the gospel, we break ourselves. If his condemnation falls on us, it crushes us.

### Applications

*My non-Christian friend*, the point of what I am saying is that Jesus Christ is essential. There's no way to build your life without him. There's no way to enter God's vineyard without him. You must not stumble or fall on this stone. You cannot survive if the stone falls on you. The only safe way to live is to stand on the stone. To build on it. To make it the foundation of your life. You do that by believing the gospel and following Jesus as your Lord with all authority over you.

*Church*, this cornerstone is the foundation of our entire existence. Without Christ as the chief cornerstone, there is no building. We are "built on the foundation of the apostles and prophets, with Christ Jesus himself as the cornerstone. In him the whole building, being put together, grows into a holy temple in the Lord" (Eph 2:20-21).

## You Cannot Trump His Authority
### LUKE 20:19-26

The religious authorities fail in their effort to question Jesus's authority. They fail so miserably that Jesus says the vineyard will be taken away from them unless they acknowledge him as the chief cornerstone.

## The Plot (20:19-20)

"Then the scribes and the chief priests looked for a way to get their hands on him that very hour, because they knew he had told this parable against them" (v. 19). Well, duh. Wherever did they get that idea? But once again, their plots are held up because "they feared the people" (v. 19). It's striking how often cowardice and murder can be in the same religious heart.

Because they're afraid, they recruit some spies (v. 20). These spies "pretended to be righteous," but they were looking for ways they "could catch him in what he said."

Since their religious authority has been destroyed, they now look to use government authority to silence the Lord Jesus Christ. So we move from religious court to the secular court.

## The Pretense (20:21-22)

They use flattery in verse 21. They're trying to butter up the Lord. Satan's agents will often make their appeal to our pride. Then they come with their trap question in verse 22: "Is it lawful for us to pay taxes to Caesar or not?" By asking this question, they hoped to discredit the Lord with the people because the people all hated the Roman oppression through taxes. If that didn't work, they hoped they could get the Lord into serious trouble with the Roman government because not paying taxes would be considered treason.

## The Perceptiveness (20:23-26)

But the Lord sees right through them (v. 23). He knows when we're playing games and trying to rig the system like a Cleveland ref.

We don't have time here to discuss all the implications of Jesus's response for our understanding of government authority, but we should say at least two things:

- *The Lord affirms Caesar's authority, even down to paying taxes.* The Lord is not an anarchist. We can never justify disobedience to civil authority with appeals to Jesus. Pay your taxes. Obey the speed limit. Serve on jury duty. Give to Caesar what is Caesar's.
- *The Lord does not equate Caesar's authority with God's authority.* Some things belong to Caesar, and some things that belong to God. Caesar may put his face and name on what is his, but this

is my Father's world. What Caesar has, God gave to him. What belongs to God, Caesar can never claim or take.

The higher authority—the *highest* authority—is God's authority. Taxes belong to Caesar; hearts and souls belong to God. God can demand of us things that Caesar could never rightfully demand. For example, the Lord can demand that we worship him. Caesar could not rightly do so. We know this intuitively, don't we? That's why in verse 26 they simply were amazed at his answer and shut up.

## You Cannot Trivialize His Authority
### LUKE 20:27-44

*The Sadducees' Scenario (20:27-33)*

Now in verse 1, the *conservative* religious leaders approached Jesus to question his authority. They failed. So in verse 27 the *liberal* religious leaders take their turn. The Sadducees were a group of Jewish people who "say there is no resurrection" (v. 27). The Sadducees are the opposition party to the Pharisees. They argue with each other all the time, but they are united against Jesus. They don't care who has authority as long as it's one of them.

So they come along to test the Lord as well. The Pharisees tried to question Jesus on the grounds of religious authority and civil authority. The Sadducees decide to challenge Jesus on the ground of scriptural authority. They try to make the Scriptures and Jesus look ridiculous by putting together an absurd scenario (vv. 28-33).

When they say, "Moses wrote for us" (v. 28), they're referring to the first five books of the Bible. They're referring to Scripture. The scenario they use builds on a law called the "kinsman-redeemer" or "levirate marriage" law. That law required just what they outlined. They are undermining one part of Scripture (the resurrection) by twisting another part of it (the kinsman-redeemer law). It's a challenge to the authority, clarity, necessity, and inspiration of the Scriptures. Our Lord responds with three basic points.

*They Don't Understand the Ages (20:34-36)*

First, he tells them they don't understand the differences between "this age" and "that age" (vv. 34-35), between earth and heaven. There are tremendous differences between what happens on earth and what happens in heaven. There are tremendous differences in our very existence. In heaven or the resurrection or "that age," there is no marriage. Marriage is an earthly reality, not a heavenly one. Incidentally, this is why sanctified singleness is ultimately better than discontented marriage. When we tear ourselves up about marrying, we're crushing this temporary life over a temporary relationship.

The reason marriage does not exist in heaven is because we are transformed in heaven. We cannot die anymore. We who believe "are like angels and are children of God" (v. 36). We are finally fit to live with our true Husband, who is Christ.

### They Don't Understand the Resurrection (20:37-40)

Second, the Lord tells them they don't understand the Bible's teaching about the resurrection. The Lord quotes the same author they quoted: Moses. He reminds them of one of the passages every Jewish person would accept as true and wonderful: the burning bush. In that passage God speaks to Moses and for the first time in the Bible states his name: Yahweh. He calls himself "the I AM," the always existing One (Exod 3:14). That's God's name. In the giving of his name, God mentions Abraham, Isaac, and Jacob—the patriarchs or fathers of the Jewish nation.

The Lord Jesus reads the Bible so closely and carefully! No Jewish person would deny that Abraham, Isaac, and Jacob lived with God. The present tense nature of the verse required belief in the resurrection. Who could deny it? That's why the Sadducees say, "Good answer. Good answer." Verse 40: "They no longer dared to ask him anything." The Lord shuts them up, too.

### They Don't Understand David's Son (20:41-44)

Third, the Lord reveals the deep truth about David's true Son. He's already shut the Sadducees up. Now he's going to shut them down. They're done with their questions; now the Lord has one of his own: "How can you say that the Christ is the son of David?" (v. 41). I imagine they looked puzzled at first. Everyone knew God promised David a son who would rule on David's throne forever. That was Judaism 101. That son would be the Christ, or the Messiah, who would bring God's kingdom and gather all of Israel. Of course the Christ is David's son.

Then the Lord, still reading his Bible so carefully, quotes Psalm 110:1 and says, "For David himself says in the Book of Psalms, 'The Lord declared to my Lord, "Sit at my right hand, until I make your enemies your footstool"'" (v. 42). Jesus helps them understand that King David eavesdropped on a divine conversation. The first Lord is the Father—Yahweh. He spoke to the second Lord, the Son—Adonai—and told him to sit in the place of honor at his right hand. It's a glimpse into the divine relationship and the Trinity of persons in the Godhead. David calls them both "Lord." If David calls the Christ "Lord," then how could David be greater? How could David be a father in that sense? How could the Christ be David's son in that sense?

He couldn't be. The Christ, David's true Son, is also God's Son. He rules far above all powers. He sits at the Father's right hand, and all his enemies will be placed under his feet. You cannot trivialize the Lord's authority by playing Bible trivia, by trying to make the Bible look absurd. He is high above all!

## Application

When we come to the Bible, do we fail to approach it with a sense of the authority it has? Is it a book of curiosities and debatable doctrines? Or does it appear to us a book of power and control because it comes from the mouth of God?

Before we "use the Bible," we must submit to the Bible. We must recognize its authority in our lives because it comes from God. When we get to know Jesus, we find out that the Lord really does honor the prophets—from John the Baptist (v. 4) all the way back to Moses (v. 37). Because he honors the prophets, the Lord also honors the Scriptures that come through them. Did you notice how often the Lord quoted Scripture (vv. 17-18,37-38,41-44)?

- His parable was but an illustration of a biblical text.
- He stands on Scripture even when it's being attacked.
- He gives attention to the details of the Bible for meaning.
- He trusts the Bible's accuracy and authority even when others are mocking it.
- He believes the whole Bible—the law of Moses, the prophets like Isaiah, and David's psalms—is sufficient for life and doctrine.
- He believes Moses really did write the first five books, Isaiah really did write Isaiah, and David really did write some psalms.

Jesus believes the Bible is true and trustworthy. He believes the Bible reveals what heaven and God are like. He does not trust another authority apart from the Bible. We will never know Jesus well until we know our Bible well and approach it the way he did.

## You Cannot Avoid His Authority
### LUKE 20:45-47

The Lord Jesus's authority cannot be questioned. It cannot be refused. It cannot be trumped—there is no higher authority. His authority cannot be trivialized or undermined. Finally, it cannot be avoided.

Many people live as if Jesus did not exist. Even among those who know his name and know about his gospel, some act as if that has nothing to do with them. Many live as if they will never have to respond to the Lord's authority.

They could not be more wrong. Luke 20 began with Jesus preaching the good news, the gospel. It ends with Jesus preaching the bad news. The good news does not appear good until a person really reckons with the bad news. The scribes put on religious shows. They want to look holy. But they're pretending—even when they pray. The scribes along with all religious hypocrites in positions of religious authority "receive harsher judgment" (v. 47). In other words, the hottest parts of hell are reserved for hypocritical religious leaders. The false minister will not escape the searing authority of God's judgment. They cannot avoid it.

Though the leaders receive "harsher judgment," there remains a condemnation for everyone who lives in sin and ignores Jesus as Lord. One day you too will come before his throne on the day of judgment. If you have bowed before his authority and followed him in faith, you will not be condemned. You will not be put to shame. You will enter his kingdom and know the power of his resurrection. But if you have stiffened your neck and hardened your heart, you will hear the final verdict: "guilty." You will hear God the Judge sentence you to condemnation in hell. There will be no escape.

The only escape is the gospel. Christ died to pay the penalty for our sins so we would not have to serve the sentence in hell. He rose from the grave to defeat death and to bring us righteousness through faith in him. All who trust him live free with God as they were meant to. Today, trust him.

## Reflect and Discuss

1. How do you feel about authority? What have been some of your most profound experiences with authority and its uses or abuses? How do those experiences shape your view of authority today?

2. Authority seems wired into creation. Why do you think that is? What do you think it tells us about God's purposes for creation and for authority?

3. Can you be a good Christian while rejecting the Lord's authority? Why or why not?

4. Is the authority of human rulers the same as God's authority? Why or why not?

5. How does the Lord teach us to relate to human governments and their authority in this passage? Are we to relate to them in this way only when they are good or effective? Why or why not?

6. When you approach the Bible, would you say you approach it with a deep sense of its authority in your life? Why or why not?

7. What are the consequences for rejecting the Lord's authority?

# The Son of Man

## LUKE 21

**Main Idea:** The end is certain and coming, so we must get ready for it.

I. **The Events Leading to the End of the World Are Certain.**
   A. Jesus's disciples and the personal signs (21:8-12,16-17)
   B. Jerusalem's desolation and the local signs (21:20-24)
   C. Universal distress and the cosmic signs (21:25-26)
II. **The Sequence of Events Is Certain.**
III. **How Can We Be Certain to Be Ready for the End?**
   A. Give it all (21:1-4)!
   B. Don't be fooled or afraid (21:8-9)!
   C. Keep on witnessing (21:13-15,18-19)!
   D. Trust God's Word (21:22)!
   E. Look for Jesus's coming (21:27-28)!
   F. Recognize the signs (21:29-33)!
   G. Watch and pray (21:34-36)!
   H. Keep listening to Jesus (21:37-38)!

Our aim in this series through Luke's Gospel has been to get better acquainted with the Lord Jesus Christ. We have hoped that getting to know Jesus would lead to a deeper love for him as our Lord and more tender, frequent fellowship with him.

History has seen many end-of-the-world cults. Even in recent history we saw the rise of a number of prominent cults that emphasized the end of the world. Some of us can recall David Koresh and the Branch Davidians in Waco, Texas. Mr. Koresh claimed to be the messiah and wooed a number of people into his cultic control. They came to a tragic end when Koresh led his followers to resist the authorities. During a siege their compound caught on fire, and a great many were killed or took their lives.

If you are a little older, you might remember the charismatic cult leader Jim Jones and the tragedy at Jonestown. That group of people in Guyana were led to drink poison-laced Kool Aid. The sayings "Don't drink the Kool-Aid" and "That person has drunk the Kool-Aid" allude to this terrible tragedy.

Such cults thrive because there remains an instinctive fascination with the idea of the end of the world. We think not only of cult groups but the guy downtown with wild eyes and hair wearing a sandwich-board sign warning that "the end is near."

These movements can make a person think that only crazy people and cult groups think about the end of the world, but, actually, wondering about the end is perfectly natural. We know that our lives end. We know that the lives of our loved ones will end. We see aspects of the world and society—wars and nuclear weapons—that really do have potential for ending life as we know it. So it's natural to wonder.

If we are spiritually minded, it's also natural to wonder what God thinks about these things. If God had a sandwich board, what would it read? If such an end is to come, how do we prepare for the end of everything as we know it?

In many respects Luke 21 focuses on the end of the world, what we should expect, and how we should prepare. The Lord Jesus has arrived in Jerusalem, where he has been teaching every day in the temple. His main message has been one of salvation through faith in him. He spends these final days teaching in anticipation of his crucifixion and resurrection. Along the way he has had confrontations with religious leaders but has now finally silenced them. Now the Lord gives his remaining energy and life to teaching the truth to his disciples so they might be strengthened by the truth and endure until the end comes.

## The Events Leading to the End of the World Are Certain

The most-repeated word in this chapter is the simple word *will*. Luke uses the word *will* nearly thirty times in the chapter. The word *will* refers to the future, but used with stress, it also carries with it the idea of certainty. What the Lord describes in this chapter is his confident certainty about the future end of the world.

If you're trying to get to know Jesus, then one of the things you need to know is that Jesus thinks the end of the world is coming. According to Jesus, we may be sure that the world as we know it has an appointed day for its conclusion.

The disciples prompt the discussion in verse 5 as they admire the temple in Jerusalem. The Lord Jesus responds to them in verse 6 by saying the temple will be utterly destroyed. No doubt that was a stunning prophecy. Jewish persons thought of the temple as God's dwelling place. King David and his son, Solomon, constructed the first temple, and those present at its dedication witnessed the glory of the Lord dwelling in it. Ezekiel prophesied that the glory of the Lord would leave that temple in response to Israel's idolatry and corruption. Indeed, the temple would be destroyed and later rebuilt. In Jesus's day the temple once again was the center of Israel's worship. Religious Jews thought the temple was God's dwelling place. How could it be destroyed again? The thought of such destruction was horrific in the minds of faithful Jewish people.

So the disciples ask two questions in verse 7: When will these things be? What will be the sign when these things take place?

Observe first the signs the Lord gives the disciples. We can group these signs into three categories: personal, local, and cosmic. The personal signs affect the disciples. The local signs affect Jerusalem. The cosmic signs affect all of creation and all nations.

### Jesus's Disciples and the Personal Signs (21:8-12,16-17)

*False teachers and antichrists* (v. 8). First, the disciples must be on guard against false christs who attempt to lead people astray. They say what David Koresh said. Of all the signs given, this is the one given with a warning. Stay away from them. Our Lord expected false teachers to enter the church right from the beginning, and they have plagued the church since the days of Christ.

The Bible never commends a liberal attitude toward false teachers. The Bible never encourages us to listen to those who present themselves as messiahs or who distort the truth about Jesus. The Lord commends discernment, carefulness, and an attitude of discrimination because he alone is Christ. He's concerned that we are not dumb sheep led astray but listening saints paying close attention to him.

*Wars and rumors of war* (vv. 9-10). Second, the sign of the coming end includes speculation about wars and tumults everywhere. All of human society will whisper about conflict and whip itself up into violence.

*Natural disasters* (v. 11). Third, the world will suffer natural disasters. Great earthquakes, famines, plagues, and signs from heaven will forecast the end. As the apostle Paul puts it, the entire creation groans as it awaits the adoption of the sons of God (Rom 8:22-23). The Lord Jesus seems to be thinking of a similar end.

*Christian persecution* (v. 12). Fourth, there will be persecution. The persecution arises because of Jesus's name. There will be oppression, suppression, and fierce state-sanctioned backlash for identifying with Christ.

*Betrayal and martyrdom* (v. 16). The coming of the end will be marked by the breaking of natural affection, of familial bonds, and of friendship. It all happens because of his name. Those who love his name will be given over to those who do not. Those who do not love his name will jail, beat, and kill those who do. Isn't it true that all of Jesus's disciples who heard him on this day died in one of these ways? All but one was martyred. The one who survived martyrdom was imprisoned on Patmos for the testimony of Christ. In the opening chapter of Acts ,the church immediately faced persecution. Nero burned Christians in his garden for entertainment. The arenas saw Christians fed to the lions. These things were prophesied by the Lord as the beginning of the end.

*General hatred toward Christians* (v. 17). Finally, Christian disciples must face a general hatred. It may feel weird to know a name so beautiful, loving, and generous while at the same time be hated for that name. Here the Lord entertains no notion that Christians will ever be popular—not at the end, not in the meantime. So, beloved, if we are Christians faithful to Christ, then the Lord wishes to disabuse us of idolatrous notions of worldly approval. Precisely because of his name the world hates us. In some ways the hatred has nothing to do with us but everything to do with the one we love and the world rejects. That name by which we are saved and which speaks of love to us is rejected, reviled, and marginalized by the bulk of the world. So we cannot expect them to hate Jesus and love us. If they hated him, they will hate us. So we must not let our hearts be troubled by this or act as if something surprising has happened. Instead, let us rejoice to be counted worthy to suffer for the name (Acts 5:41).

### Jerusalem's Desolation and the Local Signs (21:20-24)

The Lord also gives us markers of the coming end that address Jerusalem locally. The original question of the disciples was about the temple in Jerusalem. So Jesus gives answers pertinent to the holy city.

First, Jerusalem will be surrounded by her enemies (v. 20). Second, they will also be defeated (v. 24). Death and captivity will befall them. They will be trampled underfoot by the Gentiles and exiled into all nations. Hence the terrible "woe" of verse 23. All will happen "to fulfill all the things that are written" (v. 22). These calamities are not the result of a world out of control but rather of a holy God firmly in control and ready to end sin in judgment.

Our Lord does not discuss prophecy without focusing on the plight of the vulnerable—pregnant women and children (v. 23). If the Lord moderated our modern political debates, he would not likely ask candidates about their "doctrines of war." He would most likely ask them about the pictures of women and children fleeing and babies starving. The end brings a terrible woe on the world.

When you think about the end of the world, does your heart break for those who will be caught up in it? He does not parse fine theological points but weeps over Jerusalem.

### Universal Distress and the Cosmic Signs (21:25-26)

The Lord also gives signs that affect the universe. These are cosmic signs in the sun, moon, stars, seas, and waves (v. 25). Our Lord uses the imagery of apocalyptic scenes to signify this devastating end. It's as though the heavens are shaken.

The nations are bewildered because of our roaring seas. We might see global warming debates as a kind of bewilderment about the seas and the creation. Moreover, we see people fainting with fear and with expectation of what is coming on the world (v. 26). This is how people with no hope must inevitably respond to the destruction of the world—fear and foreboding.

The Lord says these things *will* happen.

## The Sequence of Events Is Certain

Throughout the chapter the Lord gives us a sequence of these events. This is *not* a prediction of *when* the world will end. The Lord himself says that no man knows the day or the hour when these things will come (Matt 24:36). In fact, prophesying the specific timing of the end is one of the signs of the false teachers and false christs. By contrast, the Lord focuses on the sequence of events rather than the specific time.

*First will be the false teachers and the rumors of wars* (v. 9). "It is necessary that these things take place first." Yet these things are not the end. "The end won't come right away." The events are spread out over time. Indeed, some of what's said in this chapter refers directly to Jerusalem and the people in Jesus's audience that day. For example, the Lord says in verse 32: "Truly I tell you, this generation will certainly not pass away until all things take place." He referred especially to the persecution of the disciples and the destruction of the temple. All of that did happen in that generation. The temple was destroyed in AD 70 when Romans surrounded and destroyed Jerusalem.

But other parts of this refer to the end of the world. So in verse 27, "Then they will see the Son of Man coming in a cloud with power and great glory." The second coming has not yet happened. We still await the Lord's return. These things do not happen all at once. They are spread out from the day the Lord spoke these words through our day until the end itself. But first are the false teachers and the rumors of war.

*Second will be the persecution, natural disasters, and so on* (vv. 10-12,16-17).

*Third comes the destruction of Jerusalem* (vv. 20-24).

*Fourth begins "the times of the Gentiles"* (v. 24). Gentiles will occupy Jerusalem, as they do until this day. God will use the Gentiles as a judgment against Israel, as it was prophesied (v. 22). All will happen according to God's divine plan. Moreover, the times of the Gentiles will feature Gentiles being brought into the kingdom of God. When Israel is broken off, then the non-Jewish people will be grafted in (Rom 11:11,17-19).

In verses 25-26 we see the cosmic distress that is to come. Then, finally, the Lord describes the second coming and the eternal kingdom (vv. 27-28).

This is the sequence the Lord gives us. We don't need more than this. It is enough to occupy our imagination and stir our spiritual devotion. The main point is not the apocalyptic language or the sequence of events. Our Lord puts this teaching to *pastoral* use. So we need to ask ourselves, "So what? Why does this matter? How does this help us or ready us for the day of the coming of the Lord?"

## How Can We Be Certain to Be Ready for the End?

The Lord gives us eight ways to prepare ourselves for the end.

### Give It All! (21:1-4)

First, give it all! This all started with Jesus observing the rich people and one poor widow giving in the temple. The widow placed two small coins out of her poverty into the offering. Jesus commends the woman for her generosity toward God. Here's another scene where Luke uses a marginalized woman to illustrate the greater virtue of the kingdom. It's no sacrifice to give to God out of your generosity, but our Lord watches this widow with intentionality. He focuses others' attention on her. She emerges as the hero who gives God her all.

Randy Alcorn in *Money, Possessions, and Eternity* meditates on this scene in a convicting way (pp. 6–9). He asks us to consider what our counsel to this woman might have been if she had asked us what she should do with these last two coins. Would we say something like, "The Lord knows these are your last two coins and would understand if you purchased bread instead"? Many of us would. Yet the Lord commends this woman for giving her last in worship to God. Giving all she had demonstrated her surrender to God. It was an act of great faith. If the Lord had provided those two copper coins, then he could provide two thousand or twenty thousand copper coins. The coins were not her salvation; God was. What is always most vital is that we should be given over fully to trusting God himself.

This is what the gospel demands. The call of Christ requires us to turn away from the world, from sin, and from our own control to trust solely in him. The gospel calls us to give ourselves over to God, acknowledging that he has purchased our lives with the blood of his Son. Now our lives belong to him, and we live constantly giving ourselves over to him as a lifestyle of faith. If we would follow Jesus, we really must forget everything and everyone else as a source of security and provision. We must forget everything else as a "lord"; Christ alone is Lord. To be ready for his coming, we must belong to Christ. To belong to Christ, we must die to ourselves and submit to him in faith.

### Don't Be Fooled or Afraid! (21:8-9)

We must not be fooled or afraid because of false teachers. That prompts us to ask ourselves, To whom do we listen? Who has our attention? To whom do we give our ear? What are our podcasts and playlists? What are we downloading and streaming? Do we give ourselves over to clear teachers of God's Word or to people who distract us or muddy the gospel?

Let me suggest that most religious programming fails to meet the tests of this chapter. This chapter presumes we are looking for and longing for the glorious appearance of our Lord Jesus Christ. So much of our day's religious programming focuses us on things on earth rather than the coming of the Lord. Too many teachers would have us believe we should not be "so heavenly minded we are of no earthly good." Yet this chapter suggests that to be of earthly good we must be even more heavenly minded. We are to be undistracted, undeterred, and unswayed by the falsehoods out there. This world and all that's in it is passing away, but the world to come and the Christ who's in it last forever. So we must "seek the things above, where Christ is, seated at the right hand of God" (Col 3:1). Our hope is that our lives are longer than this world because they stretch into eternity with Christ and the Father.

So don't be fooled or afraid. Nod with certainty when you hear the rumors of wars and calamity. Our Lord predicted it centuries ago so we would not be afraid but fasten our hearts on him.

### Keep on Witnessing! (21:13-15,18-19)

The list of calamities depresses us until we come to verse 13. Amid all the turmoil the Lord says, "This will give you an opportunity to bear witness." Huh! How often when you pray for opportunities to tell others about Jesus do you expect those opportunities to come in the form of persecution, mistreatment, war, and the like? If you are like me, I suspect you seldom or never picture it that way. We tend to pray for the "easy button." We imagine the tracks of our sharing are divinely oiled so that everything is smooth. There's no friction or difficulty. We simply attend the family barbecue, someone asks us, "What must I do to be saved," and then a revival breaks out!

That would be nice, but that's not how it happens. This text suggests we will attend the barbecue and all the food is gone, the fireworks have gotten wet, everyone is grumpy and complaining, and then you have an urge to speak of Jesus! So people begin to mock you as a "preacher." Before you arrived, they were sippin' on gin and juice. Now you, the Christian, have come and ruined their fun. That's how God more often than not answers your prayers for an opportunity to witness.

Beloved, we are salmon swimming upstream. The current of this chapter and of the world is against us. We are fighting against the rapids to make it home to Zion, and along the way we must convince some other fish to turn against the current and swim upstream with us. We will have to witness in the face of rushing opposition.

The Lord calls us to this, but he does not leave us alone. He says to his disciples, "Don't even think about what you will say. I will give you the words to speak at that time by the power of my Spirit." The Lord promises the kind of wisdom their enemies cannot withstand.

He promises betrayal, death, and universal hatred. Then the Lord promises not a hair will be harmed on their heads (vv. 18-19). It's a remarkable juxtaposition—persecution, famine, and death on the one hand, and not a single hair harmed on the other. How do we hold those two things together? Because our lives are eternal, the losing of this earthly life means the passing into eternal life and glory. The promises of God are not bound by this world; they are not even primarily fulfilled in this world. So the promises of God in Christ cannot be taken by this world. That includes our lives. We may well be taken in persecution or worse, but it will be gain for us (Phil 1:21)! We may be persecuted or put to death, but we will not be truly harmed. If we witness to the end, we gain our lives (Luke 21:19).

## Trust God's Word! (21:22)

That's what our Lord does when he refers to the Scriptures. All God has said will come to pass. Not one word will fall to the ground unfulfilled. Heaven and earth may pass away, but not God's words (v. 33). We hold in our hands the sure, standing, enduring, never-failing, never-erring Word of God. If we would be ready for the end, then we should stake our lives on the Word of God. Hide it in your heart that you might not sin against God. Stand on it as the one sure foundation. Hold it above your head as the exercise of Christ's lordship in your life. Hold it out front as your guide; it will be a lamp for your feet and a light on your path. If you would live well until Christ comes, then live by this book.

Go to the Lord's Word every morning. The last verse of the chapter features Christ going in the morning to the temple to teach and the crowds that come to hear him. We do not have a temple to visit and Christ there preaching, but we have a Bible to open, and he teaches us through it. We can go every morning in the temple of our own bodies to learn from him. Do that until he comes.

## Look for Jesus's Coming! (21:27-28)

For the lost world the coming of the Lord will be fearsome, but verse 28 encourages the saints with the promise that these signs indicate that our redemption is near! We have been bent by the calamity and the turmoil too. Perhaps that's why we are told to "stand up" (v. 28). The Lord calls us to lift our heads. Like David we must look to the hill from where our help comes. We look up because our redemption is close. All the signs point to this reality—Christ is near! All we hope for draws quickly near. We get to live through tragedy like people who know there's something better on the other side. We get to live through suffering like people who know they will be robed in the perfect righteousness of Christ. We are people who know that, even if we don't manage to stand up and lift our heads; then in the kingdom God with his own hands will wipe away every tear from our eyes (Rev 21:4) and lift our heads (Ps 3:3)!

### Recognize the Signs! (21:29-33)

Signs only help us if we heed them. As a boy, I used to love the cartoon *Mr. Magoo*. I rolled on the floor laughing as this functionally blind, wealthy old man drove his car through all kinds of calamity with barely a hint of concern. Mr. Magoo went through life blind. So do a good number of Christians. But the wise saints, like the "sons of Issachar" (see 1 Chr 12:32), know the times and the seasons, and they heed them. We must be a people who know the end is surely coming, and we must rightly interpret our Lord's signs so that we are ready when he comes.

### Watch and Pray! (21:34-36)

Readiness requires prayerfulness. We must be on guard against hearts weighed down by the cares of this life and of that coming day. The things we learn here are not intended to overthrow our hearts but to establish them. We must remain awake. We must pray for strength so we escape the calamities to come and stand assured before Christ. The best preparation for the life to come is a present life of prayer.

### Keep Listening to Jesus! (21:37-38)

The Lord continues teaching, and the people keep coming. He keeps teaching today by his Word and his Spirit. We are meant to keep listening. Give attention to God's Word, and you will be ready when he comes.

## Conclusion

If you are not yet a Christian, this chapter applies to you. Right now you are not ready for the end of the world because you are still in your sins. So you must give it all to Christ. Surrender to him. Confess your sins. Acknowledge the righteousness of God's judgment against you. Then consider that your sins were atoned for on the cross and your righteousness secured in the resurrection. Put your trust in Christ and follow him in the obedience that comes from faith. Then, no matter what happens in your life and in the world, you may be certain that you are Christ's and he is yours. Believe in Christ, and the end will simply be the beginning of eternity for you.

## Reflect and Discuss

1. What comes to mind when you think about the end of the world?
2. Is the end of the world and the second coming of Christ an encouraging idea to you? Why or why not?
3. The Lord gives his disciples several things to focus on or do as they wait for the end and his return. Which of those things seem most necessary to your life right now? Why?
4. Why do you suppose people follow doomsday cult leaders when Jesus warns so clearly against such leaders?
5. How might Christians help protect people from the mistake of following cult leaders?

# The Lamb of God

## LUKE 22:1-38

**Main Idea:** In his being betrayed, Jesus guarantees that betrayal does not have the last word.

---

I. **The Betrayal of Jesus Was Prompted by Satan (22:1-6).**
   A. Sanctified time (22:1)
   B. Sinful leaders (22:2)
   C. Satanic influence (22:3)
   D. Secret plot (22:4-6)
II. **The Betrayal of Jesus Was Predicted in the Scriptures (22:7-23).**
   A. In-time/temporal fulfillment (22:7-13)
   B. End-times/eschatological fulfillment (22:14-18)
   C. Christological fulfillment (22:17-22)
III. **The Betrayal of Jesus Purchases Us a Kingdom (22:23-30).**
   A. On Christian leadership
   B. On solidarity with Christ
IV. **The Betrayal of Jesus Protects Us from Satan (22:31-34).**
V. **The Betrayal of Jesus Provides Us a Mission (22:35-38).**

---

Betrayal depends on the exploitation of the best virtues. Where there isn't love, trust, and hope, betrayal cannot be effective. If we are skeptical, critical, judgmental, or not trusting, it's not easy for us to be betrayed. So betrayal is one of those human experiences that takes the best of our humanity and exploits it in a way that produces pain. A spouse who has suffered adultery knows that the pain of adultery is doubled because of the love and trust it took advantage of and the assumption of faithfulness it exploited.

Such is the case when we think of the relationship between citizens and authority. Some were rightly concerned about the news of Secretary of State Hilary Clinton's handling classified emails in a way that undermined public confidence and trust. We witness an office holder, conferred trust and respect, exploit and betray public support. Or think of the police-involved shootings of unarmed African-American men. As we watch those situations unfold, we are reminded that government can only be effective insofar as its people trust it. Only when the people honor the government and the government stewards that trust by returning respect and honor can a state last. So when we watch a sworn officer of the state take a life illegitimately, we are not merely watching a tragedy on our streets. We are watching something happen to public trust and public virtue. And no matter what side you're on, it feels like a betrayal—betrayal of officers who need our support or betrayal of vulnerable communities who need our protection.

Betrayal exploits the greatest virtues. That's why it hurts so long and takes so long to recover from it. It's a painful human experience.

But betrayal is not limited to human experience. We have not suffered it alone, no matter what form it takes. Christ Jesus the Son of God was himself betrayed. God himself has been betrayed by his people. Yet we find redemption in how the Lord responds to betrayal. By means of betrayal, God both teaches us about the frailty of humanity and redeems humanity itself, repairing the broken and breached trust and restoring the honor and dignity of human life. For God enters the system of our betrayal, our world of betrayal, and in his own being betrayed creates a new world, a new humanity where all things are proper and right in his control.

Recall that Jesus is in Jerusalem teaching in the synagogue every day. He has put an end to the public opposition that religious leaders express toward him. But that does not mean those leaders are done with their opposition. In Luke 22 we witness the beginning of the end of our Lord's earthly life. We peer into Judas's betrayal, but we also glimpse Jesus's redemption.

## The Betrayal of Jesus Was Prompted by Satan
### LUKE 22:1-6

*Sanctified Time (22:1)*

It was nearly time for the Festival of Unleavened Bread, also called Passover. For Jewish people this was a sanctified or holy time. The Festival and Passover stretch back centuries to the time when Israel was in slavery in Egypt and God sent Moses to deliver them. They stretch back to the tenth plague in the exodus when God sent forth the angel of death to strike dead the firstborn of every household except those under a particular exemption. God instructed Israel to prepare a meal of bitter herbs and to eat the meal fully dressed that night because the Passover would happen hurriedly (Exod 12:3). The Lord also commanded Israel to spread the blood of a lamb on their doorposts. God promised that when the angel of death was probing all the homes of Egypt, if he saw the blood on the doorposts, he would pass over those homes to strike those not covered by the blood (Exod 12:5-13).

Verse 1 opens in this holiest of seasons. The entire nation celebrates the day God saw the blood of the lamb and spared their firstborn sons and delivered them from slavery in Egypt. It's a sanctified time.

### Sinful Leaders (22:2)

You'd expect the religious leaders to be preparing for this time of worship. You'd expect them as holy men to be with their families, perhaps reading Exodus 12 with them. Instead, "the chief priests and the scribes were looking for a way to put [Jesus] to death." Holy dates are coming; hateful men are scheming. What a shocking contrast between the celebration of verse 1 and the sinister darkness of verse 2.

There's a problem with their plot. The scribes and chief priests "were afraid of the people." The people respected Jesus. They thought Jesus was a prophet. Early every morning they came to the temple to hear Jesus preach (21:38). So the priests and scribes were afraid to kill him outright. They needed a secret way to assassinate the Lord.

### Satanic Influence (22:3)

The scribes and priests were not acting alone in their hatred for the Lord. Satan—the devil—was on the scene too. In our day of scientific fascination, I know it's not popular to say things like this, but Satan is real. The devil actually exists.

Satan was an angel of God. He was created to serve God, but one day he decided he wanted to be God. He led one-third of all angels in rebellion against God and was thrown out of heaven. Hell was prepared for Satan and his angels.

Satan opposes Jesus and seeks to destroy him. Satan "entered Judas, called Iscariot, who was numbered among the Twelve." Judas served in our Lord's inner circle as one of the original twelve apostles. How the devil entered Judas is not told, but Satan influenced and controlled him. Satan put it into Judas's heart to betray the Lord.

### Secret Plot (22:4-6)

The result of all of this—of the priests' and scribes' murderous cowardice, of Judas's betrayal, of Satan's influence—is a secret plot to betray the Lord. The priests had an inside man and an inside job waiting to be carried out. As Matthew tells us, Judas sold out the Lord for thirty pieces of silver. That was the hit price. Now Judas looked for a secret place away from the crowd to betray Christ.

## Applications

*Fear God.* If we fear man more than we fear God, we will serve man or ourselves rather than God. If we fear man more than God, then we will do some wicked things even at holy times. We will hardly even recognize God when he is incarnate among us. Christians are called to fear God rather than man. We cannot please man and God at the same time; we must serve God rather than man (Gal 1:10). The entire duty of man is to fear God and keep his commandments (Eccl 12:13). The fear of the Lord is the beginning of wisdom (Prov 19:23). So let us be a people who cultivate the fear of the Lord, a people who revere their Creator in all things. Let our households be built on the fear of the Lord (Josh 24:14-15) because "the fear of the LORD leads to life; one will sleep at night without danger" (Prov 19:23).

*Resist Satan.* As we said before, Satan is real. He first appeared as "the most cunning of all the wild animals" (Gen 3:1), and he comes to steal, kill, and destroy (John 10:10). To ignore him is a mistake. It is foolish to pretend he doesn't exist. His handiwork is everywhere around us. Just think about the reality of greed and betrayal we see throughout society. Do you think greed and betrayal come from God? Of course not! Betrayal is Satan's idea and Satan's plan.

As those who have the Bible, we know his tricks. Beware the adversary. Resist him and he will flee you (Jas 4:7). He cannot enter a Christian who has the Spirit of God. Judas did not have the Spirit, but we do. Greater is he who is in us than he who is in the world (1 John 4:4). So we resist with greater power. Do not give him a toehold in your life (Eph 4:27). Do not believe his lies. Do not believe his whispers. He betrayed Christ; he will betray every Christian. Resist the devil, and he will flee.

## The Betrayal of Jesus Was Predicted in the Scriptures
### LUKE 22:7-23

This entire chapter makes many allusions to the Old Testament. It presents us the fulfillment of prophecies and themes that run throughout the Scriptures. If you're interested in seeing the unity and trustworthiness of the Bible, Luke 22 provides a great place to settle and study.

The Scripture is fulfilled in this passage in at least three ways.

### In-Time/Temporal Fulfillment (22:7-13)

First, Luke 22 fulfills the Scriptures *in time*. This is the temporal fulfillment of God's promised plans. Everything that happened at that time was a fulfillment of what the Bible had predicted centuries before. We've already seen in Exodus 12 where, in the days of Moses, God required Israel to observe the Passover. In all of the preparation and eating of verses 7-14, we have Exodus 12 fulfilled or obeyed by Jesus and his followers in that time.

They selected a place to observe the Passover (vv. 8-13). Interestingly, even finding a place was a fulfillment of a small prophecy of the Lord. They sacrificed a lamb as the Bible required (v. 7). They sat and ate together (v. 14).

### End-Times/Eschatological Fulfillment (22:14-18)

But there is also an *eschatological* fulfillment of the Scriptures. *Eschatological* is a theological term that has to do with "end times" or "last things." Prophecy often has multiple fulfillments. So not only do Jesus and his disciples fulfill the Scriptures by eating the meal in their own time, but the Lord also points us to a future fulfillment of Scripture.

In verse 15 the Lord anticipated eating the meal with his disciples before he suffered, but the Lord also anticipates eating and drinking again when it is "fulfilled in the kingdom of God" (v. 16) and when "the kingdom of God comes" (v. 18). So Jesus looks forward to another time at the end when he will eat with us in the kingdom. The Passover gives way to the Lord's Supper, which in turn points forward to the marriage supper of the Lamb. That is the ultimate or end-time fulfillment.

### Christological Fulfillment (22:17-22)

The Lord Jesus himself gives us a third fulfillment of the Scriptures. The Scriptures are fulfilled *in him*. Even the Passover meal was truly about Jesus. The bread was a symbol for his body broken for us; the cup was a symbol of his blood poured out for us.

The ancient Passover in Egypt foreshadowed and symbolized the true Passover in Christ. The blood spread on the doorposts of homes, which turned away the angel of death, finds its ultimate meaning in the blood spilled on the cross, which turns away God's wrath against sinners. The lamb slain in Egypt pointed to the Son of God, the true Lamb of God, crucified for us. So John the Baptist proclaims, "Here is the Lamb of God, who takes away the sin of the world!" (John 1:29). All the other lambs and sacrifices were but commercials, pictures, and symbols of the one true Lamb nailed to the cross and resurrected in power and glory. We rejoice and proclaim, "Christ our Passover lamb has been sacrificed" (1 Cor 5:7). Luke 22 records the preparation for our Lord's sacrifice.

Even the betrayal by Judas mentioned in verse 21 was a fulfillment of Scripture. The psalmist saw a day when even his own familiar friend would betray him (Ps 41:9; see John 13:18). Jesus says David's words were written about him (24:44). In truth Satan influenced Judas, but God was in control. Jesus was not killed simply because he was betrayed. He was killed because he was appointed to die for our sins (Acts 4:27-28). Even the most wicked and desperate acts of men cannot overthrow the plans of God. Even the cruelest betrayals come through the sovereign hands of God. God is always at work in such suffering to bring to pass his ultimately good plans. He works through tragedy to accomplish our salvation and bless his people.

We celebrate Romans 8:28. The "all things" of Romans 8:28 includes some evil things, bad circumstances, betrayals, breaking of confidence, selling out of the Savior, and stabbings in the back. The sovereign Lord works those together for our blessing, for all those who would believe in Christ. Never, never, never think Satan has the last word! He doesn't even have the first word. God—in, through, and over our suffering—speaks the truth of his love and goodness.

Beloved, if you are new to the Bible, I pray that you can see that Jesus's fulfillment of the intricate details, the overarching patterns, and the specific prophecies of the Bible means Jesus and the Bible's message are trustworthy. The Bible is true.

Feel free to inspect it, challenge it, and look for discrepancies and contradictions. Here's what you will discover: the testimony of the Bible remains consistent and accurate. It's accurate not only within itself but also with historical testimony outside the Bible. This book is true. Its message is true. You can trust it. If you trust it, it will point you to Jesus the Lamb of God who comes as God's sacrifice to take away the sins of the world. On the cross the Lord made atonement for our sins. All who trust Jesus's sacrifice to turn away God's wrath and follow Jesus in faith will be saved. Their sins will be forgiven. They will be counted righteous in God's sight by faith in Christ. They will be born again to live for God.

Is there anyone you think you should trust more than Jesus?

## The Betrayal of Jesus Purchases Us a Kingdom
### LUKE 22:23-30

In the times of these events, darkness no doubt filled the minds of all who understood what was to happen. When the Lord mentioned "suffer" (v. 15) and said his betrayer was among them (v. 21), no doubt darkness entered the room. The disciples wondered to themselves who would cross the Lord. That must have been an awkward dinner-table conversation! Can you imagine your leader or rabbi saying to you once again that he will suffer because one of you sold him out? They would all deny the charge and perhaps eyeball one another.

Then, amazingly, their conversation moves from denying they would betray Jesus to arguing which of them was the greatest (v. 24)! Isn't pride a blinding and dangerous sin! They actually argue about the Lord's replacement before he is gone!

The Lord's response was so gracious in verses 25-30. He wants the disciples to think rightly about the Christian life. So Jesus boils kingdom life down to two things: service and solidarity. Jesus makes clear that life and leadership in God's kingdom does not look like life and leadership in the sinful world. His followers do not lead like Gentile unbelievers who "lord it over" others (v. 25). Gentiles rule one another in power-hungry, power-grabbing pride and call themselves "benefactors." They oppress others and try to convince others it is for their good. Jesus says, "It is not to be like that among you."

In the kingdom of heaven, the Lord Jesus himself is the only Lord. Even he does not rule harshly and "lord it over" others. Instead, the Lord Jesus is "among you as the one who serves" (v. 27). If our Lord were at a banquet, he would not sit at the chief place at the table and wait for others to serve him. He would, rather, dress in a servant's uniform and attend to all the other guests. He's the Lord of the table, but he is the kind of Lord who wraps a towel around his waist and washes the feet of others. In the kingdom of God, the greatest people are the greatest servants. In a world full of people who would argue for their own greatness based on age, class, privilege, race, gender, education, and almost anything else, the Lord shines bright as the one who forsakes all of those prejudices and gives his life for others. The Lord turns the entire world upside down with his emphasis on service.

Beginning in verse 28, the Lord graciously commends the disciples as those who "stood by [him] in [his] trials." When the religious leaders opposed him, they did not run away from him. They stayed in solidarity with the Savior. When his family said he was crazy, the disciples did not distance themselves from him socially. When city mobs would get out of control and riot, they did not run away seeking their own safety. They were with the Lord in his trials, sharing the danger and rejection he faced. They expressed unity with him. In that solidarity the Lord promised to give them a kingdom. Just as the Father has given Jesus the kingdom for obeying the Father's will and accomplishing his plans, so the Lord promised to confer a kingdom on his disciples for standing with him in solidarity. In this kingdom we will eat and drink together with Christ, enjoying the final fulfillment of the fellowship we have with him.

## On Christian Leadership

Among Christians, leaders serve. The man who would lead God's people who wishes to be served violates the nature of leadership in the kingdom. The pastor who would accrue for himself riches and wealth, comfort and ease, fame and popularity on the backs of God's people betrays Christ. What we do and who we are as leaders is not for the benefit, comfort, and ease of the leader. Pastors must be among the people as those who serve.

Being called "pastor" is wonderful. The office of pastor ought to be respected. But a "leader" betrays the office and the honor and the trust of Christ and the people of Christ if he uses that trust for his own gain. If you see that in us as your pastors, then stop following us. Call us to repentance and to account. Never follow a man who chases his own name. Never follow a man who chases his own belly. Never follow a man who lives for himself. Christ did not live that way. Christ made himself a servant. Such a man is indeed a gift to a church. Receive such a man as a gift from the Lord.

We nominate persons to serve as deacons or elders in our church who reflect our Lord's heart and habit in this passage. Are they not the kinds of men who lay down their lives to serve the church? Do they not quietly go about their days doing good for others and building others up? We trust that in his grace God gives us pastors who not only watch over our souls but lay down their lives for us. Let us honor such men.

Cherish them. Let us encourage them in their service and praise God for his gifts.

## On Solidarity with Christ

Let us be Christians who stand in solidarity with Christ. I have been scratching my head trying to think through the police shootings of the recent past. I have sometimes been befuddled. I try to use social media in a way that I hope over the course of time speaks the whole counsel of God. I don't make any pretensions of doing that well. Sometimes I write and almost with the first comment I regret not striking the correct balance or saying things well.

This past week, and for a long time, I found myself standing between *legitimate* desires for multiple people. It's right for people to challenge me about whether something I've written duly honors good police officers or whether I've called into question the integrity of all officers. The challenge isn't always done well, but I don't bristle with the challenge. I hear the call to stand with those placed in authority over us (Rom 13:1), especially those whose actions are just and true.

It's also right when people write and say, "We need to stand with those who have been victimized by officers who seem to go rogue in their treatment of citizens." So we hear the call for Christians to stand in solidarity with victims, to cry out for the voiceless (Prov 31:8-9).

We stand between what can feel like competing calls to solidarity with either officers or victims. These calls go out unreflectively and uncritically without regard to the facts of each case. Have you figured out how to thread the needle of these competing calls? I certainly haven't.

Reading this text did help me figure one thing out: we are called to stand in solidarity *with Christ.* As we stand with him, as we take upon ourselves his name, as we endeavor to live as fully as we can the whole counsel of God, that solidarity with Christ armed with the wisdom of his Word helps us go as far as we need to go in solidarity with others. But we are not fundamentally expressing loyalty to man; we are most fundamentally expressing loyalty to Christ. That means we must have a critique and commendation for everyone. His word surely steps on the toes of all of us, affirming us and rebuking us, whether we think about the color of skin or the color of uniforms. Or, to put it another way, it is not the fulfillment of Christian solidarity with Christ to refuse to offer a necessary word of encouragement or rebuke to whomever is before us. We all have natural empathies with different groups in different situations, but those empathies are not to be trusted. *Christ* is to be trusted. We will have natural and instinctive responses, even well-formulated responses. Christ and his word are to be trusted. We must interrogate our assumptions and our loyalties to be sure we stand with Jesus in these tumultuous times. We work out our lesser loyalties under our greater authority to the Lord. As it was for Jesus's original disciples, the promise is a glorious, unshakeable, unending kingdom.

In all of our attempts to live faithfully in the world, we are *not* fundamentally fighting for control of the United States. We are *not* fundamentally fighting for control of human government. We are *not* fundamentally fighting for reform of police departments and policing or the change of local communities. Those are not ultimate things. Those are all proper things in their proper place. What we actually live for is another kingdom, another Ruler, and a city whose foundations are not laid with human hands! We live for another kingdom where we will rule with Christ. In that kingdom sorrow will have met its end. Death will be forever eliminated. Tears will be forgotten. In that kingdom we will only know his love, his grace, and his mercy. At this Last Supper Christ lifts our eyes to that day and that rule as our hope. Let's make sure our hearts are set on that kingdom in solidarity with Christ.

## The Betrayal of Jesus Protects Us from Satan
### LUKE 22:31-34

Jesus addresses Simon Peter in verses 31-34. He tenderly repeats Simon's name. The Lord states a startling fact: Satan has taken a personal interest in Simon's destruction. Indeed, Satan would like to destroy all the disciples in order to destroy the entire Christian church in its infancy.

Simon's response is just as startling. He seems undaunted by Satan's interest and expresses confident self-reliance. He swears he will stand with Jesus no matter what—even unto death. Perhaps he has taken the Lord's comment about standing with him in his trial too much to heart. As they print on every mutual fund prospectus, "Past performance is no guarantee of future results." Simon seems oblivious to that fact. Simon thinks his past performance means a future of never failing Christ.

But we know the story. Simon will hear that rooster crow, and he will know it's the referee's whistle catching him in the foul. He will deny the Lord three times just as Jesus predicted.

Betrayal does not belong exclusively to Satan and to Judas. We may experience or commit betrayal as Christians. All our sins are betrayals, but here is the key: Judas went on to destruction, but even as Jesus informs Simon of his coming betrayal, the Lord also says that he has prayed for Simon's faith to stand. What a remarkable thing! The Lamb of God prays and intercedes for us. In our conflict with Satan and temptation to sin, even when we seem unable to pray, there remains One who prays for us! Christ the Lord has chosen intercessory prayer as his continuing ministry at the right hand of the Father.

During our worst failures in sin and temptation, Christ was already praying for us. He always pleads for us. His blood always intercedes for us. We have an advocate with the Father (1 John 2:1). As with Peter and Job, invisible warfare rages around us. We are not always aware of it. Satan prowls about looking for Christians to devour (1 Pet 5:8), looking for ways to steal, kill, and destroy (see John 10:10). But Christ is always on the job to pray for us and keep us. What a merciful Savior! What a wonderful God!

When he is betrayed, Jesus becomes a perfect Priest for us. He suffers what we have suffered, so he is able to identify with us and to intercede for us.

Perhaps you are a backslider. You have turned from Christ. Your heart by some degree has hardened toward Christ. For a season, perhaps you have indulged your sin. You may be reminded even now of your betrayal. The memory of his love haunts you. Perhaps you have been tempted to think that there is no way back, that you have gone too far in sin, and that Christ would not have you. Beloved, those are the whispers of Satan, not of Christ. See what the Lord says to Peter: "When you have turned back, strengthen your brothers" (v. 32). The Lord already anticipates Peter's restoration and usefulness. Did not Christ come to Peter after the resurrection and three times affirm his love for Peter and Peter's love for him?

Though it would be enough to restore Peter, the Lord goes further to make wonderful use of Peter in his kingdom. If you have backslidden, your life is not over. Your usefulness to Christ is not over. The Lord still has plans for you just as he still has love for you. If you come to the Lord, he will not crush you or reject you; he will receive you. And more than receive you, the Lord will renew you, and he will reuse you for his glory and your joy. This is what the Lamb of God is like. He is the friend of sinners, and the backslider can come to him.

## The Betrayal of Jesus Provides Us a Mission
### LUKE 22:35-38

Jesus reminds his disciples of a short-term mission trip he once sent them on. On that previous trip, our Lord provided for them supernaturally. They testify that they lacked nothing they needed.

Now, however, the Lord sends them with money bag, clothing, and supplies. It's not that he will no longer provide for them. He will now provide through the regular means of the church itself. So we go out into the whole world proclaiming this Lamb in partnership together. This is why we want international missions in the DNA of every local church. We partner together to make Christ known to the world.

## Conclusion

Praise be to God for the Lamb who was slain! In his being betrayed, he guarantees us that betrayal does not have the last word. Instead, he guarantees us redemption and a home in his kingdom where our enemies cannot reach. This kingdom and our home are coming. It belongs to all those who belong to Christ.

## Reflect and Discuss

1. What things come to mind when you hear the word *betrayal*? How would you define *betrayal*, and what would you say are some of its effects on people?
2. In what ways did Jesus's early disciples betray him? Do you think this helps Jesus sympathize with us in our experiences?
3. How did God use the betrayal of Jesus to our advantage? What words would you use to describe this turn of events?
4. Do you have any family members or friends who do not think the Bible is true or historically accurate? What are their arguments? How might a chapter like Luke 22 address their concerns?
5. What do you imagine life in the final kingdom of God will be like?

# The Rejected Savior

## LUKE 22:39-71

**Main Idea:** The Lord Jesus Christ accepted complete rejection so that sinners with faith in Christ might receive complete acceptance.

---

I.   **Jesus Was Rejected by the Father (22:39-46).**
II.  **Jesus Was Rejected by Judas (22:47-53).**
    A.  Betrayal (22:47-48)
    B.  Violence (22:49-51)
    C.  Cowardice (22:52-53)
III. **Jesus Was Rejected by Peter (22:54-62).**
IV.  **Jesus Was Rejected by Mockers (22:63-65).**
V.   **Jesus Was Rejected by Priests (22:66-71).**

---

We all have fears. One fear nearly everyone has in common is the fear of rejection. Men feel it every time they hope to ask someone out on a date. Perhaps you felt the fear of rejection when you went on a job interview for a position you really wanted. Most people would never want to work as telemarketers; they face rejection all day long.

Where does fear of rejection come from? Researchers tell us it comes from a basic desire to belong and a desire to avoid appearing or feeling like failures. We don't want to be rejected by social groups or cast off by others. So fear grows in our hearts, and we shrink back from rejection.

However, rejection is a part of life. I asked my wife out six times before she said yes! We have all felt it. But here is the question: What if rejection could be redemptive? What if being rejected actually led to your blessing?

Not everything we desire is good for us. Getting everything we want can ruin us. Spoiled children who grow up receiving everything they want and yelling a possessive "Mine!" toward everything they see tend not to be the most generous people in the neighborhood. A touch of rejection might have been good for them.

The events in our text occur in two locations—the Mount of Olives (v. 39) and the home of the high priest, Caiaphas (v. 54)—and five scenes: Jesus praying before he is betrayed; Judas betraying the Lord with a kiss; Peter denying the Lord three times; the soldiers mocking and beating the Lord; and the priests and scribes condemning the Lord. At the heart of the passage is one central action: everyone around Jesus rejects him.

## Jesus Was Rejected by the Father
### LUKE 22:39-46

You will remember that verses 1-38 record the Lord Jesus having the Last Supper with his disciples. As he eats with his followers, two things are revealed: (1) he is the true Passover Lamb who takes away the sins of the world, and (2) Judas will betray him to his enemies.

Verse 39 tells us they have finished that Supper. They have come out of the upper room where they had the meal. Jesus had a habit or routine: "as usual" he went "to the Mount of Olives." His disciples followed him.

On that fateful night the Lord had prayer on his mind. He instructs the disciples to pray (vv. 40,46). With the cross just hours away, you'd think the Lord would ask them to pray for him, but he doesn't. He tells them to pray so that they "may not fall into temptation" (v. 40). The Lord is not the only one in danger that night. The disciples will face threats from within—temptations of various sorts.

At the center of this scene are Jesus's prayers. He walked off by himself and asked God, "Father, if you are willing, take this cup away from me—nevertheless, not my will, but yours, be done" (v. 42). The other Gospel writers tell us Jesus made this petition three times that night. "If you are willing . . . if you are willing . . . if you are willing." The time of prayer was so strenuous that an angel from heaven had to strengthen him, and in agony he sweated great drops of blood.

The "cup" has two references. On the one hand, it refers to the cup of God's wrath. The Bible often symbolizes God's wrath as a cup full of strong, destructive drink. Like wine that intoxicates and causes men to stumble, so the wrath of God will make men stagger in his judgment (Isa 51:17; Rev 14:9-10). In order to save sinners from their sin, the Lord Jesus will have to "drink," or suffer, that wrath in our place. The cup contains God's righteous fury against all the sins of the world for all time. Christ will suffer for it all. The Lord knew that he came into the world for this hour and purpose (John 12:27). But this hour and purpose are so unimaginably stressful that even the Son of God asks three times that this cup be removed from him. Can you imagine being judged for every sin of every person who ever lived? That is the cup of God's wrath.

But this is also the cup of God's salvation. The bitter wrath results in our sweet rescue from condemnation and hell. In that agonizing scene of prayer, God the Father did something that had never happened between Father and Son. The Father rejected his Son. Though the Son of God prayed three times to have this cup removed, each time God the Father returns a silent *no* from heaven. The prayer that saves sinners was actually a prayer denied. The Father said no to Jesus in order to say yes to us. We tend to think God's plans are accomplished by his saying yes to us, but here with his only Son, the Father accomplishes our salvation by saying no. Jesus must drink the cup. Our greatest deliverance came from an unanswered prayer.

### Applications

The entire scene teaches us a great deal about prayer.

*Prayer protects us from temptation* (vv. 40,46). The Lord instructs his disciples to pray so they would not be tempted. We are never far from some beguiling suggestion from the world, the flesh, and the devil. We are never far from some whisper that would destroy us. So we must pray as an inoculation against temptation.

*Prayer is submission* (v. 42). "Not my will, but yours, be done." Here's how we know whether we're praying in ultimate trust in God or we think our ways are best: Can we conclude our prayer request this way? If we are sure our way is the right way, then we don't want to hazard the idea that God may have a different plan in mind. True prayer is not bringing God in line with our plans but rather submitting our plans to the Lord's designs.

*Prayer is always answered yet sometimes with a* no (v. 42). We must learn to welcome the *no* just as much as we welcome the *yes*. The Lord may do more with a *no* than we could ever dream. And since he is infinitely good, we can expect his *no* to be filled with that goodness. If God withholds something from us, the withholding is better than our receiving. We must trust that.

*God's saying no to our prayer request does not equal abandonment* (v. 43). See how the angels ministered to our Lord, "strengthening him." The Father was right there with the Son even though he did not grant the Son's request. We can be tempted to think the silence of heaven and the *no* to our prayers represents God's abandoning us. But God promised never to forsake us or abandon us. He remains just as present with us in the *no* as he is in the *yes*.

*God's saying no to our prayer requests does not equal a bad outcome.* How quickly our spirits are downcast when we think our prayers are unanswered. Here the Lord pleads, and heaven answers no; but on the other side of that *no* is our redemption. It's not a bad outcome. Ultimately it's the greatest outcome imaginable. Christ will suffer and die, but for the joy set before him, Christ endured the cross and despised the shame (Heb 12:2). On the other side of the cross is our salvation in Christ. We must learn that a *no* from God does not equal a bad result.

*Prayer requires effort and self-denial* (vv. 44-46). The disciples were tired from excessive sorrow. That's why they found it difficult to pray. However, prayer is warfare against our flesh. We must not let our flesh have the last word when it comes to prayer. That itself would be giving in to temptation. We war against the flesh and press in to the Spirit to pray. We must pray until we *pray*.

See the Savior in Gethsemane on his knees sweating blood and hearing a *no* from the Father. See in that *no* his rejection and our salvation. He rescues us by enduring our punishment and shame. He removes our guilt and condemnation by what he suffered on the cross. Three days later God raised him from the dead, proving his sacrifice was accepted and we are justified in him. Hope in him and follow him. He will make you new and whole. Trust him.

## Jesus Was Rejected by Judas
### LUKE 22:47-53

In the middle of calling the disciples to pray, Judas came leading a crowd against Jesus (v. 47). You'll remember from verse 6 that Judas has agreed with the Lord's enemies to look for a time to secretly betray the Lord. That betrayal depends on Judas's exploiting his close, intimate relationship with Jesus.

### Betrayal (22:47-48)

First, Judas exploits his membership among Jesus's disciples. Verse 47 calls him "one of the Twelve." That's the inner circle. Those are the twelve men the Lord Jesus chose to carry out his mission as apostles. Judas exploits this trust.

Second, Judas had intimate knowledge of the Lord's routine. He knew the Lord liked to retreat to the Mount of Olives. He knew when the Lord would be there. In fact, Judas had been there with the Lord many times himself. He used that intimate knowledge to betray the Lord to those who wanted to murder him.

If that wasn't enough, Judas used an intimate gesture—a kiss—to betray the Lord. Think of all the things we communicate with a kiss:

- A couple signifies their marriage with a kiss.
- A married couple communicates their love with a kiss on the lips, or their romance with a kiss on the neck.
- Kissing a person's hand may communicate admiration or respect.
- Many people communicate friendship with a kiss on the cheek. That would have been true in the culture and time of Jesus's day.
- The early church was encouraged to greet one another with a holy kiss.

Here's the thing: no matter how you kiss, a kiss always symbolizes something good. Not until Judas betrays our Lord does betrayal become associated with a kiss. He exploits the greeting of friendship and loyalty.

With that gesture Judas rejects Jesus as his Lord and Savior. With a gesture meant to communicate intimacy and partnership, Judas actually communicates rejection and the breaking of fellowship.

### Violence (22:49-51)

But just as striking as Judas's betrayal is the Lord's composure. Verse 49 says, "When those around him saw what was going to happen, they asked, 'Lord, should we strike with the sword?' Then one of them struck the high priest's servant and cut off his right ear."

At this point the disciples are like, "Ride or die!" They wake up, and they recognize that Judas has sold out the Lord. They're like, let's do this. The other Gospel writers tell us that Peter cut off the ear of the high priest's servant. I love what Leonce Crump says about this passage: "If your first reaction in a scrape is to cut a man's ear off, then chances are you've done that before!"

But here's the thing: the Lord's kingdom is not accomplished by violence. The disciples had asked once before if they should call down fire from heaven to consume the Samaritans who rejected Jesus. The

Lord told them they didn't know what spirit they were acting in. He has not come in violence but in love. So he says, "No more of this!" (v. 51). Our Lord is in control. He limits the evil being done. Under his rule there will be no violence. The Lord Jesus stands for what's good and right, even when it costs him his life.

Not only does the Lord oppose violence; he heals the victims of it. Right in the middle of this potential riot, the Lord Jesus performs a miracle by putting a man's ear back on his head.

Now here's my question: Why didn't everyone who came to arrest Jesus change their minds? At least the servant should have switched sides. I don't care what's going on, but I am going to join forces with the guy who just put my ear back on my head. He's the good guy. It's an amazing and stubborn fact of life: people don't always believe in God even when he does good things for them. His kindness is meant to lead us back to him in repentance (Rom 2:4), but some people reject him and his kindness.

## Cowardice (22:52-53)

One reason people don't change their minds and follow Jesus is cowardice. They commit to their secret plans, and they're afraid to change direction. The Lord rebukes the chief priests and officers of the temple and elders for their cowardice.

The "hour—and the dominion of darkness" (v. 53) refers to that moment when the betrayal of Jesus and his sacrifice are carried out. They could not take him before it was time, but at the appointed time the Lord gave himself over to them to accomplish the Father's will. The power of darkness has the upper hand now, but it's only an "hour." It's only for a brief time, and it's only for God's purpose. Satan thinks he has conquered the Son of God. What he has really done is help complete the plan of God. Even cowardice and darkness are made to do God's bidding.

## Application

Betrayal, violence, and cowardice never win. Jesus suffers rejection at the hands of one of his close friends. That should never be. It should never be among us. Let us make all our expressions of affection and loyalty to Christ genuine and true. And let us make our loyalty to one another true. We live in a world where loyalty is in short supply. People sell you out quickly and cheaply, just as Judas did. But among God's people, among those of us who see our Savior betrayed, this should never be.

## Jesus Was Rejected by Peter
### LUKE 22:54-62

We come now to the third rejection in this passage: Peter's three rejections of the Lord.

After the temple guards seized the Lord, they "led him away, and brought him into the high priest's house," and "Peter was following at a distance" (v. 54). That's loaded with meaning. He's gradually disassociating himself from the Lord. But let this be known: We cannot safely follow Jesus from a distance. We are meant to be close to him.

The Lord had warned Peter that Satan was looking to destroy him, and Peter responded confidently: "Lord, I'm ready to go with you both to prison and to death" (v. 33). Peter is like those brothers that be talkin' 'bout, "I ain't scared to go to prison." But you remember what the Lord said in return in verse 34: "I tell you, Peter, the rooster will not crow today until you deny three times that you know me."

In the courtyard the people make a fire. They plan to be there a while. "Peter sat among them" (v. 55). Psalm 1:1 says,

> How happy is the one who does not
> walk in the advice of the wicked
> or stand in the pathway with sinners
> or sit in the company of mockers!

Apparently Peter has forgotten that verse. He goes from following or walking with the crowd some distance from Jesus, to standing in the courtyard, to sitting among them. That's when the three denials happen.

First, "a servant" girl (v. 56) takes a good look at Peter. You can see her leaning in by the light of the fire, observing Peter. When she's sure, she says, "This man was with him too." Peter denies it in verse 57. He sounds indignant. "Woman, I don't know him." What a lie!

Second, an unnamed man, simply called "someone else," saw Peter. He didn't have to study Peter's face the way the servant girl did. He merely saw Peter and knew Peter was one of the Lord's followers. He says, "You're one of them too" (v. 58). But Peter denies the Lord again, saying, "Man, I am not!" Two opportunities to be loyal. Two opportunities to claim Jesus as his Master. Two lies. Two rejections. The rooster is stirring.

Verse 59 begins, "About an hour later." Perhaps Peter began to relax in that hour. Perhaps he thought no one else would bother him. Maybe he thought his lies had worked. Maybe in that hour the earliest rays of dawn began to crack the sky. A third man speaks up: "This man was certainly with him, since he's also a Galilean." This unnamed man not only recognized Peter as a disciple but also Peter's connection with Galilee and Jesus's ministry in that area. The followers of Christ are better known by the world than we recognize. "But Peter said, 'Man, I don't know what you're talking about!'" The third denial. As the words left Peter's mouth, "Immediately, while he was still speaking, a rooster crowed" (v. 60).

I imagine the sound of a rooster has never been more terrifying or heartbreaking. Verse 61: "Then the Lord turned and looked at Peter." Everything that needed to be said was in their eyes. All they needed to understand was transferred in a look. What if Peter had responded differently to the servant girl's look or the man's look of recognition, or taken a moment to acknowledge that, yes, he looked like a Galilean? If Peter had been honest in those earlier looks, could he have avoided this final look? If he had thought nothing of the knowing looks of the people in the courtyard, could he have avoided the knowing look of the Lord?

That look from the Lord was followed by Peter's memory of what the Lord had said regarding a rooster. Then came the bitter tears of a man who'd rejected his Lord.

In the looks and the tears we're meant to learn something of ourselves: we cannot try to avoid looking like Christ's followers and ever hope that the Lord would look at us with approval. In fact, Jesus says that if we deny him on earth before men he will deny us in heaven before God (21:9).

## On Weakness and Wickedness

But there's a tremendous difference between Judas and Peter in this chapter. Judas intentionally sold Jesus out. Judas was "the son of destruction" (John 17:12). He was an unrepentant man destined for condemnation. But Peter failed the Lord despite his honest commitment to the Lord. That's why the Lord restores Peter before the story is over. Peter really did want to ride or die with Jesus. He really intended to stand with Jesus. But in the hour of darkness, Peter's courage failed him.

There's a tremendous difference between wickedness (Judas) and weakness (Peter). Wickedness receives condemnation. Weakness receives help and comfort. Nothing could be more important than making an accurate diagnosis of our failures. Do they come from wickedness or weakness? Is our heart darkened with sin, or are our frames but dust?

The Lord rejects the wicked, but he will receive the weak. He invites them, "Come to me, all of you who are weary and burdened, and I will give you rest" (Matt 11:28). In fact, Christ knew Peter's weakness, and he knows our weakness. He places himself in this position of rejection so that he might be familiar with our weakness and help us with it. Are you weak? Christ is strong! Are you unable to stand in the hour of temptation? Run to Christ, who defeats your temptation. Do not try to stand in your own strength. Fall into your weakness and discover the strong arms of God. Weakness is but an invitation to trust the Lord Jesus Christ with what we cannot trust ourselves: our souls.

## Jesus Was Rejected by Mockers
### LUKE 22:63-65

The Lord's friends were not the only ones to reject him on that night. Consider the nature of this rejection. It's both physical and personal. They not only beat the Lord; they also mock him. The previous rejections were personal in the sense that they betrayed the intimacy of friends. This rejection is personal in the sense that it assaults Jesus psychologically and attacks our Lord's character. They aim to discredit and disgrace the Lord.

Specifically, they're mocking the Lord as a prophet. A prophet was one who brought the word of God to the people. These soldiers reject the idea that Jesus Christ really brought God's message.

They play a little game. They blindfold him and take turns hitting him. Then they say, "Prophesy! Who was it that hit you?" (v. 64). No doubt that seemed like a funny taunt, but can you imagine the day of judgment when they appear before Christ and he says, "By the way, I know it was you who hit me"?

Verse 65: "And they were saying many other blasphemous things to him." To blaspheme someone is to slander him, to speak against his person. Luke simply gives us that summary statement. You can imagine the things that were said would not be fitting to say or to write.

### Good News for Blasphemers

Many of us have committed blasphemy against the Lord—especially before we were convinced of our sin and came to believe he is indeed a prophet and the Son of God. When I was a Muslim, I blasphemed him by rejecting that he was the Son of God. How many of us have used Jesus's name in vain? Some of us mocked the Lord with accusations like, "If Jesus is really God, why doesn't he . . . ?"

We see this rejection of the Lord, and we tend to feel anger; perhaps we think these men deserve to be condemned. If they never repented then they were, in fact, condemned. But there's good news for blasphemers, too:

> Therefore, I tell you, people will be forgiven every sin and blasphemy, but the blasphemy against the Spirit will not be forgiven. Whoever speaks a word against the Son of Man, it will be forgiven him; but whoever speaks against the Holy Spirit, it will not be forgiven him, either in this age or in the one to come. (Matt 12:31-32)

What kind of God forgives blasphemers? Only the kind of God who willingly suffers that blasphemy in order to save the blasphemer. Only the Lord Jesus Christ is so full of love and mercy that he makes a way for those who dishonor him to share in his honor.

Maybe that's you. Hear the promise again: "Every sin and blasphemy will be forgiven people. . . . Whoever speaks a word against the Son of Man will be forgiven." Through faith in the Son of God, there is forgiveness for the worst blasphemer. The only rejection that is final is his rejection of us in the judgment. Repent and submit to his lordship before it's too late.

## Jesus Was Rejected by Priests
### LUKE 22:66-71

Finally, the established religious leadership put Jesus on religious trial. According to verse 67, their main concern is whether Jesus is "the Messiah." The Lord is put on trial for who he claimed to be.

They, of course, don't really want to know the answer to the question. The Lord knows that these men are willfully blind. They are committed to unbelief. It does not matter what he tells them. They will find a way to reject or avoid it.

Here is the hardest heart of all: the heart that refuses all proof and reason, the heart that refuses to admit what it knows. These men have hardened their hearts in this way.

But the hardness of man's heart cannot stop the advancement of God's plan. Despite their unbelief, the Lord goes on to say, "But from now on, the Son of Man will be seated at the right hand of the power of God " (v. 68). In other words, there's nothing you can do to keep me from reigning in honor with God.

In using the title "the Son of Man," Jesus does tell them that he is the Christ and the Son of God. That's why they respond the way they do in verse 70. They knew that the "Son of Man," a title taken from Daniel 7, was a reference to the Deity. They ask: "Are you, then, the Son of God?" The Lord hangs them with their own words: "You say that I am." Then comes the final rejection. They said, "Why do we need any more testimony, since we've heard it ourselves from his mouth?" (v. 71).

Larry King once said that the person he'd most like to interview is Jesus Christ. Mr. King said he'd ask one question: Were you really born of a virgin? For Mr. King the answer to that question would define human history. That's the further testimony Mr. King would like even though that's the plain testimony of the Bible in the Old and New Testaments.

You see, it's easy to reject Jesus by claiming to need more information. Many people hide behind what they don't know in order to avoid what they do know. These elders knew Jesus claimed to be the Son of God. They also knew Jesus performed miracles to prove it. But they didn't want to follow the evidence. They only wanted to confirm their rejection of him. There are many like them today.

What about you? Will you reject Jesus? Will you pretend that you need more information while clinging to your bias? Or will you be honest? There's more than enough information and testimony to know the truth. It's why this Gospel was written—so we could be certain that the things we've been taught about Jesus are true. What further testimony do you need?

## Conclusion

Do not reject Christ. Believe in him. Sincerely seek answers for your questions. When you have them, trust them. If you accept Christ, he will accept you. If you reject him, he will reject you.

## Reflect and Discuss

1. If you can, think back to your life before you became a Christian. Were there ever any incidents where you rejected the gospel? Why did you reject it?

2. How does the Father's rejection of Jesus's prayers in the garden of Gethsemane ultimately lead to our salvation and Jesus's glory?

3. Have you ever been rejected or had to reject someone for your good or their good? What was that like? How did the vision of a good outcome help you during the rejection? How does this help us with our rejections as a Christian?

4. What is it about God the Father and the Lord Jesus Christ that enables them to receive those, like Peter, who once rejected them? What aspects of God's character does the forgiveness of rebels, backsliders, and blasphemers reveal?

# The Crucified Christ

## LUKE 22:66–23:56

**Main Idea:** When we embrace the truth with humility, it leads us to commit ourselves into God's hands for safekeeping.

---

I.  **The Courts: There Can Be No Justice Where There Is No Truth (22:66–23:25).**
    A.  Let us receive the truth (22:66-71).
    B.  Let us stand on the truth (23:1-5).
    B.  Let us never abandon the truth (23:6-25).
    D.  What true justice requires
II.  **The Crucifixion: There Can Be No Forgiveness Where There Is No Humility (23:26-43).**
    A.  The chain of mourners (23:26-31)
    B.  The circle of mockers (23:32-38)
    C.  The conversation of thieves (23:39-43)
III.  **The Commitments: There Can Be No Genuine Commitment Where There Is No Focus (23:44-56).**
    A.  Jesus commits his spirit to the Father (23:44-48).
    B.  Joseph commits Jesus's body to the ground (23:49-53).
    A.  The disciples commit themselves to the Sabbath (23:54-56).

---

Based on the judgment of all-white juries, eight black teenage boys were sentenced to death for the rape of two white women on a freight train in 1931 (a ninth boy, only twelve, was judged too young for the electric chair). The trials took place in just a day, with a lynch mob demanding the surrender of the teenagers outside the jail before the trials. The only lawyers who would defend the accused included a retiree who hadn't tried a case in years and a Tennessee real-estate lawyer unfamiliar with Alabama law.

The convictions led to demonstrations in the heavily black neighborhood of Harlem in New York City, and the case eventually made it to the Supreme Court, where the convictions were reversed because of the lack of an adequate defense. Amid enormous public interest, charges were dropped against four of the men. Three were resentenced to life in prison; a fourth, Clarence Norris, was resentenced to death, later reduced to life in prison. Governor George Wallace pardoned Norris in 1976. To this day the Scottsboro case is still shorthand in public dialogue for unfair, racially biased convictions and sentencing.

We now reach the section of Luke's Gospel when Jesus faces his capture and arrest. The authorities place him on trial, which results in his conviction and later his crucifixion. The text reveals three courtroom scenes. These scenes reveal three lessons.

## The Courts: There Can Be No Justice Where There Is No Truth
### LUKE 22:66–23:25

### Let Us Receive the Truth (22:66-71)

*Jewish or lower court.* The first part of our text focuses on a series of court scenes. The first court scene is the Jewish "elders of the people" (v. 66). This group of leaders is also called "the Sanhedrin," and they were the highest religious court in Israel. As we saw in the previous section, they want to know whether Jesus claims to be the Messiah. Jesus knows them: these are people who willfully oppose the truth. Nevertheless, the Lord answers their question. He not only claims to be the Messiah, but he also uses the title "Son of Man" (v. 69). The Jewish leaders understand Jesus's claim, but they reject it.

You can do anything with the truth—even condemn a perfectly innocent man like Jesus. The truth is more than facts. Facts must be interpreted. They must be interpreted accurately before you arrive at the truth. The religious leaders receive a plain statement about who Jesus is. They know the facts from his own mouth, but they deny the truth and condemn an innocent man.

### Let Us Stand on the Truth (23:1-5)

*Pilate's court/state supreme court.* They would have killed the Lord then, but there was a problem: the Romans had conquered Israel, and because the Jews were under Roman occupation, they could not carry out a death sentence themselves; only Rome could do that.

So the Jewish court refers the case to the state supreme court. They bring the Lord to Pilate. Verse 2 says they actually change the charges. They accuse Jesus of "misleading our nation, opposing payment of taxes to Caesar, and saying that he himself is the Messiah, a king." Of course, the first two charges are not true, and the last charge is manipulative. They're trying to paint Jesus as a public menace and a threat to the Roman government. In fact, another Gospel writer tells us that they tried to put Pilate in an awkward position. They tried to say that Pilate would not be loyal to Caesar if Pilate didn't condemn Jesus.

So Pilate questions the Lord: "Are you the king of the Jews?" The Lord admits it plainly with the words, "You say so" (v. 3). Again, another Gospel writer tells us that Pilate felt like he was the superior: he told Jesus he had power over the Lord's life. But the Lord responds by saying, "You would have no authority over me at all if it hadn't been given you from above" (John 19:11), and, "My kingdom is not of this world" (John 18:36). The Lord is not only Messiah but also King of Heaven and Earth.

Pilate finishes his interrogation and actually finds Jesus not guilty (v. 4). Verse 5 says the priests kept insisting that the Lord was a threat to the government. At this point public opinion is interfering with justice.

### Let Us Never Abandon the Truth (23:6-25)

*Herod's court/court of jurisdiction* (23:7-12). But as they pressure Pilate, they slip up. They mention Galilee (v. 5). When Pilate heard that, he reassigned the case to a different jurisdiction: he sent the case to Herod. Herod was a vile and corrupt man, but he kept his finger on the pulse of things, and he knew about Jesus. He wants Jesus to do some miracle for his amusement (v. 8). That's the only reason Herod questioned the Lord (v. 9). But the Lord remained quiet as the religious leaders accused him and as Herod and his soldiers mocked him. The entire place is a circus. No one is interested in the truth or justice. Everyone has an agenda. The only righteous person in the place was the one being mocked and tried.

Finally, Herod has had his fun. So he mocks Jesus and sends him back to Pilate. Herod and Pilate became friends on that day (v. 12).

*Summary judgment* (23:13-16). When they went back to Pilate, Pilate called together the Jewish leaders (v. 13). Pilate gave his verdict in verses 14-16. He finds no guilt in Jesus. Neither did Herod. Pilate doesn't see a reason to put the Lord to death, so he looks to make a compromise. He decides to punish Jesus and release him.

Now isn't that an amazing conclusion? Pilate's decision essentially affirms the Lord's truthfulness. But what a stunning blindness and hardness of heart! Instead of standing on what's right and delivering justice, Pilate refuses to embrace the truth. John's Gospel records a telling exchange between Pilate and Jesus:

> *"You are a king then?" Pilate asked.*
> *"You say that I'm a king," Jesus replied. "I was born for this, and I have come into the world for this: to testify to the truth. Everyone who is of the truth listens to my voice."*
> *"What is truth?" said Pilate.* (John 18:37-38)

The Bible says, "The truth will set you free" (John 8:32), but that's only the case if you acknowledge it. Pilate did not acknowledge the truth, so he didn't free Jesus and didn't free himself. He remained bound to the deceits of the day.

*Court of public opinion* (23:18-25). Sometimes the official courts are less powerful than the court of public opinion. The court of public opinion is really the last court in this scene. They had charged Jesus with being a threat to the king and stirring up the people against the government. Those were false charges. Now here they are asking for the release of a man "who had been thrown into prison for rebellion and murder" (v. 25).

Pilate tried to talk to them, but they shouted him down. "Crucify, crucify him!" (v. 21). They've become a mob. Mob justice is no justice at all. Pilate insisted on the Lord's innocence, but they kept crying out for his death. Their voices "won out" over truth (v. 23). Their voices prevailed over justice. Their voices prevailed over the power of Rome. Pilate gave them what they demanded. He released Barabbas and "handed Jesus over to their will" (v. 25).

## What True Justice Requires

The only way to have justice in any situation is to care more about truth than we do about ourselves. If we sacrifice truth, then we will miscarry justice.

The only persons who can make sure our systems of justice actually deliver justice are those inside and outside who will be voices for truth. A judiciary with people ruled by their own political interests will soon give the people what they want rather than what is right. A public ruled by their own selfish desires will soon twist the courts to serve their desires. Justice requires nobility of character and the courage of truth-based conviction.

We cannot be protestors accusing others without regard for the entire truth. We cannot be public servants rendering judgments in the fear of man. And Lord help us if the interests of an untruthful public align with the interests of unfaithful servants. If they handed over the perfectly innocent Christ to death, what do you think will be done to lesser men? Courts can only give us justice if they care about truth.

## The Crucifixion: There Can Be No Forgiveness Where There Is No Humility
### LUKE 23:26-43

The action moves from the courtroom to the execution. We witness three conversations leading to the crucifixion.

### The Chain of Mourners (23:26-31)

Jesus is led away followed by a crowd like a long chain of mourners. The Roman soldiers seized Simon of Cyrene. Cyrene was in modern-day Libya, in North Africa. Simon was just happening by, "coming in from the country" (v. 26). He may not have even known what was going on. Perhaps he was a large strong man because they make Simon carry our Lord's cross as Jesus followed behind. Simon, Jesus, the soldiers, and "a large crowd of people followed him, including women who were mourning and lamenting him" (v. 27). The scene is heavy with grief.

Yet it's not Jesus for whom people should grieve. When the Lord speaks, he makes plain that the people need to weep for themselves. Verse 29 says times will get so bad that they will go from rejoicing at the birth of children to blessing women who cannot have children. People will want the mountains to fall on them. He says in verse 31 that if these kinds of things can happen "when the wood is green"—to an innocent man like Jesus—then what will happen later "when it is dry"—to sinners like themselves? So they should weep for themselves and for the future of humanity.

All this means that condemnation is coming upon Israel and the world. Beloved, the first act of humility before God is to admit that his judgment is righteous and sure.

### The Circle of Mockers (23:32-38)

The Lord's comments in verses 28-30 give us context for what he says at "the place called The Skull" (v. 33). They reach Golgotha. They lift the Lord and the two criminals up on crosses. The people stood by, watching helplessly. All around the Lord are soldiers and religious folks. You cannot tell them apart by their actions. The soldiers mock him and divide his garments (vv. 34-35). The religious rulers scoff at him (v. 35). They use everything Jesus claimed about himself to ridicule and shame him. The Lord Jesus Christ is sentenced to death for being who he said he was—the Messiah of God, the chosen one, the Son of God.

The soldiers mock by saying, "If you are the King of the Jews, save yourself!" (v. 37). They place a sign over his head that was meant to add insult to injury: "This is the King of the Jews" (v. 38). Perhaps that was meant by the Romans to put Jewish people in their place by making an example of Jesus. The religious leaders object to the sign, but Pilate insists on it. God, by the scribbling of mockers, makes the cross a throne.

In this entire scene our Lord says one thing. Verse 34: "Father, forgive them, because they do not know what they are doing." In verses 28-30 the Lord says that judgment is coming. But God forgives. In the middle of his torment, the Son of God prays for sinners. In verse 34 he says that forgiveness is possible.

### The Conversation of Thieves (23:39-43)

The Lord and the two other criminals have a conversation. The first criminal "began to yell insults at him" (v. 39). He's hanging on the cross receiving his own death sentence, and with his final breath he decides to mock the Lord along with the crowd. "Aren't you the Messiah? Save yourself and us!" Some people go all the way to their condemnation being stupid and unrepentant.

The second criminal has much better sense. He rebukes the first:

> *"Don't you even fear God, since you are undergoing the same punishment? We are punished justly, because we're getting back what we deserve for the things we did, but this man has done nothing wrong."* (vv. 40-41)

Then, showing how much sense this man has, he adds, "Jesus, remember me when you come into your kingdom."

I don't know why some people doubt deathbed conversions. This man in the last hours of his life came to believe that Jesus was indeed the Christ, the Son of the living God. He came to believe that Jesus really did have a kingdom, one that he could possibly enter. He saw his sin and admitted his wrong. And he did the only thing he could do—the only thing he needed to do: plead with Christ for forgiveness and mercy. Aside from Jesus, this thief is the only humble man in the entire scene! He's humble enough to admit his sin and humble enough to turn to Jesus for forgiveness.

The Lord speaks only one line in the entire conversation: "Truly I tell you, today you will be with me in paradise" (v. 43).

Put the scenes together: Judgment is coming. God is forgiving. Paradise is offered. But the only ones who receive it are the humble who admit their sins and confess that Jesus is the Son of God who died on the cross to atone for their sins and was raised from the grave three days later. If you, beloved, are humble enough to confess your sins and turn away from them, calling on the name of the Lord, God promises he will forgive you of your sin and robe you in his righteousness. And that day paradise will be your home.

This is what we Christians call "the gospel," which means the "good news." And it is *really good*. Thieves hanging on a cross can lay hold of this good news. Criminals in the moment of their execution can be forgiven because of this good news. People in the moment of their death can latch on to this good news and discover eternal life. This same news and promise of paradise are offered to you. If you are not yet a Christian, I pray you have this kind of humility. I pray you're able to admit that you are a sinner. I pray you're able to acknowledge that God's condemnation is righteous and is coming. And I pray you can see that you cannot save yourself but you need a Savior. I pray you put your faith in Christ. The Bible promises that all who call on the name of the Lord will be saved. Do not doubt it; just do it. Call on the name of the Lord, and you will be saved.

Christian, you have already received this good news, and God has already given you this humility. We should not act as if we are superior because of our humility. We should not repeat the arrogance we sometimes have shown to people who are not Christians. We were stubborn as mules and rejected the truth in our sin, too, but we have received grace from the Lord. He has given us his kindness, and it has enabled us to admit the truth about ourselves. We once boasted of our goodness and relied on our moral actions to turn away God's wrath, and all the while we claimed to be good, we rejected the gospel and the only path to salvation. But the Lord has claimed us, changed us, and given us eyes to see the truth in Jesus Christ. When we were enabled to see the truth about ourselves, we were better able to see the truth about Christ. Now our enduring experience with God is freedom from guilt, shame, and agony through faith in Jesus Christ who redeems us.

## The Commitments: There Can Be No Lasting Commitment Where There Is No Focus
### LUKE 23:44-56

*Jesus Commits His Spirit to the Father (23:44-48)*

The sun's light failed for three whole hours in the middle of the day. Christ has been crucified. The hour of death has come. All of heaven cloaks its face. When the sun was to be its strongest, darkness covers the entire land.

God gives a sign that something miraculous has happened. God tears the curtain in the temple in two. The curtain once divided the most holy place—where God was thought to dwell and only a high priest could enter—from the outer court where others could worship. Now in the crucifixion, in the tearing of his flesh, Christ has torn the curtain between God and man. Now all who worship God may go into his presence as priests.

Then Christ cries in a loud voice, "Father, into your hands I entrust my spirit" (v. 46). What a declaration of faith and act of trust! The Son of God models for us what should be our confession too. Come what may, into the hands of our loving Father, we commit ourselves to God. So it was with Christ: in the hour of his death, our Lord focuses his attention on his Father. The Father who sent him into the world, prepared a body for him, ordained that he should suffer and die—that same God is worthy of our commitment.

No matter our circumstance and what befalls us, let us by God's grace learn to declare, "Father, into your hands I entrust my spirit." For those hands will never lose us. No one will ever slip through those omnipotent fingers. No one will ever pluck us from those hands. That's the kind of focus on the Father that drives and sustains commitment.

*Joseph Commits Jesus's Body to the Ground (23:49-53)*

Though a member of the council, Joseph did not agree with the decisions of his fellow leaders. He did not participate in their actions. He was looking for the kingdom of God. He knew Jesus was a teacher of truth.

So Joseph requests the Lord's body from Pilate and buries the Lord in an unused tomb. Though burying the Lord was a godly religious thing to do, Joseph is focused on the Lord's body rather than on the hope of the resurrection. It would have been better if Joseph had buried the Lord still looking to the future, to Christ, and to the Father.

He does not know it yet—so we don't wish to be too hard on Joseph—but in three days Joseph's grief will be lifted. In three days the tomb will be empty. In three days Christ will be raised again in glory and power. That will change Joseph's focus. He will then see Christ more clearly than he did on the day of the Lord's death. He will see the Lord not in grave clothes but clothed in his glory.

### The Disciples Commit Themselves to the Sabbath (23:54-56)

Next we have the Jewish women in the scene. It's the day of preparation for the Passover, so they cannot handle the body or they will be unclean for the Passover. The Sabbath approaches, and they must make preparation. In a couple of days, they will visit the tomb, but in the meantime they return to the law in preparing for the Sabbath. It's so easy to slip back into religion, isn't it?

But we don't want to be too hard on these women. We were not alive on the day Christ was crucified. We cannot easily imagine the grief of someone who actually knew Jesus and loved him. We cannot imagine the thunderclap in their souls or the broken places in their hearts. So they return to the familiar. They, too, are not yet focused as they ought to be on Christ. But they will be when they visit the tomb and find it empty.

But what about us? We must be truth people who receive and stand on the truth and do not abandon it. We confess the truth that God is coming in judgment, but he does also forgive and offer paradise. Will we remain focused on Christ and his gospel? Will that focus drive us deeper in our commitment to Christ and his gospel, no matter what happens until he comes?

We can be like these Jewish women who quietly slide into religious observance. We can be like Joseph, overwhelmed in mourning and forgetting the resurrection. Or we can be like Christ, committing our spirits into God's hand for safekeeping. For this is what the truth leads us to when we embrace it.

## Conclusion

If you have never committed yourself to Christ, I beg you to do that. Commit yourself to Christ and his salvation, and you will never be disappointed. If you are a Christian and, like the people in this text, you are experiencing suffering, you too commit yourself to Christ. For Christ's love and the life he gives far outlasts our suffering. Whether it is the mourning of death, confusion, or disappointment, commit yourself to the one who will faithfully keep you. Whenever we take the Lord's Supper, we commit ourselves afresh to him. We do so knowing more than any of the people in this chapter. We know he rose from the grave, and we know he was victorious over our enemies. What we do at the supper we have the joy of doing all the time and any time we want to be safe in his hands.

## Reflect and Discuss

1. Why must Christians be people committed to the truth? What happens if a Christian keeps a slippery grip on truth?
2. What do you think is the relationship between truth and justice? Did we see truth and justice displayed in Christ's trials? Did we see them played out in Christ's crucifixion?
3. C. John Miller believed that "repentance was humility in action" (Miller, *Repentance*, 96). What do you think about that statement? Why might humility be necessary to repentance and receiving forgiveness?
4. Do you believe in "deathbed conversions"? Why or why not? What do the two thieves on the cross teach us about the best use of our last moments of life if we are blessed to have our faculties when that time comes?
5. Unlike the persons in this chapter, we live on the other side of the cross and resurrection. Does that fact help us face and endure grief? If so, how?

# The Resurrected Lord

## LUKE 24

**Main Idea:** Jesus rose from the dead on the third day, and he has changed lives down to this day. Are you open to the claims of Christ?

---

I. **The Tomb Was Open and Empty (24:1-12).**
   A. Surprising scene (24:3)
   B. Surprising men (24:4-5a)
   C. Surprising message (24:5-7)
   D. Surprising report (24:8-12)
II. **The Scriptures Were Opened and Fulfilled (24:13-27).**
III. **Their Eyes Were Opened, and They Recognized (24:28-35).**
IV. **Their Minds Were Opened, and They Believed (24:36-49).**
V. **Heaven Was Opened, and Jesus Ascended (24:50-53).**

---

We've come now to the end of Luke. Luke 24 recounts the one thing on which all of Christianity stands or falls: the resurrection. Without the resurrection there is no Christianity. In fact, our own Bible tells us in 1 Corinthians 15 that if the resurrection did not happen and we believe it did, then we are fools.

So, in a sense, everything in Luke's Gospel builds up to this one, final miracle. Nothing that happened before the resurrection has any meaning if Christ did not rise from the grave. His virgin birth is meaningless. His perfect obedience to God is meaningless. His miracles and teaching are meaningless. Even his crucifixion means nothing if Christ remains dead. It all hangs on the events of this final chapter.

So, did the resurrection happen?

It might be helpful to remember why Dr. Luke decided to write this Gospel. He told us in Luke 1:1-4.

> *Many have undertaken to compile a narrative about the events that have been fulfilled among us, just as the original eyewitnesses and servants of the word handed them down to us. It also seemed good to me, since I have carefully investigated everything from the very first, to write to you in an orderly sequence, most honorable Theophilus, so that*

*you may know the certainty of the things about which you have been instructed.*

This book of the Bible was written that "Theophilus" (lover of God) might have certainty concerning the teachings of the faith. As Luke points out in that introduction, we can have certainty because Christianity is a historical faith ("events that have been fulfilled"), a verifiable faith ("eyewitnesses"), and a biblical faith ("servants of the word"). Those same truths apply to the resurrection. We have historical, biblical, and verifiable evidence to make us certain that Jesus Christ is the resurrected Lord of all.

Think of watching the news over the course of a day when some major story is developing. That morning the story breaks. The reporter tells you that something big has happened but they're still gathering the details. About midday they are interviewing eyewitnesses who add detail and human interest. Maybe a suspect or a key figure has been identified. Then by the evening news they've managed to put together a more complete report of what has happened.

Luke 24 is like that developing news story. In verses 1-12 we get the early report of something big happening. "The tomb is open and is empty." In verses 13-27 we find two witnesses who get some background on the main subject of the story. "The Scriptures were opened and fulfilled." But also in verses 28-35 they are able to verify the name of the person involved. "Their eyes were opened and Jesus revealed." In verses 36-49 there is the first-person interview with the main focus of the story. Jesus appears in person in the newsroom. "Their minds were opened, and they believed." Finally, in verses 50-53 the story comes to its end. Then "heaven was opened, and Jesus ascended."

Will you believe this good news? Are you open to the claims of Jesus Christ?

## The Tomb Was Open and Empty
### LUKE 24:1-12

"The first day of the week" (v. 1) according to the Jewish calendar is Sunday. It's "early dawn" (ESV) when the women go to the tomb to properly prepare Jesus's body for burial. Matthew tells us they wondered how they would get into the tomb since they'd seen a large boulder rolled into place to seal it. But the fact that they went anyway and went early tells you something about the devotion of these women.

### Surprising Scene (24:3)

When they arrive, they encounter three surprises. First, they are surprised to find the stone has been rolled away from the tomb. Another Gospel writer tells that an angel had flicked this massive stone away as you or I would flick lint off our shirts. That's the first miracle in the scene.

But then they're surprised to find that the tomb was empty. The body of the Lord Jesus was missing. That was no doubt distressing. They were already in mourning; now their loved one's body was gone.

### Surprising Men (24:4-5a)

Next they're surprised by "two men . . . in dazzling clothes." You can see how Luke writes with restraint as a historian. He first tells us how they appeared to the women. Later in verse 23 he tells us these were angels. Like everyone in the Bible who sees angels, the women "were terrified and bowed down to the ground" (v. 5). Nobody can look at the glory of even an angel and remain on their feet. What will it be like to see the glory of God?

### Surprising Message (24:5b-7)

Then came the surprising message in verses 5-7. The question—"Why are you looking for the living among the dead?" (v. 5)—serves as both a correction and an announcement. You're looking in the wrong place. No one goes to find a living person in a graveyard. "He is not here, but he has risen!" (v. 6).

This was not what the women were expecting. The reason they weren't expecting it was because they had not remembered the Lord's teaching. He had told them in Galilee and several times throughout his earthly life that he must suffer, die, and rise again three days later. They should have been waiting those three days in anticipation instead of mourning. But they forgot the gospel, and their forgetting took them to the tomb.

It's not until they remember the Lord's teaching about the empty tomb that their lives change. Nothing could be more important in the Christian life than remembering the gospel. One of our great challenges as Christians is keeping the truth of our Lord uppermost in our minds. We leak. We forget. We wander and stray. But if we keep our feet in the path of his teaching, then we'll never be overcome in times of trouble and sorrow. We will be the only people rejoicing even in the face of death if we keep our minds fixed on his gospel!

### Surprising Report (24:8-12)

The ladies remember (v. 8), and as soon as they remember, they take a surprising report back to "the Eleven" and to "all the rest" of the disciples back in the city of Jerusalem (v. 9). Mary Magdalene, Joanna, and Mary the mother of James were chief among the women. You may remember their names from Luke 8:2. These are some of the women who financially supported Jesus's ministry. They traveled with the Lord and were dedicated to him. They were known and respected.

But they were not believed (v. 11). The apostles and the disciples acted like male chauvinists toward these women. And that's not me being hard on these men; that's the testimony of history. In that day a woman's word would not be accepted in a court of law, for example. Women were regarded, as they sometimes are by prejudiced men in our day, as emotional, given to hysteria, and intellectually untrustworthy. This, by the way, is a proof that these things happened. In that day if you wanted your report to be credible, you would not have had a woman be the main witness to the story. If you were making it up, you would have used a male to first report the incident because of prejudice against women.

Even in our own day, we have a way to go in honoring women as full image bearers of God and servants to Christ. Even today there is real prejudice, antagonism, and chauvinism against women in the church—even though the church would have closed its doors in Jerusalem if it had been up to the men going to the tomb early in the morning to prepare the body. This ought not be so. Since God's Word sets free, there's no contradiction between the full liberty of our sisters and full submission to the limits of Scripture. May the Lord give his church the grace to dignify and magnify the work of God in and through women *while at the same time* embracing the Scriptures to define our roles. Let us root out any injustice in our own hearts toward our sisters.

These male followers of Jesus reacted just as the world would have reacted, and they nearly missed the greatest news story ever told: the resurrection. Verse 12 says, "Peter, however, got up and ran to the tomb." I think Peter ran with desperation and longing. Oh, for another memory with his Lord to replace the last memory of his failure and cowardice! Peter found the linen cloths by themselves—which would be strange if some grave robbers had taken the body as a hoax or to ridicule the disciples. That's why Peter went home "amazed at what had happened."

At the end of scene 1, when the initial reports come in, everyone is startled and marvels, but no one really knows yet what has happened. All that's really known is the tomb was open and empty.

## The Scriptures Were Opened and Fulfilled
### LUKE 24:13-27

Remember, Luke set out to teach us that we can believe with certainty the Christian faith because it is a *biblical faith*. That means that what happened on that Sunday morning was in keeping with what God said he would do in the Scriptures centuries before these events. That's what we learn in the second scene.

It is still "that same day" (v. 13). The news story is still developing. There were two disciples going to Emmaus, which was about seven miles from Jerusalem. They're talking together about everything that's happened when "Jesus himself came near and began to walk along with them" (v. 15). Verse 16 tells us, "But they were prevented from recognizing him." Now they didn't prevent themselves from recognizing Jesus; someone else did. God kept them from recognizing Christ at this point. In a spiritual sense they are walking and talking blind.

The Lord asks them what they're discussing. We don't know much about the disciple in verse 18 named Cleopas. But Cleopas will forever be remembered for what he said next: "Are you the only visitor in Jerusalem who doesn't know the things that happened there in these days?" Imagine being known for asking Jesus whether he knew about the crucifixion. That's hilarious! Jesus is the only one in the world who truly does know!

Our Lord has a sense of humor. He plays along and asks them, "What things?" (v. 19). Verse 17 tells us they're discouraged. They're like the ladies at the tomb. They don't understand what's happened either. But they break things down for Jesus as they knew them. First, they say that Jesus was from Nazareth and that he was a mighty prophet who taught and did miracles. His ministry was done before God and all the people. His ministry had integrity. But their own religious leaders betrayed him when they "handed him over to be sentenced to death, and they crucified him" (v. 20). Then they tell the Lord about the women at the tomb

(vv. 22-24). These men know the facts of the gospel, but they don't yet recognize the face of the gospel.

Their problem is not intellectual. The problem is not that they don't know some things they need to know. The problem, beloved, is spiritual. That's why Jesus begins with the rebuke of verse 25: "How foolish you are, and how slow to believe all that the prophets have spoken!" They believe some things but not all things. They don't yet believe the resurrection, and in referring to the prophets, Jesus is referring to the Old Testament, to the Bible in his day. So the Lord says, "Wasn't it necessary for the Messiah to suffer these things and enter into his glory?" (v. 26). It was necessary because God said he would do it in the Old Testament. It was necessary because God was bound by his word. So the Lord gives them what must have been the mother and father of all Bible studies ever! "Then beginning with Moses and all the Prophets, he interpreted for them the things concerning himself in all the Scriptures" (v. 27).

Two observations are critical: First, Jesus believes the whole Bible is about him. That means we cannot think it's all about us. The Lord Jesus went from Moses (Genesis) through the whole Scripture teaching about himself. This means we don't properly read our Bibles until we see how it connects to Jesus's life, death, and resurrection. The Bible tells one story all about Jesus as the star. You and I are in the Bible too—we are the ones whose sins killed Jesus—but he is the subject and the hero.

Second, Jesus believes our faith should not be rooted in personal experience only; our faith should be rooted in the Bible. We have a biblical faith. We believe these things because the Bible predicted them and they were fulfilled in history. We don't make up the meaning of these things. The meaning is there in the Bible itself. God will not let the message that saves the world rest on human experience and oral testimony. He wrote it down beforehand so we could verify it. He wrote it down so we could pass it on from generation to generation. Christianity is God saying to all the world, "I told you so! I told you I would deliver you, and I did it just like I said."

What do you root your faith in? Is your faith simply rooted in some personal experience? Or is your faith actually built on the Word of God and Jesus Christ as he is revealed in the Word of God?

The tomb was open and empty. The Scriptures were opened and fulfilled.

## Their Eyes Were Opened, and They Recognized
### LUKE 24:28-35

I trust you see something by now. The facts of the gospel and even a biblical interpretation of the gospel are not enough to truly see Jesus. We need God—the same God that caused them not to recognize Jesus at first (v. 16)—to open our eyes spiritually.

That's what's happening in this section of Scripture. We can't get to know Jesus merely through Bible study and intellectual understanding. We must have revelation from God.

They are near Emmaus. The Lord Jesus is still playing with them. Verse 28: "He gave the impression that he was going farther." Our Lord really does have a playful side to him.

J. C. Ryle states that Christ "does not always force His gifts upon us, unsought and unsolicited. He loves to draw out our desires, and to compel us to exercise our spiritual affections, by waiting for our prayers" (*Luke*, 373). In other words, the Lord likes to be sought and desired, and he was drawing that out of the disciples. Perhaps that's why he does not come to us so quickly and easily in our times of prayer and Bible reading. He's pulling out of us our truer and deeper desire for him.

So he pretends with these disciples, and in verse 29 they "urged him" to stay with them. So the Lord does. And when they sit down to eat, the Lord blesses and breaks bread with them. "Then their eyes were opened, and they recognized him" (v. 31). This is the passive voice again: they did not open their own eyes; someone—God—opened their eyes for them. The moment they had their eyes opened, they recognized Jesus, and the moment they recognized Jesus, "he disappeared from their sight."

Can you imagine the look on their faces? What amazement there must have been! I am sure they looked at one another and said, "Did you see that? That was the Lord Jesus! He's alive!" And they thought about how they felt while Jesus talked with them. They said, "Weren't our hearts burning within us while he was talking with us on the road and explaining the Scriptures to us?"

I once had Mormon missionaries visit my home to tell me about Mormonism. They offered me a copy of their supposed Scriptures and said, "When you read it, see that your heart burns, and then you'll know it's true." Friends, a burning heart is no proof of religious claims. It might be that heavy lunch you had. It was Christ's *presence* with them that gave them this warm feeling. They had walked and talked with God. And even the veiled presence of the resurrected Lord has enough glory in it to heat a person's soul. His presence was everything even when they couldn't recognize it.

Right away, "they got up and returned to Jerusalem" (v. 33). They'd just walked seven miles to Emmaus. Now they've seen the resurrected Lord, and they high-step it back the seven miles to Jerusalem. They've got good news to tell! When they get back to Jerusalem, they find "the Eleven" and others gathered in the upper room. While they were on the road to Emmaus, the Lord had also appeared to Simon Peter, and he had given a report. So they shared what had happened with them also (v. 35).

The story is developing. We had the empty tomb. But now we've got two other appearances—one to Peter and one to the two disciples going to Emmaus. The newsroom continues to put together its breaking story: The tomb was open and empty. The Scriptures were opened and fulfilled. Their eyes were open, and they recognized Jesus.

## Their Minds Were Opened, and They Believed
### LUKE 24:36-49

Now it's time for that in-studio interview with the main character of the story. "As they were saying these things, he himself stood in their midst. He said to them, 'Peace to you!'" (v. 36).

First, notice the phrase "he himself." See also in verse 15 when "Jesus himself came near" the two going to Emmaus. The phrase teaches us that this was no fantasy or delusion; this was Jesus himself—in the flesh. The Lord proves that to them when he says,

> *"Look at my hands and my feet, that it is I myself! Touch me and see,*
> *because a ghost does not have flesh and bones as you can see I have."*
> *Having said this, he showed them his hands and feet.* (24:39-40)

When we speak of the resurrection, we speak of a literal, physical or bodily rising from the dead. This is no ghost. This is not merely a "spiritual resurrection." It is the Lord Jesus himself.

Second, notice the greeting the Lord gives: "Peace to you!" Verse 37 says, "They were startled and terrified and thought they were seeing a ghost." Now Luke doesn't give us a detail that John 20:26 gives us—they were in the room with the doors locked because they were afraid of the Jewish leaders. The door is locked, but Jesus just comes on in the room.

You would have been afraid too! And you might have thought he was a ghost too! So you would have needed to hear him say, "Peace to you."

But you would have needed to hear him say that for another reason.

> This was a wonderful saying, when we consider the men to whom it was addressed. It was addressed to eleven disciples, who three days before had shamefully forsaken their Master and fled. They had broken their promises. They had forgotten their professions of readiness to die for their faith. They have been scattered, "every man to his own," and left their Master to die alone. One of them had even denied him three times. All of them had proved backsliders and cowards. And yet behold the return which their Master makes to his disciples! Not a word of rebuke is spoken. Not a single sharp saying falls from his lips. Calmly and quietly he appears in the midst of them, and begins by speaking of peace. "Peace be unto you."
>
> He is far more willing to forgive than men are to be forgiven, and far more ready to pardon than men are to be pardoned.
>
> Free, full, and undeserved forgiveness to the very uttermost is not the manner of man. But it is the manner of Christ. (Ryle, *Luke*, 379)

No word from the Lord is as sweet to the weak as "peace to you."

The Lord bids them peace. He then shows them his body. They're so excited they can't believe it. They're overcome with joy.

Then we get another hilarious point in the story: "He asked them, 'Do you have anything here to eat?'" (v. 41). Well, if you think about it, it's been over three days since he had anything to eat. So he eats while they talk among themselves.

After the Lord finished his fish, verses 44-49 tell us he held another Bible study with them. He had given them physical proof of his resurrection in verses 38-39. Now, once again, the Lord gives them biblical evidence of his resurrection. In the process of teaching them, "He opened their minds to understand the Scriptures" (v. 45). Their minds were opened, and they believed.

I believe the Lord held this second study not only so they would understand the Scriptures as head knowledge but also so they would be prepared for their mission. He tells them that they must preach repentance and forgiveness of sins to all nations starting right there in Jerusalem.

They can't remain locked in that room afraid. They must go out to the people who murdered Jesus and to all the world telling others that he is risen and there is forgiveness with God. That's their purpose. And they must do this in the power of the promise of God—who is the Holy Spirit.

Christians since that night have done just that. That's why we exist: to tell the world that Christ is risen from the dead and that everyone must repent of sin and seek his forgiveness by faith if they wish to live with God. We are, by biblical faith, witnesses of these things.

The tomb was open and empty. The Scriptures were opened and fulfilled. Their eyes were opened, and they recognized. Their minds were opened, and they believed. Are you open?

## Heaven Was Opened, and Jesus Ascended
### LUKE 24:50-53

If Christ is alive, where is he now? The answer of verses 50-53 is that he's in heaven at the right hand of the Father. These last few verses are deceptively simple. In these verses are volumes of theology, too.

Jesus has carried our humanity into glory. He rose in the same body that he showed to the disciples. Jesus is ruling over all things in heaven. And as Paul tells us in his letters, everything is being placed under his feet. Jesus is in heaven interceding for us.

The story is not over. The end of Luke 24 is merely the beginning of the church. We are meant to worship him with great joy until all nations do the same. We don't need to go to the temple in Jerusalem to bless God. We have become the temple of God in whom he lives. We bless him everywhere we go.

"This is our story, this is our song, praising our Savior all the day long" (Fanny Crosby, "Blessed Assurance").

## Reflect and Discuss

1. If the tomb had held Jesus's body, what do you think that would have meant for Christianity? (See 1 Cor 15.)
2. How does Christ's resurrection affect our lives today?
3. How would you say you've gotten to know Jesus better in the course of this study?
4. Take some time to give God thanks for showing you more of himself. Any knowledge we have of the Lord comes by the gracious work of the Holy Spirit in our lives.

# Works Cited

Alcorn, Randy. *Money, Possessions, and Eternity.* Carol Stream, IL: Tyndale, 2003.

Baxter, Richard. *The Reformed Pastor.* Carlisle, PA: Banner of Truth, 2002.

Bonhoeffer, Dietrich. *The Cost of Discipleship.* New York: Touchstone, 1959.

Calvin, John. *Institutes of the Christian Religion.* Edited by John T. McNeill. Louisville, KY: Westminster John Knox, 1960.

Chantry, Walter J. *Today's Gospel: Authentic or Synthetic?* Carlisle, PA: Banner of Truth, 1970.

Chesterton, G. K. *The Autobiography of G. K. Chesterton.* San Francisco: Ignatius, 2006.

———. *What's Wrong with the World.* 1910. Repr., n.p.: Pantianos Classics, 2016.

Coates, Ta-Nehisi. *Between the World and Me.* New York: Spiegel and Grau, 2015.

Ertelt, Steven. "57,762,169 Abortions in America Since Roe vs. Wade in 1973." Accessed September 26, 2017. http://www.lifenews.com/2015/01/21/57762169-abortions-in-america-since-roe-vs-wade-in-1973.

"Fanny Crosby: America's Hymn Queen," *Glimpses of Christian History,* Issue 198. Accessed September 26, 2017. http://www.christianity.com/church/church-history/timeline/1801-1900/fanny-crosby-americas-hymn-queen-11630385.html.

Henry, Matthew. *A Commentary upon the Holy Bible.* 6 vols. N.p.: Religious Tract Society, 1835.

Johnson, Terry. *The Parables of Jesus: Entering, Growing, Living and Finishing in God's Kingdom.* Fearn, Ross-shire, Scotland: Christian Focus, 2007.

Lewis, C. S. *Christian Reflections.* Grand Rapids, MI: Eerdmans, 1967.

———. *God in the Dock.* Grand Rapids, MI: Eerdmans, 2014.

Lipka, Michael. "A Closer Look at America's Rapidly Growing 'Nones.'" Washington, D.C.: Pew Charitable Trust, 2015. Accessed April 16, 2017. http://www.pewresearch.org/fact-tank/2015/05/13/a-closer-look-at-americas-rapidly-growing-religious-nones.

MacArthur, John. "Question and Answer Session." Together for the Gospel Conference. April 2008. Accessed September 22, 2017. http:// ia600206.us.archive.org/29/items/TheologyBites34/T4g08 _hardTruthSoftPeople.mp3.

Merton, Thomas. *The Seven Storey Mountain*. Boston: Houghton Mifflin Harcourt: 1998.

Morris, Leon. *Luke*. Tyndale New Testament Commentaries. Grand Rapids, MI: Eerdmans, 1974.

Ryle, J. C. *Expository Thoughts on the Gospels: Luke*, vol. 1. Carlisle, PA: Banner of Truth, 2012.

Smith, Gregory A., and Alan Cooperman. "The Factors Driving the Growth of the Religious 'Nones' in the U.S." Washington, D.C.: Pew Research Center, 2016. Accessed April 16, 2017, at http://www.pewresearch.org/fact-tank/2016/09/14/the-factors-driving-the-growth -of-religious-nones-in-the-u-s.

Spurgeon, Charles H. "Number One Thousand; or, 'Bread Enough and to Spare.'" *Miracles and Parables of Our Lord*, vol. 3. Grand Rapids, MI: Baker, 2003.

Warner, Judith. *Perfect Madness: Motherhood in the Age of Anxiety*. New York: Riverhead, 2005.

Williams, Moseley H. "The Man Born Blind: Application." *The Sunday- School World* 40, no. 8 (August 1900): 302.

# SCRIPTURE INDEX